THE NEW
Dynamics *of*
Multilateralism

THE NEW
Dynamics *of* Multilateralism

DIPLOMACY, INTERNATIONAL ORGANIZATIONS, AND GLOBAL GOVERNANCE

James P. Muldoon, Jr.
JoAnn Fagot Aviel
Richard Reitano
Earl Sullivan

WESTVIEW
PRESS

A Member of the Perseus Books Group

Published by Westview Press,
A Member of the Perseus Books Group

Find us on the World Wide Web at www.westviewpress.com.

Every effort has been made to secure required permissions to use all images, maps, and other art included in this volume.

Westview Press books are available at special discounts for bulk purchases in the United States by corporations, institutions, and other organizations. For more information, please contact the Special Markets Department at the Perseus Books Group, 2300 Chestnut Street, Suite 200, Philadelphia, PA 19103, or call (800) 810-4145, ext. 5000, or e-mail special.markets@perseusbooks.com.

Designed by Pauline Brown
Typeset in 10.5 point Garamond

Library of Congress Cataloging-in-Publication Data

The new dynamics of multilateralism : diplomacy, international organizations, and global governance / James P. Muldoon . . . [et al.].
    p. cm.
  Includes bibliographical references and index.
  ISBN 978-0-8133-4481-2 (alk. paper)
  1. Diplomacy. 2. International organization. 3. International relations. I. Muldoon, James P.
  JZ1305.N46 2010
  327—dc22

2010015112

10 9 8 7 6 5 4 3 2 1

Contents

v

Preface

Increasingly, the term *multilateralism* seems to be popping up everywhere—on talk radio and television, in newspapers and magazines, on blogs and even YouTube—as a way to describe the foreign policy of a country or international cooperation, generally. This is rather amazing when one considers how rarely the word was uttered in previous years outside the world of think tanks, foreign policy wonks, international affairs specialists, and international relations scholars. But multilateralism is much more than a mere description of foreign policy, diplomacy, or international cooperation. The concept encompasses an array of global issues, actors, and processes that make up the international system and refers to a particular approach to organizing and managing the complex relationships and interactions on the international level. For those of us who have long been engaged in the subject, the surge of interest in multilateralism has created some exciting opportunities to reach a wider audience for our work and to collaborate with a variety of scholars and practitioners in international relations and other academic disciplines. This has certainly been the case for us.

This book is the culmination of over a decade of collaborations to create classroom materials on the multilateral aspects of contemporary international relations that were both useful and accessible for university students, starting with the publication of *Multilateral Diplomacy and the United Nations Today* in 1998, followed by a second edition in 2005. The impetus for this undertaking has remained consistent throughout—closing what we called a "reality gap" where students' understanding of the intricate and often confusing methods and processes of multilateral diplomacy and international politics lags behind their grasp of the issues and problems on the global agenda. We concluded that what was missing was a practitioner's perspective on the ins and outs of multilateral diplomacy—how it is conducted and how it has adjusted and performed in the post–Cold War political and economic climate of the United Nations system. We believe our approach of combining the perspectives of academics and practitioners has made a difference and revealed the nuances of multilateral diplomacy at the United Nations. This volume carries forward this framework to an examination of the more general notion of multilateralism and the practical dimensions of the increasingly complex realities of the global condition in the twenty-first century. In other words, it focuses on the dynamics of global politics as they relate to today's global issues, international institutions, and global governance.

The book is organized into five parts. The first provides brief accounts of the history and evolution of multilateralism within three academic fields—diplomacy studies, international organizations, and global governance. Parts 2 through 4 concentrate on the role of three key groups of actors—states, nonstate actors, and the secretariats of international organizations, respectively—in multilateral diplomacy and global governance. Each of these parts includes contributions from both scholars and practitioners, who examine the particular role of an actor and the effects of that role as it changes on the international system and global issues and problems. The final part of the book contains our reflections on the current state of multilateralism and the implications of its complex dynamics for the international system and global governance. This volume covers a wide range of subjects, including international peace and security, the global economy, human rights, the environment, humanitarian assistance, and economic development, which we hope will prove useful to students and scholars of international relations, to practitioners, and to interested members of the general public.

With multilateralism in vogue, this book comes out at a very propitious time. But it is also a very busy time for those actually involved in multilateral activities, including the contributors to this book, who took time from their extremely full schedules to join this enterprise. Obviously, this book would not have been possible without their participation, for which we are most grateful. And we remain indebted to our publisher, Westview Press, and especially to our editor, Anthony Wahl, for their unwavering support and sticking with us over all these years.

James P. Muldoon, Jr.
JoAnn Fagot Aviel
Richard Reitano
Earl Sullivan

FEBRUARY 2010

PART ONE
The Mechanics of Multilateralism: Past and Present

Introduction

James P. Muldoon, Jr.

What does it mean when a scholar or analyst of international relations says that we live in a "multilateral world" or that the United States has abandoned "multilateralism"? One might have an intuitive understanding of what these words mean but be hard-pressed to define them. Most people, including those who write or speak about world affairs, only have a superficial understanding of what multilateralism is and how it works. Even in academic circles the concept of multilateralism and its role in today's world is poorly understood. The implications of this lack of understanding are not simply academic; there are real-world consequences—U.S. policies of the past several years, for instance. In other words, multilateralism—how it is conceived, how it works—is important. As John Ruggie (1993) and his colleagues argued nearly twenty years ago, multilateralism matters.

Since this is the fundamental premise of this entire volume, it is only reasonable to begin by looking at the history and evolution of multilateralism to establish a baseline of the phenomenon and its ongoing relevance. The chapters in this part of the book set the stage in that they describe the development of multilateralism conceptually and practically, while at the same time showing how it shapes, and is shaped by, changes in world politics and world order. As Robert Cox pointed out in 1992, "Multilateralism is not just a passive, dependent activity. It can appear in another aspect as an active force shaping world order" (1996, 494).

Chapter 1 focuses on multilateral diplomacy and chronicles the rise of the multilateral form within the institution of diplomacy. In this chapter, Geoffrey Wiseman explains how multilateralism has become "a primary, interrelated norm of diplomatic culture" and the various affects it has had on the institution and practice of diplomacy since its emergence during the twentieth century. Chapter 2 shifts the focus to international institutions and organizations. Michael Schechter provides a detailed account of multilateralism's conceptual development in the field of international organizations, highlighting the way structural changes in the international system have led to "a redefinition of international organizations and a revision of the conventional understanding of multilateralism." The third chapter, by Volker Rittberger and Andreas Kruck, situates multilateralism within the narrative of global governance. They show the evolution of multilateralism as an institutional form and mode of global governance and illustrate how the shape of multilateralism is changing.

A reading of the chapters in this part will make it abundantly clear that multilateralism has become, and is, a core feature of diplomacy, international organizations, and global governance and a defining aspect of an emerging global order. Multilateralism's meanings are not, and should not be, confined to a particular mode of interaction between three or more states or to a particular structure or organization involving three or more states; to do so misses too much of the dynamics of world politics, particularly the growing influence and expanding role of nonstate actors. Its meanings have changed, adjusting to the context and the new cast of characters on the world stage. Finally, and perhaps most importantly, the key to understanding multilateralism and its relevance today is the dynamics of the roles and relationships of the actors who define and shape the world politically, economically, and socially.

References

Cox, R. W., with T. J. Sinclair. 1996. *Approaches to world order.* Cambridge: Cambridge University Press.
Ruggie, J. G., ed. 1993. *Multilateralism matters: The theory and praxis of an institutional form.* New York: Columbia University Press.

1

Norms and Diplomacy:
The Diplomatic Underpinnings
of Multilateralism

Geoffrey Wiseman

Multilateralism is a primary, interrelated norm of diplomatic culture, along with use of force only as a last resort and in self-defense, continuous bilateral dialogue between officially recognized representatives, dialogue that is as open and transparent as possible, and civility and tact as the essence of diplomatic discourse. Part of the difficulty in understanding multilateralism's diplomatic underpinnings, or foundational assumptions, is that multilateralism is what constructivist theorists call a taken-for-granted norm (Finnemore and Sikkink 1998). In other words, aspects of the multilateral norm have become so deeply internalized that we no longer appreciate their causative and constitutive effects (Wiseman 2005, 415; cf. Mearsheimer 1994–1995).

To gain an understanding of the diplomatic underpinnings of multilateralism, I address four specific questions:

1. How has multilateralism been conceptualized in the field of diplomatic studies?
2. How has the evolution of the institution of diplomacy (in the modern sense) defined the operation and/or development of multilateralism?
3. Are there significant changes in the perception and/or practice of multilateralism within diplomatic studies?
4. How has diplomatic studies responded to the debate about the changing role(s) of states, nonstate actors, and international secretariats?

Definitional Issues

I use the term *diplomatic studies* to mean a subfield within the wider academic field of international relations (IR). This term implies the self-conscious study of, or research into, interactions and relationships between entities with standing in global politics (primarily sovereign states and international organizations) that are intended to reduce conflict and promote cooperation. I use the more neutral phrase "study of diplomacy" in referring to writings by authors who show an awareness of the multilateral process's diplomatic underpinnings but do not necessarily self-identify with diplomatic studies. In fact, it may be helpful to distinguish between a *tradition* (comprising intellectually connected scholars said by others to constitute a tradition, often ex post facto) and a *field* (comprising epistemically connected scholars who organize themselves into a self-identified professional network).[1] At some risk of oversimplification, diplomatic studies can generally be distinguished from such fields as international organizations and global governance by virtue of the priority it accords to the *practice* (procedures, tactics, means) of IR and diplomacy as distinct from the *theory* (substance, strategy, ends).[2]

Conceptualizing Multilateral Diplomacy

In diplomatic studies, diplomacy is closely associated with a Westphalian, territorial, and sovereign-state set of conceptual assumptions generally connoting the idea that states should settle problems using peaceful means (e.g., persuasion) rather than coercion (e.g., military force). Additionally, scholars of diplomacy tend to distinguish between *foreign policy*, meaning the formulation of a state's grand strategy, or worldview, and *diplomacy*, meaning the practical implementation of foreign policy, usually by professional diplomats (Nicolson [1939] 1969, 3–5; Wiseman 2005, 410–411).

The idea that representatives from two or more political entities should meet to work out differences, using tools of persuasion and dialogue, had a long premodern history that led to the establishment of a resident embassy during the Italian Renaissance (Mattingly 1955; Anderson 1993; Cohen 2001). Such classical diplomacy writers as François de Callières focused on bilateral diplomacy, which came to mean the conduct of relations between two states, generally via resident missions (Keens-Soper and Schweizer 1983). Modern scholars of diplomacy have helpfully chronicled and assembled the classical writings from Niccolò Machiavelli and Hugo Grotius to Ernest Satow, Harold Nicolson, and Henry Kissinger on such practical topics as the ideal ambassador, the art of negotiating, the right of legations, and the law of nations (Berridge, Keens-Soper, and Otte 2001).

In the twentieth century, and in the wake of real-world practice, the study of diplomacy added a second dimension to the bilateral form to arrive at multilateral diplomacy, which now means relations among three or more states at permanent or ad hoc international conferences (Berridge and James 2003, 176–177). While multilateral diplomacy is generally seen to have expanded its scope, functions, and influence since the 1919 Paris Peace Conference at the end of World War I, diplomacy scholars are quick to note that multilateralism can be traced to such major conferences as the Congress of Westphalia in 1648 and the concert system arising from the Congress of Vienna in 1815 (Davis Cross 2007). They also draw attention to the important technical conferences of the late nineteenth and early twentieth centuries (Hamilton and Langhorne 1995, 90–98; Berridge 2005, 151–156).

The idea that adding a more institutionalized multilateral dimension to traditional bilateral diplomacy would strengthen peace and international cooperation arose most dramatically with proposals for a League of Nations following World War I. Previously, the widely held view had been that war and conflict were less likely if diplomatic dialogue and communication were conducted continuously between sovereign states, including hostile ones, notably through bilateral exchange of diplomatic missions in the respective capitals.

Such critics as U.S. President Woodrow Wilson, however, objected to the old diplomacy, seeing it as a cause of war itself. For them, the old diplomacy implied a reliance on the eighteenth- and nineteenth-century idea that countries form alliances and go to war to prevent any one power from predominating and upsetting the precarious power balance. The problem was that these alliances, often negotiated in secret, were ultimately unstable. Wilson argued for a new diplomacy, one characterized by more openness and less secrecy; self-determination for the peoples of the disintegrating German, Austro-Hungarian, and Ottoman empires; and the institutionalization of multilateral diplomacy, notably with the establishment of the League of Nations with a permanent secretariat in Geneva (Sofer 1988).

Nicolson, like Satow before him, in many ways personified early, traditional diplomatic studies with its focus on the role and techniques of professional diplomats serving in the foreign ministry at home and in embassies abroad. Nicolson came to be a staunch critic of the multilateral method, deeming it susceptible to propaganda and distorting pressures from ill-informed publics. He argued that "diplomacy by conference" ("the American method") was damaging and dangerous and would undermine the discretion and confidentiality required for effective diplomacy (Nicolson [1954] 1966, 119, 99; Otte 2001, 151–180).

Bolshevik revolutionaries also criticized the old diplomacy, but for different reasons. After the 1917 Russian Revolution, Vladimir Lenin and Leon Trotsky challenged the need for the traditional sovereign state, seeing it as a tool of the bourgeoisie and thus of diplomacy itself. Indeed, as foreign commissar in 1918, Trotsky famously promised to issue a few declarations and to shut down the foreign ministry (Hamilton and Langhorne 1995, 148–153). This did not happen, as we know, but diplomacy's very existence was challenged. The Bolsheviks regarded Wilson's promotion of multilateral diplomacy as a Western attempt to cloak a bourgeois institution in sheep's clothing. Notwithstanding the objections of Western skeptics and Soviet revolutionaries, diplomacy came to be seen in both bilateral and multilateral terms after World War I. In short, multilateral diplomacy's rise in the interwar years, notably in the League of Nations (but also in such technical bodies as the International Labor Organization), constituted a major paradigm shift toward "institutionalized multilateralism" (Thakur 2002, 283).

Following World War II and during the Cold War, IR theory in the United States paid relatively little attention to the theoretical, let alone practical, dimensions of multilateral diplomacy. There were, however, important exceptions, such as Hans Morgenthau's classic *Politics Among Nations* ([1948] 2006, chs. 31 and 32). Influential research was done on European integration (Haas [1958] 2004), but this fell under the IR and international organization rubrics, not diplomatic studies (Barnett and Finnemore 2008, 41–57). It focused on institutional design and cooperation effects at the macro level, not on the micro level social practices of the organizations' diplomats and bureaucrats—the fodder of diplomacy scholars. Thus, only a few scholars addressed bilateral and multilateral diplomatic norms, rules, and relationships from a procedural perspective, concentrating on "the technicalities and minutiae of the day-to-day duties and responsibilities of the diplomat [as] chronicled in numerous manuals, memoirs, and biographies of practitioners" (Muldoon 2005, 7). This emphasis on practice distinguishes diplomatic studies as a subfield of IR, differing significantly in method, temperament, and focus from such well-established fields as international organization and such recently established fields as global governance.

Since the Cold War's end and the related rise of globalizing economic forces and their impact on trade, scholars of diplomacy have tended to see themselves as members of a distinctive field of study. Much of their work has focused on multilateral diplomacy, sometimes at the expense of bilateral diplomacy. Additionally, thoughtful writings by former practitioners describe multilateral practices in astute detail with a view to improving the process (Walker 2004).

In spite, or perhaps because, of U.S. ambivalence toward the United Nations, a strong body of writings about the United Nations emerged during the late and post–Cold War periods. (For a good summary, see Weiss and Daws 2007; also see, for example, Ruggie 1993; Luck 1999; Schlesinger 2003; Malone 2004; Hurd 2007; Bosco 2009; and Patrick 2009.) It is notable that much of this literature tends not to see the United Nations in diplomatic terms, in the senses used here. Moreover, the scholarship fits not under diplomatic studies but under the rubric of IR or UN studies.[3]

As noted earlier, diplomatic studies differs from other fields in not taking diplomacy for granted. Scholars of diplomacy have drawn attention to various practical innovations in multilateral diplomacy—for instance, peacekeeping (James 1990), informal groups (Leigh-Phippard 1999), and the use of the United Nations and other venues for back-channel contacts (Bell 1999). In so doing, these scholars generally perform as epistemic torchbearers—that is, scholars of a subject whose importance goes unrecognized by others. The field of diplomatic studies has been overshadowed by others like UN studies, foreign policy analysis, international organizations, and international political economy.

Until about twenty years ago, the study of diplomacy tended to "address" multilateral diplomacy rather than "conceptualize" its worthwhile focus on practices. Traditionally, diplomatic studies has shown less interest in conceptualizing and theorizing itself and on doing so in ways that draw on, and speak to, other fields of study. This has now changed significantly, and interesting new work is being done by theorists with interdisciplinary sensibilities and, in some cases, intimate insider knowledge.

The Institution of Diplomacy

Diplomacy may be seen in a wide sense as an institution that helps provide order in the international society of states and in a narrow sense as the process by which individual sovereign states or other entities with standing conduct relations by peaceful means (Jönsson and Hall 2005, 25).

Perhaps more than any other branch of IR, English School theory—with epistemic and intellectual connections to what I am calling diplomatic studies—has given most weight to the notion of diplomacy as an institution. Most boldly of all, Martin Wight described the diplomatic system as the "master-institution" of IR (1986, 113). In *The Anarchical Society*, Hedley Bull described diplomacy as one of five key institutions underpinning and maintaining international order, along with the balance of power, international law, war, and the great powers (Bull [1977] 2002; on the English School, see also Dunne 1998; Neumann 2003; Buzan 2004; Sharp 2009).

Although the first generation of English School writers (e.g., Wight, Bull, Herbert Butterfield, and Adam Watson) wrote about the United Nations and multilateral diplomacy, they tended to give more weight to the traditional diplomatic culture of bilateral diplomacy, especially as practiced by the Great Powers. In the edited volume *Diplomatic Investigations*, Herbert Butterfield wrote about "the new diplomacy" from a historical perspective. He wondered "in what way operations at the UN may have required a new kind of diplomacy, or resulted in the development of new techniques," but he did not pursue the question (1966, 192).

In addition to conceptualizing diplomacy as a key requirement for order, Bull developed the concept of a diplomatic culture. Interestingly, he saw the diplomatic corps in the world's capitals and "universal international organizations, especially the United Nations," as symbolizing the existence of the society of states and manifesting diplomatic culture (Bull [1977] 2002, 166, 176; see also Der Derian 1996; Wiseman 2005). In *Diplomacy: The Dialogue Between States*, former British diplomat Adam Watson argued that "collective diplomacy in its various forms is gaining in importance over bilateral diplomacy; but even collective diplomacy takes place largely outside the United Nations" ([1982] 2004, 156). However, in writing about the post-1945 proliferation of new states arising from decolonization, Bull and Watson argued in their edited volume *The Expansion of International Society* (1984) that postcolonial states generally adopted Western diplomatic institutions and methods. For Bull, the colonized and nonaligned world's "revolt against the West" occurred in many locations, the United Nations being just one of them. Still, as Watson argued in the early 1980s, "more than half of the states now members of the United Nations have either resumed or acquired independence since 1945" ([1982] 2004, 158; see also Roberts and Kingsbury 1993).

Yet, by the end of the twentieth century, much diplomacy involving "postcolonial" states occurred within the multilateral UN system. Thus, it can be argued that the United Nations, today comprising 192 member states, is "in effect international society's membership committee" (Wiseman 2007, 254), a role once performed through accumulated recognition declarations and practices in bilateral capitals. Examples include UN membership for the People's Republic of China in the early 1970s; Namibia, the Koreas, and Russia and the other Soviet successor states in the early 1990s; and subsequently Timor Leste and Montenegro.

A Multilateralized World Diplomatic System?

Whether diplomacy has become more multilateral than bilateral has been a recurring question. But it has often been subsumed in a debate about the putative decline of diplomacy, a debate concluding at times that the international order has become less bilateral, more multilateral, and even more regional. In this view, diplomacy changed from bilateral to multilateral but did not decline (Hocking 1999). Growth in the number of international organizations has helped make the case: 37 in 1909, 123 in 1951, and 244 in 2006. However, bilateralism's days are far from numbered (Leguey-Feilleux 2009, 102, 361).

Since the Cold War ended, the United Nations' fortunes have waxed and waned with changing international circumstances, although, arguably, the Security Council has retained, even added to, its paramount status (Malone 2004; Bosco 2009). But even when multilateralism at the United Nations was challenged (as during the oil-for-food scandal and the 2003 invasion of Iraq), the growth of regional multilateral diplomacy, notably in the European Union (EU), was impressive (Hocking and Batora 2009). The EU is distinctive because of its intricate web of diplomatic and paradiplomatic networks. But also important is the rise of other regional diplomacies, outside Europe and not necessarily tied to the UN system, which was originally thought to have spawned them. The Association of Southeast Asian Nations (ASEAN) is a case in point. Unlike the EU case, ASEAN regional diplomacy has grown without the formal institutionalization earlier thought necessary (Zhang 2008, 131). In Africa, too, a number of subregional arrangements have emerged in southern and western Africa, coalescing—even if fitfully—with the establishment of the African Union (Lee, Taylor, and Williams 2006; cf. Hamilton and Langhorne 1995, 202–209; Langhorne 2005, 301).

Comparing the European, Southeast Asian, and African cases of regionalized diplomacy, it is evident that assumptions about the evolution of the institution of diplomacy in the wider sense are present. The EU model was constructed on a theory of peace that would make war between France and Germany unthinkable. The ASEAN regional diplomatic model has been more deeply rooted in the norm of "nonintervention" and "norm localization" (Acharya 2004). And the African Union "model" has in some ways been forced into action by major political, economic, and humanitarian crises, suggesting research opportunities for scholars of diplomatic studies. The diplomatic underpinnings (assumptions and practices) of regional versus UN processes are likely to be significant and must be better understood.

While there is much evidence that the world diplomatic system is becoming more multilateral, the bilateral diplomatic model is not obsolete. Bilateralism is clearly important in, for instance, the U.S.-Russian, U.S.-Chinese, India-Pakistan, and Ethiopian-Somali relationships. Moreover, diplomacy's continuing bilateral vocation lies partly concealed by the diplomatic "declinist thesis" and by current scholarship eager to show the influence of globalizing and regionalizing forces. Michael Wesley (2007) makes this case in describing a bilateral turn in Australia's Asian diplomacy from 1996 to 2006. For other writers connected to diplomatic studies, the bilateral resident diplomat survives and in some ways is being asked by governments to do even more. Canadian Robert Wolfe (1998) has argued that significant numbers of resident bilateral ambassadors remain abroad. Kishan Rana, a former Indian diplomat responsible for a number of studies of diplomacy, reinforced the point, noting that in 1999 the "great majority of ambassadors on full-time assignments resident abroad engage in classic diplomacy, at bilateral posts"; he further noted that in 1999 there were some 7,700 resident ambassadors, "an average of 41 ambassadors in each of the world's capitals" (2007, 37; see also Sharp 1997; Sharp and Wiseman 2007). Finally, many developing countries wisely seek to conduct bilateral affairs in multilateral venues to stretch their diplomacy dollars.

A Unilateralized World Diplomatic System?

If the international system has become more multilateralized and regionalized, it can also be said to have become unilateralized. The main issue here is the United States' post–Cold War hegemonic rise in world affairs, which clearly affected the conduct of multilateral diplomacy, notably under President George W. Bush. Putting aside the obvious question of whether any unilateral act is commensurate with diplomacy, there is widespread agreement that the institution of diplomacy, with UN multilateralism at its core, came under intense declaratory attack from neoconservatives within the Bush administration, especially in the lead up to the 2003 U.S.-led invasion of Iraq.[4] Not unrelated is Alan Henrikson's notion that diplomacy is becoming more and more like American domestic politics (2006, 20–26).

The Bush administration's dismissive approach to the United Nations revealed the depth of global acceptance of the multilateral norm; that is, for many of the world's governments and publics, multilateralism had assumed taken-for-granted status. Paradoxically, the Bush view may have resurrected the multilateral norm to the point where many rallied to it, the most important evidence being President Barack Obama's election in 2008. Obama has embraced both diplomacy and multilateralism, a shift strongly signaled by his appointment of Susan Rice as U.S. permanent representative to the United Nations, restoring the post's cabinet-rank position (Weiss 2009, 141). In short, the Obama administration so far tends to see diplomacy as an institution, or as a general theory that international affairs should be conducted with a view to achieving a measure of both order and justice in the international system, rather than simply as a forum for promoting narrow U.S. interests.

Changes in the Perception and Practice of Multilateralism

It should be clear by now that multilateral diplomacy emerged during the twentieth century as a central norm of diplomacy, joining bilateral diplomacy (loosely equivalent to the continuous dialogue norm) as another key diplomatic-culture norm underpinning the institution and practice of diplomacy.

This norm's emergence variously affected the perception and practice of multilateralism within diplomatic studies.[5] First, there is no longer the notion (if, indeed, there ever was) that multilateral diplomacy should be restricted to the high politics of peace and security. Since 1945, multilateral diplomacy has been practiced with varying degrees of effectiveness in three domains: peace and security (e.g., Korea, Namibia, the 1990–1991 Gulf War, Cambodia, Kosovo, Rwanda); international economic development (e.g., humanitarian relief, poverty, health); and sociocultural issues (e.g., human rights, preservation of historical and cultural sites). Reflecting its wartime foundations, the UN Charter privileged peace and security, notably in the power given to the Security Council, but it also envisaged multilateral work in the other domains of international policy. Today, consensus seems to be that the UN system must address all three simultaneously.

Second, as already noted, scholars of diplomacy widely accept that multilateral diplomacy will operate within both global and regional frameworks. Again, the framers of the UN Charter envisaged regional arrangements, but they could not have anticipated the dramatic growth in regional institutions since the 1950s and the commensurate impact on diplomatic practice. Here, the EU has set the standard in formal institutional cooperation, and scholars of diplomacy have been quick to discern the trends (Hocking 1999; Hocking and Spence 2002). But as mentioned above, other regions have developed new, often informal diplomatic practices. Importantly, the rise of Asia-Pacific regional diplomacy has been unaccompanied by strong, formal institutions. Yet, the region has seen a degree of multilateral socialization, including that of such rising powers as China (Zhang 2008, 131; see also Johnston 2008).

Third, the growth in multilateral economic and trade diplomacy in recent decades has been striking. When one considers Nicolson's remark that in his day it was regarded "by the older diplomatists" as "undignified" that they "should concern themselves with questions of commerce" ([1954] 1966, 109), two points become clear: Modern diplomats are performing ever-increasing multilateral economic diplomacy, and scholars of diplomacy are following this trend closely (Lee and Ullrich 2009).

A fourth area where the perception and practice of multilateralism within diplomatic studies has changed relates to transparency. Again, Nicolson derided Wilson's attempts to import parliamentary practices into multilateral diplomacy, including summitry. Multilateral diplomacy practices (e.g., voting, parliamentary-style speechmaking, speaking directly to publics) are now taken for granted and closely studied by diplomacy scholars (Bourantonis 2006). One could also note the understudied diplomatic role of national members of parliament (Weisglas and de Boer 2007). These "parliamentary" changes are reflected in the title of historian Paul Kennedy's book: *The Parliament of Man* (2006). Nonetheless, there remains a degree of opacity at the United Nations, especially concerning Security Council operations. Ironically, this opaque side allows below-the-radar diplomacy to be conducted between representatives of states and political entities lacking formal diplomatic relations with each other (Berridge 1994, 94–98).

In such ways, diplomatic studies has chronicled many changes occurring in the practice of multilateral diplomacy, although more so with respect to the EU than the United Nations. Comparative research on why the European countries have moved forward with a multitude of institutional reform plans affecting the EU's diplomatic practices while the United Nations has had difficulty reforming its charter and institutions in any fundamental way would be of interest.

Nonstate Actors

Among those who study diplomacy, there is widespread agreement that even if the sovereign state remains the key actor, nonstate actors "increase the complexity of diplomacy and diversify the way in which it is carried out" (Leguey-Feilleux 2009, 101). A number of diplomacy scholars have contributed to this conceptual debate (Sharp 1997; Langhorne 1997; Coolsaet 1999; Cooper and Hocking

2000). My term for encapsulating state-nonstate relationships is *polylateral diplomacy*, which I define as

> the conduct of relations between official entities (such as a state, several states acting together, or a state-based international organisation) and at least one unofficial, nonstate entity in which there is a reasonable expectation of systematic relationships involving some form of reporting, communication, negotiation, and representation, but not involving mutual recognition as sovereign, equivalent entities. (Wiseman 2004, 41)

One advantage of this term is that it distinguishes the nature of state-nonstate interactions and relationships from the two basic forms of diplomacy: bilateral (between two states) and multilateral (between three or more states). Another advantage is that it clearly indicates that the relationship is a form of diplomacy, that the participants are thinking and acting diplomatically in that they are performing functions associated with diplomacy: They represent, communicate, report on, negotiate with, and promote friendly relations between entities with standing. We now live in a world diplomatic system in which all three types of diplomacy are conducted simultaneously, even if the scope of each varies from issue to issue and region to region. If the twentieth century saw the formal acceptance of multilateral diplomacy as a complement to traditional bilateral diplomacy, then the newly turned century has seen the advent of polylateral diplomacy.[6]

Because of multilateral diplomacy's "parliamentary" nature, nongovernmental organizations (NGOs) have more conceivably become diplomatic actors. Since the UN Charter provided for consultative status for NGOs with its Economic and Social Council (ECOSOC), the resultant growth has been impressive—NGOs accredited to ECOSOC numbered 2,719 in 2005. But the actual impact of NGO consultative status, including the accreditation process, is not well understood from a diplomatic studies perspective, despite fine work done in other fields from which much can be learned (Willetts 2000). The record of the World Bank and International Monetary Fund in opening their annual meeting is even more impressive (Leguey-Feilleux 2009, 107, 109). Are these nonstate entities co-opted by the system, or have they shifted the system in any meaningful way? Do these new diplomatic actors mimic or emulate the state (Johnston 2008, 45–73)? We need to learn a lot more about mutual socialization in a multilateral setting.

Scholars from several fields of study, as well as former UN officials and professional journalists, have written on the UN secretary-general's role and the unique brand of leadership and diplomacy expected of the incumbent (e.g., Urquhart 1984; Newman 1998; Traub 2006; Chesterman 2007; Meisler 2007). More needs to be learned, however, about the subtle changes in daily diplomatic practices that have occurred within the UN Secretariat (e.g., Muldoon 2005). We also need to know more about the public information (or public diplomacy) practices of international secretariats within the multilateral system. Some of these have been innovative, even involving some risk; perhaps the best examples are the celebrity-based Goodwill Ambassador and Messenger of Peace programs designed to promote UN objectives with wider publics (Cooper 2008; see also Pigman and Kotsopoulos 2007).

Additionally, we need to know how diplomats and officials at multilateral institutions are trained and how they make microdecisions and manage daily work practices that, cumulatively, are consequential (Araim 2005; Jonah 2008). Decision-making theories tend to focus on big decisions. Scholars of diplomacy should make a virtue of their expertise in procedural detail and develop projects and methods contributive to an emerging literature that conceptualizes multilateral diplomacy's routine practices (Wiseman 2007, 254–260; for pioneering conceptual work on Norwegian diplomats, see Neumann 2005; Neumann 2007; see also Pouliot 2008; Rancatore 2009, 283).

Diplomatic studies still accords primacy to the sovereign state as the chief actor in world affairs, but scholars in the field are fully aware of the contested nature of sovereignty. These scholars tend to see states as more porous than they were only twenty or thirty years ago (as a result of globalization and the Cold War's end). Diplomacy and its "machinery" of professional diplomats are still relevant to managing issues in world affairs, but relations can no longer be conducted solely with other states, in a bilateral or a multilateral context. Diplomacy is now multilayered (Hocking 1999; Copeland 2009). A question for future research is, What is beyond polylateralism? In other words, how will we conceptualize and define sustained interactions and relations not involving a sovereign-state actor? Would this be diplomacy or something else?

Conclusion

There is abundant evidence supporting the claim that multilateral diplomacy is now one of diplomacy's five key norms. And there are good reasons to believe that the development of multilateral diplomacy has had a positive effect on the four other key norms of diplomacy.

First, the UN Charter set a clear standard for the key norm that force should be used only in self-defense, and even though that marker has been honored more in the breach, its significance is extremely important to the modern diplomatic dialogue about war. Second, UN multilateral diplomacy is conducted alongside much traditional bilateral diplomacy, further encouraging the norm of continuous diplomatic dialogue. Third, the debate about a new diplomacy that occurred after World War I strengthened the norm that diplomacy should be as open as possible to the publics or, at the very least, that the results of diplomatic negotiations should be conveyed to, and not hidden from, publics. Excepting perhaps the Security Council, the multilateral UN system has promoted this openness norm (White 2005, 391–392). Fourth, many UN observers note that its deliberations are conducted with civility. This norm, like multilateralism, has a strong taken-for-granted quality, so that when it is transgressed—by, for example, a Nikita Khrushchev or Hugo Chávez—it tends to be reinforced.

There are now essentially three forms of recognized diplomacy: bilateral, multilateral, and polylateral, although the last of these, already functioning widely, is not yet fully conceptualized or, indeed, fully accepted. All three forms are practiced within the UN system, and in that context, diplomatic studies should continue focusing on the practical dynamics and characteristics of multilateralism while also pursuing a new trend toward theorizing practice. The good diplomat of the late twentieth century had to be able to conduct bilateral and multilateral diplomacy simultaneously at the United Nations and elsewhere; many diplomats today must be able to conduct simultaneously all three forms of diplomacy. The institution of diplomacy now has—and needs—three major, interconnected strands.

Notes

1. Thus, a field of diplomatic studies is manifested, for example, by membership in the diplomatic studies section of the International Studies Association or by association with *The Hague Journal of Diplomacy*. Both are relatively new professional networks, suggesting that diplomatic studies may still be more of a tradition than a field. For a disciplinary review of the relationship between diplomacy and international relations, see P. Sharp (1999). For a taxonomic review of the field, see S. Murray (2008). Note that authors cited in this chapter are indicative rather than comprehensive; for a full list of readings on the United Nations, see T. G. Weiss and S. Daws (2007, appendix 1).

2. In distinguishing between theory and practice, I am sensitive to Robert W. Cox's warning that "theory is always *for* someone and *for* some purpose" (1981, 128).

3. The United Nations University produced an impressive book list, conscious of multilateralism's diplomatic underpinnings but not necessarily focusing on them as the main variable (Newman, Thakur, and Tirman 2006).

4. Compare with UN historian Stephen Schlesinger (2008), who has argued compellingly that the Bush administration, bluster notwithstanding, actually worked closely with the United Nations to achieve policy goals.

5. Most of these claims are supported to some extent by a review of *The Hague Journal of Diplomacy*, which is perhaps "the only academic journal devoted entirely to diplomacy" (Melissen and Sharp 2006, 1).

6. An important antecedent framework was advanced by Susan Strange (1992), who argued that diplomacy had become three sided (or triangular), involving not only traditional state-state relations but also state-firm and firm-firm diplomacy.

References

Acharya, A. 2004. How ideas spread: Whose norms matter? Norm localization and institutional change in Asian regionalism. *International Organization* 58 (spring): 239–275.

Anderson, M. S. 1993. *The rise of modern diplomacy, 1450–1919*. London: Longman.

Araim, A. 2005. The journey of an Iraqi diplomat: From bilateral to multilateral diplomacy and on to the United Nations Secretariat. In *Multilateral diplomacy and the United Nations today*, ed. J. P. Muldoon et al., 42–60. Boulder, CO: Westview Press.

Barnett, M., and M. Finnemore. 2008. Political approaches. In *The Oxford Handbook on the United Nations*, ed. T. G. Weiss and S. Daws, 41–57. Oxford: Oxford University Press, 2008.

Bell, M. 1999. A bilateral dialogue regime: U.S.-Vietnamese relations after the fall of Saigon. In *Innovation in diplomatic practice*, ed. J. Melissen, 195–213. Basingstoke, UK: Macmillan.

Berridge, G. R. 2005. *Diplomacy: Theory and practice*. 3rd ed. Basingstoke, UK: Palgrave.

———. 1994. *Talking to the enemy: How states without diplomatic relations communicate*. New York: St. Martin's Press.

Berridge, G. R., and A. James. 2003. *A dictionary of diplomacy*. 2nd ed. Basingstoke, UK: Palgrave Macmillan.

Berridge, G. R., M. Keens-Soper, and T. G. Otte. 2001. *Diplomatic theory from Machiavelli to Kissinger*. Basingstoke, UK: Palgrave.

Bosco, D. L. 2009. *Five to rule them all: The UN Security Council and the making of the modern world*. Oxford: Oxford University Press.

Bourantonis, D., ed. 2006. The chair in multilateral negotiations. Special Issue, *The Hague Journal of Diplomacy* 1, no. 2: 143–170.

Bull, H. [1977] 2002. *The anarchical society: A study of order in world politics*. 3rd ed. New York: Columbia University Press.

Bull, H., and A. Watson, eds. 1984. *The expansion of international society*. Oxford: Clarendon Press.

Butterfield, H. 1966. The new diplomacy and historical diplomacy. In *Diplomatic investigations*, ed. H. Butterfield and M. Wight. Cambridge, MA: Harvard University Press.

Buzan, B. 2004. *From international to world society?* Cambridge: Cambridge University Press.

Chesterman, S., ed. 2007. *Secretary or general? The UN secretary-general in world politics.* Cambridge: Cambridge University Press.

Cohen, R. 2001. The great tradition: The spread of diplomacy in the ancient world. *Diplomacy and Statecraft* 12, no. 1: 23–38.

Coolsaet, R. 1999. The transformation of diplomacy at the threshold of the new millennium. Discussion Papers No. 48. Leicester, UK: Leicester Diplomatic Studies Program.

Cooper, A. F. 2008. *Celebrity diplomacy.* Boulder, CO: Paradigm Publishers.

Cooper, A. F., and B. Hocking. 2000. Governments, non-governmental organizations and the re-calibration of diplomacy. *Global Society* 14, no. 3: 361–367.

Copeland, D. 2009. *Guerrilla diplomacy: Rethinking international relations.* Boulder, CO: Lynne Rienner.

Cox, R. W. 1981. Social forces, states and world orders: Beyond international relations theory. *Millennium* 10, no. 2: 126–155.

Davis Cross, M. K. 2007. *The European diplomatic corps: Diplomats and international cooperation from Westphalia to Maastricht.* Basingstoke, UK: Palgrave Macmillan.

Der Derian, J. 1996. Hedley Bull and the idea of diplomatic culture. In *International society after the Cold War: Anarchy and order reconsidered*, ed. R. Fawn and J. Larkins. Basingstoke, UK: Macmillan Press.

Dunne, T. 1998. *Inventing international society: A History of the English school.* Basingstoke, UK: Macmillan.

Finnemore, M., and K. Sikkink. 1998. International norm dynamics and political change. *International Organization* 52, no. 4: 887–917.

Haas, E. [1958] 2004. *The uniting of Europe: Political, social, and economic forces, 1950–1957.* Notre Dame, IN: University of Notre Dame Press.

Hamilton, K., and R. Langhorne. 1995. *The practice of diplomacy: Its evolution, theory and administration.* London: Routledge.

Henrikson, A. K. 2006. Diplomacy's possible futures. *The Hague Journal of Diplomacy* 1, no. 1: 3–27.

Hocking, B. 1999. Catalytic diplomacy: Beyond "newness" and "decline." In *Innovation in diplomatic practice*, ed. J. Melissen, 21–42. Basingstoke, UK: Macmillan.

Hocking, B., and J. Batora, eds. 2009. Diplomacy and the European Union. Special Issue, *The Hague Journal of Diplomacy* 4, no. 2: 113–120.

Hocking, B., and D. Spence, eds. 2002. *Foreign ministries in the European Union: Integrating diplomats.* Basingstoke, UK: Palgrave Macmillan.

Hurd, I. 2007. *After anarchy: Legitimacy and power in the United Nations Security Council.* Princeton, NJ: Princeton University Press.

James, A. 1990. *Peacekeeping in international politics.* London: Macmillan.

Johnston, A. I. 2008. *Social states: China in international institutions, 1980–2000*. Princeton, NJ: Princeton University Press.

Jonah, J. O. C. 2008. Secretariat: Independence and reform. In *The Oxford Handbook of the United Nations*, ed. T. G. Weiss and S. Daws, 160–174. Oxford: Oxford University Press.

Jönsson, C., and M. Hall. 2005. *Essence of diplomacy*. Basingstoke, UK: Palgrave Macmillan.

Jönsson, C., and R. Langhorne. 2004. *Diplomacy*. 3 vols. London: Sage.

Keens-Soper, M. A., and K. W. Schweizer, eds. 1983. *François de Callières: The art of diplomacy*. New York: Leicester University Press.

Kennedy, P. 2006. *The parliament of man: The past, present, and future of the United Nations*. New York: Random House.

Langhorne, R. 2005. New directions in multilateral diplomacy: The changing roles of state and nonstate actors in diplomatic practice. In *Multilateral diplomacy and the United Nations today*, ed. J. P. Muldoon et al., 298–308. Boulder, CO: Westview Press.

———. 1997. Current developments in diplomacy: Who are the diplomats now? *Diplomacy and Statecraft* 8, no. 2: 1–15.

Lee, D., I. Taylor, and P. D. Williams, eds. 2006. *The new multilateralism in South African diplomacy*. Basingstoke, UK: Palgrave Macmillan.

Lee, D., and H. Ullrich. 2009. The diplomacy of WTO accession. Special Issue, *The Hague Journal of Diplomacy* 4, no. 1: 1–5.

Leguey-Feilleux, J.-R. 2009. *The dynamics of diplomacy*. Boulder, CO: Lynne Rienner.

Leigh-Phippard, H. 1999. The influence of informal groups in multilateral diplomacy. In *Innovation in diplomatic practice*, ed. J. Melissen, 94–110. Basingstoke, UK: Macmillan.

Luck, E. C. 1999. *Mixed messages: American politics and international organizations, 1919–1999*. Washington, DC: Brookings Institution Press.

Malone, D., ed. 2004. *The UN Security Council: From the Cold War to the 21st century*. Boulder, CO: Lynne Rienner.

Mattingly, G. 1955. *Renaissance diplomacy*. London: Jonathan Cape.

Mearsheimer, J. 1994–1995. The false promise of international institutions. *International Security* 19, no. 3 (winter): 5–49.

Meisler, S. 2007. *Kofi Annan: A man of peace in a world of war*. Hoboken, NJ: Wiley.

Melissen, J., and P. Sharp. 2006. Editorial. *The Hague Journal of Diplomacy* 1, no. 1: 1–2.

Morgenthau, H. [1948] 2006. *Politics among nations*. 7th ed. New York: McGraw Hill.

Muldoon, J. P. 2005. Introduction to *Multilateral diplomacy and the United Nations today*, ed. J. P. Muldoon et al., 1–11. Boulder, CO: Westview Press.

Murray, S. 2008. Consolidating the gains made in diplomacy studies: A taxonomy. *International Studies Perspectives* 9, no. 1: 22–39.

Neumann, I. B. 2007. "A speech that the entire ministry may stand for," or why diplomats never produce anything new. *International Political Sociology* 1, no. 2: 183–200.

————. 2005. To be a diplomat. *International Studies Perspectives* 6, no. 1: 72–93.

————. 2003. The English school on diplomacy: Scholarly promise unfulfilled. *International Relations* 17, no. 3: 341–369.

Newman, E. 1998. *The UN secretary-general from the Cold War to the new era.* Basingstoke, UK: Macmillan.

Newman, E., R. Thakur, and J. Tirman, eds. 2006. *Multilateralism under challenge?* Tokyo: United Nations University Press.

Nicolson, H. [1939] 1969. *Diplomacy.* London: Oxford University Press.

————. [1954] 1966. *The evolution of diplomacy.* New York: Collier Books.

Otte, T. G. 2001. Nicolson. In *Diplomatic theory from Machiavelli to Kissinger,* ed. G. R. Berridge, M. Keens-Soper, and T. G. Otte, 51–80. Basingstoke, UK: Palgrave.

Patrick, S. 2009. *Best laid plans: The origins of American multilateralism and the dawn of the Cold War.* Lanham: Rowman & Littlefield.

Pigman, G. A., and J. Kotsopoulos. 2007. "Do this one for me, George": Blair, Brown, Bono, Bush and the "actor-ness" of the G-8. *The Hague Journal of Diplomacy* 2, no. 2: 127–145.

Pouliot, V. 2008. The logic of practicality: A theory of practice of security communities. *International Organization* 62 (spring): 257–288.

Rana, K. S. 2007. *Asian diplomacy: The foreign ministries of China, India, Japan, Singapore and Thailand.* Msida, Malta: DiploFoundation.

Rancatore, J. P. 2009. Using "pace" in diplomatic analysis. *The Hague Journal of Diplomacy* 1, no. 2: 283–305.

Roberts, A., and B. Kingsbury, eds. 1993. *United Nations, divided world: The UN's roles in international relations.* Oxford: Clarendon Press.

Ruggie, J. G., ed. 1993. *Multilateralism matters: The theory and praxis of an institutional form.* New York: Columbia University Press.

Satow, E. M. [1917] 1957. *A guide to diplomatic practice,* ed. Nevile Bland. London: Longmans, Green and Co.

Schlesinger, S. C. 2008. Bush's stealth United Nations policy. *World Policy Journal* 25, no. 2: 1–9.

————. 2003. *Act of creation: The founding of the United Nations.* Boulder, CO: Westview Press.

Sharp, P. 2009. *Diplomatic theory of international relations.* Cambridge: Cambridge University Press.

————. 2001. Making sense of citizen diplomats: The citizens of Duluth, Minnesota, as international actors. *International Studies Perspectives* 2, no. 2: 131–150.

————. 1999. For diplomacy: Representation and the study of international relations. *International Studies Review* 1, no. 1: 33–57.

————. 1997. Who needs diplomats? The problem of diplomatic representation. In *Diplomacy,* vol. 3, *Problems and Issues in Contemporary Diplomacy,* ed. C. Jönsson and R. Langhorne, 58–78. London: Sage.

Sharp, P., and G. Wiseman, eds. 2007. *The diplomatic corps as an institution of international society.* Basingstoke, UK: Palgrave Macmillan.

Sofer, S. 1988. Old and new diplomacy: A debate revisited. *Review of International Studies* 14, no. 3: 195–211.

Strange, S. 1992. States, firms and diplomacy. *International Affairs* 68, no. 1: 1–15.

Thakur, R. 2002. Security in the new millennium. In *Enhancing global governance: Towards a new diplomacy?* ed. A. F. Cooper, J. English, and R. Thakur, 106–132. Tokyo: United Nations University Press.

Traub, J. 2006. *The best intentions: Kofi Annan and the UN in the era of American world power.* New York: Farrar, Straus and Giroux.

Urquhart, B. 1984. *Hammarskjold.* New York: Harper and Row.

Walker, R. A. 2004. *Multilateral Conferences: Purposeful international negotiation.* Basingstoke, UK: Palgrave Macmillan.

Watson, A. [1982] 2004. *Diplomacy: The dialogue between states.* London: Methuen.

Weisglas F. W., and G. de Boer. 2007. Parliamentary diplomacy. *The Hague Journal of Diplomacy* 1, no. 2: 93–99.

Weiss, T. G. 2009. Towards a third generation of international institutions: Obama's UN policy. *The Washington Quarterly* 32, no. 3: 141–162.

Weiss, T. G., and S. Daws. 2007. *The Oxford handbook of the United Nations.* Oxford: Oxford University Press.

Wesley, M. 2007. *The Howard paradox: Australian diplomacy in Asia, 1996–2006.* Sydney: ABC Books.

White, B. 2005. Diplomacy. In *The globalization of world politics*, ed. J. Baylis and S. Smith, 387–403. 3rd ed. Oxford: Oxford University Press.

Wight, M. 1986. *Power politics.* 2nd ed. Harmondsworth, UK: Penguin Books.

Willetts, P. 2000. From "consultative arrangements" to "partnership": The changing status of NGOs in diplomacy at the UN. *Global Governance* 6, no. 2: 191–212.

Wiseman, G. 2007. Esprit de corps: Sketches of diplomatic life in Stockholm, Hanoi, and New York. In *The diplomatic corps as an institution of international society*, ed. P. Sharp and G. Wiseman, 246–264. Basingstoke, UK: Palgrave Macmillan.

———. 2005. Pax Americana: Bumping into diplomatic culture. *International Studies Perspectives* 6, no. 4: 409–430.

———. 2004. "Polylateralism" and new modes of global dialogue. In *Diplomacy*, vol. 3, *Problems and issues in contemporary diplomacy*, ed. C. Jönsson and R. Langhorne, 36–57. London: Sage.

Wolfe, R. 1998. Still lying abroad? On the institution of the resident ambassador. *Diplomacy & Statecraft* 9, no. 2: 23–54.

Zhang, Y. 2008. Anticipating China's future diplomacy: History, theory, and social practice. In *China's "new" diplomacy: Tactical or fundamental change?* ed. P. Kerr, S. Harris, and Qin Y, 131–149. Basingstoke, UK: Palgrave/Macmillan.

2

Systemic Change, International Organizations, and the Evolution of Multilateralism

Michael G. Schechter

We are living in an era of structural transformation. Not simply has pre–World War II multipolarity and Cold War bipolarity been replaced by unipolarity, but missiles, nuclear technology, globalization, and attendant global norms about such phenomena as humanitarian intervention and popular participation in governance have eroded the "pillars of state sovereignty" (Zacher 1992). Concomitant with these structural changes has been a redefinition of international organizations and a revision of the conventional understanding of multilateralism. This chapter chronicles the ways in which changes in the international system, and especially in the roles of nonstate actors, have been reflected in the works of international organization scholars in general and the concept of multilateralism in particular.

Multilateralism is traditionally understood as a dialogue among government representatives who "hope to work out common approaches to common concerns" (Holmes 2009, 9). Multilateralism, involving representatives from three or more countries, is seen to complement "the enormous amount of bilateral [one government representative to one other] diplomacy that thousands of government officials conduct every day to promote and protect their nations' interests and priorities" (Holmes 2009, 9).[1]

> While a bilateral relationship between many countries is clearly entered into in order to produce some direct, tangible, military, economic, or cultural gain, the benefits to be gained from a state's participation in multilateral arrangements are often far less obvious. Especially when

resources are scarce, decision makers will often wonder if the time and money spent at the United Nations or in regional organizations is well spent, and whether the pursuit of the collective global or regional interest will present unacceptable limitations and barriers to the satisfaction of their country's primary developmental and security ambitions (Braveboy-Wagner 2009, 1).

In addition to underscoring the controversies that surround engaging in multilateral diplomacy, these statements make clear that multilateralism can take place in any number of forums, including around the tables of global and regional international organizations. But multilateral conversations and negotiations can just as easily take place in the corridors of international organizations, outside of any formal international organization (as with the six-party talks relating to North Korean nuclear policy), in conference calls, or even over cyberspace. Thus, multilateralism should not be confused with formal international organizations. "This distinction is fundamentally important in order to differentiate a discussion about a crisis in multilateralism as a general principle from a discussion about a crisis in a special formal international organization" and vice versa (Newman 2007, 11). The former involves a debate as to whether governments can better achieve their ends acting on their own, unilaterally, negotiating one-on-one with another government, bilaterally, or multilaterally. The latter crises involve questions about whether participation in a particular international organization (like the United Nations or the European Union) is worthwhile, recognizing as Jacqueline Braveboy-Wagner does that multilateral diplomacy within intergovernmental organizations has costs as well as potential benefits. The distinction is also essential to understand the development of normative orders in the so-called Third World, especially Asia, Africa, and the Middle East, where formal regional organizations remain weak (Acharya 2006), but multilateral diplomacy has resulted in a confluence of views on issues related to trade, human rights, and the use of force. As this chapter shows, however, the meanings of international organization and multilateralism are not simply distinguishable but also dynamic and contentious.

International Organizations and International Institutions

The traditional focus of international organizations was on intergovernmental organizations, understood to be organizations comprising members representing three or more governments. Those with only two governments represented are called bilateral organizations; thus, negotiations going on within them are bilateral negotiations. Intergovernmental organizations have been differentiated in a number of other ways. Some speak of universal intergovernmental organizations, where the membership is open to all governments, as contrasted to regional intergovernmental organizations, where the membership is restricted. Sometimes inclusion is dictated by geography (e.g., the African Union comprises governments on the African continent), but other times this is less the case (as with the Organization for Economic Cooperation and Development). In their classic textbook on decision making in intergovernmental organizations, Robert Cox and Harold Jacobson differentiate intergovernmental organizations in two "ideal types": forum organizations and service organizations. "Some organizations are established to provide a forum or framework for negotiations and decisions, others to provide specific services." Forum organizations, which are of more immediate interest to us in this chapter, "carry on many activities ranging from the exchange of views to the negotiation of binding legal instruments" (i.e., multilateralism as traditionally understood). However, Cox and Jacobson go on to note that governments often use forum organizations "for the collective legitimation of their polices or for propaganda" (1973, 5–6).

Far outnumbering intergovernmental organizations are international nongovernmental organizations, more often referred to, somewhat imprecisely, as nongovernmental organizations (NGOs). In such organizations, the members do not represent governments, although the funding for NGOs can come from government sources. To further complicate matters, in some organizations—most notably the International Labour Organization—representatives are both from governments and not. In this instance, labor unions, corporations, and governments are represented in a long-standing tripartite arrangement. It should be noted that the generic term *international organizations* is often used to describe both intergovernmental organizations and international nongovernmental organizations. Indeed, the Union of International Associations (UIA) takes this approach in the *Yearbook of International Organizations*, one endorsed decades ago by the Economic and Social Council of the United Nations. The UIA subdivides international organizations into federations of international organizations (a category that does not exclude for-profit international bodies), universal membership organizations, intercontinental membership organizations, and regionally defined membership organizations.

It should also be noted that some scholars "confusingly" refer to international organizations as international institutions, whereas Maurice Duverger's classic definition of institutions—"the collective forms or basic structures of social organization as established by law or by human tradition"—is obviously more encompassing, including relationships that need not manifest themselves in formal organizations of bricks and mortar, with letterheads and international staffs, as do international organizations (Archer 2001, 1–2). That is, intergovernmental organizations are a subset of international organizations, which, in turn, are a subset of international institutions, which have been defined as "persistent and connected sets of rules, formal and informal, that prescribe behavioral roles, constrain activity, and shape expectations" (Keohane 1990, 732).

Multilateralism

The definition of multilateralism also suffers from confusion and imprecision. In the United Nations, something is only considered multilateral if it is duly authorized by a multilateral forum. Otherwise, it is called multinational—for instance, the multinational (non-UN) observer team that served in the Sinai (Ruggie 1993, 39n18). Robert Keohane, one of the most prominent scholars of international relations of the twentieth century, defines multilateralism in a way that best approximates what policy makers and the media mean when they use the term: "Multilateralism can be defined as the practice of co-ordinating national policies in groups of three or more states, through ad hoc arrangements or by means of institutions" (1990, 731). Bates Gill and Michael Green adopt the language of "minilaterals" to describe ad hoc multilateral arrangements among like-minded countries "to address and resolve specific, commonly faced challenges" (Gill and Green 2009, 10). Behind this is the principle that the smaller and more homogenous the group, the easier it is to achieve consensus, and that consensus could be at a relatively higher common denominator than a larger coalition of preset members (Karns and Mingst 1990, 313). What Gill and Green seem to have in mind are the so-called coalitions of the willing that the United States has found particularly attractive of late, given that it is no longer as in control of intergovernmental organizations as it once was (Gill and Green 2009, 10). But Emanuel Adler writes of ad hoc arrangements in a broader sense, what he calls "communitarian multilateralism," "primarily institutionalized efforts to socially construct multilateral communities, either as a corollary of the expansion of communities of practice—like-minded groups of individuals who engage in the same practice—and/or as inclusive forms of security, which security communities, such as the European Union (EU), use in their attempt to stabilize their environments."

Adler's examples make clear what he has in mind, for in writing of security partnerships, he is not limiting himself to the North Atlantic Treaty Organization (NATO) but rather also discusses so-called constructed social spaces or regions, like a "greater Middle East" or "the Mediterranean region" or the "European neighborhood" (Adler 2006, 37–38). Thus, for Adler, ad hoc multilateral arrangements are socially constructed, underscoring not simply the difference between formal multilateral institutions and socially constructed ones but also between those constructed, in an ad hoc manner, by the global hegemon and those mutually constructed by like-minded actors, not necessarily powerful in any materialist way.

Multilateralism is understood by liberal institutionalists to bring stability, reciprocity in relationships, and regularity in behavior. It is understood as "necessary because all states face mutual vulnerabilities, all share interdependence, and all need to benefit from—and thus support—public goods. Even the most powerful states in the world cannot achieve security, environmental safety and economic prosperity in isolation or unilaterally, and so the international system rests upon a network of regimes, treaties and international organizations" (Newman 2007, 10). Braveboy-Wagner, whose interest is in multilateralism in the South (i.e., countries with less power and generally less wealth), contends that "multilateralism, whether at the global or at the regional level, enables global south states to share strategic information and ideas, to draw global attention to their particular concerns, to reduce the costs or penalties for noncooperation with dominant northern partners via the assumption of collective stances . . . and to facilitate adoption of alternative courses of action that would be less likely to work if states adopted them singly" (2009, 7). Thus, whereas the costs and benefits to governments of countries at different levels of economic development vary, there is widespread agreement among many international organization scholars of multilateralism's increasing use, and presumably its value, to countries throughout the globe.

Arthur Stein has usefully written of the often overlooked value of multilateralism as a source of both international and domestic legitimacy. A government seeks to work in concert with other governments, in part because that suggests that the government's objectives "are not particularistic national interests but common interests." At the same time, multilateralism "provides domestic legitimacy to governments that need the support of citizens to sustain their foreign policies" (Stein 2008, 47–49). Keohane notes that the sources of this legitimacy are both "output" and "input," that is, derived from achievement of the substantive purposes of the institution and from the processes by which decisions are reached that result in those achievements (2006, 58). Amitav Acharya emphasizes the roles that multilateral institutions play in interpreting and extending norms: "The norms of multilateralism themselves vary, and undergo adaptation and transformation in different historical and regional contexts" (Acharya 2006, 97). While John Ruggie is famous for writing about how post–World War II multilateral institutions (especially those founded at Bretton Woods) embedded economic liberalism as a global norm, a similar point can be made about the role of multilateral institutions in embedding human rights norms. While much is made of the role of the United Nations in articulating and even codifying international human rights norms, beginning with the aspirational Universal Declaration of Human Rights, as Richard Goldstone and Erin Kelly argue, what may be even more important is the role of multilateral institutions in embedding those norms in national and regional regimes. Even "when leaders of non-democratic nations disregard international human rights norms, the norms remain significant to the extent that they are adopted by domestic constituencies and help shape reform movement advocacy. South Africa is a prominent example of the value of such international norms in bolstering reform and contributing to the transition to democracy." There is also a "tendency" for "national courts to look to international standards" (Goldstone and Kelly 2006, 270–273).

Multilateralism and International Organizations

There are other theories of international relations, most notably realism and neo-realism, which take the position that international institutions have minimal influence on world politics, even in such "low politics" issues as human rights and the economy. John Mearsheimer is probably most famous for taking this position. As he puts it, "My central conclusion is that institutions have minimal influence on state behavior, and thus hold little promise for promoting stability in the post–Cold War world" (1994–1995, 3).

Acharya obviously has a very different perspective, in language that sounds more constructivist than realist or even liberal institutionalist. Indeed, what interests him is how some of the self-same multilateral institutions that once helped institutionalize norms may now be displacing or transforming the norms that they once helped to institutionalize (Acharya 2006, 96–97). In this regard Acharya helpfully provides five "drivers" for multilateralism's promotion of normative changes: increased global and economic interdependence; emergence of new transnational challenges; changes in the global distribution of power, opening up space for new roles for multilateral institutions; global spread of democracy, providing a more conducive climate for multilateral organizations to effectuate changes within member countries; and the global spread of civil society among the globe's leading norm entrepreneurs (2006, 105–107).

The role of the United Nations and its connection to state sovereignty seems to accord with Acharya's insight. In his widely acclaimed Agenda for Peace, former UN secretary-general Boutros Boutros-Ghali boldly proclaimed, "Respect for its [the state's] fundamental sovereignty and integrity are crucial to any common international progress. The time of absolute and exclusive sovereignty, however, has passed; its theory was never matched by reality" (United Nations 1992). Obviously such a redefinition was necessary for the United Nations to embrace humanitarian intervention as an evolving norm, but at the same time it is in tension with the fundamentally statecentric nature of the United Nations itself. Indeed, the UN Charter's provision relating to state sovereignty boldly states,

> Nothing contained in the present Charter shall authorize the United Nations to intervene in matters which are essentially within the domestic jurisdiction of any state or shall require the Members to submit such matters to settlement under the present Charter; but this principle shall not prejudice the application of enforcement measures under Chapter VII. (Article 2[7])

Of the uses of the multilateral form historically, the resolution of collaboration problems is the least frequent. In the literature, that fact traditionally has been explained by the rise and fall of hegemonies and, more recently, by various functional considerations. Ruggie's analysis suggests that a permissive environment in the leading powers of the day is at least as important. Looking more closely at the post–World War II situation, for example, he suggests that "it was less the fact of American *hegemony* that accounts for the explosion of multilateral arrangements than of *American* hegemony" (1993, 8). Still, it is worth noting that while international institutions have come to cover just about every issue area of importance in international relations in the post–World War II era, "they vary across issue-areas in the extent to which they are designed to support, supplement, or supplant a world market economy" (Keohane 1990, 761).

It needs to be pointed out, however, that Keohane defines multilateralism, as it has been traditionally, that is, as involving states. For him, it is intergovernmental relations, which only reflects a subset of relations among peoples that transcend state boundaries. More recently, scholars such as Phillip Jones and David

Coleman have argued that it is insufficient to limit multilateralism to intergovernmental relations (2005, 3–4). With the erosion of the pillars of state sovereignty and international relations scholars' increased attention to interactions among and between nonstate actors, including NGOs, transnational advocacy and transnational social movements, and intergovernmental organizations, they argue that the analysis of multilateralism in the twenty-first century "needs to incorporate these institutionalized means of promoting concerns, many of which are expressed at the local level as well as the national, regional and global levels." Of course, they are not arguing that the state has lost its place, or even necessarily its primacy, in world politics as various elements of civil society have enhanced their prominence and, in some instances, their power and influence. Indeed, they argue that along with the enhanced influence and attention to civil society actors, the enhanced role of subnational political entities as advocates of the less powerful warrants the redefining of multilateralism (Jones and Coleman 2005, 4). But they argue, with examples like the Global Compact in which the United Nations has sought to work with multinational corporations and the World Bank's funding of NGOs, that intergovernmental interactions are only a subset of interactions that characterize an increasingly globalized world, and thus they believe that the concept of multilateralism needs to be broadened or it, too, will only refer to a subset of the key interactions in the contemporary world. Still, in their writings, they have distinguished economic multilateralism from political multilateralism, wherein the latter is more conventionally understood "with its emphasis on engagement through state diplomacy and through inter-governmental organizations," unlike economic multilateralism where interactions among nonstate actors are seemingly more pervasive (Jones and Coleman 2005, 3–4).

In some ways, Thomas Legler's work on democratization in Latin America raises questions of the continued relevance of Jones and Coleman's distinctions between political and economic multilateralism. Legler suggests that traditional intergovernmental (or interstate) political multilateralism assumed "executive sovereignty," that is, "the externally recognized supreme authority of heads of state and government, as well as their diplomatic representatives." Moreover, he argues that executive sovereignty, at least in the inter-American context, had long been reinforced by a "club mentality," one in which state leaders and their representatives "follow a strict set of diplomatic rules, such as mutual respect and recognition of executive prerogatives, as privileges of membership in their executive club" (Legler 2007, 124). Pierre de Senarclens is even more critical of this conventional, political multilateralism, identifying it chiefly with the United Nations:

The UN became the center of a very particular multilateral diplomacy whose principal function was to give government representatives an opportunity to deliberate, interact on a personal level, ritualize through complicated procedures and ceremonials the manifestation of their state sovereignty, maintain through rhetoric and propaganda their own national authority and their international legitimacy, find ways and means to play out their conflict on a symbolic level, and also to benefit occasionally from the program resources allocated by the system. (2007, 12–13)

As a consequence, de Senarclens argues that governments and their representatives

attach more importance to the formalities of UN multilateralism than to its substance. They use it to defend the diplomatic prerogatives associated with a traditional conception of state sovereignty. They preserve the rituals of lengthy and tedious negotiations and, in so doing, they encourage a surreal political rhetoric, which diverts the international organizations from their sector-based functions. They tend to invest in the symbolic and rhetorical aspects of the various UN bodies and even of some of its specialized agencies. They use them to put forward their own ideological agendas as fora for diplomatic exchange, and to ensure the presence of their representatives on the various commissions and ad hoc committees. This particular form of multilateralism is a serious obstacle to constructive dialogue and to the implementation of concrete programs of action. It contributes to the crisis in the legitimacy and accountability of the UN system. Diplomats in New York and Geneva are indeed regularly overstretched by the obligation to attend a daily load of different meetings on a great variety of topics. It is particularly burdensome for poor countries whose limited number of representatives have to rush from one meeting to another, with little possibility of making a substantive contribution to the debates and unable . . . to absorb the enormous number of reports being published by the secretariats. Since part of this multilateralism is devoid of substantive issues, governments tend to dispatch junior diplomats to these meetings. Lacking clear instructions, and sometimes even the appropriate technical competence, these representatives have little inclination to take the content of programs seriously. They also devote time and energy to promoting the appointment of their representatives to various UN bodies, or to the chair of one of these bodies,

rather than to the substance of the debate. The frailty of checks and bal-
ances within the system is also due to the fact that the positions taken
by diplomats in international fora are not subject to scrutiny by the
media or national parliaments. (2007, 29–30)

Thus, in de Senarclens's view, the United Nations, and by implication many other
intergovernmental organizations, suffers from being statecentric and, as a consequence, out of synch with the structural transformations of the post–Cold War
era, especially those of the so-called third wave of democracy, globalization, and
other contributing factors to the erosion of the pillars of state sovereignty. But, as
Legler suggests, de Senarclens may be overstating the case, even in the United
Nations, where there have been discussions of a so-called chamber of peoples (Peterson 2006, 144): "But just as sovereignty of the ruler has yielded historically to
democratic, popular sovereignty in many countries, state-centric club multilateralism is under pressure to become more inclusive, wherein members of civil society
participate in multilateral discussions, at times using support gained externally to
influence internal debates, the so-called 'boomerang' effect" (Legler 2007, 124).
Legler and Andrew Cooper have labeled this "networked multilateralism." Not
simply is the process different—having more involvement with civil society, being
significantly quicker and somewhat more open, and lacking an obsession for seeking consensus—but the goals are different, namely, affecting the domestic political
processes within member countries (i.e., piercing that hard shell of state sovereignty). Cooper and Legler also recognize that in many instances, traditional club
multilateralism interacts with members of civil society, which they refer to as complex, or hybrid, multilateralism (2006, 20–21, 85).

Robert O'Brien and his colleagues, focusing on the interaction between multilateral economic institutions and global social movements, discuss what they call
"complex multilateralism." Consistent with view of the primacy of states, they
note that "complex multilateralism has not challenged the fundamentals of the
existing world order, but it has incrementally pluralized governing structures."
And thus far, at least, it "has largely taken the form of institutional modification
rather than substantive policy innovation" (O'Brien 2000, 3). Jackie Smith specifically identifies the ways in which social movements have contributed to multilateralism and singles out three: "by advocating for multilateral solutions to global
problems, by cultivating popular constituencies for multilateralism, and by relating struggles to international norms and institutions." Notable examples of the
first way include the League of Nations and, more recently, the International

Criminal Court. Popular constituencies were important in generating opposition to apartheid, and social movements are important in publicizing government violations of treaty provisions and encouraging achievement of the Millennium Development Goals (Smith 2006, 396–397). Smith also takes note of social movements that contest globalization (2006, 398–401). These include what others refer to as social-justice and counterhegemonic movements. Indeed, some consider these the only true social movements (Eschle and Maiguashca 2005). Cox also refers to them as bottom-up forces: "Bottom-up forces not only counteract top-down pressures from established political authorities. They also legitimate or delegitimate authority in the state and would constitute the basis for a new multilateralism in [a future, post-Westphalian, posthegemonic, postglobalization] world system" (1997a, xx, xxv).

While accepting Keohane's differentiation between organizations and institutions and keeping an intergovernmental focus to his understanding of the concept of multilateralism, John Ruggie, another major figure in the field of international relations, suggests that Keohane's "nominal" definition may be useful for some purposes. But it "misses the *qualitative* dimensions of the phenomenon that makes it distinct." Ruggie notes that what he calls "qualitative" multilateralism is basically the same as what William Diebold calls "substantive" multilateralism, and what Ruggie calls "nominal," Diebold calls "formal" (Ruggie 1993, 6). Qualitative or substantive multilateralism means the kind of relations that are instituted among the parties on the basis of ordering principles among them, in other words, "generalized principles of conduct: that is, principles which specify appropriate conduct for a class of actions, without regard to the particularistic interests of the parties or the strategic exigencies" (Ruggie 1993, 11). The best example of this nondiscrimination is in trade relations. In the security field, Ruggie exemplifies this with reference to collective security or collective self-defense (1993, 9–10). Michael Barnett is most interested in Ruggie's attention to the purposes of multilateral arrangements. In particular, Barnett notes the interplay between global security issues in the post–Cold War period and their impact on broadening the definition of security—and, in turn, the degree to which that broadened definition has affected multilateral security organizations like the UN Security Council and NATO, including in terms of their attention to humanitarian intervention. Accordingly, he sees the evolution of what he calls "humanized multilateralism" (Barnett 2008, 139–141). Frank Schimmelfennig, on the other hand, is interested in the institutional aspects of multilateralism, especially as they relate to NATO in the post–Cold War era. He contends that the members of an organization most demonstrate multilateralist behavior when confronted with a threat to their core values. His point is that it is less the multilateralist structure (flexible or not) that determines the multilateralist behavior of its members than it is the threat to common values (e.g., ethnic cleansing in the Balkans or the attack on a member state on September 11, 2001) (Schimmelfennig 2008, 184–185). Both agree that the end of the Cold War has required international organizations to adapt to the change in power distribution in the world, unlike at the end of both world wars, when new institutions were established. Of course, the proliferation of global conferences in the postdecolonization era did in fact give rise to a new sort of institutional format and conference diplomacy.

> Multilateral diplomacy in its recent manifestations is distinctly different from the multilateral diplomacy of prewar and immediate postwar conferences. Reasons include the incidence of bloc voting, the role of ideology and its impact on bargaining flexibility, differing expectations among Third World delegates, the proliferation of independent states, the growth of multilateral bureaucracies with very definite ideological orientations, the wide publicity associated with contemporary international conferences, the growth of non-governmental organizations (NGOs), and the increased activity of domestic interest groups in the foreign policy domain. (Graham, Kauffman, and Oppenheimer 1984, 3)

Complicating matters, of course, is that the world is now hegemonic or unipolar, suggesting that the reorganization of intergovernmental organizations should be more reflective of that distribution of power if they expect the dominant global power (the United States) to see active support in its self-interest. Otherwise, one would expect it to act more unilaterally than in the past. William Ascher puts it this way: "Multilateralism under the control of a hegemonic power is not much different from disguised bilateralism. As long as the hegemon can rely on the multilateral agency to send the same message, or to send a desired message that would have been awkward to send through bilateral channels, multilateralism is a sophisticated way of making the hegemon's message less offensive and of magnifying its impact by putting the force of the multilateral agency and other member states behind the message" (1990, 137). But to counter this argument, Stein makes a kind of path-dependency argument, one that seems to accept what Mearsheimer and other realists and neorealists deny, namely, that international organizations have become increasingly autonomous actors in world politics, in part at least owing to mission creep (Stein 2008, 65). In Stein's words:

Although unilateralism remains an ever-present possibility and although international organizations reflect the power and interests of their members, the growing number of such organizations, as well as international laws and agreements, over the past century makes multilateralism an existential reality. The world consists of overlapping clubs in every region and functional domain. Indeed, the number of intergovernmental organizations well exceeds the number of states in the system, and there are so many international treaties and agreements that it is impossible to compile a complete list. Thus, although the option of unilateralism is available, the existence of such a large array of international institutions sustains a multilateralist reality. (2008, 49–50)

By the somewhat arcane expression that multilateralism is "an existential reality," Stein means that "much as governments try to deny the reality, much as they try to go it alone, in the end they are constrained by the reality they can do little of any consequence without acting in conjunction with important others" (2008, 50). Shepard Forman makes the same point:

Multilateralism is no longer a choice. It is a matter of necessity, and of fact. It exists in the thousands of conventions and treaties that nation-states have signed, in the institutions that have been established to implement and monitor these agreements, and in the international courts and tribunals that resolve disputes arising among their members. In its institutional guise, multilateralism provides access to countries that would on their own hardly be players on the world stage, while constraining arbitrary or coercive action by the most powerful. Multinational institutions provide the legal and normative framework and legitimacy for transnational action. They permit coordination and encourage cost sharing; and they limit out-riding by those who prefer not to follow the rules of the game, as well as free riding by those who would rely on the beneficence of self-interest of others. (2002, 439)

Cox underscores the structural point made, almost in passing, by these theorists: Multilateralism can only be understood within the historical structure of world order in which it exists. But, he adds, "multilateralism is not just a passive, dependent activity. It can appear in another aspect as an active force shaping world order. The agent/structure dilemma is a chicken-and-egg proposition" (1996a, 494). A critical approach to multilateralism thus directs our attention toward the establishment of a social order which is seen to be embedded in the nexus between material conditions, interests and ideas. A particular order is, under this interpretation, stabilized and perpetuated through "institutionalization." Multilateral institutions thus reflect the power relations prevailing at their point of origin and tend, at least initially, to facilitate worldviews and beliefs (for instance in the merits of neoliberal economics) in accordance with these power relations. This implies that power relations are embedded in all multilateral institutions, even if these are supposedly based on diffuse reciprocity and formal equality among the member countries. Ideas also serve diverse social purposes and thereby also influence how member states define their interests in multilateral institutions. Thus, the multilateral institutions as such matter, and not just their member states. Outcomes are determined not simply by the distribution of power among the members that constitute the institution in question, but also by the multilateral institution itself, which can affect how choices are framed and outcomes reached. (Bøås and MacNeill 2003, 5–6)

James Caporaso, building on Ruggie, says that multilateralism is distinguished from other forms of institutions by three properties: indivisibility, generalized principles of conduct, and diffuse reciprocity.

Indivisibility can be thought of as the scope (both geographic and functional) over which costs and benefits are spread. . . . Generalized principles of conduct usually come in the form of norms exhorting general, if not universal, modes of relating to other states, rather than differentiating relations case-by-case on the basis of individual preferences, situational exigencies, or a priori particularistic grounds. Diffuse reciprocity adjusts the utilitarian lenses for the long view, emphasizing that actors expect to benefit in the long run and over many issues, rather than every time on every issue. (Caporaso 1993, 53–54)

Coming from a critical theoretical (as contrasted to problem-solving) approach to international relations, Cox dissents from Keohane, Ruggie, and their fellow travelers. Because critical approaches do not derive from the existing world order, they do not assume that states are the basic entities. Instead, such approaches ask what the basic forces may be. Applying such an approach—which Cox calls the new realism—to the problem of multilateralism involves "attempting to link two dynamics: the dynamic of structural change in world order, and the dynamic of development of multilateral practices" (Cox 1997a, xvii). While recognizing the range of forces and institutions being taken into account by scholars like Jones and Coleman, O'Brien and his colleagues, and perhaps especially Smith, Cox sees that as still granting formal status to a only a limited range of existing forces. But, more importantly, the "new multilateralism" that interests Cox "is potential, not actual. It would be built from the bottom up and on the basis of broadly articulated global society." That is, although elements of it are evolving today in what some call the global civil society, for Cox the "new multilateralism" (new in the sense of unconventional, not temporally) cannot come into full bloom until there has been a fundamental structural transformation, which is dependent on a significant shift of power away from states and the people who run them, who have a vested interest in the current statecentric world. He sees this new world order as being post-Westphalian (states still exist, but not as primary actors in world politics), posthegemonic, and postglobalization. "The 'new multilateralism' will not come from piecemeal reform of old multilateral institutions but rather as part of a decomposition of civil society and political authority from the bottom up" (Cox 1997b, 258). Current thinking about multilateralism (i.e., the old multilateralism) is portrayed as pluralist, which assumes that there is a mutual recognition of the integrity and equality of different value systems, at the same time that many support globalization and its homogenizing impacts. In contrast, and taking into account conflicting civilizational constructs and normative preferences, Cox writes, "A new multilateralism will have to begin by elucidating and making more explicit the diverse coexisting ontologies—the competing interpretations of the world. This consists, in the first place, in an exercise in empathetic understanding, the ability to get inside the mind of the 'other' while retaining one's own identity" (1997a, xxv). This leaves the real challenge for the new multilateralism as being "to bridge distinct unities and identities and to achieve a common perception of reality that is not merely the imposition of a single hegemonic perspective" (Cox 1997b, 253).

Summary and Conclusions

The twenty-first century finds the simultaneous resurgence of multilateralism within intergovernmental organizations at the same time that bilateral negotiations and critical multilateral diplomacy are occurring outside of formal intergovernmental organizations. The best example of the first is the ratification of the Lisbon Treaty and the increased multilateral coordination in the European Union that comes with the unprecedented appointment of the first permanent president of the European Council and the first high representative for foreign and security policy. At the same time, important multilateral discussions are occurring in NATO, the UN Security Council, and the Group of Twenty, to name just a few. But competing for headlines is multilateralism outside of formal intergovernmental organizations, including the so-called six-party talks, involving North Korean nuclear proliferation and the 2009 Copenhagen Conference, as well as bilateralism. While the last seemed to typify negotiations in the Middle East, the North Korea government also insisted on face-to-face bilateral discussions with the United States.

This suggests that while the latest crisis of multilateralism (really meaning the crisis in selected intergovernmental organizations, most notably NATO and the UN Security Council) may have subsided, bilateralism and multilateral negotiations are not a thing of the past. Indeed, as we have seen, some governments prefer negotiating outside formal intergovernmental organizations; this includes some smaller and weaker states, those traditionally expected to be the biggest supporters of formal intergovernmental organizations, where the options for coalition building are omnipresent (Braveboy-Wagner 2009, 5–6).

While there is evidence of the invigoration of civil societies in countries throughout the globe, there is simultaneously—especially in the aftermath of the 2008–2009 global recession—a reassertion of state sovereignty and a kind of reinforcement of the pillars of state sovereignty, especially in terms of financial regulation but also in terms of immigration restrictions. As a consequence, those—like Cox—who see the "new multilateralism" as contingent on the evolution of a post-Westphalian world may have seen their prospects dim somewhat. That is, those who take a critical approach to international relations rather than a problem-solving one, not taking the world as it is but rather standing apart from the world order in which they live (Cox 1996b, 88–89), find that the world order they believe will be more successful in eliminating inequalities and achieving peace remains more an abstraction than a reality. On the other hand, as this chapter has suggested, events of the post–World War II era, especially since the end of the Cold War, have led other scholars of international organization and multilateralism to alter their focus and to take account of the complexity of events on the ground, often inventing new terminology to explain the variants in multilateralism that characterize the world order in which we now live.

Note

1. This chapter does not address issues of bilateralism. This is not because bilateralism is not important. Indeed, Beth Simmons (2006, 441) makes a strong case for the challenges bilateralism presents to multilateralism, at least in the world trade regime. Bilateralism is not discussed here as it is definitionally separable from multilateralism.

References

Acharya, A. 2006. Multilateralism, sovereignty and normative change in world politics. In *Multilateralism under challenge? Power, international order, and structural change*, ed. E. Newman, R. Thakur, and J. Tirman, 95–118. Tokyo: United Nations University Press.

Adler, E. 2006. Communitarian multilateralism. In *Multilateralism under challenge? Power, international order, and structural change*, ed. E. Newman, R. Thakur, and J. Tirman, 34–55. Tokyo: United Nations University Press.

Archer, C. 2001. *International organizations.* 3rd ed. New York: Routledge.

Ascher, W. 1990. The World Bank and U.S. control. In *The United States and multilateral institutions: Patterns of changing instrumentality and influence*, ed. M. P. Karns and K. A. Mingst, 115–140. Boston: Unwin Hyman.

Barnett, M. 2008. Is multilateralism bad for humanitarianism? In *Multilateralism and security institutions in an era of globalization*, ed. D. Bourantonis, K. Ifantis, and P. Tsakonas, 136–162. New York: Routledge.

Bøås, M., and D. MacNeill. 2003. *Multilateral institutions: A critical introduction.* Sterling, VA: Pluto Press.

Braveboy-Wagner, J. A. 2009. *Institutions of the global South.* New York: Routledge.

Caporaso, J. A. 1993. International relations theory and multilateralism: The search for foundations. In *Multilateralism matters: The theory and praxis of an institutional form*, ed. J. G. Ruggie, 51–90. New York: Columbia University Press.

Cooper, A. F., and T. Legler. 2006. *Intervention without intervening? The OAS defense and promotion of democracy in the Americas.* New York: Palgrave Macmillan.

Cox, R. W. 1997a. Introduction to *The new realism: Perspectives on multilateralism and world order*, ed. R. W. Cox, xv–xxx. Tokyo: United Nations University Press.

———. 1997b. Reconsiderations. In *The new realism: Perspectives on multilateralism and world order*, ed. R. W. Cox, 245–262. Tokyo: United Nations University Press.

———. 1996a. Multilateralism and world order. In *Approaches to world order*, ed. R. W. Cox and T. J. Sinclair, 494–523. Cambridge: Cambridge University Press.

———. 1996b. Social forces, states, and world orders: Beyond international relations theory. In *Approaches to world order*, ed. R. W. Cox and T. J. Sinclair, 85–123. Cambridge: Cambridge University Press.

Cox, R. W., and H. K. Jacobson. 1973. The framework for inquiry. In *The anatomy of influence: Decision making in international organization*, ed. R. W. Cox, and H. K. Jacobson, 1–36. New Haven, CT: Yale University Press.

de Senarclens, P. 2007. The UN as a social and economic regulator. In *Regulatory globalization: Critical approaches to global governance*, ed. P. de Senarclens and A. Kazancigil, 8–37. Tokyo: United Nations University Press.

Eschle, C., and B. Maiguashca, eds. 2005. *Critical theories, international relations and "the anti-globalisation movement": The politics of global resistance*. New York: Routledge.

Forman, S. 2002. Multilateralism as a matter of fact: U.S. leadership and the management of the international public sector. In *Multilateralism and U.S. foreign policy: Ambivalent engagement*, ed. S. Patrick and S. Forman, 437–460. Boulder, CO: Lynne Rienner.

Gill, B., and M. J. Green. 2009. Unbundling Asia's new multilateralism. In *Asia's new multilateralism: Cooperation, competition, and the search for community*, ed. M. J. Green and B. Gill, 1–29. New York: Columbia University Press.

Goldstone, R. J., and E. P. Kelly. 2006. Progress and problems in the multilateral human rights regime. In *Multilateralism under challenge? Power, international order, and structural change*, ed. E. Newman, R. Thakur, and J. Tirman, 259–288. Tokyo: United Nations University Press.

Graham, N. A., R. L. Kauffman, and M. F. Oppenheimer. 1984. *The United States and multilateral diplomacy: A handbook*. New York: Oceana Publications, Inc.

Holmes, K. R. 2009. Smart multilateralism: When and when not to rely on the United Nations. In *ConUNdrum: The limits of the United Nations and the search for alternatives*, ed. B. D. Schaefer, 9–29. Lanham, MD: Rowman & Littlefield Publishers.

Jones, P. W., and D. Coleman. 2005. *The United Nations and education: Multilateralism, development and globalization*. New York: RoutlegeFalmer.

Karns, M. P., and K. A. Mingst. 1990. Continuity and change in U.S.-IGO relationships: A comparative analysis with implications for the future of multilateralism in U.S. foreign policy. In *The United States and multilateral institutions: Patterns of changing instrumentality and influence*, ed. M. P. Karns and K. A. Mingst, 321–350. Boston: Unwin Hyman.

Keohane, R. O. 2006. The contingent legitimacy of multilateralism. In *Multilateralism under challenge? Power, international order, and structural change*, ed. E. Newman, R. Thakur, and J. Tirman, 56–76. Tokyo: United Nations University Press.

———. 1990. Multilateralism: An agenda for research. *International Journal* 45: 731–764.

Legler, T. 2007. The inter-American democratic charter: Rhetoric or reality? In *Governing the Americas: Assessing multilateral institutions*, ed. G. Mace, J.-P. Therien, and P. Haslam, 113–130. Boulder, CO: Lynne Rienner.

Mearsheimer, J. 1994–1995. The false promise of international institutions. *International Security* 19, no. 3 (winter): 5–49.

Newman, E. 2007. *A crisis of global institutions? Multilateralism and international security*. New York: Routledge.

O'Brien, R. 2000. *Contesting global governance: Multilateral economic institutions and global social movements*. Cambridge: Cambridge University Press.

Peterson, M. 2006. *The UN General Assembly*. New York: Routledge.

Ruggie, J. G. 1993. Multilateralism: The anatomy of an institution. In *Multilateralism matters: The theory and praxis of an institutional form*, ed. J. G. Ruggie, 3–47. New York: Columbia University Press.

Schimmelfennig, F. 2008. Transatlantic relations, multilateralism and the transformation of NATO. In *Multilateralism and security institutions in an era of globalization*, ed. D. Bourantonis, K. Ifantis, and P. Tsakonas, 183–201. New York: Routledge.

Simmons, B. A. 2006. From unilateralism to bilateralism: Challenges for the multilateral trade system. In *Multilateralism under challenge? Power, international order, and structural change*, ed. E. Newman, R. Thakur, and J. Tirman, 441–459. Tokyo: United Nations University Press.

Smith, J. 2006. Social movements and multilateralism. In *Multilateralism under challenge? Power, international order, and structural change*, ed. E. Newman, R. Thakur, and J. Tirman, 395–421. Tokyo: United Nations University Press.

Stein, A. A. 2008. Incentive compatibility and global governance: Existential multilateralism, a weakly confederal world, and hegemony. In *Can the world be governed? Possibilities for effective multilateralism*, ed. A. S. Alexandroff, 17–84. Waterloo, Canada: Wilfrid Laurier University Press.

United Nations. 1992. *An agenda for peace: Preventive diplomacy, peacemaking and peacekeeping*. Report of the secretary-general pursuant to the statement adopted by the summit meeting of the Security Council on 31 January 1992. UN Document A/47/277-S/24111. United Nations. June 17. www.un.org/docs/sg/agpeace.html.

Zacher, M. W. 1992. The decaying pillars of the Westphalian temple: Implications for international order and governance. In *Governance without government: Order and change in world politics*, ed. J. N. Rosenau and E.-O. Czempiel, 58–101. Cambridge: Cambridge University Press.

3

Multilateralism Today and Its Contribution to Global Governance

Andreas Kruck and Volker Rittberger

The Relevance and Transformation of Multilateralism Today

More than fifteen years ago, John G. Ruggie, in his contribution to the seminal volume *Multilateralism Matters*, defined multilateralism as "an institutional form that coordinates relations among three or more states on the basis of generalized principles of conduct" (1993, 11). Generalized principles of conduct specify appropriate behavior "for a class of actions, without regard to the particularistic interests of the parties or the strategic exigencies that might exist in any specific occurrence" (Ruggie 1993, 11). Ruggie's original conception of multilateralism thus implies a world order based on diffuse, rather than specific, reciprocity[1] and international policy coordination between sovereign states, or more precisely their executive branches of government (cf. Caporaso 1993, 55); crucially, the reference to generalized principles of conduct signals a departure from the realist conception of the international system as an unregulated anarchical realm.

Under unregulated anarchy, states do not only have to provide for their security on their own; their security-seeking efforts also generate permanent security competition, which gives rise to a situation known as the security dilemma. Other states perceive a state's efforts to enhance its security by enlarging its power (i.e., control over resources) as threatening to their own security. This leads to a vicious circle of distrust, security competition, and strife for power, which always harbors the possibility of escalation into violent conflict (Rittberger and Zangl 2006, 15). By contrast, multilateralism (in Ruggie's conception) is a constitutive feature of a normative, that is, rules-based (rather than "natural"), world order whose basic ordering principle might be characterized as "regulated anarchy" (cf. Rittberger and Zürn 1990). While there is no common world government superimposed upon sovereign states, nonetheless there exist generalized principles of conduct governing states' interactions, reducing their uncertainty, stabilizing their expectations toward one another, and removing various obstacles to cooperation (cf. Hasenclever, Mayer, and Rittberger 1997, ch. 3). Generalized principles of conduct that are characteristic of multilateralism thus supersede and contain the effects of anarchy.

This conception of a multilateral world order reliant on rules-based interstate policy coordination lies at the heart of many scholarly notions of global governance today. To say that global governance, that is, collective action on the global level, which claims authority and is aimed at dealing with common cross-border problems and at producing global public goods, is not only possible but also actually taking place necessarily implies the recognition of generalized principles of conduct and thus some normative order beyond the nation-state. Empirically, multilateralism conceived as an institutional form for coordinating and organizing relationships between (and among) states according to generalized principles of conduct is a core component of the contemporary global governance architecture (cf. Karns and Mingst 2009; Muldoon 2003). This is evidenced by the salience of multilateral international institutions, that is, international organizations such as the United Nations, the International Monetary Fund, or the World Trade Organization (WTO) and international regimes such as the climate-stabilization regime built around the Kyoto Protocol on the reduction of greenhouse-gas emissions.[2] Furthermore, it seems obvious that without effective and legitimate multilateral institutions (both international organizations and international regimes), there can and will be no effective and legitimate global governance.

At the same time, the conditions for (effective and legitimate) global governance have greatly changed in the past two decades. Economic and societal globalization, shifts in global power structures, and transformations in prevailing global ideas, as well as a changing constellation of politically potent actors on the world stage (cf. Rittberger, Kruck, and Romund 2010, chs. 2 and 3) have increasingly put the traditional executive-multilateral system[3] of interstate policy coordination under pressure. Intergovernmental institutions, which were once created by states to regain political steering capacity in times of growing interdependencies, have suffered severe crises of effectiveness and legitimacy. At least partly in response to these deficiencies, multilateralism has changed in the past two decades both in terms of how it plays out empirically and how it is conceptualized in scholarly research concerned with the actual and the desired institutional shape(s) of global governance. More recent notions of an evolving global governance architecture go beyond a world order based on exclusive interstate coordination of policies under regulated anarchy. They also include institutionalized policy coordination and cooperation between (inter)state and nonstate actors such as civil society organizations and transnational business actors (Rittberger, Nettesheim et al. 2008; Steffek 2008).

In the face of material and ideational systemic changes and new actors entering the stage of world politics, there is a growing recognition that global governance is no longer the exclusive domain of states and intergovernmental organizations. Scholars of global governance stress the regulatory capacities of nonstate actors and point to the emergence of a variety of public-private and purely private institutional modes of governance beyond the state (Bernstein and Cashore 2008; Graz and Nölke 2008; Hutter 2006; Koenig-Archibugi 2006; Nölke 2004; Pattberg 2007). As a result, not only traditional executive-multilateral institutions but also a range of "new" public-private and private transnational institutions create and implement rules for the collective management of transsovereign problems and are involved in the provision of global public goods. Both public-private and purely private governance institutions transcend statecentric conceptions of an exclusive executive multilateralism. The pluralization of actors and institutional forms of global governance leading to an ever-denser network of governance institutions suggests the emergence of a heterarchical world order. This heterarchical order is organized in and by new institutional modes of "open" or even "inclusive" multilateralism, which grant nonstate actors institutionalized channels of access to, or participation in, global decision-making processes (Rittberger, Huckel et al. 2008).

This chapter pursues a twofold objective: It seeks to demonstrate that multilateralism, as an institutional form of global policy coordination according to generalized principles of conduct, continues to inform current thinking heavily about how the world is and should be governed. Yet, it also points out that, under the pressure of systemic changes (first of all, economic and societal globalization) and due to a new constellation of politically potent actors on the world stage, the shape of multilateralism has changed considerably and quite likely will continue to do so in the foreseeable future. There seems to be a (nonlinear) trend of institutional adaptation toward an opening of intergovernmental institutions vis-à-vis nonstate actors and even the emergence of inclusive, multipartite modes of multilateralism. Inclusive, multipartite modes of global governance rely on institutionalized policy coordination and cooperation between (and among) a broad range of public and private actors.

To develop these arguments, we first outline in more detail our conception of global governance and argue that the absence of a world government by no means precludes the provision of governance on the global level. We then sketch the emergence of a growing demand for global governance, which states have initially tried to meet by taking recourse to intergovernmental, executive-multilateral institutions. We explicate how far conceptions of global governance have been and still are informed by executive-multilateralist ideas. In the next step, we go on to show what kinds of deficiencies in terms of (problem-solving) effectiveness and legitimacy arise from purely executive-multilateral global governance. This is followed by a description of more recent institutional innovations in numerous issue areas of world politics, signaling a change in the institutional shape of multilateralism. We also offer theoretically grounded explanations for general trends and situational variations in institutional change toward open or inclusive multilateralism. Finally, we argue that a heterarchical world order—distinct from both anarchical and hierarchical orders—is emerging that builds upon, but at the same time goes beyond, interstate policy coordination.

Global Governance: Conceptual Features of Governance Beyond the State

Despite the growing popularity of the concept of global governance, there is still no consensus on the meaning of the concept (Dingwerth and Pattberg 2006, 185; Finkelstein 1995, 178). Therefore, we first outline our conception of global governance, including the feasibility of governance beyond the state, before discussing the growing demand for global governance and attempts to meet this demand through executive-multilateral means.

First of all, governance should not be confounded with government. Government refers to formal institutions that partake in hierarchical norm and rule setting, monitoring of compliance with rules, and rule enforcement. Governments have the power to *make* binding rules and to *enforce* them; in other words, governments allocate values authoritatively (Brühl and Rittberger 2001, 5). The term *governance* is more encompassing than that of *government* (Rosenau 1992, 4). It refs to a variety of purposive mechanisms steering social systems toward their goals (Rosenau 1999, 296), the most important political goals being security, welfare, legal certainty ("rule of law"), political participation, and the formation of a collective identity (Zürn 1998, 41). Governance can thus be understood as a process of intentional creation and implementation of political order, that is, of sets of (collectively binding[4]) norms and rules that facilitate the coordination and cooperation of social actors (Koenig-Archibugi 2006, 3; Rosenau 1992, 3; Trebesch 2008, 8).

More precisely, governance can be defined as collective action that claims authority[5] vis-à-vis norm addressees and aims at dealing with common problems and at producing public goods. Governance is a multistep process including (1) identifying promising and sustainable approaches to solve societal problems, (2) translating these approaches into rules of conduct, (3) ensuring adherence to these rules (which may range from persuasive communication and positive incentives to enforcement), and where necessary, (4) adjusting these rules to changing circumstances (Rittberger, Huckel et al. 2008, 46). Global governance refers to governance aimed at dealing with transsovereign, (potentially) global problems and at producing global public goods. Transsovereign problems are those that transcend state boundaries in ways over which states have little control and that cannot be solved by individual state action alone (Cusimano 2000, 3). Global public goods are material or immaterial goods (such as financial stability, international peace, and climate stability) with a global scope; per definition, no one can be excluded from the consumption of public goods, and their consumption by one actor does not reduce their availability for other actors (Kaul, Grunberg, and Stern 1999; Kaul and Mendoza 2003).

Governance may take different forms comprising "governance by government," "governance with governments," and "governance without governments" (Zürn 1998, 166–180). It is therefore crucial to note that governance is not limited to governance by government; in other words, the viability of global governance is not contingent on the existence of a world government. Governance by government, as we know it from the domestic realm of nation-states, refers to a hierarchical (top-down) mode of norm and rule setting and implementation. By contrast, governance beyond the nation-state takes place in the absence of a world government. Therefore, it usually takes the form of horizontal governance with multiple governments (and intergovernmental institutions) or governance without governments, that is, regulation of social behavior in an issue area by nonstate actors. Moreover, there are hybrid modes of horizontal public-private governance with governments and nonstate actors.

Thus, governance at the global level is fundamentally different from governance at the nation-state level in that it frequently lacks means of enforcement and predominantly relies on nonhierarchical, horizontal modes of policy coordination and cooperation. Nonetheless, governance can occur in a wide range of forms on various political levels, and the absence of a world government by no means implies an absence of global governance (Reinicke 1998). This is, of course, not to deny that there are particular structural difficulties associated with governance at the global level, leading to an often inadequate supply of global governance. In comparison to "governance by government" at the nation-state level, global governance is less backed by formal authority since most international institutions do not have strong monitoring, let alone enforcement, mechanisms (Brühl and Rittberger 2001, 7). The conditions for effective and legitimate governance at the global level are very demanding—but not impossible to fulfill. In fact, it can be shown that the level of compliance with norms and rules beyond the nation-state is surprisingly high in comparison to compliance with national norms and rules (Zürn 2005, 1; cf. Zangl 2006, 2009).

The Empirical Demand for Governance Beyond the Nation-State, (Executive) Multilateralism, and the Evolution of a Normative World Order

As long as governments were able to regulate political problems and to provide public goods independently (through "governance by government"), there was little need for governance beyond the nation-state (Brühl and Rittberger 2001, 6). However, in the decades after World War II, and even more so since the 1970s, the capacities of nation-states to pursue their governance goals on their own have become challenged: International interdependence has intensified as a result of expanding exchanges and transactions among individuals and collective actors. Individual states can no longer handle the problems arising from interdependence independently (Keohane and Nye 2001).

As a result, constraints on states' autonomous decision making and the need for political regulations beyond the nation-state have increased dramatically (Mayer, Rittberger, and Zürn 1993, 393). This has led nation-states to pursue an internationalization of governance through the creation and strengthening of executive-multilateral institutions in order to (re)gain political steering capacity. This strategy of internationalization of governance (cf. Genschel and Zangl 2008, 436–437) has included pooling or, less frequently, even delegating sovereignty.

Pooling sovereignty in multilateral organs such as the UN Security Council occurs when decisions are taken by common voting procedures other than unanimity; sovereignty is delegated when supranational organs such as the European Commission or the European Court of Justice are permitted to make certain decisions autonomously, without an intervening interstate vote or a member state's unilateral veto (Brühl and Rittberger 2001, 6; Moravcsik 1998, 67).[6]

An increasing demand for international cooperation and governance beyond the nation-state has contributed to the establishment of international institutions (both intergovernmental organizations and international regimes) (Rittberger and Zangl 2006, ch. 3). Not only has the internationalization of governance manifested itself in a growing number of international institutions and a higher density of rules in most issue areas of world politics, but existing international institutions have also enhanced their autonomy vis-à-vis member states (Barnett and Finnemore 2004) and (at least in some cases) expanded the depth of regulations by intruding further into internal matters of member states (Genschel and Zangl, forthcoming). Multilateral institutions that constrain and guide their member states' behavior and organize their relationships in accordance with generalized principles of conduct (such as the principle of nondiscrimination in the General Agreement on Tariffs and Trade and the WTO) have become part and parcel of the international system. Increasing in scale, scope, and regulatory depth, international institutions have contributed to bringing about a normative international order of "regulated anarchy." In short, multilateralism has been the institutional mold for the internationalization of governance.

The Changing Institutional Shape of Multilateralism

Beyond Exclusive Executive Multilateralism: Institutional Innovations in Global Governance

However, while there can be no doubt that interstate cooperation through multilateral institutions has been, and will continue to be, a vital component of global governance, the limits of statecentric conceptions of world order and a resulting transformation of the institutional shape of multilateralism (from exclusive executive multilateralism to more open and even inclusive multilateralism) have become ever more evident. In an era of globalization or denationalization (Held et al. 1999; Keohane and Nye 2000; Zürn 1998) and a growing emancipation of transnational nonstate actors from state control, not only the nation-states' but also intergovernmental institutions' capacities to fulfill governance functions effectively and legitimately have been challenged. The existence of various recurring governance gaps (Brühl and Rittberger 2001; Kaul, Grunberg, and Stern 1999, xxvi–xxxiv) demonstrates that global governance based solely on executive multilateralism cannot achieve important governance goals and creates pressure for institutional innovation (Rittberger 2009).

Globalization has led to the emergence of new transsovereign problems and the aggravation of existing ones and has created a growing need for the provision of global public goods. Transsovereign problems like worldwide pandemics, global environmental threats, proliferation of weapons of mass destruction, or transnational terrorism dominate the global political agenda after the Cold War (Cusimano 2000, 3). Their emergence and aggravation give rise to recurring deficits concerning the "output legitimacy" of intergovernmental institutions. The output legitimacy of global governance refers to problem-solving capacities, that is, the performance of institutions in generating and implementing their policy programs with a view to dealing effectively with the (transsovereign) problems that confront them (Scharpf 1999).

Many transsovereign problems not only exceed the problem-solving—regulatory or (re)distributive—capacities of individual nation-states but also those of intergovernmental organizations. Those responsible for the problems, as well as those whose behavior is ultimately to be governed, are often transnationally active private entities that are inadequately addressed by existing international rules concerned with interstate policy coordination. The incongruence between the reach of societal exchanges and transactions and the transsovereign problems emanating from them, on the one hand, and the reach of political regulations, on the other, brings about a "jurisdictional gap." This mismatch between the cross-border and often cross-sectoral nature of complex transsovereign problems and the spatial and actor-specific limitations of problem-solving capacities of nation-states and their intergovernmental organizations leads to a lack of effective institutionalized problem management. In other words, intergovernmental organizations aiming at mere interstate policy coordination do not seem suited to deal effectively with complex, transsovereign problems emanating from the activities of private actors.

Moreover, the implementation of global policy programs often falls short of agreed-upon goals. This "operational gap" shows up in many policy domains where governing interstate institutions lack the scientific-technical knowledge and expertise, as well as the political-administrative capacities (in short, the organizational means), needed to translate general policy goals into operational policy measures that would be adequate to deal effectively with transsovereign problems.

Apart from that, an "incentive gap" can be identified. We have noted above that, overall, the level of compliance with norms and rules beyond the nation-state is surprisingly high on many accounts. Nonetheless, compared to the enforcement capacities of (developed) states, there usually exist only limited means on the global level to create external incentives for the compliance with inter- or transnational norms and rules. Therefore, it is of paramount importance that norm addressees voluntarily abide by global norms and rules without being coerced into doing so. The inclusion of actors from civil society and the business sector should positively impact on the effectiveness of an institution because it leads to an increased readiness to comply with norms and rules. Norm addressees who accord high "input" or "process legitimacy" to governance structures because they have been granted fair participation rights in the norm-creation process usually show a higher degree of norm compliance (Beisheim and Dingwerth 2008; Franck 1997, 355; Zürn 2005, 26–39). Put in negative terms, this means that the exclusion of politically potent private actors from intergovernmental policy making reduces their readiness to comply with norms and rules emanating from executive-multilateral institutions.

In addition to governance gaps that undermine the output legitimacy of global governance, "input legitimacy" deficits can be made out and give rise to increasingly fierce contestation by civil society actors (Steffek 2008, 105). Input legitimacy derives from the extent and depth of participatory opportunities as well as from the transparency and fairness of policy-making processes. It is called into question on the global level when participatory gaps arise. Participatory gaps open up when access for those affected by the problem, and by the norms and rules created for dealing with it, to policy-relevant deliberations and decision-making processes in intergovernmental organizations is not available or is heavily restricted.

Nonstate actors are affected, in many ways, by the decisions of these organizations, but they are usually not granted adequate participatory rights in these organizations' policy-making processes. Institutional arrangements that combine the delegation of substantial political competencies to the global level with very restricted access for the general public to, as well as a lack of transparency of, decision making are highly detrimental to the input legitimacy of global governance (Zweifel 2006). These input legitimacy deficits of intergovernmental organizations have increasingly become contested in the public as the spectrum of potent actors on the global level has widened and the power relations between (and among) them have shifted. The "new" politically potent actors from civil society and the business sector may ultimately serve as adversaries or as cooperation partners in domains formerly dominated by nation-states or interstate actors. This raises the question of how to develop and institutionalize new authority structures involving nation-states, intergovernmental organizations, and the business and civil society sectors that are conducive to multipartite public-private policy cooperation rather than a zero-sum competition for influence in the global system (Rittberger 2006, 46).

Global systemic changes facilitating the emergence or aggravation of transsovereign problems and changing constellations of actors in the global system have not just led to recurring governance gaps (and thus deficits in both the input and output legitimacy of executive multilateralism). These governance gaps have created functional pressure for institutional adaptation and innovation and have opened up opportunity structures for private actors' successfully making their case for institutionalized involvement in global governance. At least partly in response to functional pressures and new opportunity structures, new transnational modes of governance beyond interstate policy coordination have come into existence.

Cooperation between public and private actors aimed at dealing with transsovereign problems and supplying global public goods has increased. Moreover, this intensification of public-private cooperation is leading to institutional change in the realm of global governance. Therefore, the spectrum of institutional arrangements is no longer adequately captured by the concept of intergovernmental or executive multilateralism. Intergovernmental organizations have opened up toward private actors. Inclusive, multipartite institutions have been established that institutionalize policy coordination and cooperation between (and among) public and private actors.

It should be noted, though, that more recent open or even inclusive modes of governance do not simply replace exclusive executive-multilateral institutions. As a result of the increasing participation of nonstate actors in international institutions and the resulting institutional change in the realm of global governance, traditional executive-multilateral institutions have not vanished. Rather, three specific (inter)organizational structures can be identified as coexisting in the international system. While these organizational structures developed at different points, they did not necessarily unfold in a linear manner, so they can now be observed simultaneously.

In a large number of international organizations (and also in the most important organ of the United Nations, namely, the Security Council), exclusive executive multilateralism has been, and still is, the dominant organizational structure. This exclusive organizational structure is characterized by nonpublic negotiations and bargaining between national governmental representatives, which are consciously isolated from public scrutiny or participation. Access to these decision-making processes for nonstate actors is only of an informal nature, if it exists at all. Examples of this exclusive executive multilateralism are the UN Security Council, which provides ad hoc access for nonstate actors through the so-called Arria Formula,[7] as well as the International Atomic Energy Agency.

Alongside this exclusive executive multilateralism, a more recent feature of intergovernmental organizations has emerged, which can be described as open or advanced executive multilateralism (Rittberger, Huckel, et al. 2008, 16–17; cf. O'Brien et al. 2000; Steffek 2008). This organizational feature derives from the charter of the international organization granting nonstate actors formal consultative status and thus formal access to deliberative and decision-making bodies. The UN Economic and Social Council, specialized agencies within the UN system, and other international organizations, such as the WTO, have, to varying extents, opened up to nonstate actors and provided them with the opportunity to voice their concerns within, and offer their expertise to, the intergovernmental decision-making bodies (Alger 2002; Martens 2005, 155–156; Staisch 2003). Nonetheless, nation-states still remain the central actors and gatekeepers since they decide which nonstate actors are granted formal access to the international organization or organ and under which conditions.

Recently, the emergence of a new mode of governance beyond the nation-state can be observed: the emergence and rise of inclusive, multipartite institutions in which public (state and/or interstate) as well as private actors from the business sector and/or civil society are endowed with membership and participatory rights. In this (inter)organizational structure, nonstate actors are granted formal agenda-setting, policy-deliberation, decision-making, and voting rights in the policy-making process that by far exceed those granted to nonstate actors endowed with consultative status in institutions of "open" or "advanced" executive multilateralism.

The structure and mode of operation of inclusive, multipartite institutions can be illustrated by taking the Global Fund to Fight AIDS, Tuberculosis and Malaria (Global Fund) as an example (Huckel Schneider 2007, 2008). The Global Fund is being used as a governance mechanism aimed at expanding the resources available worldwide for fighting certain infectious diseases and channeling resources to those regions or locations most in need. After the UN General Assembly decided in June 2001 to create the Global Fund, it took up work at the beginning of 2002. As a joint endeavor of the international community, civil society, the private sector, and those affected by the diseases, the Global Fund is based upon the participation of a large variety of actors affected by the problem and by the rule-making and distributive decisions reached for dealing with it. The highest organ of the Global Fund, the Foundation Board, comprises representatives of developing and donor countries, nongovernmental organizations (NGOs), international nongovernmental organizations (INGOs), private foundations and businesses, as well as representatives of international organizations, such as the United Nations Joint Program on HIV/AIDS, the World Health Organization, and the World Bank Group.[8] While all groups of actors participate in the debates and the drafting of documents, only the states together with INGOs and private-sector actors (businesses and foundations) are endowed with voting rights.

Inclusive, multipartite institutions like the Global Fund can be said to be part (and the preliminary apex) of a trend toward increased participation of nonstate actors in global policy making in different issue areas of world politics. To be sure, it certainly cannot be claimed that this type of institution has already become the dominant mode of institutionalized cooperation in world politics. Nonetheless, inclusive, multipartite institutions are no longer isolated cases; rather, they are indicative of broader developments toward institutionalized public-private provision of global governance that, although still in their infancy, can be traced back over a longer period. The trend toward more inclusive institutions is reflected by the rise in the sheer number of organizations, public-private partnerships, and global policy networks in numerous issue areas of public policy that meet the requirements of multiactor membership and shared decision-making rights (Rittberger, Huckel, et al. 2008, 26–27; cf. Benner, Reinicke, and Witte 2004; Kaul 2006; Reinicke and Deng 2000). This trend toward institutionalized participation of nonstate actors in global governance culminating in inclusive, multipartite institutions can be observed in all three broad policy domains of international politics (security, welfare, system of rule), albeit to a differing extent.

As regards the policy domain of welfare, the following institutions can be pointed out: the Global Fund; the United Nations Joint Program on HIV/AIDS; the Global Alliance for Vaccines and Immunization; the United Nations Development Cooperation Forum, which seeks to foster the coordination and harmonization of (inter)state and nonstate actors' development policies; or the widely known Global Compact, which aims at making private business actors comply with certain human rights, ecological, labor, and anticorruption standards and requires them to issue "communication(s) on progress" (i.e., reports on how these commitments are implemented).

In the policy domain of system of rule, the UN Permanent Forum on Indigenous Issues can be referred to as an example of inclusiveness, directed toward issues concerning the rights and welfare of indigenous peoples (García-Alix 2003; Ströbele-Gregor 2004, 23; Thies 2008). The Extractive Industries Transparency Initiative (EITI) is a multipartite initiative in which developed and developing states, as well as INGOs and transnational corporations from the extractive industries sector, are represented. It aims to enhance the transparency of revenue flows from resource extraction by setting a standard of transparency for both corporations and host governments and monitoring compliance with it. This is particularly relevant for areas in which the participating corporations are conducting business and in which, at the same time, states seemingly lack the capacity or the readiness to uphold the rule of law. EITI seeks both to promote the economic well-being of populations in resource-rich areas by containing corruption and personal enrichment and to prevent security problems arising from, and fuelled by, unregulated resource extraction (cf. Feldt 2004; Haufler 2006).

Similarly, in the sovereignty-sensitive policy domain of security, the Kimberley Process Certification Scheme for the certification of the origins of raw diamonds serves as a widely known example of an inclusive institution aimed at dealing with the cross-border effects of "conflict economies" (Böge et al. 2006; Paes 2005b, 67–81; Paes 2005a; Rittberger 2004, 26–27).

We see that institutionalized participation of nonstate actors in global governance has increased and a number of inclusive, multipartite institutions have been established in recent years. To be sure, this development does not unfold in a linear, all-encompassing manner. There are considerable issue-area-specific variations and instances in which functional necessities and pressures for institutional innovation have not led to inclusive institutionalization or even to a considerable opening of intergovernmental organizations (cf. Rittberger, Kruck, and Romund 2010, ch. 10). Exclusive executive multilateralism still prevails in some issue areas despite systemic changes and its evident dysfunctionalities.

Approaches Toward Explaining the Emergence of "New" Modes of Public-Private Governance

Functionalist arguments about the effects of macrostructural systemic changes contribute to accounting for broader long-term transformations in the institutional shape of multilateralism. However, it would be mistaken to assume that private actors automatically jump in to close governance gaps in executive-multilateral governance systems. Systemic change and changing constellations of actors in world politics do create a demand for open, or even inclusive, institutions of global governance. On the other hand, the systemic-functionalist argument that inclusive institutions are established because they are expected to close existing governance gaps cannot fully account for (variations in) the emergence of these institutions (Benner, Reinicke, and Witte 2004, 193–195; Brühl 2003, 167; Brühl and Liese 2004, 165). The demand for inclusive, multipartite institutions of global governance, which stems from governance gaps arising from the system of executive multilateralism, does not automatically create a sufficient supply of these institutions. In order to explain the emergence of specific public-private institutions and variations in their establishment even though systemic pressures may be constant, an agency-centered analysis of the interests and preferences of, and the resources available to, public and private actors is necessary.

"New" modes of public-private governance for the collective management of transsovereign problems and the provision of global public goods have received considerable attention in a burgeoning global governance literature. At the same time, agency-centered theoretical explanations of (variations in) the emergence of public-private governance arrangements have remained scarce. However, there are indications that more recent research on the establishment of public-private governance arrangements has started to move beyond macrotheoretical functionalist arguments that explain the emergence of public-private governance arrangements solely with reference to functional demands arising from changing systemic structures (Schäferhoff, Campe, and Kaan 2007, 10–12). By taking actors' interests, incentives, and resource endowments into account when trying to explain cooperative public-private relationships, scholars of global governance have (explicitly or implicitly) picked up resource-exchange theory that had first been used in interorganizational research in the late 1970s (Börzel and Risse 2005; Brühl 2003; Edele 2006; Nölke 2000, 2004; cf. Aldrich 1979; Pfeffer and Salancik 1978). In particular, resource-exchange theory has been used to explain the formation of (global) public-private partnerships, transnational policy networks, and inclusive, multipartite institutions.

An explanation based on resource-exchange theory and dealing with the emergence of inclusive, multipartite institutions posits that these institutions are set up by public and private actors to "exchange" or "pool" their specific material and immaterial resources in order to deal with a certain transsovereign problem. The emergence of multipartite modes of coordination and cooperation can then be explained by the motivation of rational actors, resulting from resource deficits, to exchange or pool their specific problem-relevant resources and thus be better off than they would be through unilateral or executive-multilateral action. From the vantage point of resource-exchange theory, two conditions are crucial for the emergence of inclusive, multipartite institutions of global governance. First, there exists a consensus between and among the various public and private actors that their goals in a given policy domain, and the strategies employed to reach these goals, are compatible or, in the best case, even complementary. In other words, a "domain consensus" is necessary. Second, mutual resource dependence between various public and private actors sharing this domain consensus is held to possess explanatory power for the emergence of inclusive institutions (Edele 2006; Pfeffer and Salancik 1978). In order to effectively deal with transsovereign problems, in- stitutions of global governance are in need of access to sufficient material, regula- tive, organizational, and epistemic resources. Since public and private actors (i.e., nation-states, intergovernmental organizations, INGOs, and private business actors), on their own, do not have all of these resources at their disposal, they have to cooperate and pool their resources: If all (or at least most) of these actors take part in the policy-programming and -implementation process and share their resources, they can expect to design and implement more effective and more le- gitimate solutions to transsovereign problems. The emergence of inclusive, mul- tipartite institutions can thus be conceived of as resulting from the exchange of material and immaterial resources between public and private actors: The major resources of business actors are financial means and management expertise. INGOs, in turn, can contribute financial means (by fund-raising activities) as well as problem-specific knowledge. Public actors can offer participatory rights in decision-making processes of global governance institutions; they also dispose of legal political authority—a scarce resource, which they may share with, or even partially delegate to, private actors (Aldrich 1979, ch. 11; Edele 2006, 46–47; Pfeffer and Salancik 1978, ch. 3).

In a nutshell, according to resource-exchange theory, inclusive, multipartite institutions of global governance emerge if and when, in a certain policy domain, public and private actors agree on common policy goals and on strategies to achieve them, causing these various actors to be mutually dependent on each others' resources in order to reach compatible or even complementary goals. Resource-exchange theory can thus contribute to explaining the establishment of specific transnational institutions of global governance and complement more general arguments about systemic change, functional necessities, and changing constellations of actors—in a similar way as regime theory, or, more precisely, situational-structural theories (cf. Hasenclever, Mayer, and Rittberger 1997, ch. 3; Zürn 1992), in the late 1980s and the 1990s specified broader arguments about international institution building resulting from increasing international interdependencies.

The Emergence of a Heterarchical World Order

It was noted that while multilateralism still plays a pivotal role in current conceptions of global governance, the shape of multilateralism has changed considerably in the past two decades and moved beyond mere interstate policy coordination. The opening up of intergovernmental organizations toward private (civil society and business) actors and the creation of inclusive, multipartite institutions of global governance are constitutive elements of an emergent heterarchical world order (Rittberger, Huckel, et al. 2008, 42–54). The term *heterarchy* denotes a "third" ordering principle beside anarchy and hierarchy. It points to an alternative to mere anarchic self-help systems, on the one hand, and formally or de facto hierarchically structured systems, that is, a world state or hegemonic or even imperial rule, on the other (Holsti 1992, 56–57).[9] The concept of heterarchy is meant to capture the existence of an increasingly dense network of institutions of global governance, created and maintained by public and private actors and aimed at the rules-based collective management of transsovereign problems through horizontal policy coordination and cooperation, where different groups of actors (nation-states, intergovernmental organizations, civil society organizations, transnational corporations/private-sector actors) are sensitive to each other's values and interests and dependent on one another to achieve collective goals.

The peculiarities of a heterarchical world order consist, inter alia, in the generation and implementation of norms and rules that are not bound to a vertical, top-down policy process. Instead, its institutional framework is flexible enough to allow for a range of innovative institutional approaches toward dealing with transsovereign problems of a varying nature. Thus, different problem-solving processes are designed and activated according to situational needs in a given issue area. Apart from that, a heterarchical order is based on the activities and problem-solving capacities of a variety of public and private actors and utilizes their respective resource endowments. Leadership is exercised by those actors who are, or are perceived to be, best suited to deal with a certain issue. Formally, the different actors are largely independent of one another but find themselves within a system of complex interdependence. Concomitant to the rise of transsovereign problems, this mutual dependency promotes the creation of institutionalized policy coordination and cooperation between public and private actors.

A heterarchical world order is thus marked by the coexistence of nation-states; intergovernmental organizations; inclusive, multipartite institutions; and private governance institutions aimed at dealing with transsovereign problems and providing global public goods. The coexistence of different actors and institutional forms of global governance does not imply that nation-states and intergovernmental institutions necessarily lose importance. Rather, they remain integral elements and anchors of a network of differently constituted institutions of global governance. However, both the nation-states and their executive-multilateral institutions are undergoing significant transformations, losing their monopoly on the provision of governance and exercise of political authority (Cutler, Haufler, and Porter 1999; Genschel and Zangl 2008).

Notes

1. *Specific reciprocity* refers to the quid pro quo exchange of items of equivalent value between specified partners in a strictly delimited sequence of give and take. By contrast, *diffuse reciprocity* refers to an institutional arrangement that its members expect to yield a rough equivalence of benefits in the aggregate and over time and that involves conforming to generally accepted standards of behavior. In a system of diffuse reciprocity, states do not just focus on immediate benefits but act on the expectation that cooperative behavior will be reciprocated in the long run (Keohane 1986, 4; Ruggie 1993, 11–47).

2. Both international organizations and international regimes are international social institutions. As such, they are characterized by behavioral patterns based on international norms and rules, which prescribe behavioral roles in recurring situations and lead to a convergence of reciprocal expectations. So, when we refer to multilateral international institutions, this includes both international organizations and international regimes. However, it should be noted that international organizations and international regimes differ in two ways. International regimes always relate to specific issue areas, such as the containment of climate change or the protection of human rights. By contrast, international organizations (e.g., the United Nations) can transcend the boundaries of issue areas. Furthermore, while international organizations function as collective actors, international regimes do not possess actorlike qualities (Krasner 1983, 2; Rittberger and Zangl 2006). However, despite their ability to function as (collective) actors, international organizations should not be conceived as monolithic entities; they usually comprise several organs (a plenary organ, an executive council or board, a secretariat, a dispute-settlement body, a parliamentary assembly, etc.) with actorlike qualities.

3. *Executive multilateralism* refers to an exclusive organizational mode of intergovernmental policy making characterized by nonpublic negotiations and bargaining between national governmental representatives. See below for a more detailed elaboration of the concept that contrasts executive multilateralism with *open* and *inclusive multilateralism*.

4. It should be noted that our conception of bindingness is not limited to legal obligations but also includes politically or socially binding norms and rules that politically potent actors feel compelled to comply with.

5. As far as regulatory action is concerned, authority can be defined as the ability of an actor or an institution to induce rule addressees to take note of, and comply with, their rules (Rittberger, Nettesheim, et al. 2008, 2). In a broader sense, political authority refers to the capacity not only to make collectively binding decisions and to set rules of behavior (decision-making competence) but also to implement such decisions with appropriate organizational means (organizational competence) and to give these decisions normative justification (legitimatory power) (Genschel and Zangl 2008, 431).

6. Delegating sovereignty rarely takes place in world politics, but can be observed more often in regional integration schemes, such as the European Union (EU).

7. The Arria Formula, named for UN Ambassador Diego Arria of Venezuela, who devised it in 1992, is an informal arrangement that allows the Security Council to be briefed by nonstate (mainly civil society) actors about international peace and security issues. At regular Security Council meetings and consultations, only government representatives (of Security Council members) and UN officials can speak. The Arria Formula offers members of the Security Council the opportunity to invite other council members to an informal meeting in which one or more people (e.g., representatives of humanitarian NGOs), who are considered expert(s) in a matter of concern to the Security Council, are heard (Paul 2003).

8. Nonstate members of the board include, as of October 2009, representatives of a Zambian community initiative (CITAM+), a U.S.-based educational NGO (RESULTS), a Serbian youth association against AIDS, the Bill & Melinda Gates Foundation, and the transnational mining company Anglo American.

9. For a somewhat different conception of "heterarchy," compare J. Donnelly (2009).

References

Aldrich, H. E. 1979. *Organizations and environments.* Englewood Cliffs, NJ: Prentice Hall.

Alger, C. 2002. The emerging roles of NGOs in the UN system: From Article 71 to a People's Millennium Assembly. *Global Governance* 8, no. 1 (January–March): 93–117.

Barnett, M., and M. Finnemore. 2004. *Rules for the world: International organizations in global politics.* Ithaca, NY: Cornell University Press.

Beisheim, M., and K. Dingwerth. 2008. Procedural legitimacy and private transnational governance: Are the good ones doing better? SFB Governance Working Paper Series No. 14, Free University Berlin, Germany.

Benner, T., W. H. Reinicke, and J. M. Witte. 2004. Multisectoral networks in global governance: Towards a pluralistic system of accountability. *Government and Opposition* 39, no. 2: 191–210.

Bernstein, S., and B. Cashore. 2008. The two-level logic of non-state market-driven global governance. In *Authority in the global political economy,* ed. V. Rittberger and M. Nettesheim, 276–313. Basingstoke, UK: Palgrave Macmillan.

Böge, V., C. Fitzpatrick, W. Jaspers, and W.-C. Paes. 2006. Who's minding the store? The business of private, public and civil actors in zones of conflict. Bonn International Center for Conversion (BICC) Brief 32. Bonn: BICC.

Börzel, T. A., and T. Risse. 2005. Public-private partnerships: Effective and legitimate tools of transnational governance? In *Complex sovereignty: Reconstituting political authority in the twenty-first century,* ed. E. Grande and L. W. Pauly, 193–216. Toronto, Canada: University of Toronto Press.

Brühl, T. 2003. *Nichtregierungsorganisationen als Akteure internationaler Umweltverhandlungen: Ein Erklärungsmodell auf der Basis der situationsspezifischen Ressourcennachfrage.* Frankfurt am Main, Germany: Campus.

Brühl, T., and A. Liese. 2004. Grenzen der Partnerschaft: Zur Beteiligung privater Akteure an internationalen Organisationen. In *Die Entgrenzung der Politik: Internationale Beziehungen und Friedensforschung,* ed. M. Albert, B. Moltmann, and B. Schoch, 162–190. Frankfurt am Main, Germany: Campus.

Brühl, T., and V. Rittberger. 2001. From international to global governance: Actors, collective decision-making, and the United Nations in the world of the twenty-first century. In *Global governance and the United Nations system,* ed. V. Rittberger, 1–47. Tokyo: United Nations University Press.

Caporaso, J. A. 1993. International relations theory and multilateralism: The search for foundations. In *Multilateralism matters: The theory and praxis of an institutional form,* ed. J. G. Ruggie, 51–90. New York: Columbia University Press.

Cusimano, M. K. 2000. Beyond sovereignty: The rise of transsovereign problems. In *Beyond sovereignty: Issues for a global agenda,* ed. M. K. Cusimano, 1–40. Boston: St. Martin's.

Cutler, A. C., V. Haufler, and T. Porter, eds. 1999. *Private authority and international affairs.* Albany: State University of New York Press.

Dingwerth, K., and P. Pattberg. 2006. Global governance as a perspective on world politics. *Global Governance* 1, no. 2: 185–203.

Donnelly, J. 2009. Rethinking political structures: From "ordering principles" to "vertical differentiation"—and beyond. *International Theory* 1, no. 1: 49–86.

Edele, A. 2006. All hands on deck—the establishment of global public-private partnerships for development from a resource exchange perspective. MA thesis, University of Tübingen (Germany), Institute of Political Science.

Feldt, H. 2004. Publish what you pay: Rohstoffe und die Offenlegung von Zahlungsströmen. In *Unternehmen in der Weltpolitik,* ed. T. Brühl, H. Feldt, and B. Hamm, 246–263. Bonn: Dietz.

Finkelstein, L. S. 1995. What is global governance? *Global Governance* 1, no. 3: 367–372.

Franck, T. M. 1997. *Fairness in international law and institutions.* Oxford: Oxford University Press.

García-Alix, L. 2003. *The permanent forum on indigenous issues.* Copenhagen: International Working Group for Indigenous Affairs.

Genschel, P., and B. Zangl. Forthcoming. *Der "postheroische" Staat: Vom Herrschaftsmonopolisten zum Herrschaftsmanager.* Frankfurt am Main, Germany: Suhrkamp.

————. 2008. Metamorphosen des Staates: Vom Herrschaftsmonopolist zum Herrschaftsmanager. *Leviathan* 36, no. 3: 430–454.

Graz, J.-C., and A. Nölke, eds. 2008. *Transnational private governance and its limits.* London: Routledge.

Hasenclever, A., P. Mayer, and V. Rittberger. 1997. *Theories of international regimes.* Cambridge: Cambridge University Press.

Haufler, V. 2006. The transparency principle and the regulation of corporations. In *Global governance and the role of non-state actors*, ed. G. F. Schuppert, 63–80. Baden-Baden, Germany: Nomos.

Held, D., A. McGrew, D. Goldblatt, and J. Perraton. 1999. *Global transformations: Politics, economics and culture.* Cambridge, UK: Polity Press.

Holsti, K. J. 1992. Governance without government: Polyarchy in nineteenth-century European international politics. In *Governance without government: Order and change in world politics*, ed. J. N. Rosenau and E. O. Czempiel, 30–57. Cambridge: Cambridge University Press.

Huckel Schneider, C. 2008. Legitimacy and global governance in managing global health. PhD diss., University of Tübingen (Germany), Institute of Political Science.

————. 2007. Global public health and innovative forms of governance. Paper prepared for the Sixth Pan-European Conference on International Relations, September 12–15, Turin, Italy.

Hutter, B. M. 2006. The role of non-state actors in regulation. In *Global governance and the role of non-state actors*, ed. G. F. Schuppert, 63–79. Baden-Baden, Germany: Nomos.

Karns, M. P., and K. A. Mingst. 2009. *International organizations: The politics and processes of global governance.* Rev. ed. Boulder, CO: Lynne Rienner.

Kaul, I. 2006. Exploring the policy space between markets and states: Global public-private partnerships. In *The new public finance: Responding to global challenges*, ed. I. Kaul and P. Conçeicão, 219–268. Oxford: Oxford University Press.

Kaul, I., I. Grunberg, and M. A. Stern. 1999. Introduction to *Global public goods: International cooperation in the 21st century*, ed. I. Kaul, I. Grunberg, and M. A. Stern, xix–xxxviii. Oxford: Oxford University Press.

Kaul, I., and R. U. Mendoza. 2003. Advancing the concept of public goods. In *Providing global public goods: Managing globalization*, ed. I. Kaul, P. Conçeicão, K. Le Goulven, and R. U. Mendoza, 78–112. Oxford: Oxford University Press.

Keohane, R. O. 1986. Reciprocity in international relations. *International Organization* 40, no. 1: 1–27.

Keohane, R. O., and J. S. Nye. 2001. *Power and interdependence: World politics in transition.* 3rd ed. New York: Longman.

————. 2000. Globalization: What's new? what's not? (and so what?) *Foreign Policy* 118: 104–119.

Koenig-Archibugi, M. 2006. Introduction: Institutional diversity in global governance. In *New modes of governance in the global system: Exploring publicness, delegation and inclusiveness*, ed. M. Koenig-Archibugi and M. Zürn, 1–30. Basingstoke, UK: Palgrave Macmillan.

Krasner, S. D. 1983. Structural causes and regime consequences: Regimes as intervening variables. In *International regimes*, ed. S. D. Krasner, 1–22. Ithaca, NY: Cornell University Press.

Martens, K. 2005. *NGOs and the United Nations: Institutionalization, professionalization and adaptation.* Basingstoke, UK: Palgrave Macmillan.

Mayer, P., V. Rittberger, and M. Zürn. 1993. Regime theory: State of the art and perspectives. In *Regime theory and international relations*, ed. V. Rittberger, 391–430. Oxford: Clarendon Press.

Moravcsik, A. 1998. *The choice for Europe: Social purpose and state power from Messina to Maastricht.* Ithaca, NY: Cornell University Press.

Muldoon, J. P. 2003. *The architecture of global governance: An introduction to the study of international organizations.* Boulder, CO: Westview Press.

Nölke, A. 2004. Transnational private authority and corporate governance. In *New rules for global markets: Public and private governance in the world economy*, ed. S. A. Schirm, 155–175. Basingstoke, UK: Palgrave Macmillan.

———. 2000. Regieren in transnationalen Politiknetzwerken? Kritik postnationaler Governance-Konzepte aus der Perspektive einer transnationalen (Inter-)Organisationssoziologie. *Zeitschrift für Internationale Beziehungen* 6, no. 2: 331–358.

O'Brien, R., A. M. Goetz, J. A. Scholte, and M. Williams. 2000. *Contesting global governance: Multilateral economic institutions and global social movements.* Cambridge: Cambridge University Press.

Paes, W.-C. 2005a. "Conflict diamonds" to "clean diamonds": The development of the Kimberley Process Certification Scheme. In *Resource politics in sub-Saharan Africa*, ed. M. Basedau and A. Mehler, 305–324. Hamburg, Germany: German Institute of Global and Area Studies.

———. 2005b. Internationale Initiativen zur Eindämmung von Res-sourcenkonflikten und "Neuen Kriegen": Ein Überblick. *Die Friedens-Warte* 80, no. 1–2: 61–81.

Pattberg, P. 2007. *Private institutions and global governance: The new politics of environmental sustainability.* Cheltenham, UK: Edward Elgar.

Paul, J. 2003. The Arria Formula. Global Policy Forum. October 2003. www.global policy.org/component/content/article/185/40088.html (accessed October 12, 2009).

Pfeffer, J., and G. R. Salancik. 1978. *The external control of organizations: A resource dependence perspective.* New York: Harper & Row.

Reinicke, W. 1998. *Global public policy: Governing without government?* Washington, DC: Brookings Institution Press.

Reinicke, W. H., and F. Deng. 2000. *Critical choices: The United Nations, networks, and the future of global governance.* Ottawa, Canada: International Development Research Center.

Rittberger, V. 2009. Legitimes Weltregieren durch inklusive, multipartistische Institutionen? In *Wer regiert die Welt und mit welchem Recht? Beiträge zur Global Governance-Forschung*, ed. V. Rittberger, 261–282. Baden-Baden, Germany: Nomos.

———. 2006. Weltorganisation in der Krise—Die Vereinten Nationen vor radikalen Reformen. In *Weltordnung durch Weltmacht oder Weltorganisation? USA,*

Deutschland und die Vereinten Nationen, ed. V. Rittberger, 41–62. Baden-Baden, Germany: Nomos.

———. 2004. Transnationale Unternehmen in Gewaltkonflikten. *Die Friedens-Warte* 79, no. 1–2: 15–34.

———. 2000. Globalisierung und der Wandel der Staatenwelt: Die Welt regieren ohne Weltstaat. In *Vom ewigen Frieden und Wohlstand der Nationen*, ed. U. Menzel, 188–218. Frankfurt am Main, Germany: Suhrkamp.

Rittberger, V., C. Huckel, L. Rieth, and M. Zimmer. 2008. Inclusive global institutions for a global political economy. In *Authority in the global political economy*, ed. V. Rittberger and M. Nettesheim, 11–54. Basingstoke, UK: Palgrave Macmillan.

Rittberger, V., A. Kruck, and A. Romund. 2010. *Grundzüge der Weltpolitik: Theorie und Empirie des Weltregierens*. Wiesbaden, Germany: VS Verlag für Sozialwissenschaften.

Rittberger, V., M. Nettesheim, C. Huckel, and T. Göbel. 2008. Introduction: Changing patterns of authority. In *Authority in the global political economy*, ed. V. Rittberger and M. Nettesheim, 1–9. Basingstoke, UK: Palgrave Macmillan.

Rittberger, V., and B. Zangl, with M. Staisch. 2006. *International organization: Polity, politics and policies*. Basingstoke, UK: Palgrave Macmillan.

Rittberger, V., and M. Zürn. 1990. Towards regulated anarchy in East-West relations. In *International regimes in East-West politics*, ed. V. Rittberger, 9–63. London: Pinter.

Rosenau, J. N. 1999. Towards an ontology of global governance. In *Approaches to global governance theory*, ed. M. Hewson and T. Sinclair, 287–301. Albany: State University of New York Press.

———. 1992. Governance, order, and change in world politics. In *Governance without government: Order and change in world politics*, ed. J. N. Rosenau and E. O. Czempiel, 1–29. Cambridge: Cambridge University Press.Ruggie, J. G. 1993. Multilateralism: The anatomy of an institution. In *Multilateralism matters: The theory and praxis of an institutional form*, ed. J. G. Ruggie, 3–47. New York: Columbia University Press.

Schäferhoff, M., S. Campe, and C. Kaan. 2007. Transnational public-private partnerships in international relations: Making sense of concepts, research frameworks and results. SFB Governance Working Paper Series No. 6, Free University Berlin, Germany.

Scharpf, F. W. 1999. *Regieren in Europa—effektiv und demokratisch?* Frankfurt am Main, Germany: Campus.

Staisch, M. 2003. Reaching out, or not: Accounting for the relative openness of international governmental organizations towards NGOs. MA thesis, University of Tübingen (Germany), Institute of Political Science.

Steffek, J. 2008. Zähmt zivilgesellschaftliche Partizipation die internationale Politik? Vom exklusiven zum partizipativen Multilateralismus. *Leviathan* 36, no. 1: 105–122.

Ströbele-Gregor, J. 2004. Indigene Völker und Gesellschaft in Lateinamerika: Herausforderungen an die Demokratie. In *Indigene Völker in Lateinamerika und En-*

twicklungszusammenarbeit, ed. Gesellschaft für technische Zusammenarbeit (GTZ), 1–27. Eschborn, Germany: GTZ.

Thies, H. 2008. Towards more inclusive institutions? Insights from the treatment of indigenous issues at the UN. Paper prepared for the 2008 International Studies Association Annual Meeting, March 26–29, San Francisco, California.

Trebesch, C. 2008. Economic governance. SFB Governance Working Paper Series No. 11, Free University Berlin, Germany.

Zangl, B., ed. 2009. *Auf dem Weg zu internationaler Rechtsherrschaft? Streitbeilegung zwischen Politik und Recht.* Frankfurt am Main, Germany: Campus.

———. 2006. *Die Internationalisierung der Rechtsstaatlichkeit: Streitbeilegung in GATT und WTO.* Frankfurt am Main, Germany: Campus.

Zürn, M. 2005. Introduction: Law and compliance at different levels. In *Law and governance in postnational Europe: Compliance beyond the nation-state,* ed. M. Zürn and C. Joerges, 1–39. Cambridge: Cambridge University Press.

———. 1998. *Regieren jenseits des Nationalstaates: Globalisierung und Denationalisierung als Chance.* Frankfurt am Main, Germany: Suhrkamp.

———. 1992. *Interessen und Institutionen in der internationalen Politik: Grundlegung und Anwendung des situationsstrukturellen Ansatzes.* Opladen, Germany: Leske + Budrich.

Zweifel, T. D. 2006. *International organizations and democracy: Accountability, politics, and power.* Boulder, CO: Lynne Rienner.

PART TWO
The Role of State Actors in Twenty-First Century Diplomacy

Introduction

Richard Reitano

In his new book on Henry Kissinger and 1973, the fateful year in global (and American domestic) politics, historian Alistair Horne quotes a message by U.S. Secretary of State (and National Security Advisor) Henry Kissinger to then Soviet ambassador to the United States Anatoly Dobrynin: "Anatoly, the madmen in the Middle East seem to be at it again. . . . I want you to know what we have done" (2009, 296). The crisis between the United States and the Soviet Union, in which the American military forces were brought to DEFCON 3,[1] was diffused through bilateral diplomacy between the Americans and the Russians. Some reference was made to the United Nations, but it played a relatively minor role in diffusing what some have argued was the greatest confrontation between the two superpowers since the 1962 Cuban Missile Crisis. Multilateral diplomacy eventually did work, but only after the two superpowers put state sovereignty and their perceived national interests aside for the time being and worked with the Israelis and the Arab states, particularly Egypt, to end the 1973 war in the region.

The inherent conflict between state sovereignty and the uses of multilateral diplomacy remains an issue in the early years of the twenty-first century. The problems discussed and evaluated in this part of the book, including "rogue" states, global terrorism, nuclear proliferation, genocide, economic globalization, climate change, and human rights, are more complex, and the dangers to global peace and stability may, in fact, be greater than those engendered by the conflicts that characterized the post–World War II era dominated by the Soviet-American bipolar balance of power.

Joseph Melrose and Andrew Melrose remind us in their chapter that "it was not until the Peace of Westphalia in 1648 that the complete international social order we recognize today was created, through the introduction of the 'state' into this flow of authority." This "authority" is vested in every nation, where the right of rule, many believe, is granted "from God to the ruler." They note that the major attempt to bring about international peace and security through the creation of the United Nations in 1945 was not, in reality, about a new form of collaborative multilateral diplomacy. Ambassador Melrose and Andrew Melrose conclude that "the authority of the United Nations resides in the will of its member-states. It has little independent authority." They do believe, however, that "as 'centers for harmonizing actions,' international organizations have been able to effectuate actual change" in the behavior of states.

In his chapter, Stephen Rock describes the difficulties encountered by the global community in dealing with so-called rogue states. He observes, "Rogue states pose substantial challenges for twenty-first-century diplomacy. They do not conform to international standards that are critical to the security of states and the well-being of their citizens, and they typically resist efforts to convince them to do so." Rock notes that rogue states are not a "new phenomenon," but information about weapons of mass destruction is now available on an unprecedented basis in human history, and the restraints on behavior imposed by the superpowers after World War II no longer hold because of the resulting demise of the bipolar division of global power after the Cold War ended. He concludes that of the three ways of dealing with rogue states (force, coercion, and diplomacy), the "strategy of engagement, which seeks economic, political, and diplomatic cooperation" with these regimes may offer the most promising means for success by the international community through concerted diplomatic action. State sovereignty and national interests, however, remain as major stumbling blocks in curbing bad behavior by rogue states.

Donna Schlagheck suggests in her chapter that the "failure of multilateral efforts" to enforce treaties, conventions, and multistate cooperation regarding terrorism, nuclear proliferation, and genocide has "also led to new, emerging forms of multilateralism." She points out, for example, that "seventy-five states now cooperate on [an] ad hoc basis to identify and apprehend terrorists seeking to acquire, or criminals attempting to sell them, fissile material." Schlagheck describes the dangers posed by terrorists but also concludes that "the lack of social and political rights [and] the lack of the rule of law and democratic reform" do contribute to recruiting terrorists in troubled and divided regions of the world. Despite the enormous problems involved, states are now cooperating in a series of "new multi-lateral approaches to the evolving threats [posed by] proliferation and terrorism." She does note that the "innovations in multilateral diplomacy" designed to deal with the nuclear and terrorist issues have failed to address the tragic and continuing consequences of genocide. Schlagheck believes that "selfish state sovereignty" remains a major obstacle in the "development of an effective and rapid response to genocide" by the international community.

David Kennett is concerned with "the [economic] challenges that currently confront the global economy," and he is pessimistic about the "possibility of state or multistate solutions," particularly for the problems posed by climate change. He describes the "consolidation" of the nation-state historically, which resulted from "the imposition of a central taxing authority." Kennett notes that "even today within supranational bodies, important economic decisions are largely made on a national basis." He concludes that the global economic crisis, which exploded in 2008, resulted largely from "Americans [spending] more than our country produced" and that "Chinese funding of U.S. public and private debt" compounded the crisis. Unfortunately, a multistate solution is not at hand because there is no "agreement on the exact nature of the disease and on the appropriate medicine." Be it climate change or the economic meltdown, Kennett believes, "It would be much easier if there were a supranational body to which all nations surrendered substantial sovereignty." He notes that "domestic politics," "enforcement mechanisms," and "free riding" are ultimately the major barriers to multistate solutions necessary for promoting global economic recovery and confronting the threats resulting from climate change.

Timothy Longman and Natalie Zähringer agree with Bruce Cronin that sovereignty "has provided a measure of stability, predictability, and order within the anarchic system of nation-states." Nevertheless, they point out that, as Jackson Nyamuya Maogoto has estimated, the emphasis on state sovereignty resulted in "approximately 170 million" deaths in the twentieth century. The idea that states are "free to govern within their own territories" is a fundamental principle of sovereignty that has characterized the Westphalian state system since 1648. Longman and Zähringer present arguments that support the conclusion that the conflict between state sovereignty and the respect for human rights has, historically, more often than not resulted in a victory for the advocates and practitioners of state sovereignty. The revolutionary changes in communications and the willingness of "private citizens" within states and nongovernmental organizations to take stands against, and to increase global awareness about, human rights abuses, however, are major factors today in challenging traditional notions of state sovereignty. The authors believe that "the growth of international civil society fighting for human rights is having an impact, and if a growing number of people take up human rights as a cause, the changes to the international system may ultimately be much more significant."

Finally, as Leslie Gelb observed, the real danger to global peace and stability is "nations drowning in a flood of terrorism, tribal and religious hatred, lawlessness, poverty, disease, environmental calamities, and governmental incompetence" (2009, 59). The list is endless. It also includes corruption, ignorance, the absence of education and schools, and the oppression of women. The debate regarding state sovereignty, as our authors in this part point out, is nothing new. What is new is the attention now paid by the global community to what results from hiding behind the cloak of state sovereignty and national interest, as is the awareness of what the international community must do through multilateral diplomacy to end threats, to stop the violence, and, fundamentally, to recognize that we are citizens not only of our respective nations but also of a global community. Recognizing and accepting our "responsibility to protect" the "least among us," in the final analysis, holds out the possibility of protecting us all.

Note

1. Defense readiness condition, or DEFCON, 1 is war.

References

Gelb, L. H. 2009. Necessity, choice, and common sense. *Foreign Affairs* 88, no. 3 (May–June): 56–72.
Horne, A. 2009. *Kissinger 1973: The Crucial Year.* New York: Simon & Schuster.

4

Unplanned Obsolescence? The Future of the State in a Multilateral World

Joseph H. Melrose and J. Andrew Melrose

History

We live today in the most "interconnected" period in human history. The communication and transportation revolution that helped spawn this globalization has allowed us to reach beyond borders in a way that would have been unthinkable even one hundred years ago. But although our daily lives have become more interconnected and complicated—or so it seems—many of the mechanisms that enable us to reap the benefits of globalization remain hidden. This underlying transformation has occurred through a slow process of continually adding layers upon layers onto a system of interstate interaction that has been in place for centuries.

At the onset of the American Revolution, Benjamin Franklin was postmaster general of the colonies. The most famous American in the world, winner of the Copley Gold Medal, member of the Royal Society, and the tamer of electricity who held honorary degrees from Oxford, Cambridge, and St. Andrew's, was what we would today consider nothing more than a solid but respectable civil servant. This was a man who, as John Adams perhaps hyperbolically wrote, had a reputation "greater than that of Newton, Frederick the Great or Voltaire, his character more revered than all of them. There's scarcely a coachman or a footman or scullery maid who does not consider him a friend of all mankind." The second postmaster general of the United States under the Constitution, Timothy Pickering, was appointed special commissioner to the Iroquois Confederacy—the equivalent of a special envoy today—during his term in office and parlayed his postal work into becoming the secretary of war,[1] then secretary of state, the stepping stone to the presidency.[2] Other early postmasters were similarly impressive; governor, Supreme Court justice, and congressman were just a few of the roles these men had or would play. From 1829 to 1971, the appointment was even a cabinet-level position. Yet, how many have even heard of the current postmaster, John E. Potter, a career member of the postal service? Despite what has been universally acknowledged as a successful tenure in which he has demonstrated excellent leadership qualities,[3] few American political watchers would even contemplate the idea that he could be a serious candidate for a major diplomatic or political position, let alone recognize him in line at the supermarket. With communication faster and more commonplace, the importance of the postmaster general in many ways has increased; yet, no one would even think of suggesting that Bill Gates, Warren Buffet, or even Angelina Jolie be made postmaster general. Why has the importance of this position changed so much? There must be something more to the diminishing fortunes of the position than mere advances in technology.

The Growth of an International Organization

The answer is rooted in the founding and growth of an international organization dedicated to harmonizing and regulating the modalities of interstate mail. The Universal Postal Union (UPU)[4] was founded by twenty-two countries through the Treaty of Berne in 1874, which came into force one year later. It was the third permanent international organization created and is currently a specialized agency of the United Nations, with 191 member states.[5] The Treaty of Berne set a common rate for international mail, with an additional charge for excessive weight or distance, guaranteed delivery, and regulated interpostal service compensation for travel across the sea. However, it did not regulate domestic postage rates, the appearance of postage stamps, or the means of transportation within individual countries. By standardizing the international aspects of member states' postal services, the UPU replaced many of the diplomatic functions of the postmaster general in the name of efficiency.

Prior to the UPU the international exchange of mail was governed by a series of bilateral treaties, which led to complications regarding the practical aspects of efficiently transporting mail from, for instance, the United Kingdom to Australia. Compensation disagreements over cross-transit fees and the use of new routes often required further bilateral treaties. By harmonizing these issues globally, the UPU was a rousing and instant success. Before its existence the transmission of a simple letter from one country to another required bilateral treaties with, and stamps from, every country it transited through, all calculated at different rates, and involved the constant fear that the authorities in one of the many countries it passed through might confiscate, delay, or destroy the letter temporarily in its charge. The UPU pooled the transportation resources of its members for the greater good. There was now a single territory, as it were, for mail. As more and more countries joined the UPU, the role of the national postmaster general evolved from a political, diplomatic, and bureaucratic position to a strictly bureaucratic one. Most of the international issues raised by the transportation of mail across international boundaries were taken care of by the UPU. Since then, innovations in technology and the rise of private-sector competitors like FedEx, UPS, and DHL have further reduced the importance and necessity of a national postal service.

Though this recounting of the history of the international postal service may seem a mundane and obscure soliloquy, of interest to only the most die-hard philatelists, "It is not unfair to say that the Universal Postal Union works in an obscurity which is a direct result of its efficiency" (Williamson 1930, 68). The founding and growth of the UPU represents an important milestone in international relations. For one of the first times ever, a group of states joined together mutually and voluntarily to limit their sovereignty in order to increase efficiency. What started as a small practical solution to an increasingly complicated process grew into a worldwide organization that specifically superseded aspects of an essential right of the state, the ability to regulate the circumstances under which something crosses its borders. Yet, despite this concession of sovereignty, the UPU's influence was solely limited to the international aspects of the mail system. "As a non-political organisation, it does not interfere in matters that fall within the domestic domain of national postal services. For example, Posts set their own postage rates, decide which and how many postage stamps to issue, and how to manage their postal operations and staff" (UPU 2001). As technology and patterns of use have changed, the question that arises for the UPU is how will it adapt to changing circumstances? Will it be expanded into the private realm? Will it exist as an anachronism like the UN Trusteeship Council or can (should) it be repurposed to cover new forms of communication?

Other Organizations

The UPU is just one of many international organizations created since the Central Commission for Navigation on the Rhine (Rhine Commission) was founded during the Congress of Vienna in 1815. Like many international organizations, the Rhine Commission was created in order to minimize potential sources of conflict that might arise over access to vital resources with the hope that harmonization and regulation would help reduce tension. The most successful and common types of international organizations have followed this pattern of attempting to minimize disputes through harmonization. The Customs Convention on Containers, Convention on International Civil Aviation, International Telegraph Convention, and Brussels Satellite Convention are just a few of the international agreements that work in the background of our everyday lives to increase efficiency and remove potential sources of tension. These conventions, as well as the various small-scale international organizations that either spawned, or were spawned by, them, are the fundamental building blocks of our globalized world. While they have not gone so far as to create a new world order, without them numerous commonplace activities like radio transmission, passenger air travel, or routine commercial shipping would be potential acts of war or causes for conflict. Yet, it is interesting to note that they uniformly limit, through international regulation, one of the inherent roles of the state, the security of borders, by creating exceptions to the state's discretionary power—which raises the question, Do these organizations, and more famous ones like the United Nations and World Trade Organization (WTO), represent a new level in the flowchart of state power and authority? In short, is the obsolescence of the state inevitable?

The Origins of State Power

Before we can answer that question, we need to examine briefly where the power of the state comes from. The evolution of the modern state into the lodestone of social organization has been a slow process occurring through incremental concessions to the ruling order that have expanded over time. During the early parts of human history, the concepts of state and nation were unheard of. There was no state or nation but only a ruler, and the ruler was directly connected to the creative force. Whether he (or she) was considered an earthly god, a descendent of a god, a descendent of the first being, a conduit to the divine, or something else, the ruler's legitimacy derived from a personal connection with the creative force. Power flowed directly from the divine. The ruler had absolute power and was the individual guarantor, through his connection to the local deity, of the long-term stability of the civilization. As society expanded, the tension between the ruler and the ruled grew. Especially concerning to many of the emerging political class was the idea that rulers' connection to the divine exempted them from the laws they themselves enacted.

This concern led, in England, to the Magna Carta in 1215, which enunciated the concept that the ruler was bound by earthly as well as divine laws. Through this, the idea of limiting power by legal regulation was first established. Meanwhile the Declaration of Arbroath of 1320 in Scotland introduced the concept of the nation as a collective grouping of people and the repository of the divine right of rule. The nation grants that right from God to the ruler. Both of these concepts initially had a relatively limited and specifically focused impact. Their lasting importance—and relevance to this discussion—entails not what they did at the time but the principles they laid out and how those principles eventually evolved into the system we know today. Simply put, these documents helped create a system in which authority derived from divine power, which flowed to the nation and from the nation to the ruler, who made and enforced the law. Not until the Peace of Westphalia in 1648 was the complete international social order we recognize today created, through the introduction of the state into this flow of authority. Although ostensibly nothing more than a peace treaty ending the Thirty and Eighty Years wars, it did so through the recognition that the state is a sovereign entity and, as such, has the right to govern affairs within its borders. This was a peace not between rulers but between states, over which the rulers merely held power. At the time they probably did not recognize the revolutionary change this represented, but it was fundamentally different from the previous order.

Under the Westphalian system, power no longer flowed to the ruler and then the state but from the state to the ruler, and on matters within the territory of the state, there was a right of sovereignty—basically, of noninterference by other states. This right of sovereignty has been the guiding principle of international relations and a touchstone of philosophy for the past 350 years. Obviously, this is an extreme simplification of the concept of the flow of authority, which has been the subject of countless philosophical, academic, and legal treatises. The important point to take is that every single treaty, convention, charter, and constitution since has been based on the concepts introduced in those documents (i.e., that authority flows from the people to the state to the government). The question today is, How do international organizations fit within the flow of authority and what is their long-term relationship with the state?

Although numerous international organizations are working in the background on a whole host of issues, none is as singularly important or extensive as the United Nations. In its discussion of the future role of the state, this chapter focuses on the four main purposes of the United Nations spelled out in Article I of its charter. Each purpose, as well as the strengths and weaknesses of actions taken in pursuit of these goals, will be briefly examined. By determining why some aspects have been more successful than others, we will hopefully be able to see a pattern regarding interaction between the state, the concept of sovereignty, and international organizations. As the most famous and primary international organization in the world, the United Nations will, in many ways, serve as proxy for the entire system.

The United Nations

The UN Charter was signed, in the aftermath of World War II, with great fanfare on June 26, 1945. Its stated purpose was to "maintain international peace and security," "develop friendly relations among nations," "achieve international cooperation," and "be a centre for harmonizing the actions of nations." Its position on the Westphalian system was clear and direct: "The Organization is based on the principle of the sovereign equality of all its Members." Nothing in the charter explicitly authorized action in matters essentially within the domestic jurisdiction of the state. In form, little of the prevailing order had actually changed. The difference was that now potential future advances could be made through a permanent organization.

Maintain International Peace and Security

The United Nations' immediate mission was to provide a forum for states to work together to resolve disputes peacefully and hopefully prevent the outbreak of another devastating world war. The atomic age had just begun. Hope was high that a new phase of enlightened human history was beginning in which the wonders of the atom would provide unlimited power, abundant food, and countless other technological marvels. War would be no more. The United Nations would solve all the problems of the past. As such, much of its early work revolved around lingering disputes arising out of World War II and the soon-to-end colonial system in places such as Palestine and Kashmir.

Despite the unbounded optimism of those early days, it is safe to say that the organization was not altogether successful at resolving these protracted problems since they continue to plague us today. The system relied on enlightened states to resolve their differences through discussion with a mutual acknowledgment that achieving lasting peace was more important than temporary interests. But on controversial and emotional issues, such as self-determination and territorial integrity, it soon became apparent that states were unwilling to sublimate their own self-interest to what was arguably the common good.

The authority of the United Nations, as an organization of sovereign states, resides in the will of its member states. It has little independent authority. The United Nations is not a cooperative in which each individual state gives up a portion of its own sovereign power for the commonweal. It is an association in which each member state has a common interest but frequently acts alone. When it comes to maintaining international peace and security, the United Nations has confronted many obstacles. Although the charter envisions collective action to remove threats to peace and suppression of aggression, in practice this has not been accomplished. No doubt the Cold War, which prevented consensus decision making on most issues, had a huge impact on the ability to take collective action, but more than that has limited the effectiveness of peacekeeping operations.

Peacekeeping operations in practice tend to be more about tamping down the outbreak of fighting than resolving the issues that led to war; in effect, the United Nations' role in practice has been to mediate and not to arbitrate. Two of the longest standing and most contentious disputes in international relations today, Kashmir and Israel/Palestine, have tested the United Nations from almost the very beginning and highlight this point. Both situations involve emotional territorial disputes arising, in general, out of the colonial era. Both have, on occasion, devolved into military conflict that threatened to engulf entire regions. Initially, the United Nations gamely tried to resolve the crises through high-powered diplomatic negotiations, led by Chester Nimitz and Ralph Bunche, respectively,[6] and cease-fire resolutions. Yet, no matter what was tried, the fact remained that both situations involved legitimate territorial disputes in which two separate groups of people had equally valid claims to the same area of land with divided support among the world at large. Since neither party to the disputes was clearly interfering in the domestic affairs of a separate state, the Westphalian theory of state sovereignty, which was part and parcel of the charter through Article II, still applied. The United Nations was powerless to do anything more than urge peace and moderate cease-fires. If ever there was a case in which the necessity of ensuring global peace and security should overcome state sovereignty, Kashmir and Israel/Palestine should have been the poster children.

The problem was not just one of legal authority. There was also the practical matter of being able to actually project power. The United Nations, like most international organizations, is entirely dependent on its member states for its successes and failures. These two situations required authorization and funding for peacekeeping troops and supplies by the United Nations, as well as the support of the parties to the conflict. Moreover, even when peacekeeping troops remained in place during conflicts, the question of whether they had the ability to engage in military engagements was undefined, sometimes to disastrous effect.

In both Kashmir and Israel/Palestine, it was the parties' withdrawal of support that led to failure. In Kashmir this manifested itself in a plebiscite that was never held, while in Israel/Palestine, it was the removal of peacekeepers themselves. As Secretary-General U Thant pointed out, following the withdrawal of the UN Emergency Force (UNEF) from the Sinai in 1967, which helped lead to the Six Day War, the legitimacy of the force depended on the voluntary cooperation of Egypt as the host government. When Egyptian president Gamal Abdel Nasser requested the removal of the UNEF, there was little choice but to withdraw, even though another war in the Middle East was inevitable. Similarly, when Indian prime minister Jawaharal Nehru refused to hold an agreed-to plebiscite in 1953, the United Nations was powerless to act.

Perhaps, the two most shameful events for UN peacekeeping operations entailed the inability or unwillingness of peacekeepers to prevent genocidal actions in the places they were ostensibly protecting in Bosnia and Rwanda. In Sierra Leone, in an embarrassing comedy of errors, a convoy of UN peacekeepers literally dropped their pants and ran after being confronted by a band made up, in part, of child soldiers. The message has been clear: UN authority in the realm of peace and security rests not on the independent power of the organization but on a voluntary grant of sovereign authority by the individual member states. When that grant is removed or goes unrecognized, no independent source of authority exists. The United Nations can only affect change by encouraging cooperation and harmonization among a group of interested member states.

In this regard there have been successes, primarily when a single state or regional organization takes the place of UN peacekeepers. Whether we are talking about Australia in East Timor, Nigeria and the Economic Community of West African States (ECOWAS) in Sierra Leone and Liberia, or the North Atlantic Treaty Organization (NATO) in Kosovo, the most effective peacekeeping operations have been those taken up by individual states. States are the only entities able to project force and maintain a standing army, while international organizations tend to operate under the constraints of consensus and the principle of sovereign noninterference. In practice, the ability of the United Nations to both approve and enact missions in the realm of maintaining peace and security has been limited to observation and mediation. Its role has not been to forcibly stop the fighting but to function as a human shield separating combatants.

It comes therefore as no surprise that the most successful ongoing peacekeeping mission has taken place outside the scope of the United Nations or an established international organization. The Multinational Force and Observers (MFO) was created by the Egyptian-Israeli Peace Treaty of 1979 as an anticipated backup solution in the event that the United Nations was unwilling to create a new peace-keeping force following the failure of the UNEF. MFO is not a traditional peacekeeping force made up of troops from a variety of countries with differing motivations or levels of commitment. Its troops operate with the sovereign authority of each state equally and are funded directly by the parties and the United States, acting in its capacity as guarantor. The MFO has shown that maintaining peace and security requires the ability to project force as well as the ownership, commitment, and support of the parties involved. This motivational factor, sup-plemented by financial ownership, is the most important determinant of whether a peacekeeping operation will succeed.

The success of MFO has helped herald the emerging potential of regional or-ganizations, conducting discrete missions composed of smaller groups of inter-ested parties working together as sovereign entities, to affect change. By moving to a system in which regional powers or organizations are the primary method of projecting force, often under the political cover of legitimacy from the United Nations, peacekeeping operations, such as MFO, are more successful because they replicate the Westphalian system. When it comes to peacekeeping, the United Nations has discovered the limitations of trying to function as a supranational or-ganization: There is just too much invested in the traditional system to overturn traditional conventions. As an arbitrator that determines exceptions to the rule of domestic noninterference, however, it can be quite effective.

Before moving on, it is important to mention quickly one other important development: the rise of the private military company (PMC). Mercenaries, as they are more fantastically known, have been operating around the world, often in a supplementary role, for most of history. Their utility has always relied on an ability to rapidly muster and deploy without potential domestic fallout. Tra-ditionally incorporated ad hoc into a state's standing army, they enabled it to expand the size and skill level of its military without political cost or long-term financial investment. In modern times, the high cost of standing armies, military hardware, and specialized knowledge required for operation has led to a resur-gence of the PMC. This opens up the opportunity for the United Nations to take a much more active role in peacekeeping but raises serious questions regarding the role of the state and the reliance of the United Nations on its authority. In much the same way as new technologies and the ability of private companies to replicate delivery functions have diminished the importance of the postal service, PMCs represent a potential new avenue for the projection of force by an international organization, and the debate over their use should be followed closely.

Develop Friendly Relations Among Nations

The second main purpose of the United Nations, "to develop friendly relations among nations based on respect for the principle of equal rights and self-determination of peoples, and to take other appropriate measures to strengthen universal peace" (UN Charter Article 1[2]), has been fraught with problems similar to those that bedevil peacekeeping. How can one reconcile the principle of self-determination with that of state sovereignty? Certainly, in some ways this is fairly easy, since the right of a state to determine its own means of self-organization is more or less directly connected to the principle of noninterference in the domestic affairs of another state as defined through Westphalia. However, in a practical manner, the issue of self-determination most often arises when one segment of an existing state desires independence or its own set of rules. This is one of the reasons why Kashmir, Israel/Palestine, Bosnia, and Cyprus have been such vexing problems for the international system. Which principle trumps, state sovereignty or self-determination? In general, the United Nations has tried to stay out of these delicate and emotional issues brought about by groups declaring their wish to separate from a greater existing state. When circumstances lead to actual conflict, the United Nations has tried to balance the two principles by suggesting, or offering to organize, plebiscites. Unfortunately, as with peacekeeping, the state in question must provide its assent, and that has not always been forthcoming.

East Timor and Cameroon are two of the few examples in which the broader state has not only consented but also supported the efforts. Just like with peacekeeping, the principle of supporting self-determination enshrined in the charter is often superseded by the reality that state sovereignty is the foundation of the organization, and states are usually unwilling to sublimate their self-interest. UN support for self-determination has been successful in places like East Timor because the state involved has been committed to the process and willing to accept the result whatever it may be. It has been unsuccessful in places like Kashmir and Cyprus because the states involved have been resistant and unwilling to accept a potential outcome. In reality the United Nations' support for self-determination has been haphazard, successful when the Wesphalian system is embraced and unsuccessful when it is not.

Achieve International Cooperation

When it has come to dealing with issues of "an economic, social, cultural or humanitarian character" (UN Charter Article 1[3]), many of the same dynamics and problems we have seen in both peacekeeping and self-determination have occurred. Much has been talked about, hyped, and hoped for, but in practical terms, little has actually been done. The basic problem is that different people have different ideas about what phrases and terms actually mean. Without some sort of enforcement mechanism to adjudicate meaning, applicable definitions are left up to individual states. The Universal Declaration of Human Rights (UDHR) was adopted by the General Assembly in 1948 and is widely considered one of the most important documents of the modern era, a landmark in human history accorded the unique honor of becoming a permanent part of the international space station. It elucidates hopes and desires for the human condition and in many ways represents the extent that humanity has grown since the beginning of civilization. Through the UDHR and its complementary documents, the International Covenant on Civil and Political Rights and the International Covenant on Economic and Social Rights, the world came together and set out the basic principles that govern our individual interactions with the state. Simply put, they make up a bill of rights for all humanity. But what have they actually done, and do the rights apply internationally and domestically?

In many ways the UDHR is a formal iteration of concepts developed over time that have become customary international law. Most of the articles in the document are neither controversial nor new and were written with such generality as to be open to widely divergent interpretations. In reality, it is an aspirational statement of society's hopes and not a legal obligation that can be enforced. Its authority is based upon a consensus on rhetoric not definition, but that does not mean it is not important. Its real value has been in framing and bringing to the fore the issue of individual human rights. From a practical perspective the document itself guarantees nothing in and of itself because there is no enforcement mechanism, such as an international judicial system, through which an individual may petition a grievance. Yet, in many countries the UDHR has been directly incorporated into the domestic legal code. In that manner it has functioned as a ready-made template for states looking to formalize the guarantee of rights. As an international treaty it is nothing more than rhetoric, but as suggested language it has had a profound impact, working not as an international guarantee of rights but as a series of domestic guarantees. In short, its strengths and weaknesses, much like those of the international organization, follow those of the traditional Westphalian system. When incorporated into the domestic code, it is given the full force of sovereign authority, but when excluded, it is nothing more than political rhetoric.

Center for Harmonizing Actions

Despite the failure of the United Nations, and the broader international system it represents, in accomplishing the previous three purposes, it has actually been extremely successful in its fourth and least well-known one. As "centers for harmonizing actions," international organizations have been able to effectuate actual change. Although they receive little public attention, the Convention on Containers, Convention on Civil Aviation, World Customs Organization, and Universal Postal Union have created the semblance of a supranational authority that rises above the Westphalian system. The main reason for their success has been that they tend to deal with issues that may be controversial but are unemotional. Furthermore, they are of a discrete and easily definable nature. Though states may have different and irreconcilable opinions about what freedom of speech entails, the concept of what constitutes a shipping container is easily negotiable. This has allowed deliberations to focus on practical matters, free from concern about potential consequences regarding domestic political issues, such as whether hate speech is protected speech. Harmonization on these matters does not threaten the integral sovereignty of states. Whether or not an international standardized definition of a shipping container exists, the state will have to create one. By outsourcing, as it were, this definition to an international organization, the state gains both efficiency and utility. Sovereignty is impeded but without any potential cost.

In general, these sorts of harmonization organizations are noncontroversial and obscure. Like the best secret agents, they are ordinary. But one has increasingly drawn attention, the World Trade Organization, a relatively new organization that grew out of the General Agreement on Tariffs and Trade (GATT). The main goal of the GATT was to harmonize international trade through agreement on the basic classification of goods and limitations on tariff fluctuations, taking care to exclude sensitive areas like agriculture from the initial discussions. Enforcement was primarily through a form of mutually assured destruction. Should a state dishonor its obligations on one good, then other states would dishonor their obligations to that state. States maintained their obligations because the benefits outweighed the risks. The incentives for demanding compliance from other states were almost the opposite of those for self-determination or human rights. In those situations the worry was that if a state went too far in trying to push compliance, it would open itself up to retaliation. If the United States pushed China on self-determination in Tibet, then China could push the United States on voting rights in the District of Columbia. In the Sixty-First UN General Assembly, this actually occurred: Iran sponsored a resolution on the Situation of Indigenous Peoples and Immigrants in Canada, while Belarus sponsored a resolution on the Situation of Democracy and Human Rights in the United States of America.

As GATT successfully determined how goods would be classified and what would be covered and bound tariffs to a certain level, it soon became clear that agreement would need to grow and begin tackling areas of trade it had previously ignored, like intellectual property, subsidies, agriculture, trade practices, and most importantly determinations of whether a state was engaging in unfair trade practices. For this reason, the WTO was created, and as it has grown, it has truly represented the potential future role of international organizations and begun to expand the boundaries of the Westphalian system. The reason the WTO is so important to the question of the future role of the state is simple. Unlike most other agreements, the WTO has an independent enforcement mechanism. Thus far, this enforcement mechanism has functioned completely within the boundaries of the Westphalian system. Should a state be found to have violated the agreement, then an aggrieved state or states could impose retaliatory and transparent protectionist measures against the offending party at a rate proportional to the harm caused.

In other words, the primary remedy is a limited exemption from the obligations for the aggrieved party. However, albeit the usual remedy, it is the only one possible. Although the dispute-settlement procedures are set up in such a way as to ensure that disputes are settled diplomatically, there is still the possibility, if all else fails, of requiring monetary compensation. In a recent case brought by several countries against the United States over upland cotton subsidies, several of the developing countries involved requested monetary damages as a remedy. Even though the settlement panel has avoided taking that route and the United States has taken measures to remedy the original dispute, the application of monetary damages in the future is still a possibility. The impact of such a situation on an organization already grappling with major issues regarding the potential expansion of the agreement to controversial and emotional issues like intellectual property rights and agricultural subsidies is impossible to predict. But should the application of monetary damages come to pass, it would represent the first significant departure from the Westphalian system, and whether or not we realized it at the time, the world would have changed overnight.

Conclusion

Despite the way it sometimes appears, the international order imposed by the Peace of Westphalia in the mid-seventeenth century is still in place. Whatever advances humanity has made since then with regard to acknowledging human rights, working toward global peace, or delivering mail, none has challenged the role of the state as the foundation of an international relations system organized around the principle of sovereignty. But one thing is sure, if something does arise to shift the paradigm, it is guaranteed to be obscure and seemingly mundane. The obsolescence of the state, whether planned or unplanned, will not occur in the foreseeable future. Instead, the role of the state and the concept of sovereignty will continue to evolve slowly to meet the future needs of our changing global society. Only a truly cataclysmic event that threatened the entire world and changed our perceptions could threaten the Westphalian system and radically change the role of the state in its interplay with international organizations on issues other than harmonization.

Notes

1. The Department of War was renamed the Department of Defense in 1949.

2. Following George Washington and John Adams, neither of whom had the opportunity, the next four presidents had all previously served as secretary of state.

3. In 2007 he was awarded the Roger W. Jones Award for Executive Leadership by American University.

4. Founded as the General Postal Union, the UPU was renamed in 1878 to reflect its rapid expansion.

5. All UN member states besides Andorra, the Marshall Islands, Micronesia, and Palau are members, along with the non-UN member states of the British Overseas Territories (Anguilla and Bermuda, among others), the Netherlands Antilles and Aruba (combined), and Vatican City.

6. Adm. Chester Nimitz was the recently retired five-star fleet admiral of the U.S. and Pacific Allied navies, while Dr. Ralph Bunche was one of the high-ranking Amer-

icans in the UN Secretariat when the United Nations was founded. In 1948 Dr. Bunche took over the role of UN mediator following the assassination of Count Folke Bernadotte, a famous Swedish diplomat, by the militant group Lehi.

References

Universal Postal Union. 2001. UPU at a glance. UPU. www.upu.int/about_us/en/ upu_at_a_glance.html (last accessed August 25, 2009).

Williamson, F. H., Brig. Gen. 1930. *The international postal service and the Universal Postal Union*. London: Royal Institute of International Affairs.

5

The Challenge of "Rogue States" for a Troubled International Community

Stephen R. Rock

On October 9, 2006, the Democratic People's Republic of Korea (DPRK) detonated a nuclear device. The international community reacted swiftly. Within a week, the UN Security Council had unanimously adopted Resolution 1718, expressing its "gravest concern." The Council demanded that North Korea conduct no further nuclear tests and refrain from future testing of ballistic missiles, the most likely delivery system for a North Korean nuclear warhead. It banned the export of arms, nuclear technology, and luxury goods to the DPRK, and it froze North Korean assets that might be used to support its nuclear program. Defying the United Nations, the DPRK continued to test ballistic missiles, including the Taepodong 2, a multistage intercontinental ballistic missile, and on May 25, 2009, it conducted a second nuclear test.

Thomas Henriksen has observed that "since time immemorial there have been polities that have stood outside the international community" (2001, 349). Rejecting norms of behavior to which most members of the community subscribe, they have been labeled "pariah states," "outlaw states," "backlash states," and, most recently, "rogue states" (Lennon and Eiss 2004, vii). Rogue states pose substantial challenges for twenty-first-century diplomacy. They do not conform to international standards that are critical to the security of states and the well-being of their citizens, and they typically resist efforts to convince them to do so.

At the same time, some "rogue regimes are reformable" (Jentleson and Whytock 2005–2006, 81). Beginning in the 1970s, the Libyan government, under the leadership of Muammar Qaddafi, sought to obtain weapons of mass destruction

(WMDs). It supported a variety of terrorist organizations and attempted to assassinate the heads of state of a number of African and Middle Eastern countries. It was responsible for a series of terrorist incidents, most notably an attack on a West Berlin nightclub in 1986, the December 1988 bombing of Pan Am Flight 103 over Lockerbie, Scotland, and the September 1989 explosion of the French airline Union des Transports Aériens (UTA) Flight 772 over Niger.

Yet, after nearly three decades as a global pariah, Libya made a "concerted effort to enter the good graces of the international community" (Kaplan 2007). In 1999, the Libyan government turned over for trial two suspects in the destruction of Pan Am Flight 103. Four years later, the regime renounced terrorism and declared that it was severing its ties to terrorist groups. It accepted responsibility for the Lockerbie bombing and established a fund to compensate families of the victims. It announced that it was abandoning its pursuit of WMDs and would allow international observers to monitor the demolition of its facilities. In 2007, after the United States had reestablished full diplomatic relations with Tripoli, Libya was elected as a nonpermanent member of the UN Security Council.

Rogue States in the Twenty-First Century

Although rogue states are not a new phenomenon, they may be a more prominent feature of this century than the last. One reason is that the dissemination of knowledge concerning the design and construction of nuclear weapons, as well as other types of WMDs, puts the acquisition of such weapons within the reach of most countries. A second is that during the second half of the twentieth century, the bipolar division of much of the world into two camps limited both states' need and their ability to act in a "roguish" manner. States that might, for example, have sought to obtain nuclear weapons did not feel compelled to do so because they were protected by the nuclear umbrella or the conventional forces of one of the superpowers, which were in turn able to influence the behavior of their allies and clients. The end of the Cold War produced dramatic changes for states such as North Korea, which, following the collapse of the Soviet Union, found itself both more vulnerable and less constrained.

The concept of the rogue state originated with the Clinton administration. In 1994, Anthony Lake, then national security adviser, authored an article in *Foreign Affairs* titled "Confronting Backlash States." These "recalcitrant and outlaw states," Lake argued, lacked the capabilities of a superpower but were nonetheless a matter of grave concern because their behavior was "often aggressive and defiant." According to Lake, backlash states shared a number of characteristics: autocratic or authoritarian leaders, denial of human rights, promotion of radical ideologies, opposition to popular participation in governance, and the inability to cooperate effectively with others. Perhaps most importantly, they possessed a "siege mentality" that caused them to seek weapons of mass destruction and ballistic missiles to deliver them. Among the states Lake identified as falling into this category were Cuba, Iran, Iraq, Libya, and North Korea (1994, 45–46).

Backlash states may not have been a bad descriptor, but the term did not convey much seriousness of threat or urgency in confronting it. Perhaps for this reason, even before the appearance of Lake's article, President Clinton had begun to warn about the "clear and present danger" represented by "rogue states such as Iran and Libya." The new term "evoked an image of a rogue elephant and was meant to accentuate the states' vicious and out of control nature" (Henriksen 2001, 358). *Rogue states* rapidly entered the U.S. diplomatic lexicon, employed by policy makers, journalists, academics, and the general public.

In June 2000, the Clinton administration announced that it was abandoning the term *rogue states* in favor of *states of concern*. According to the State Department, the former appellation was outdated and inappropriate because it lumped together quite diverse states in a single category (Litwak 2000, 375). Nevertheless, when George W. Bush succeeded Clinton, the rogue state concept was quickly resurrected. Indeed, following the attacks on the World Trade Center and the Pentagon on September 11, 2001, rogue states and their terrorist allies became the focus of Bush administration foreign policy. In its 2002 exposition of its national security strategy, the administration cited the emergence, during the 1990s, "of a small number of rogue states that, while different in important ways, share a number of attributes." These states, the document asserted, "brutalize their own people and squander their natural resources for the personal gain of the rulers; display no regard for international law, threaten their neighbors and callously violate international treaties to which they are party; are determined to acquire weapons of mass destruction, along with other advanced military technology, to be used as threats or offensively to achieve the aggressive designs of these regimes; sponsor terrorism around the globe; and reject basic human values and hate the United States and everything for which it stands." Contending that, unlike America's Cold War adversaries, rogue states and terrorist organizations armed with weapons of mass destruction could not be deterred from attacking the United States or its allies, the Bush administration articulated a strategy that envisioned striking U.S. enemies before they could attack (White House 2002, 13–14, 15).

Although described by the administration as "preemption"—striking an adversary that was itself about to attack—the strategy was in fact one of "prevention"—denying opponents the capacity to attack the United States or destroying the capabilities that they already possessed. The U.S. invasion of Iraq in March 2003 was justified, at least initially, by that country's alleged possession of WMDs and the need to forestall their use.

The notion of "rogue states" is problematic in certain respects. It is a one-size-fits-all designation that obscures the diversity of the regimes to which it has been assigned. The term does not enjoy widespread international currency; rather, it is employed almost exclusively by American politicians, statesmen, and academicians to describe countries at odds with the United States. Some writers have suggested that, according to the criteria by which rogue states are typically defined, the United States is a rogue state, since it possesses nuclear weapons, flouts international law, disregards the wishes of the United Nations, uses force aggressively, and has, in recent years, withdrawn from or refused to enter into international treaties (Chomsky 2000).

The purpose of this chapter, however, is not to question the utility of "rogue states" as an analytic category. Its central concerns are (1) the challenges for the international community posed by states that have been described as "rogues," and (2) the various ways in which the international community might respond, with particular emphasis on the role of diplomacy.

What Challenges Do Rogue States Present?

Rogue states, as noted above, are defined by their refusal to behave according to international norms. The most important of these are recognition and protection of basic human rights, rejection of terrorism, and nonproliferation of weapons of mass destruction, particularly nuclear nonproliferation. Some scholars deny that international norms exist, but this position confuses the absence of universal subscription to norms with the absence of norms. The international community has an extensive body of law and a complex framework of institutions designed to encourage (though not, for the most part, to enforce) compliance. Most states comply with most norms most of the time. The fact that instances of noncompliance occur does not imply the absence of international norms any more than noncompliance with domestic law demonstrates the absence of such law.

The challenge posed by rogue states to the international community is twofold. Most immediately, the behaviors of such states endanger others. Rejection by outlaw states of norms of antiterrorism and nonproliferation are particularly worri-some. Terrorist activities threaten the security of states and those that inhabit them. While a few scholars, most notably Kenneth Waltz, believe that the prolif-eration of nuclear weapons would create stable deterrence in many parts of the globe, the vast majority of analysts believe that the increased danger of accidental or unauthorized nuclear war, or of the escalation of conventional war to the nu-clear level, far outweigh any potential benefit (Waltz and Sagan 2003). In com-bination, terrorism and nuclear weapons—nuclear terrorism—have especially devastating potential. Graham Allison (2004) has termed nuclear terrorism "the ultimate (preventable) catastrophe."

Over the longer term, if rogue states become sufficiently large in number or their activities force other states to violate generally accepted rules of behavior, the rules themselves may be undermined, eventually becoming meaningless. Thus, for example, if Iran were to acquire nuclear weapons, Saudi Arabia, Egypt, and other Arab states might feel compelled to do so too. Similarly, North Korea's nas-cent nuclear arsenal could cause South Korea and Japan to reconsider their re-nunciation of nuclear weapons. If enough nuclear dominoes were to fall, nonproliferation would presumably cease to be a norm. Countries still might de-cide not to pursue nuclear weapons, but one constraint on their doing so would have been removed. Ultimately, the deterioration of international norms regarding human rights, terrorism, and WMD proliferation would almost inevitably lead to increased human suffering and death.

The Use of Force in Confronting Rogue States

Members of the international community, individually and collectively, have at their disposal three basic strategies for dealing with rogue states: the use of force, coercion, and engagement. The use of force, which sees little or no room for diplo-macy, can serve two primary purposes. One is to overthrow the rogue regime and install a government more compliant with international standards of behavior. The second, in the case of WMD proliferation, is to destroy the weapons, the fa-cilities being used to produce them, or both.

Regime change (or rollback) was pursued most prominently by the United States and its supporters in the invasion of Iraq and removal of the government of Saddam Hussein in 2003. The strategy appears, as of this writing, to have been at least a partial success: A new, nonrogue regime is in place. But the Iraqi case—as well as that of Afghanistan—also demonstrates the enormous difficulties associated with rollback. In late 2008, the Congressional Research Service (CRS) reported that the United States had expended $864 billion on operations in Afghanistan and Iraq and on other aspects of the so-called global war on terror. Adjusted for inflation, this figure exceeds the amount spent by the United States in any conflict since World War II. By 2018, the CRS projected, the cost would likely be in the neighborhood of $1.7 trillion—$2.4 trillion if one factors in the interest on monies borrowed to finance the effort. By early summer 2009, more than 5,700 U.S. and coalition military personnel had lost their lives, and tens of thousands had been wounded. Afghan and Iraqi casualties are more difficult to determine, but in May 2009, Iraq Body Count put the number of documented civilian deaths from military action, paramilitary action, and sectarian violence in Iraq alone at between 92,000 and 100,000.

Despite this vast expenditure of blood and treasure, in neither Afghanistan nor Iraq is the long-term stability of the new government or, indeed, the country assured. It is by no means clear that the international community has been made safer. By driving the Taliban and their Al Qaeda allies out of Afghanistan, the Afghan war has helped to destabilize Pakistan, a nuclear power, and it is likely that the Iraq War has added urgency to Iran's quest for nuclear weapons.

Moreover, regime change—except as part of a legitimate war of self-defense— violates one of the central norms of the international community: nonintervention in the internal affairs of individual states. This norm, which has been at the heart of the Westphalian order for more than 350 years, is enshrined in Article 2.7 of the UN Charter: "Nothing contained in the present charter shall authorize the United Nations to intervene in matters which are essentially within the domestic jurisdiction of any state." Although Article 42 of the charter does permit the Security Council to authorize the use of military force against sovereign states in situations where they threaten to breach the peace, the Security Council has never exercised this authority. In the case of Iraq, after acrimonious debate, the Council rejected a U.S.-sponsored resolution that would have authorized the use of military force. While it is beyond the scope of this chapter to identify all the reasons for this rejection, the belief that invasion and conquest of Iraq would be an unjustifiable violation of Iraqi sovereignty clearly played a role. As a strategy for dealing with rogue states, regime change is problematic in the sense that it requires the violation of one international norm in order to enforce others.

Preventive military action—destruction of, for example, the weapons or facilities of a prospective or nascent nuclear power—encounters the same difficulty, particularly when, as in the case of Iran, there exists ambiguity regarding the objectives of a nuclear program. The right of a state to develop nuclear power for peaceful purposes, particularly the production of civilian energy, is made explicit in the preamble to the Nuclear Nonproliferation Treaty (NPT). The major weaknesses of preventive military action, however, are more practical. One, illustrated by Israel's bombing of Iraq's Osirak nuclear reactor in 1981, is that a preventive attack is unlikely to be a long-term solution. Although destruction of a rogue state's WMD facilities might discourage the government from pursuing WMDs in the future, it is at least as likely to cause the state to accelerate its pursuit, in order to be in a position to deter future attacks. Nuclear (and other WMD) facilities can be rebuilt, and having had them destroyed once is likely to make a state determined to avoid a repeat performance. Even states that have not previously been attacked typically take precautions that would make a successful air strike difficult to achieve. Iran's nuclear facilities are spread around the country, and many are carefully concealed. Some of North Korea's nuclear installations are built into the sides of mountains. It is possible that certain sites are simply unknown to observers outside of either country.

A successful strike against either North Korea or Iran would probably disperse radioactive material, causing significant civilian casualties, as well as rendering surrounding areas unfit for industry, agriculture, and human habitation. It would almost certainly provoke retaliation. North Korea has an army of more than 1 million, and it has thousands of long-range artillery pieces and short-range missiles capable of hitting Seoul, which stands only thirty or forty miles south of the demilitarized zone. An attack on the DPRK's nuclear facilities would be likely to produce a conflagration on the Korean Peninsula and could result in serious damage to the South Korean capital as well as the loss of many thousands of lives. Any attempt to destroy Iran's nuclear facilities would presumably cause the Iranian government to launch a barrage of ballistic missiles at Israel and to step up its support for terrorist organizations such as Hezbollah. The entire Middle East and Persian Gulf region could be rendered even less stable. It is not surprising, given the difficulties associated with preventive action, that the UN Security Council has, despite condemning both Iran and North Korea for their nuclear programs, steadfastly refused to contemplate authorizing military strikes and that the United States and Israel have—at least thus far—declined to undertake them.

Diplomacy in Confronting Rogue States: Coercion

Given the undesirability, for reasons both principled and practical, of employing military force against rogue states in many instances, it is important to consider the potential of approaches relying more heavily on diplomacy. In coercion, the central point of diplomacy is to construct a coalition of states working together to exert pressure on the outlaw nation.

The standard tool of coercion is economic sanctions. Sanctions can serve several purposes. Targeted sanctions, such as the freezing of foreign assets of certain individuals or corporations and limitations on those individuals' ability to travel abroad, are intended to pressure government officials and elites directly. More broad-based sanctions aim to pressure the government indirectly by damaging the economy and creating domestic dissatisfaction with the regime. With regard to the specific problem of WMD proliferation, sanctions such as the prohibition on the importation of fissile materials and nuclear technologies are designed to slow down the weapons-acquisition process, as well as to signal a determination to react even more strongly if weapons are procured or employed.

Broad-based sanctions are often regarded as unethical because, unlike targeted sanctions, they do not discriminate but harm an entire population, most of whose members are not responsible for the objectionable behavior of the regime. The larger problem with economic sanctions, however, has been the inability, in many instances, of members of the international community to collaborate in putting together a potentially effective sanctions program.

North Korea is a case in point. Although the DPRK is often described as the world's most isolated country, it maintains commercial ties with many states, including China, most members of the European Union, and even South Korea. Foreign investment is on the rise. Multinational corporations are interested in taking advantage of cheap North Korean labor, and a British firm recently signed a long-term contract to explore deposits of oil and natural gas. Between 2007 and 2008, the DPRK's foreign trade increased by nearly a third. As a result, the country's gross domestic product has been rising at an average annual rate of roughly 1.5 percent. This has allowed the regime to replace and repair some of the country's deteriorating infrastructure, which was previously an obstacle to significant economic growth. North Korea is a poor state, but it is not being squeezed economically in a way that would cause the government to consider seriously abandoning its nuclear weapons program, renouncing terrorism, or improving its human rights record.

The failure of members of the international community to impose a rigorous sanctions regime on North Korea illustrates the fact that states often place higher value on national objectives than they do on upholding international norms. China, for example, is responsible for nearly 75 percent of North Korea's foreign trade and furnishes the country with essential energy supplies in the form of petroleum. Any multilateral effort to coerce North Korea will almost certainly fail without Chinese participation. Beijing has been reluctant to pressure the DPRK because it values North Korea as a buffer between itself and South Korea, a U.S. ally, because the presence of a heavily armed North Korea significantly complicates American geostrategic planning in the Far East, and because economic collapse in North Korea would likely send a flood of refugees across the border into China.

China is not alone. The United States, despite its consistent rhetorical commitment to the norm of nuclear nonproliferation, has refused to punish Israel for its development of an undeclared nuclear arsenal. It maintains close and increasingly cooperative relations with India and Pakistan, even though, in 1998, both countries conducted nuclear tests in violation of the NPT. Only if members of the international community are willing to give priority to the protection of global norms over their own short-term interests will multilateral efforts at coercion be likely to succeed.

When rogue states obtain weapons of mass destruction, as in the case of Saddam Hussein's Iraq and the DPRK, the aim of multilateral coercive diplomacy is likely to shift to containment, particularly through deterrence. Although the Bush administration, in justifying its policy of preemption, contended that rogue regimes were irrational and not susceptible to deterrence, there is little or no evidence to support that proposition. *Rationality* is a term too commonly used and too rarely defined. For successful deterrence, it is not necessary that leaders of rogue states carefully weigh the costs and benefits of various courses of action. It is necessary only that they value their lives and wish to maintain their grip on power. If they can be convinced that the danger to their lives and hold on power would be seriously jeopardized by their own use of WMDs or by the transfer of WMDs to terrorist groups, then they are unlikely to use or transfer them. Kim Jong-Il and his successors may be dissolute and completely unconcerned with the plight of North Korea's largely poor and malnourished population, but this does not mean that they do not care about themselves. While suicide bombers are prepared to give their lives for their causes, there is little or no evidence that either the Iranian government or the Muslim clerics who dictate policy are prepared to sacrifice themselves or their positions.

Presenting a strong, unified front can be critical in attempting to contain a rogue state. A state without major diplomatic or military patrons will find it hard to resist the demands of the international community. In 1991, Iraq's military forces were evicted from Kuwait by a coalition of thirty-four states acting under the authority of UN Security Council Resolution 678. Thereafter, the application of UN-authorized economic sanctions and the enforcement of UN-authorized no-fly zones in northern and southern Iraq helped keep up the pressure. Saddam Hussein neither employed weapons of mass destruction nor transferred them to terrorists but apparently ordered his arsenals destroyed. The failure of U.S. forces, following the 2003 invasion, to find any WMDs appears to validate the argument of John Mearsheimer and Stephen Walt (2003) that waging war against Iraq was unnecessary because Iraq could be contained. This does not mean that all rogue states can be contained, but it is cause for optimism.

Diplomacy in Confronting Rogue States: Engagement

Coercion, it can be argued, is not really diplomacy. After all, it does not involve negotiating with the rogue state except to communicate the demands of the international community. The meaning of diplomacy is better captured by the strategy of engagement, which seeks economic, political, and diplomatic cooperation with the rogue regime and may even offer it incentives to improve its behavior.

During the 1990s, after failing to secure international support for stringent economic sanctions and considering and rejecting preventive military action, the Clinton administration adopted a policy of engagement toward North Korea. The strategy culminated in the 1994 Agreed Framework, by which the DPRK agreed to shut down its nuclear program and halt the reprocessing of plutonium in return for the provision of two proliferation-resistant light-water nuclear reactors and a supply of heating oil, as well as expanded commercial and diplomatic contacts with the United States. The accord eventually unraveled, for reasons that remain the subject of debate, but it probably delayed North Korea's acquisition of nuclear weapons for at least a few years.

The principal criticism of engagement is that it is nothing more than a modern form of appeasement, which, rather than satisfying an aggressive state, is likely to whet its appetite and cause it to make ever-increasing demands. To forestall this possibility, it may often be wise, when employing engagement, to back it with threats of coercive measures. In other cases, coercive measures may help to create a situation in which subsequent efforts at engagement stand a better chance of success. The reform of Libya illustrates the potential effectiveness of such an approach.

In the 1980s, the U.S. government, under President Ronald Reagan, adopted a largely unilateral strategy toward Libya that relied on economic sanctions and punitive air strikes. The policy's ultimate objective was regime change via the provocation of a coup d'état against Libyan leader Muammar Qaddafi. It failed in large part because it did not seriously damage the Libyan economy and because Qaddafi was able to manage domestic opposition to his rule by focusing Libyan anger at the United States and clamping down on dissent (Jentleson and Whytock 2005–2006, 58–61).

Under the George H. W. Bush and Clinton administrations, the U.S. government abandoned its effort to spark an internal overthrow of the Libyan regime and moved to a reform-oriented strategy based on coercion (Jentleson and Whytock 2005–2006, 63–65). Crucially, Washington sought to involve the international community. In January 1992, the UN Security Council adopted Resolution 731, condemning the destruction of the Pan Am and UTA aircraft and demanding that Libya accede to American, British, and French demands that the suspected perpetrators be handed over for trial. When this did not produce the desired results, the Security Council passed Resolution 748, imposing a series of sanctions, including the suspension of international flights to and from Libya. Additional sanctions were enacted in 1993, when the Security Council adopted Resolution 883, requiring UN member states to freeze Libyan funds and prohibiting them from selling to Libya technologies and materials important to the extraction and refining of oil and natural gas. With Washington having already established its willingness to use military force and multilateral sanctions in place, the stage was set for engagement.

Beginning in the late 1990s, members of the international community negotiated with Libya in an effort to bring it back into the fold. Lengthy discussions with representatives of the United Nations and the United Kingdom resulted, in 1999, in the Libyan government's decision to turn over two suspected Lockerbie bombers for trial in The Hague. Crucial to Tripoli's willingness to take this action were promises relayed to Libya by UN Secretary-General Kofi Annan that the United States and Britain would confine their questioning of the suspects to issues directly related to the trial and that the trial would "not be used to undermine the Qaddafi regime." When the two suspects arrived in the Netherlands, the United Nations, in a gesture of goodwill, lifted the sanctions that it had previously imposed (Jentleson and Whytock 2005–2006, 70, 76).

Shortly after this breakthrough, the U.S. government embarked on secret negotiations with Libya. The talks centered on Libya's WMD programs and its sponsorship of international terrorism. British negotiators soon joined the proceedings, along with representatives of the Egyptian and Saudi governments.

Libyan offers to abandon its WMD programs and end its terrorist activities were not initially accepted because issues concerning the Lockerbie bombing remained unresolved. But Qaddafi nevertheless began cutting ties with terrorist organizations. In August 2003, following a series of discussions with representatives of Britain, the United States, and the United Nations, the Libyan government agreed to pay compensation to families of the Lockerbie victims and subsequently delivered a letter to the United Nations acknowledging its role in the attack (Kaplan 2007).

The willingness of members of the international community to provide inducements to the Libyan regime was critical to diplomatic success. Negotiators from Britain, the United Nations, and the United States promised that "acceptance of civil responsibility" for the Lockerbie bombing "would not be used as grounds for legal action against the Libyan government." Between August and December, when final agreement was reached on Libyan WMD disarmament, U.S. officials offered repeated assurances that the United States wanted "policy change and not regime change" (Jentleson and Whytock 2005–2006, 76). Thereafter, other promises made by the United States and Britain in the course of negotiations—particularly the lifting of U.S. unilateral sanctions and the restoration of full diplomatic relations—were kept. The strategy, in the end, was a mix of carrots and sticks, and while coercion may have brought Libya to the bargaining table, it seems clear that "positive sanctions"—that is, promises and rewards—were necessary to seal the deal.

Toward the Future

As Bruce Jentleson and Christopher Whytock note, a variety of factors beyond diplomacy were responsible for the Libyan government's willingness to abandon its roguish behavior and conform to international standards. Of particular importance were economic problems experienced by Libya in the late 1990s as a result of a decline in world oil prices, problems that were exacerbated by U.S. and UN sanctions. Economic difficulties contributed to heightened internal dissatisfaction and an increasing Islamist threat to Qaddafi's leadership. In brief, the global and the domestic Libyan environment were favorable to Libyan reform.

Still, diplomacy was critical in two respects. First, diplomatic efforts led by the United States and Britain succeeded in unifying much of the international community. The United Nations imposed sweeping multilateral sanctions against the Libyan regime, which eventually felt compelled to seek their removal. Second, negotiations between representatives of the international community—primarily

Britain, France, the United States, and the United Nations, but also the governments of various countries in the Middle East—and the Libyan government reassured Libya that its compliance with international standards of behavior would not make it vulnerable but would in fact be rewarded.

One cannot conclude from the Libyan case that all rogue states could be reformed if only diplomacy were employed effectively. Even a broad international coalition brandishing both carrots and sticks and sensitive to the evident insecurities of the North Korean regime might fail to convince Pyongyang to give up its nuclear weapons. Still, if members of the international community can find a way to work in concert as they did with respect to Libya, the prospects for success will be considerably brighter.

And what of Iran, which has an active nuclear program aimed, according to most analysts, at achieving a nuclear weapons facility and which supports several anti-Israeli terrorist organizations? It appears that diplomacy has a chance if two conditions are met. First, the international community must join together in opposition to Iran's nuclear ambitions. To some extent, this has already occurred, as various UN resolutions and the imposition of multilateral sanctions indicate. Second, the representatives of this community must be willing to meet with Iranian negotiators in an effort to determine what if anything might induce Iran to abandon its nuclear program. If security assurances are required—which would not be surprising, given the harsh rhetoric aimed at the Iranian regime by the United States in recent years, the U.S. invasion and conquest of neighboring Iraq, the hostility of largely Arab, Sunni states to Persian, Shiite Iran, Israel's nuclear arsenal, and so forth—then such assurances should be seriously considered. Pronouncements by U.S. President Barack Obama that the United States is not at war with Islam may be a step in the right direction. If Iran's nuclear program is motivated by factors other than insecurity, then these motives must be addressed. One especially interesting suggestion is that Iran's uranium enrichment facilities continue to operate, but that they be placed under international supervision (Luers, Pickering, and Walsh 2008). The proposed multilateral enrichment program might satisfy both Iranian national pride and the desire for a secure source of fuel for the production of electricity in Iran's nuclear reactors.

Rogue states will almost certainly be with us for the foreseeable future. Confronting them with force may in some cases be effective, but military action is likely to encounter practical difficulties as well as normative objections. In most instances, diplomacy will be the superior option. Whether diplomacy succeeds or fails will depend in part on two factors: (1) the willingness of members of the international community to put aside their own strategic, economic, and other interests to collaborate in the enforcement of international norms, and (2) their willingness to engage rogue states, to understand the sources of their behavior, and, to the extent possible, to address them.

References

Allison, G. 2004. *Nuclear terrorism: The ultimate (preventable) catastrophe.* New York: Time Books/Henry Holt & Co.

Chomsky, N. 2000. *Rogue states: The rule of force in world affairs.* Cambridge, MA: South End Press, 2000.

Henriksen, T. H. 2001. The rise and decline of rogue states. *Journal of International Affairs* 54, no. 2 (spring): 349–373.

Jentleson, B. W., and C. A. Whytock. 2005–2006. Who "won" Libya? The force-diplomacy debate and its implications for theory and policy. *International Security* 30, no. 3 (winter): 47–86.

Kaplan, E. 2007. How Libya got off the list. Council on Foreign Relations. October 16. www.cfr.org/publication/10855.

Klare, M. 1995. *Rogue states and nuclear outlaws: America's search for a new foreign policy.* New York: Hill and Wang.

Lake, A. 1994. Confronting backlash states. *Foreign Affairs* 73, no. 2 (March–April): 45–55.

Lennon, A. T. J., and C. Eiss, eds. 2004. *Reshaping rogue states: Preemption, regime change, and U.S. policy toward Iran, Iraq, and North Korea.* A Washington Quarterly Reader. Cambridge, MA: MIT Press.

Litwak, R. S. 2001. What's in a name? The changing foreign policy lexicon. *Journal of International Affairs* 54, no. 2 (spring): 375–392.

———. 2000. *Rogue states and U.S. foreign policy: Containment after the Cold War.* Washington, DC: Woodrow Wilson Center Press.

Luers, W., T. R. Pickering, and J. Walsh. 2008. A solution for the U.S.-Iran nuclear standoff. *New York Review of Books* 55, no. 4 (March 20): 19-22.

Mearsheimer, J. J., and S. M. Walt. 2003. An unnecessary war. *Foreign Policy* 34 (January–February): 50–59.

Waltz, K. N., and S. D. Sagan. 2003. *The spread of nuclear weapons: A debate renewed.* New York: W. W. Norton & Co.

White House. 2002. *National security strategy of the United States of America.* Washington, DC. September. www.globalsecurity.org/military/library/policy/national/nss-020920.pdf.

6

Global Terrorism, Nuclear Proliferation, and Genocide: The Threats Posed to States and Global Stability

Donna M. Schlagheck

As the twentieth century came to a close, three existential threats to states and global stability increasingly challenged diplomats and the limits of multilateral diplomacy. In 1998, Pakistan and India built and detonated nuclear bombs, which expanded the "nuclear club" and undermined the Nuclear Nonproliferation Treaty (NPT) of 1970. In 2001, Al Qaeda orchestrated attacks on the World Trade Center in New York and the Pentagon in Washington, D.C., prompting the Bush administration to initiate a "global war on terrorism." And, as the new millennium began, genocidal campaigns led to the death and displacement of people across the community of nations, with hundreds of thousands of Bosnian refugees in the Federal Republic of Germany, Rwandan Tutsi deaths still unnumbered, and a new genocide taking shape in Darfur, Sudan. The failure of multilateral efforts to enforce the 1948 Convention on the Prevention and Punishment of the Crime of Genocide was undeniable.

The inability of multilateral treaties, conventions, and cooperation to prevent or even restrain terrorism, nuclear proliferation, and genocide has also led to new, emerging forms of multilateralism, including the Proliferation Security Initiative (PSI) and the International Criminal Court (ICC), designed to hold accountable individuals engaged in terrorism and genocide, among other crimes. Innovative approaches to managing these threats to collective security have been informal, such as the PSI, as well as traditionally formal and institutional (e.g., the ICC has charged the current president of Sudan, Omar al-Bashir, with counts of genocide in Darfur). The dynamics of multilateralism clearly include the capacity to change, to adapt in the face of crisis and failure.

This chapter explores the changing dynamics of multilateralism and the roles played by leading state actors and intergovernmental organizations in that process. In addition, particular attention is paid to the provocative and productive role played by nonstate actors in the evolution of multilateralism, particularly in the issue area of the globalized threats posed by nuclear proliferation, terrorism, and genocide.

Nuclear Proliferation

Stunning the international community, India and Pakistan detonated nuclear bombs in 1998. The International Atomic Energy Agency (IAEA) had been established by the United Nations in 1957 as a specialized agency to share expertise on the peaceful uses of atomic energy and to prevent the diversion of fissile material. Following multiple wars and intractable differences over Kashmir, both India and Pakistan conducted an arms race and pursued nuclear weapons technology, culminating in the 1998 tests successfully conducted by each state. The proliferation "embargo" had failed, but far more disturbing were subsequent revelations regarding the "father" of Pakistan's nuclear program, Dr. A. Q. Khan. Not only had this scientist led the development of Pakistan's nuclear weapons program, but for personal profit he had also sold technology and materials to Iran, Libya, and North Korea. In the following decade, Libya elected to forego all weapons of mass destruction (WMDs), Iran actively pursued what it termed "peaceful uses of atomic energy," and North Korea tested both ballistic missiles and a nuclear warhead. What was the response of the international community?

UN Secretary-General Kofi Annan appointed a High-Level Panel on Threats, Challenges and Change to assess emerging threats to global peace and security. In its 2004 report, the panel warned of a "cascade of [nuclear] proliferation" and recommended a freeze on construction of any uranium-enrichment and -reprocessing facilities (United Nations 2004, para. 12). Since almost sixty states now operate or are building nuclear reactors, and forty of them possess the scientific and industrial capacity to build nuclear weapons if they so choose (United Nations 2004, para. 109), the status quo poses enormous potential risk to states and global stability. Multilateral diplomacy figures prominently in the report's recommendations, which include giving states more incentives to sign and abide by the NPT, collective efforts to reduce conflict and the demand for nuclear weapons, enhanced IAEA inspections, a moratorium on repro-cessing, and a Security Council pledge to take collective action to punish any state that uses or threatens to use nuclear weapons (United Nations 2004, para. 112–124). By mid-2009, not one of the recommendations had been implemented.

Interestingly, in paragraph 132, the panel's report noted that this threat "is currently being addressed on a voluntary basis by the Proliferation Security Ini-tiative (PSI). We believe that all States should be encouraged to join this vol-untary initiative." What is the PSI? Remarkably, it was an initiative led by the administration of George W. Bush, which earlier had exited the Anti–Ballistic Missile Treaty in 2002, refused to engage in the Kyoto Protocol on climate change, join the ICC, or obtain Security Council approval to invade Iraq. Nonetheless, in May 2003 President Bush announced, "When weapons of mass destruction or their components are in transit, we must have the means and the authority to seize them" (Bush 2003). PSI was conceived as an ad hoc collective effort to address a threat, leveraging the military (especially naval and aerospace) and intelligence resources of its members, which would act on their own initia-tive, or collaboratively, on a stand-by basis to capture or interdict fissile mate-rials. Over 90 states (including Britain, France, and Russia) now participate in the PSI, which complies carefully with international maritime law and UN Se-curity Council Resolution 1540 (2004), strongly urging states to cooperate to reduce proliferation.

In 2006, Russia and the United States agreed to a second-generation version of PSI, the Global Initiative to Combat Nuclear Terrorism. Seventy-five states now cooperate on a similar ad hoc basis to identify and apprehend terrorists seek-ing to acquire, or criminals attempting to sell, fissile material.

The Secretary-General's report and the Security Council have supported and legitimized this innovative approach to collective security. Despite great tension between the United States and the United Nations following the 2003 invasion of Iraq, the American proposal was welcomed and is now held up as a new model for collective security. Within the U.S. foreign policy community, leading figures, including Henry Kissinger (former national security adviser and secretary of state for Presidents Richard Nixon and Gerald Ford), George Shultz (former secretary of state for President Ronald Reagan), William Perry (former secretary of defense for President Bill Clinton), and Sam Nunn (former senator and arms-control ex-pert) published a framework in 2008 in which they suggest a "new nuclear agenda" should evolve through which the ultimate goal of NPT, a world without nuclear weapons, can be achieved. Both bilateral (U.S.-Russia) and multilateral

(Security Council) action to control the nuclear fuel cycle are necessary, while simultaneously the former Cold War adversaries must return to a bilateral process of building down their arsenals, which constitute 90 percent of nuclear weapons worldwide. In 2008, U.S. presidential candidates John McCain and Barack Obama both agreed with this modification of multilateral diplomacy. In 2009, U.S. President Obama and Russian president Dmitry Medvedev agreed to initiate negotiations on strategic weapons reductions, with special attention focused on verification and monitoring protocols, and after a year of intense negotiations, the United States and Russia reached agreement on a new Strategic Arms Reduction Treaty that was signed by Presidents Obama and Medvedev in April 2010.

Terrorism

The use or threat of violence against symbolic targets to achieve a political goal (i.e., terrorism) has been both an instrument of state governance and a tactic employed against states for millennia. Roman historian Josephus provided one of the earliest written accounts of Jewish resistance to Roman occupation using terrorism. The term itself was first used to describe the French revolutionary leadership's "reign of terror" (*régime de la terreur*) against counterrevolutionaries. In the twentieth century, terrorism evolved into a transnational threat, providing the spark that ignited World War I through the assassination of Archduke Franz Ferdinand in Sarajevo. Following World War II and the struggles for independence waged by numerous colonies, terrorism became a widely recognized means of repression and a useful tool in the struggle for national self-determination.

Using technology to their advantage, terrorists hijacked aircraft, occupied embassies, and exploited global television and other news media to garner attention for their cause. Frustrated in their struggle against Israel, Palestinian groups were among the first to use terrorism internationally to attract attention and aid for their nationalist cause, which Arab states had not or could not provide. In 1970, hijacked airliners were blown up in Jordan, and in 1972 Palestinians, aided by the West German "Red Army Faction," carried out an assault on the Olympic Games held in Munich. The inability of West German state authorities to secure the games or to rescue the Israeli athletes held hostage (all eleven died) demonstrated with the utmost drama the emergence of a serious new threat to stability in the international community.

The targeted states and the United Nations did not sit idly in the face of this new threat. In 1968, Cuba and the United States forged an agreement to deter hijacking via a bilateral agreement either to prosecute or to extradite any hijackers who brought an aircraft illegally to their soil. Subsequent UN resolutions and multilateral conventions would condemn such conduct, but a nonstate actor, the International Airline Pilots Association, effectively ended hijacking for ransom and attention by announcing a policy that pilots would not fly to or from states that gave sanctuary to hijackers. In 2001, Al Qaeda agents hijacked four fully fueled U.S. airliners to use as WMDs. Airline companies soon armored all cockpit doors, and several considered allowing pilots to carry weapons. The threat against air travel was soon eclipsed by the prospect of terrorists acquiring other types of WMDs.

In "A More Secure World: Our Shared Responsibility," the Secretary-General's High-Level Panel on Threats, Challenges and Change summarizes the danger posed by terrorism in stark terms: Terrorism attacks the values that lie at the heart of the UN Charter, namely, respect for human rights and the rule of law, adherence to rules of war that protect civilians, tolerance among peoples and nations, and the peaceful resolution of conflict (2004, para. 145). The report identifies two key dynamics that make the threat of terrorism so urgent: the rise of groups like Al Qaeda (i.e., armed, nonstate transnational networks capable of sophisticated violence) and the possibility that such groups are seeking and may acquire WMDs (i.e., nuclear, radiological, biological, or chemical weapons). The report calls for the United Nations and its secretary-general to take a leadership role to design a comprehensive strategy to fight terrorism.

In describing what such a comprehensive strategy must include, the report's authors identify the major impediments to effective multilateral diplomacy: the lack of social and political rights; the absence of the rule of law and democratic reform to provide a nonviolent avenue for redress of grievances regarding, among other things, occupation, poverty, and unemployment; and state collapse (United Nations 2004, para. 148). All these impediments, for example, drove the Palestinian leadership to resort to international terrorism and were repeatedly cited in General Assembly debate as reasons not to condemn the resort to "armed struggle" to achieve national self-determination by and for the Palestinian people.

Despite attacks on airlines, embassies, governments, and businesses, General Assembly and Security Council resolutions tended to repeat the language of General Assembly Resolution 48/122 (December 20, 1993), which condemned all acts of terrorism and called upon member states to prevent, combat, and eliminate it, and Security Council Resolution 1269 (1999), which called on member states to cooperate to prevent and suppress terrorism. Torn between the conflicting values of nonviolent resolution of conflict, state sovereignty, and the right of all peoples to self-determination, multilateral diplomacy and the United Nations took no significant counterterrorism action until the unimaginable attacks of September 11, 2001.

The magnitude of the shock and the implications of Al Qaeda's attacks on 9/11 are still being assessed. At the United Nations, only a few miles from "Ground Zero" at the World Trade Center, the international community took its first steps toward a "preventive diplomacy," and the "responsibility to prevent" has now entered the common vernacular of the agents of multilateral diplomacy. The dozen international conventions against terrorism that were already in place and the 1999 sanctions against persons and states sponsoring terrorism (i.e., Osama bin Laden and the Taliban) were "reactive" and lacked provisions to monitor compliance.

After September 11, 2001, the Security Council adopted Resolution 1373 obliging all states to comply with a new regime of counterterrorism measures, and the Counterterrorism Committee was created to channel technical aid and verify compliance with the new standards. The United Nations is now considering the high panel's recommendation that the Counterterrorism Committee be empowered to work as a clearinghouse for state-to-state sharing of military, police, and border-control assistance to further strengthen counterterrorism efforts. As has often been the case, however, member states' noncompliance has undermined the effectiveness of the body's attempts to repress and prevent terrorism.

As a result of 9/11, the United Nations postponed the opening session of the Fifty-Sixth General Assembly, while the Bush administration organized its "global war on terrorism," a unilateral effort, initially, to identify the members, leaders, and funders of Al Qaeda. The organization's sanctuary in Afghanistan under Taliban rule was attacked by a Security Council–approved coalition that disintegrated when President Bush adopted a "preemptive war" strategy against Iraq in 2003. The Bush administration, via the "Uniting and Strengthening America by Providing Appropriate Tools Required to Intercept and Obstruct Terrorism" (USA PATRIOT) legislation hurriedly passed by Congress in October 2001, began a multidimensional war on terrorism that included military strikes, arrests and kidnappings of suspected Al Qaeda jihadis, detention without trial, torture, "rendition" (movement of detainees to locations for harsher interrogation), surveillance of foreign and domestic electronic communications, and intelligence sharing with other states at levels never before practiced. Spain and the United Kingdom, victims of post-9/11 Al Qaeda attacks on their public transportation, and Germany, where 9/11 pack leader Ramsi al-Yousef and others had lived and trained, joined a multilateral intelligence-sharing enterprise to combat extremist terrorism. France, Russia, and China, each with indigenous fears of Islamic discontent among North African immigrants, Chechens, and Uighurs, respectively, also joined a first-of-its-kind post–Cold War intelligence "cooperative." By 2009, the mastermind of 9/11, Khaled Sheikh Mohammed, and hundreds of suspected Al Qaeda "enemy combatants" were in U.S. custody in facilities like Guantánamo Bay, Cuba. A majority of the detainees have been processed out of detention; yet, over two hundred remain at "Gitmo," posing an ongoing problem for President Obama, who announced plans to close Guantánamo's detention facility in 2010. President Obama has encountered problems both in repatriating detainees whose home states do not want their return and in confronting growing resistance on the part of American legislators who do not want the detainees in the United States either.

The U.S.-led multilateral intelligence effort included the Permanent Five (P-5) members of the UN Security Council. Although France and Russia would succeed in blocking George Bush's quest for a Security Council resolution endorsing the 2003 attack on Iraq to preemptively destroy that state's alleged WMD programs and topple Saddam Hussein, the P-5 intelligence-sharing enterprise proceeded.

By 2006, the multilateral leadership role formerly played by the United Nations had been reduced to a Counterterrorism Committee project named the Global Counterterrorism Strategy. In this effort, emphasis lay in two areas: (1) redressing conditions that contribute to the resort to terrorism (i.e., preventive diplomacy), and (2) coordinating planning for emergency response in the case of a terrorist attack employing WMDs.

The danger of a terrorist group's acquiring and using a weapon of mass destruction produced another innovative, non-UN multilateral project, led again by the parties most threatened: the Russian Federation and the United States. The Global Initiative to Combat Nuclear Terrorism, initiated by the United States and Russia, convened in Morocco in October 2006 to pursue three goals: (1) to enable participating states to share intelligence, (2) to create a global framework to integrate counterterrorism expertise and capabilities, and (3) to coordinate three approaches to the threat—counterterrorism, counterproliferation, and non-proliferation. Thirteen states met in Morocco in 2006 to sign a statement of principles for the Global Initiative to Combat Nuclear Terrorism, and the IAEA was invited as an observer. Like the PSI, signatories are considered "partners" and are expected to contribute and share intelligence and expertise in order to

1. develop or strengthen security controls over nuclear and radiological material
2. improve security at civilian nuclear facilities
3. improve detection capabilities
4. provide enhanced law enforcement capacity to search and seize nuclear devices or material considered key to eradicating the WMD black market
5. deny terrorists sanctuary or support
6. ensure prosecution of terrorist and those assisting them

As of May 2009, the global initiative was a multilateral effort joined by seventy-five states, with the European Union and IAEA holding observer status. The members collaborate on the UN General Assembly's First Committee, promoting universal ratification of the International Convention for the Suppression of Acts of Nuclear Terrorism, and the IAEA has now established an Illicit Trafficking Database (ITDB) following directives from the 2005 NPT Review Conference.

Within both the United Nations–led multilateral programs and the independently driven global initiative, the convergence of two existential threats—nuclear proliferation and terrorism—is being addressed through multilateral diplomacy. The urgent emphasis on prevention of such threats via collaboration, either under the auspices of the United Nations or not, is critical in light of the ITDB 2008 report that noted 275 incidents of unlawful activity related to possession of fissile or radiological material, 332 incidents of stolen or lost nuclear material, and 398 incidents of improper disposal. The risk posed by terrorists or criminals who obtain such material is prompting sovereign states to engage in or design multilateral solutions to these threats. The balance of sovereignty and self-preservation may be shifting.

Genocide

The United Nations and member states have demonstrated their ability to design new multilateral approaches to the evolving threats of proliferation and terrorism. Both traditional treaties and conventions, as well as ad hoc collaborations such as the PSI and the Global Initiative to Combat Nuclear Terrorism, have enhanced collective security. Tragically, though, such innovations in multilateral diplomacy to address genocide have not occurred, despite extensive scholarship, the establishment of nongovernmental organizations (NGOs) (e.g., Amnesty International and the International Crisis Group), and the evident transnational impacts that genocide has in our interdependent globalized environment. Although significant conceptual and normative change has taken place, the ability of the international community to take action to prevent or halt genocide has not developed into an effective capacity.

Genocide is defined in the universally binding Convention on the Prevention and Punishment of the Crime of Genocide (adopted in 1948) as "acts committed with intent to destroy, in whole or in part, a national, ethnical, racial or religious group" (Article II). Recognizing that states primarily control the infrastructure necessary to carry out genocide, usually against a subgroup of their own population, the United Nations soon moved to establish a subcommission within the Commission on Human Rights (CHR) for the Prevention of Discrimination and Protection of Minorities. Much later, in 1967, the CHR would actually place violations of human rights on its agenda, and working groups with fact-finding authority were appointed. Working groups within the Economic and Social Council and the CHR produced studies that identified early-warning indicators of impending genocide and recommended remedies and "urgent procedures" in 1993 (United Nations 2003). Meanwhile, genocides have continued to occur, including in Bangladesh, Cambodia, Rwanda, and the former Yugoslavia. In all these cases, the United Nations was stymied by its own charter's emphasis on protecting the sovereign rights of states to govern, often expressed in reports blaming large-scale killings on "civil wars," in which the United Nations must not intervene. As early as 1981, human rights scholar Leo Kuper (1981) condemned the United Nations for its lack of moral leadership. Despite NGO and media coverage of unspeakable atrocities, the United Nations could only endorse initiatives to intervene, as in 1991 when Kurds in northern Iraq received protection against Saddam Hussein under a "no-fly zone" carried out by the U.S.-led coalition that had ejected Iraqi forces from Kuwait. Mostly, the United Nations took a reactive, post hoc approach by establishing international criminal tribunals (for Rwanda and Yugoslavia) to prosecute the crimes against humanity. New thinking and new approaches would not emerge until the late 1990s.

In 1999, as Serbs began moving troops and tanks toward Kosovo in direct violation of a 1998 agreement negotiated by Ambassador Richard Holbrooke not to take such action, refugees began to flood into Albania and Italy. U.S. President Bill Clinton believed another "ethnic cleansing" (as Serbs had called the 1992–1995 purging of Muslims from Bosnia-Herzegovina) was about to unfold. The Clinton administration prevailed on its NATO allies to conduct a three-month series of bombing raids on Belgrade to force the Serbs to pull back from Kosovo and allow the refugees to return home. Defending this action in the face of strenuous international criticism, on June 20, 1999, Clinton declared, "If the world community has the power to stop it, we ought to stop genocide and ethnic cleansing" (Clinton 1999). Clinton had articulated a normative value superior to state sovereignty and a moral obligation to prevent humanitarian disaster when possible. The breakdown of the "sovereignty barrier" had begun. Although more than 10,000 Kosovars died, nearly all the 850,000 displaced would return home.

The following year, in light of public debate and lessons learned in NATO's "after-action reports," the government of Canada appointed the International Commission on Intervention and State Sovereignty (ICISS), which published its 2001 report under the title *The Responsibility to Protect*. The case of the former Yugoslavia had offered many insights following its multiple genocides. For Bosniaks (Muslim citizens of Bosnia-Herzegovina), the 1995 intervention led by the United States and NATO (with Security Council consent) had ended the fighting, but few of the hundreds of thousand of refugee Bosniaks from the northern half of Bosnia-Herzegovina have returned to their homes and villages now under Serb control in the Republika Srbska. Most refugees remain in Europe, creating a continuing strain on asylum states like Germany. Few non-Muslims (under 10 percent) now live in the capital, Sarajevo, which has lost, perhaps forever, its rich mixture of Christian Orthodox, Catholics, and Muslims. Ironically, Sarajevo's Jewish community coordinated a substantial relief program for Muslims who endured the three-year siege of Sarajevo. The Croatian "cleansing" of ethnic Serbs from the Krajina region had happened in 1994; it took them less than two weeks to kill or expel over 100,000 fellow Yugoslavs who happened to be Christian Orthodox. The shocking speed of the Croatian army's offensive contrasted sharply with the arduously slow process of Security Council debate, authorization of intervention, and actual deployment of forces. That contrast, as well as the need for a rapid-response humanitarian-intervention capacity, constituted powerful arguments for revising the conventional multilateral approach to genocide. Like nuclear proliferation and terrorism, preventive diplomacy was essential, as was the logistical ability to deploy force swiftly in the face of impending genocide.

In 2004, the call for a new approach and its corollary "responsibility to protect" figured prominently in the ICISS report. The concepts of human security and sovereign states' responsibility to ensure it lie at the heart of the report's argument that states failing in that duty will be deemed to have lost their sovereign rights to govern as they please within their territorial borders. The report has led to new thinking about sovereignty, not as an absolute right but instead as a privilege states earn by protecting their people (Kuperman 2009, 34). Doing so brings them legitimacy and a claim to sovereignty. The report urges a change in the terms of the debate from "right to intervene" to "responsibility to protect" (ICISS 2001, para. 2.33). It also notes that this responsibility requires developing the power to prevent (rather than react) and entails an obligation to rebuild.

How did the international community and the United Nations respond to the report? The 2005 World Summit saw General Assembly action of the sort decried by its critics: 2005 General Assembly Resolution 60 (A/RES/60/1) acknowledged the principle of the responsibility to protect and "to use appropriate diplomatic, humanitarian and other peaceful means, in accordance with Chapters VI and VII of the Charter, to help to protect populations from genocide, war crimes, ethnic cleansing and crimes against humanity." Member states worried about impingements on sovereignty insisted, though, that the use of force only be approved "on a case-by-case basis" and with Security Council agreement (United Nations 2005, para. 139).

Further disappointing advocates of building a rapid-response capability to intervene at or before the onset of genocide—promoted as early as the 2000 Brahimi Report (United Nations 2000)—the General Assembly has been stymied in attempts so far to implement the means to fulfill the responsibility to protect. Confronted with a resurgence of violence in Sudan that has forced 2 million residents of the Darfur region to flee their homes and villages, the United Nations has undertaken a "partnership" with the African Union (AU), on the premise that an indigenous response promises both greater speed and more cultural sensitivity. As with Rwanda in 1994, the political will to act has been weak. Despite the relentless attacks on refugees and relief workers, the United Nations has, as of 2009, deployed half the 20,000 troops authorized, and Sudanese president al-Bashir has ordered all aid workers and UN-AU personnel out of the country. The 2008 indictment of al-Bashir by the ICC appears to have had a most unintended consequence: Aid to refugees is trickling to a halt while the Sudanese government's genocidal policies defy both the United Nations and those demanding it meet its responsibility to protect.

Conclusion

Multilateral diplomacy has responded to new threats in the global community via innovative solutions and new ways of thinking about human security. Frustrating advocates and critics alike, selfish state sovereignty continues to thwart development of an effective and rapid response to genocide. When their existence is threatened, however, by nuclear proliferation or terrorism, states demonstrate a greater willingness to collaborate and sacrifice some aspects of their sovereignty. State survival trumps human security, but the inertia is perhaps just beginning to shift. Leadership and the political will to act, especially in confronting genocide, will likely determine whether multilateral diplomacy can fully exercise the right to protect.

References

Allison, G. 2006. The will to prevent. *Harvard International Review* 28, no. 3.

Bush, G. W. 2003. Remarks by the president to the people of Poland. White House. May 31. http://georgewbush-whitehouse.archives.gov/news/releases/2003/05/20030531-3.html.

Clinton, W. J. 1999. Interview of the president by Wolf Blitzer. *CNN Late Edition*. June 20. http://clinton4.nara.gov/WH/New/html/19990620c.html.

International Commission on Intervention and State Sovereignty (ICISS). 2001. *The responsibility to protect*. Report of the International Commission on Intervention and State Sovereignty. Ottawa, Canada: International Development Research Center. Available online at www.iciss.gc.ca.

Kuper, L. 1981. *Genocide: Its political use in the 20th century*. New Haven, CT: Yale University Press.

Kuperman, A. J. 2009. Rethinking the responsibility to protect. *Whitehead Journal of Diplomacy and International Relations* 10, no. 1 (winter/spring): 33–43.

Ramcharan, B. G. 2008. *Preventive diplomacy at the UN*. Bloomington: Indiana University Press.

Totten, S. and P. R. Bartrop. 2005. The United Nations and genocide: Prevention, intervention, and prosecution. In *Genocide at the millennium: A critical bibliographical review*, ed. S. Totten, 113–146. Piscataway, NJ: Transaction Publishers.

United Nations. 2005. Resolution adopted by the General Assembly 60/1. 2005 World summit outcome. UN Document A/RES/60/1. United Nations. October 24. http://daccess-dds-ny.un.org/doc/UNDOC/GEN/N05/487/60/PDF/N0548760.pdf.

———. 2004. *A more secure world: Our shared responsibility*. Report of the secretary-general's High-Level Panel on Threats, Challenges and Change. UN Document A/59/565. United Nations. December 2. www.un.org/secureworld.

———. 2003. Report of the committee on the elimination of racial discrimination. UN Document A/48/18. United Nations. September 15. http://documents-dds-ny.un.org/UNDOC/GEN/N93/502/16/pdf/N9350216.pdf.

———. 2000. Report of the panel on United Nations Peace Operations. UN Document A/55/305–S/2000/809. United Nations. August 17. www.un.org/peace/reports/peace_operations.

7

Challenges to the Global Economy: Can the State Fix Them?

David A. Kennett

Globalization

The post–World War II era, especially the last three decades, has seen a remarkable increase in the level of international economic activity, albeit from the low levels created by the dramatic contraction in trade and other international economic transactions during the Great Depression years of the 1930s. International flows of goods, services, capital, and labor have all increased substantially during this period. A surge in activity followed the advent of reform in China and its subsequent emergence as a leading exporter onto the world stage. In that country alone exports went from less than 5 percent of gross domestic product (GDP) in 1979 to more than 35 percent in 2006 (Bramall 2008) and roughly 40 percent today. Similarly, the breakdown of the systems of central planning in the Soviet Bloc gave a push to trade.

As recently as 2008 the surge in international economic activity seemed secure and irreversible, but today threats that might upset this apparent stability are more visible. This chapter discusses some of the challenges that currently confront the global economy. The challenges are of different types and scales and their amenability to state or multistate solutions varies. Some affect merely the scope and success of the current trading and global financial structure and address them. The most serious challenge discussed in this chapter, however, is climate change, which threatens the survival of the planet. In general, the problems are of such a magnitude that the possibility of state or multistate solutions are, in fact, relatively limited, and effective solutions will require, at the very least, cooperation on a scale that we have not witnessed to this point.

The Rise of the Economic Nation-State

Before embarking on a deeper discussion of what actually threatens the global economy and what the nation-state can and cannot achieve, it is worthwhile to review in brief the genesis of the historical economic development of nation-states because there are clear parallels with the need today to increase jurisdictional scope to eliminate problems. The feudal economic organization that preceded the economic nation-state placed limits on the gains offered by the division of labor, economies of scale, and trade based on comparative advantage. Feudal jurisdictions were small and militated against economic growth through duplicative taxing authorities, the nonstandard system of weights and measures, the differences in both the letter and the application of the law, and the unreliability of the currency as a store of value and, therefore, as a medium of exchange. Even language was nonstandard within many European countries. The feudal system also prevented an efficient allocation of labor since almost all rural labor was subject to the rules of serfdom and therefore immobile in both occupational and geographic terms.

These problems were reduced by the imposition of a centralized state capable of requiring uniform standards across the disparate feudal territories. The date of this transition is hard to fix, but we can think of it as originating in western Europe in the sixteenth century in Tudor England and the Low Countries, then extending through Jean-Baptiste Colbert's reforms in eighteenth-century France to Otto von Bismarck's domestic economic policies in the unification of Germany in the nineteenth century. In any event, most historians and political scientists believe that the Westphalian state system was established after 1648.

The most important proximate cause of consolidation of the nation-state was the relative inability of the sovereign to tax, which limited the capacity to conduct public works, make war, or even live according to the standard to which monarchs should be accustomed. To this end, the sovereign used force (including newly acquired military capacity) to unify the state. The imposition of a central taxing authority carried the important subsidiary benefit of reducing the imposition of local taxes (often nothing more than ransom), which had served as a serious detriment to trade. The advent of the nation-state brought with it also the first vestige of the assumption of recognizable macroeconomic responsibility on the part of national governments. The dominant economic doctrine of the new state was called mercantilism—literally, the doctrine of merchants—but it was a broad collection of ideas rather than a tightly defined orthodoxy. Mercantilism can be thought of as having two agendas or projects—internal and external. The internal project was focused on the elimination of the barriers to internal commerce. The external project was the creation of a positive balance of foreign trade that would maximize the accrual of precious metals at home (which would flow in as the counterpart of the surplus in trade), while creating a positive balance of employment, thus maximizing domestic economic activity. As the free trade doctrines of Adam Smith and David Ricardo gained acceptance, this mercantile policy was roundly attacked and suffered an intellectual eclipse. In practical terms, however, it was more durable and experienced a revival in the 1930s as governments scrambled to fight domestic unemployment. It is important to note that the charge of "neomercantilism" constitutes a major criticism of China's currency policy today.

Many of the limits to growth posed by the piecemeal nature of feudal economy were overcome by the creation of the larger national unit. Laws, languages, weights, measures, and commercial codes were standardized. National currency became a more acceptable store of value and means of exchange. Internal tariff and nontariff barriers to trade were eliminated. As a result, internal trade ballooned, and national prosperity increased. The nation-state remained the unquestioned unit of responsibility until late in the twentieth century, when some national power was relinquished to supranational organizations as diverse as the European Union and the World Trade Organization. However, even today within supranational bodies, important economic decisions are largely made on a national basis. There are clear parallels between this transition to the nation-state and the problems of the world economy today. Just as the inefficiencies encountered in the feudal system of organization could not be resolved without the imposition of power from above (the nation-state), it is hard to see how our current challenges can be met without at least comprehensive and well-enforced international agreements or the relinquishing of sovereignty by nation-states to some form of supranational body.

Product Safety and Quality Standards

The first of the challenges to the global trading system to be discussed relates to product quality. These (along with issues of weights and measures) were addressed in the creation of the nation-state but have emerged in the international arena in a different form. In the fall of 2007, the global trading system was briefly shaken by product-quality issues involving Chinese exports. Among the problems were toothpaste containing toxic diethylene glycol, pet food and dairy products containing melamine, seafood containing antimicrobial agents, and toys coated with lead paint. There was a consumer reaction against Chinese products in the United States, although the quantitative effects were smaller than might have been assumed based on the amount of coverage in the press.

The threat to the global system was simple. If American and European consumers had no faith in the quality and safety of Chinese products, then a reaction would set in, causing a reduction in trade and threatening Chinese entry as a major global power. Fortunately, this is one challenge potentially rectifiable by market reaction alone: American firms responsible for importing from China have a reputation to protect. Should that corrective prove ineffective, it would remain clearly in the interest of the Chinese government to defend the "made in China" brand, and quick steps could be taken on product-quality matters at the national level. The second avenue of state action (the United States and other importing nations performing more rigorous testing before licensing entry) proved largely unnecessary; the threat of action was enough. In this case, state action was perfectly adequate to meet the challenge posed by the threat.

Trade Imbalances

A second important threat to the stability of the global economy lies in the substantial imbalances in global trade. Two such imbalances stand out. The first is that between the developed nations and the burgeoning manufacturing nations of East Asia, and between China and the United States. The other is the relationship between oil consumers and the oil producers, of which the United States and Saudi Arabia are the most important examples. This is less pressing than the U.S.-China issue. The problem of recycling petrodollars has been with us since the 1970s, and the United States has learned to handle the problem reasonably well.

One of the great success stories of globalization, the sustained growth of the Chinese economy, has been highly dependent on a trade imbalance with the United States. China has followed a neomercantilist policy, maintaining a lower value for the yuan in order to facilitate an export-led growth strategy. Seventeenth-century English mercantilists would have recognized this as promoting a favorable balance of employment. Equally, American prosperity for the first eight years of the new century was also dependent on the capital counterpart of the trade deficit, which was Chinese funding of U.S. public and private debt. So close was this symbiosis that economic historians Niall Ferguson and Moritz Schularick (2007) coined the word "Chimerica" to refer to these two economies whose prosperity was symbiotically linked. The East Chimericans (China) would do the producing and the saving (as well as the bulk of the investment), while the West Chimericans (the United States) would handle the consumption end of things. Not only was this the key, for a while, to U.S. and Chinese prosperity, but Ferguson and Schularick considered it to be "the real engine of the world economy" and ascribed to it the stability that was tested and found wanting during the economic disaster of 2008.

As 2008 played out, it became clear that the Chinese government's policy of depressing its exchange rate had had the desired effect of building a current account surplus. Furthermore, the influx of Chinese savings into the United States had had the effect of depressing dollar interest rates and thereby fueling a surge in asset prices. In turn, Americans saw prosperity in the growing value of their houses and mutual funds and, able to borrow cheaply against this value, saw little need to save. This set the scene for 2008, when asset prices "readjusted" and provoked a meltdown that shook the balance sheets of many financial firms and gave rise to a crisis. The meltdown was the more severe because financial creativity had produced complex and opaque derivative products, but the root cause can be seen in the Chinese financing of the U.S. asset bubble. "The present crisis grew out a serious and unsustainable imbalance in the United States and world economies. Specifically, over recent years, until the outset of the recession, Americans spent more than our country produced or was capable of producing at full employment" (Volcker 2009). Although the crisis originated in the United States, it quickly permeated the global economy, producing the deepest and most sustained downturn of the postwar era.

The world is now waiting to see if another shoe is about to drop. The Sino-American trade imbalance pumped so much money into dollar-denominated assets that there are fears that the dollar, backed as it is by a weak economy, cannot continue to be the world's main reserve and trading currency and that as it unwinds, with no obvious successor, further disruption must result.

Despite a recent fall in Chinese exports, Sino-U.S. trade is still well out of balance, and if the U.S. economy recovers, the gap will widen once more as exports are sucked in. Although a return to the "Chimerican" status quo ante would offer temporary relief, it would be the first step toward a replication of the crisis. Must such imbalances always constitute a threat to the global economy, or is there some way of disarming them, and would such a solution be at the state level, or would it require supranational authorities?

There are clear "state solutions," but they are unattractive in political terms and may therefore be infeasible. The American state solution is to reduce U.S. consumption and increase savings in the consumer, governmental, and corporate sectors. This would be a credible response to years of overconsumption, but its implementation in the short term would prolong a global recession for which, ironically, the most likely engine of recovery is the spendthrift American consumer. Lowering the federal deficit would require a sharp increase in the tax burden on Americans; a voluntary increase in saving would imply a sharp fall in consumption. The total shift would have to be around 4 percent of GDP. Although this could solve America's problem, it would require additional action if the world economy were to escape without serious damage. Since the U.S. dollar is the world's de facto reserve currency, America's deficit is required to provide liquidity to the global system. Were the United States to bring its current account more into balance, some additional global currency would be needed, and the slack would have to be taken up either by another currency (the euro?) or by some artificial store of value, such as an expansion of the International Monetary Fund's special drawing rights. Even a state solution for America's imbalance would require an international solution for international reserves.

The possible Chinese state solution would be to let the value of the yuan appreciate, thereby allowing an increased lowering of the trade surplus and reducing Chinese purchases of dollar-denominated assets. However, such a policy would raise real wages and unit labor costs, lessening the price competitiveness of Chinese products on the international market. Chinese authorities fear any reduction in exporting activity will have a multiplied effect on Chinese employment and will cause lower growth. While Chinese growth has been spectacular and sustained, the World Bank thinks that any slippage below 9.5 percent annual growth of GDP will lead to increasing unemployment (*Economist* 2008) and therefore to growing social unrest. GDP growth in 2009 was below this threshold, though surprisingly strong at 8.7 percent, but with unemployment on their minds, the chance is slim that Chinese authorities will allow a revaluation of their currency. So, individual state solutions are limited by domestic politics.

Could there be a multilateral state solution to this problem? If there were a greater agreement on the exact nature of the disease and on the appropriate medicine, it might, in fact, be easier to achieve a cooperative global solution. In an innovative essay, economist Richard N. Cooper (1989) compared the impasse of international macroeconomic cooperation to the rise of cooperation in global health agreements. Before there was clear agreement on the causes of epidemics, international conferences on public health achieved little. He suggested that international macroeconomics is a parallel situation. Until the nature and transmission mechanism of economic problems are well understood, cooperative international action is unlikely. Thus, until the United States, China, and other parties are in full agreement that the imbalance creates a global problem and that one party or another should act to modify it, an effective policy solution is unlikely.

Financial Regulation

While payment imbalances were the fundamental cause of the 2008 crisis, the ineffective regulation of the large financial institutions that embody serious systemic risk has been seen as a more proximate cause. The previous two decades had seen a dismantling of preexisting national regulatory structures and a failure to regulate new derivative products. In testimony before the U.S. House of Representatives Committee on Oversight and Government Reform in October 2008, Alan Greenspan, who headed the Federal Reserve from 1988 to 2006, confessed that his presumption of optimally self-regulating markets was flawed. He told the House, "I don't know how significant or permanent it is. But I've been very distressed by that fact." He also admitted that he had "made a mistake in presuming that the self-interest of organizations, specifically banks and others, were such as that they were best capable of protecting their own shareholders and their equity in the firms" (2008).

The admission that lax regulation in the United States was at least a partial cause of the 2008 collapse prompted U.S. authorities to review the regulatory structure. In January 2010 the Obama administration introduced new regulations that, while stopping short of the reintroduction of Glass-Steagall, put severe limitations on the activity of large banks. However, the rapid international transmission also drew attention to the need for coordinated international regulation. Systemic risk can be generated in many jurisdictions, not merely the United States, and heavier regulation in any one country might merely serve to drive the riskier operations to other less regulated jurisdictions. This calls into question whether the threat to international stability can be met by national policy alone or so-called macroprudential action must be coordinated. While it is in each nation's interest to have a stable banking structure, it might be advantageous for a single nation to allow highly leveraged operations if the gain were great and the risk fell mainly outside the country.

It is interesting to note the role of Iceland in the international transmission of the 2008 crisis. A very small country with little history of international banking and inexperienced regulators, Iceland allowed its institutions to assume vastly too much risk, and the resulting collapse not only imposed a heavy cost on Iceland's taxpayers but also added considerably to international instability. In the Great Depression of the 1930s, it was Creditanstalt, a bank in relatively small Austria, whose instability precipitated a global collapse.

Believing international coordination is necessary, the Group of Twenty (G-20) nations have created a new Financial Stability Board (FSB) to cover all G-20 countries and the European Commission. It is chaired by Mario Draghi, governor of the Bank of Italy, with a secretariat based at the Bank for International Settlements headquarters in Switzerland.

Its brief is to examine all "systemically important" financial institutions, instruments, and markets, and its purview will include, for the first time, the most important hedge funds. Although its concern is macroprudential, part of its focus must be microprudential, concerned with the behavior of individual companies when they are large enough to threaten the system. So, each major firm will have to register and report its strategy, debt, and risk levels to the FSB. The board will appoint subgroups to monitor each important firm's financial and operational structure and any contingency funding arrangements.

Will this international approach prove superior to the national approach? There are reasons for skepticism. First, the group that the FSB has to supervise is much bigger than that of its predecessor, the Financial Services Forum. The new membership will include Argentina, China, India, Mexico, and Russia. Conventional thinking is that the success of collective action is inversely related to the number of players—merely deciding on standards is more difficult—but in the interconnected world of finance, proceeding without these emergent economic powers would invite failure.

Second, and perhaps more importantly, the FSB has neither enforcement capabilities nor adequate funds to perform bailouts. This means that the most it can do when it finds a miscreant is turn it over to national authorities, which will then have to curtail its operation or commit national taxpayer funds to the rescue. It is hard to imagine, for example, China feeling cooperative in the long term with a Swiss-based body that exposes its banking system and demands contraction and refinancing by the national government at considerable expense. Simple game theory suggests that agreements that do not include any punishment mechanisms for cheating are destined to fail.

Climate Change

There has been considerable dispute about the short- and long-term consequences of human action on the environment and the future of the planet. However, today it is fair to suggest that a consensus has emerged that much of global warming is anthropogenic, meaning caused by humanity, and that unless we successfully control the output of greenhouse gases (GHGs) and other forms of pollution, the change in our physical environment will be catastrophic to our economic situation, if not fatal to the planet itself.

The issue of global warming presents two classes of problems familiar to economists. A healthy global environment is a classic *public good*, a good shared by all and from which none can be excluded. The benefits cannot therefore be effectively priced. "Free riding," that is, benefiting from the actions of others while contributing less than a "fair share," will be an inherent danger. The cause of the threat to the atmosphere, pollution itself, is an *externality*, an unrequited third-party effect of other people's economic transactions. As carbon stored within the earth as coal, oil, and natural gas and upon the earth in the form of old-growth forest is burned, largely for energy, the level of GHGs in the earth's atmosphere increases, producing the greenhouse effect and global warming. There are really only two ways of tackling this:

1. by drastically reducing the burning of fossil and old-growth-forest carbon at least to slow the buildup of atmospheric carbon dioxide
2. by finding some effective way of lowering the level of GHGs, mostly carbon dioxide, in the atmosphere, by pumping them into the earth or increasing the growth of carbon-rich matter that will hold it

The second alternative, while intriguing, is technologically quite remote in terms of the scale required at present. If action is to be taken on the global environment in the near term, it will have to take the form of reduced carbon consumption either through reduced energy needs or through increased efficiency in energy creation and reduced destruction of old-growth forest. The latter contributes about 18 percent of incremental GHGs—more than the 14 percent added by the global transportation sector. This illustrates some of the complexity of the problem. Indonesia and Brazil are the world's third- and fourth-largest emitters of GHGs (behind the deindustrializing United States and industrializing China), respectively, because of their extensive deforestation.

Economists argue that an effective reduction in carbon consumption requires establishing a carbon "price" that will make all users of carbon pay some measure of the price of the externality created by the consumption of carbon. As the Stern Report noted, "Putting an appropriate price on carbon—explicitly through tax or trading, or implicitly through regulation—means that people are faced with the full social cost of their actions. This will lead individuals and businesses, advocates argue, to switch away from high-carbon goods and services, and to invest in low-carbon alternatives" (Stern 2006).

It would be much easier if there were a supranational body to which all nations surrendered substantial sovereignty on these issues. In the absence of such an organization, the plausible solution is to broker international agreements that commit all signatories to attaining national goals, which collectively work toward achieving appropriate international targets. The Stern Report considered that "the choice of policy tool will depend on countries' national circumstances, on the characteristics of particular sectors, and on the interaction between climate-change policy and other policies. Policies also have important differences in their consequences for the distribution of costs across individuals, and their impact on the public finances." This was the approach taken in the Kyoto agreement, which was concluded within the UN Framework Convention on Climate Change and was an early step in establishing international action on global warming.

It is important to note that to resolve the crisis, GHG reduction would have to be both more stringent and more comprehensive than that required by the Kyoto accords. Only the "industrialized countries" accepted binding targets; developing countries (which include China, now the world's largest polluter) were exempt. The United States, the largest polluter in the world until 2006, refused to ratify the treaty. Significantly, those that retained a binding target were at the time the largest per head polluters, and since many were moving into postindustrialization, the capacity to reduce industrial pollution was apparent. Even so, the pledge made by the developed nations at Kyoto to dial back pollution to its 1990 levels was only achieved because of the collapse in economic output in Eastern Europe and the former Soviet Union. The United States, in fact, did better than many Kyoto signatory nations, including Canada.

An international conference, the fifteenth "conference of parties," held in December 2009 in Copenhagen sought to establish the next steps forward by building on the Kyoto Protocol. There was a wide variety of problems to tackle. First, what Kyoto has so far achieved may be too little, too late. The group of developed nations that accepted a binding target (that is, without the United States) at Kyoto accounted for about 30 percent of total GHG emissions. Due to their partially successful policy of curtailment and the growth of emissions in developing countries, developed nations constituted only 20 percent of global emissions by 2005, and with each succeeding year, their share of the total will continue to fall. So, compliance by the industrialized nations will result in a smaller and smaller contribution to achieving global emission objectives.

Second, the consensus among scientists is that the target of 20 percent reduction by 2020 against the baseline of 1990 is about half of what is needed to stabilize the situation. Third, there is the issue of international equity. Since the establishment of the 1990 baseline, most of the growth of GHGs has been from the "developing countries," of which China is the leader, but much of Asia and Latin America are involved as well. While these nations have been the source of increased GHGs, their contribution per capita is still well below that of the richer nations, despite recent trends.

A relatively small group of countries struggled hard at Copenhagen to produce some kind of accord in the face of Chinese intransigency. U.S. President Barak Obama, who negotiated directly, called the end result "a meaningful and unprecedented breakthrough." However, those who thought that the convention would be able to come up with hard and enforceable targets were sadly disappointed. The accord contained a loose commitment to hold global warming to within 2°C above preindustrial levels, but in terms of a mechanism to effect this, little was achieved.

One bright spot was the funds made available to developing nations. Initially, $10 billion (rising to $100 billion) a year has been made available to fund the UN Collaborative Program on Reducing Emissions from Deforestation and Forest Degradation in Developing Countries and to enable developing nations to meet rising energy prices. Consumers and taxpayers in the developed world will have not only to pay some form of carbon tax to reduce their own pollution but also to finance international aid required for developing nations to pay higher carbon prices and to keep their old-growth forests intact.

Given the problems of an international solution, is a multistate solution available? In technical terms, yes! Each state could voluntarily reduce its own pollution to ensure that the world does not heat up. In political terms, this is unlikely because any nation can become a free rider and benefit from the sacrifices made by other nations, while contributing little or nothing to solving the problem. This is the more likely because it is easy for any nation to perceive itself as an aggrieved party. Early industrialized nations can now point to substantial emission reductions, while latecomers often assert the right to pollute on a par with richer nations. Nations in Europe or North America, which have demolished their old-growth forests, can now point to the importance, for example, of retaining Amazonia as a global "lung." China and the United States, as the largest polluters, are key players, but that fact has enabled them to be slow in getting on board because agreements without them are largely meaningless. American policy at Copenhagen was to pledge to cut U.S. GHG emissions from 2005 levels by 17 percent by 2020—although the 2005 levels are higher than those of 1990, the date used by the group that ratified Kyoto as a benchmark. China would support no target numbers beyond a commitment to reduce its energy intensity of GDP by 45 percent, but it did countenance the possibility of international inspection.

If emitter states like China do not act on GHGs, is there any solution open at the state level? Canadian economists Jeff Rubin and Benjamin Tal have proposed a tariff of roughly 17 percent, which would offset the implicit subsidy associated with China's lower GHG-emissions standards. Such a policy would force the polluter to "internalize the externality" of pollution by treating the tariff as a cost of exporting. Although any single nation could adopt this policy, collective action would be preferable and more decisive, perhaps as coordinated action by the Organization for Economic Cooperation and Development.

If, however, there is a multistate solution to climate change, it will depend on each nation's agreeing to do its part to fulfill the agreed-on international agenda or being coerced by the coordinated tariff policies of other states. But establishing an equitable international agenda is fraught with problems. A major one is the fact that nations have different states of development and economic prosperity. "Cap and trade" is the preferred route in Europe and, it seems, of the Obama administration. However, this appears inequitable to many developed nations because the permits are usually allocated initially without charge to the firms that have in the past used the most carbon and therefore polluted the most.

Conclusion

From our review of the feasibility of state solutions to challenges to trade we can conclude the following:

1. In the case of product standards, the preferable solution lies in the market, but if this fails there is an available state solution, which, because it is in the interest of at least one party, will likely be followed.
2. In the case of financial regulation, there are state solutions that would be globally beneficial, but either imperfect information or free riding for

short-term gain might induce some states to adopt a globally inefficient policy. Coordinated multistate action is preferable, but enforcement tools must be defined for regulation to prove successful.

3. Balance-of-payment imbalances can be rectified by state action, but appropriate action may be infeasible for domestic political reasons. Successful policy might be more easily achieved if the causes and consequences of the imbalances are fully agreed on.

4. Finally, in the case of climate change, the possibility of free riding makes the simple state solution of unilaterally reducing emissions improbable. The multistate solution of meeting agreed-on targets appears politically difficult to achieve. In the absence of a supranational body with coercive powers, coordinated countervailing tariffs imposed by groups of states against recalcitrant polluting nations could create a feasible system.

References

Bramall, C. 2008. *Chinese economic development.* New York: Routledge.

Cooper, R. N. 1989. International cooperation in public health as a prologue to macroeconomic cooperation. In *Can nations agree? Issues in international economic cooperation,* ed. R. N. Cooper, B. Eichengreen, C. R. Henning, and G. Holtham, 178–254. New York: Putnam.

Economist. 2008. The great wall of unemployed. *Economist.* November 29, 80.

European Environmental Agency (EEA). 2007. *Greenhouse gas emission trends and projections in Europe.* EEA. November 27. www.eea.europa.eu/publications/ eea_report_2007_5.

Ferguson, N., and M. Schularick. 2007. Chimerica and the global asset market boom. *International Finance* 10, no. 3: 215–239.

Greenspan, A. 2008. Testimony to House Oversight Committee. October 23. http://oversight.house.gov/images/stories/documents/20081024163819.pdf.

Romm, J. 2009. The United States needs a tougher greenhouse gas emissions reduction target for 2020. Center for American Progress. January 19. www.american progress.org/issues/2009/01/romm_emissions.html.

Stern, N. 2006. *Stern review on the economics of climate change.* Executive Summary. HM Treasury. October 30. www.hm-treasury.gov.uk/sternreview_index.htm.

Volcker, P. A. 2009. Statement before the Joint Economic Committee, Washington, D.C., February 26. http://jec.senate.gov/public/?a=Files.Serve&File_id=e9b83 30c-f68c-49bf-818f-c1af11794406.

8

Explaining State Responses
to Human Rights

Timothy Longman and Natalie Zähringer

The concept of human rights—the idea that all people are entitled to a minimum standard of decent treatment simply by virtue of their humanity (Donnelly 2003, 7)—has become an increasingly important influence on international affairs. Following World War II, diplomats developed a series of international legal documents that spell out the basic expectations that all people can have of their governments, particularly in reference to individual freedom. This international human rights law has increasingly become the basis on which both domestic and international actors place pressure on governments to reform how they treat their populations. Since the end of the Cold War, the international community has become ever more willing to enforce human rights standards, holding a growing number of individuals accountable for human rights violations in international courts and even justifying military intervention on humanitarian grounds (Ishay 2004).

The growing importance of human rights on the international stage seems to challenge one of the fundamental principles that have long undergirded the international system of states: sovereignty. For several centuries, relations between states have been shaped by the idea that each state has autonomy over internal affairs and that no state has a right to interfere in the domestic affairs of other states. This principle of sovereignty is the starting point for realism, the dominant approach to the study of international relations, which holds that sovereignty "has provided a measure of stability, predictability, and order within the anarchic system of nation-states" (Cronin 2007, 293). Realists argue that since each state acts to promote the interests of its own nation-state, sovereignty protects weak states from destructive interference by strong states, while allowing strong states "to define and pursue their interests unilaterally without being subjected to the will of a majority" (Cronin 2007, 294).

Critiques of the international system based on sovereignty, commonly known as the Westphalian system, have become common in recent years, pointing out that claims of sovereignty have been used to justify terrible atrocities and arguing that higher principles should now take precedence over sovereignty. Jackson Maogoto, for example, points out that "sovereign excesses in the twentieth century resulted in the murder of approximately 170 million persons by their sovereign" (2008, 213). Human rights doctrines appear to challenge the principle of sovereignty directly by regulating how states can treat their own citizens within their territories. The growing influence of human rights principles appears to many observers to mark a decline in the Westphalian system, as the international community has increasingly acted to enforce human rights standards within individual countries, through diplomatic pressure and humanitarian interventions to stop human rights violations and through the imposition of judicial accountability following abuses (cf. Lyons and Mastanduno 1995; Jacobsen, Sampford, and Thakur 2008).

Given the extent to which states have historically defended sovereignty, how can the growing willingness to intervene on behalf of human rights be explained? Why has the international community moved so aggressively since the end of the Cold War to create international courts that hold domestic actors accountable for offenses committed within their own countries? Has the international political commitment to sovereignty waned? Have states suddenly embraced an approach to international relations based on liberal ideals rather than principles of national interest? Are both the Westphalian system of states and the realist approach to international relations in crisis?

In this essay, we argue that the expansion of support for human rights and the increase in humanitarian interventions do not mark a sharp break with the Westphalian idea of sovereignty—at least not yet. In fact, the new emphasis on protecting human rights is driven less by idealistic commitments than by national self-interest, the very principle that derives from sovereignty and that the realist approach contends motivates international affairs. Whether or not the preservation of the Westphalian system is a good thing remains a matter of much debate, but at least up to the present, international pressures for human rights, international war crimes courts, and humanitarian intervention have presented only limited challenges to the principle of sovereignty. Nevertheless, some important changes in international relations are taking place, particularly in terms of soft law, driven both by national self-interest and by an increasingly powerful international movement for human rights within civil society, and these changes are placing increasing pressure on states to provide at least a minimum respect for human dignity.

Sovereignty and the Realist Approach to International Relations

Sovereignty has served as a central organizing principle for the international system of states for nearly four centuries. The principle of sovereignty holds that states are free to govern within their own territories as they choose, without interference from other states, while maintaining, at least in theory, equality with other states. The principle of sovereignty was made explicit in the 1648 treaties, known as the Peace of Westphalia, that ended the Thirty Years War, in which European states fought for decades to impose religious and political practices on one another. International law emerged to regulate interactions between states, but historically whatever happened within individual states—except as it affected foreign nationals—was outside the scope of international law and was regarded as the responsibility of whatever power, be it a monarchy, dictatorship, or democracy, was sovereign over a given territory. As Stephen Krasner states, "Nonintervention, or the principle that no state should be subject to interference in its internal affairs, follows directly from the assumption that each state is a sovereign actor capable of deciding on its own policies" (1995, 232).

While international respect for sovereignty has never been absolute, governments have jealously guarded their sovereignty for obvious reasons. Enjoying sovereignty means that rulers are free from excessive external influence. Although governments have sometimes used claims of sovereignty to defend themselves from criticisms regarding their abuse of power, advocates of the Westphalian system maintain that it has served on the whole to preserve international peace because it has prevented powerful states from simply imposing their will on smaller and weaker states and has limited the number of armed conflicts between states.[1]

Realism, the dominant approach to international relations for the past half century, takes sovereignty as a basic supposition, regarding sovereign states as the primary actors in international politics. As a consequence, international law remains largely consensual, with states being bound only by the treaties they have chosen to ratify. With no higher authority in place to regulate their actions and interactions, the international system is anarchic. According to Gene Lyons and Michael Mastanduno, the basic ideas in the realist approach are that "states are motivated by what they perceive to be their interests, and behavior and outcomes are determined by the distribution of power among states" (1995, 17).

This central tenet of the realist approach arose in part in reaction to idealist perspectives that viewed state actions as motivated by values and ideals. Realists are skeptical about "the prospects for moral and political improvement" (Loriaux 1992, 406), seeing power as the key element in international affairs. For example, Reinhold Niebuhr argued against the idea that states could act on principles other than self-interest: "In every human group, there is less reason to guide and to check impulse, less capacity for self-transcendence, less ability to comprehend the needs of others and therefore more unstrained egoism than the individuals, who compose the group, reveal in their personal relationships" (1932, xxv).

The emergence of human rights as a growing factor in international affairs seems to present a challenge to such realist thinking. While societies have long enjoyed the possibility of establishing limitations on the actions of their own states through constitutions, bills of rights, and other means, the principle of sovereignty limited states' ability to impose such institutions on other states. Human rights doctrines attempt to establish international standards of conduct for states, and the enforcement of human rights appears to involve individual states or groups of states seeking to force particular practices or structures on other unwilling states in apparent violation of their sovereignty. As Andrew Moravcsik states, "International human rights institutions are not designed primarily to regulate policy externalities arising from societal interactions across borders, but to hold governments accountable for purely internal activities" (2000, 217).

The Emergence of a Human Rights Discourse

The concept of human rights, the idea that all people are inherently deserving of a basic level of dignified treatment, has roots in historic religious and moral ideas of human dignity and in the Enlightenment ideas of natural rights and limited government (Ishay 2004). Yet, the idea that people have rights not because they are God's creation or because they are citizens of a certain country but simply because they are human is a fairly recent concept. As Jack Donnelly asserts, "One searches in vain for human rights in (Western) classical or medieval political theory and practice" (2003, 76). According to Donnelly, the concept of human rights was a practical response to the emergence of market capitalism and highly powerful, centralized states. Western states were the first to industrialize and develop centralized, bureaucratic states; hence, they were the first to develop legal mechanisms to limit state power and defend the vulnerable. Support for human rights has spread internationally as the state system and global capitalism have expanded (Donnelly 2003, 57–70).

Modern human rights are distinguished by their combination of a moral commitment to human dignity with a legal structure delineating individual rights. Early international moral movements, such as the fight to end the slave trade (Hochschild 2005), were able to force policy changes, but without a permanent legal framework, they proved insufficient to make lasting improvements in the human condition. The earliest attempt to use international law to protect human rights was the Geneva Convention of 1864, orchestrated by Swiss businessman Henri Dunant, who, horrified by the suffering he witnessed in the aftermath of a battle in the Italian wars of independence, urged the creation of an international treaty that regulated the treatment of wounded soldiers and offered protection to medical personnel (Gumpert 1938). Additional conventions sought to limit the brutality of warfare in international treaties that together are considered the "law of war." While these treaties regulated interactions between states, they helped set a precedent for the later development of human rights treaties, since their purpose was to protect human dignity by limiting how states could engage in warfare.

Modern human rights regimes built on earlier ideas about limiting government and protecting individual human dignity but arose as a direct reaction to the brutality of World War II. In the Nuremberg and Tokyo war crimes tribunals organized by the victorious Allies, prosecutors were hampered by the lack of a legal basis for holding German and Japanese government officials and officers accountable for the Holocaust and other massacres of civilians in territories under their control. Although the trials included testimony about German and Japanese atrocities and created a new category of crimes (i.e., crimes against humanity), the legal basis for such crimes was questionable, and convictions were achieved more on the charges that were more clearly based on existing international law—"crimes against peace" and "waging wars of aggression" (Minow 1998, 25–34). The fact that participation in the Holocaust was difficult to prosecute, because it had been carried out by Germany and other Axis powers against their own citizens and did not violate domestic law, was particularly important as an impetus for creating international human rights law that would supersede domestic law. In the aftermath of the Holocaust, many people felt that certain acts—such as the commission of genocide—were not permissible by any government, regardless of the principle of sovereignty (Ishay 2004, 173–244; Power 2003, 17–60).

In the years immediately after World War II, the international community began to adopt human rights law, but the legal regimes set up to enforce that law remained weak, posing little challenge to the principle of sovereignty. The preamble to the UN Charter claims that the organization was created "to reaffirm faith in fundamental human rights, in the dignity and worth of the human person, in the equal rights of men and women and of nations large and small," and Article 1 adds that the United Nations is intended "to achieve international cooperation . . . in promoting and encouraging respect for human rights and for fundamental freedoms for all, without distinction as to race, sex, language, or religion." Yet, Article 2 goes on to state, "The Organization is based on the principle of the sovereign equality of all its Members." Among its first actions, the United Nations authorized drafting the Universal Declarations of Human Rights (UDHR), a broad statement of civil, political, social, and economic rights that was adopted in 1948. While providing a long list of rights that all signatories claim to respect, the UDHR lacks any consistent, ongoing, and effective enforcement mechanisms, as it remains merely a General Assembly resolution. In an attempt to create a stronger legal basis for international human rights enforcement, the United Nations sponsored two human rights treaties in 1966, the International Covenant on Civil and Political Rights and the International Covenant on Economic, Social, and Cultural Rights, but the enforcement mechanisms they established remained relatively weak (Donnelly 2003, 129–135). Both treaties put self-evaluation mechanisms in place through the submission of regular reports to either a treaty-based or UN-based body.[2] This pattern of "self-validated compliance" (Armstrong, Farrell, and Lambert 2007, 158) reoccurs in other treaties on specific human rights issues, such as genocide, torture, and racism, where the rights are spelled out in greater detail, but the treaty bodies lack the coercive muscle to force compliance. As international law is constructed by, and applies to, states, they play a powerful role in the establishment of the human rights regimes. International organizations such as the United Nations may be sponsors of human rights treaties, but ultimately the individual state has to consent to their implementation.

In the context of the Cold War, both the Eastern and Western Bloc states were more interested in gaining allies in Africa, Asia, and Latin America than in protecting human rights, leading both sides to install or prop up governments in places like Chile, Indonesia, and Sudan that perpetrated massive human rights abuses against their own populations. For example, even when President Jimmy Carter claimed to make human rights the centerpiece of his foreign policy in 1977, he did so selectively, often overlooking abuses by U.S. allies (Stoyanov 2005).

Despite the general lack of international enforcement of human rights, there were a few instances of human rights intervention by the international community prior to 1990, though the self-interested motivation of most of these humanitarian interventions also seemed to outweigh moralistic concerns. During the Pakistani civil war of 1971, India intervened to support the outgunned East Pakistan, helping to create the independent state of Bangladesh. India's intervention helped to prevent slaughter in Bangladesh but also divided in half a state that most Indians viewed as an enemy (Cronin 2007, 295). In 1978, Tanzania supported a rebellion by Ugandans seeking to depose brutal dictator Idi Amin, driving him from power. This intervention was in response to growing Ugandan incursions into Tanzania as well as the expanding problem of Ugandan refugees fleeing into Tanzania. In 1979, Vietnam invaded Cambodia to drive the Khmer Rouge from power, ending four years of rule by one of the bloodiest regimes in modern history, but the Khmer and Vietnamese governments had been unfriendly, and Vietnam installed a puppet regime in Phnom Penh. Despite their supposed humanitarian intentions, each of these interventions had obvious advantages for the states that intervened, and all were condemned by other countries and international organizations as violations of sovereignty. The one case in which the international community joined together in support of human rights without obvious self-interested motivations was the antiapartheid movement of the 1970s and 1980s. Perhaps because the apartheid system in South Africa had become anomalous, and because the methods used included diplomatic isolation and economic and cultural boycotts but not military intervention, the antiapartheid movement received few criticisms for violating the South African government's sovereign right to rule as it pleased. The economic isolation of South Africa did, in fact, contribute to the demise of the apartheid regime and helped lead to eventual majority rule in 1994 (Shepherd 1991).

The end of the Cold War led to a resurgence of interest in human rights enforcement, particularly in the judicial realm. Despite the precedent set by the Nuremberg and Tokyo trials, more than forty years passed before another international human rights trial was organized. In May 1993, the UN Security Council created an ad hoc International Criminal Tribunal for the former Yugoslavia (ICTY) in an effort both to hold accountable individuals who had committed atrocities in Croatia and Bosnia-Herzegovina and also to help bring an end to the violence by eliminating impunity. A year later, the Security Council established another ad hoc court in response to genocide committed in Rwanda, the International Criminal Tribunal for Rwanda (ICTR). The creation of the ICTY and ICTR inspired a wave of legal actions, both domestic and international, to hold accountable perpetrators of massive human rights abuses in the aftermath of war and authoritarian rule. In cooperation with domestic governments, the United Nations created hybrid criminal courts in Cambodia, Kosovo, Sierra Leone, and Timor Leste. This explosion of ad hoc international courts helped build momentum for an international conference in Rome in 1998 that produced a treaty creating the permanent International Criminal Court (ICC). Since beginning operation in 2002, the ICC has taken up cases in the Central African Republic, Democratic Republic of Congo, Sudan, and Uganda. This development shifts the focus of human rights accountability onto individuals rather than states. Some critics interpret the move toward individual accountability as a deliberate attempt to circumvent state sovereignty, and the question of prosecuting political leaders remains controversial (Nill 1999).

The arrest in 1998 of former Chilean president Augusto Pinochet in the United Kingdom on charges raised by a Spanish court for crimes committed in Chile was significant both for the way it internationalized justice and for its challenge to the principle of impunity for heads of state. Although Pinochet was ultimately released and allowed to return to Chile, Yugoslav president Slobodan Milošević was tried by the ICTY, former Liberian president Charles Taylor was tried by the Special Courts for Sierra Leone in The Hague, and the ICC has brought charges for the first time against a sitting president, Omar al-Bashir of Sudan. A number of European states have also adopted a policy of universal jurisdiction that allows them to enforce criminal law against individuals who committed human rights violations in foreign countries against foreign citizens. Trials against Rwandans involved in the 1994 genocide have been held in Belgium, Canada, Finland, and Switzerland, while Spain has brought cases involving human rights abuses in Argentina and Guatemala (Kamminga 2001).

The new international judicial activism is only one of the aspects of the emergence of human rights as a major factor in international relations. Whereas President Jimmy Carter's inclusion of human rights issues in U.S. diplomacy was regarded as innovative, human rights have now become a regular element of diplomatic relations. Human rights issues are almost always on the agenda of summits between Western states and countries with questionable human rights records like China, Egypt, Russia, and Saudi Arabia. Some countries with particularly bad human rights records, such as Burma (Myanmar), North Korea, and Zimbabwe, face broad diplomatic isolation. This is facilitated largely by international human rights groups such as Amnesty International and Human Rights Watch, which have become increasingly influential, bringing both extensive media coverage to issues they target and bearing considerable diplomatic pressure (Roth 2000, 225–248; Wiseberg 1992, 372–390).

Sovereignty Redefined?

In the two decades since the end of the Cold War, analysts have contended that state sovereignty is under threat from a variety of sources. The emergence of increasingly powerful supranational entities such as the European Union has created an apparent threat to sovereignty from above, while a supposed explosion of subnational identity groups and separatist movements demanding autonomy has challenged state sovereignty from below. Other scholars argue that the process of globalization has challenged sovereignty, as technological improvements in transportation and communication have diminished the significance of borders and made states increasingly interdependent (Krasner 1995, 230–231).

The increasing prominence of the international human rights regime is often cited as among the most serious challenges to the traditional respect for sovereignty in the international system. In a discussion of "sovereignty under siege," Letitia Lawson and Donald Rothchild write, "An emerging international individual rights regime has begun to limit the rights of sovereign states to act as they wish with their citizenry" (2005, 223–235). For many advocates of human rights and international law, this is a welcome development. In discussing the impact of international human rights law on the state, Maogoto argues, "Though the classic ideas about sovereignty die hard, the difficult and often bitter struggle waged in the 20th century against the edifice of the State, in a bid to curb its power and freedom of action through the concept of international accountability by penal process, has had its moments of triumph which have played a large part in clipping State sovereignty" (2008, 3).

For many realists, who believe that the principle of sovereignty protects both weak and powerful states, the emergence of the human right regimes poses a threat to the world system. R. J. Vincent argues that promotion of human rights challenges traditional foreign policy principles, writing that "there is an inescapable tension between human rights and foreign policy" (1986, 129). Under President George W. Bush, the United States government worked actively to undermine the International Criminal Court, because it believed that the ICC would undermine U.S. sovereignty. As David Nill claims, defending the Bush position, "The formation of the ICC opens the door to new and troubling questions concerning the future of international justice and its influence on national sovereignty" (1999,

120). Charles Call (2004, 101–113) notes that the development of international justice is deeply flawed and actually promotes injustice, since only those from weak states are prosecuted, while those from powerful states enjoy impunity.

As a review of both the history of sovereignty and actual human rights enforcement indicates, fears (or hopes) of the demise of sovereignty as the dominant organizing principle for the international community are premature. States, both large and small, still actively defend the principle of sovereignty and reject international interference. Many states that face international criticism for their human rights records and, more recently, leaders threatened with possible prosecution in international courts have defended themselves with claims of sovereignty. Zimbabwean president Robert Mugabe, for example, has characterized criticisms of his human rights record as imperialist efforts by world powers (the West) to exploit his country. Sudanese president Omar al-Bashir, indicted by the ICC in 2009 for his role in the violence in Darfur, has likewise rejected the accusations as unwarranted international interference in his country's internal affairs. As M. Cherif Bassiouni observes,

> Curiously, when it comes to international criminal justice, states rediscover sovereignty, and jealously defend it, not on the grounds that they have priority in the exercise of criminal jurisdiction, but as a bar to justice, whether be it exercised by a national or international institution. . . . In short, state sovereignty remains an obstacle to international justice, not because of the inherent nature of sovereignty, or its exigencies, but because it is interpreted and used as a means of achieving goals that contradict those of international criminal justice. (2003)

Although state leaders still insist that sovereignty is firmly in place, international lawyers and practitioners argue that there has been a shift away from absolute sovereignty, as iterated by former UN secretary-general Boutros Boutros-Ghali: "The time of absolute and exclusive sovereignty, however, has passed; its theory was never matched by reality" (1992, para. 17). This idea was further extended by the report of the International Commission on Intervention and State Sovereignty (ICISS), which linked the rights of sovereign states to a duty to protect their people. Failure to do so would provide the international community with a justifiable reason to act (ICISS 2001, 13, 29).

Some scholars furthermore insist that the promise of "equality of all states" remains mere fiction, particularly in the case of weak or "failed" states. The realist perspective, while considering sovereignty key, has also held that power relations have been important, and powerful states have never fully respected the sovereignty of weaker states. According to Krasner, "Interventions have occurred when there is an asymmetry of power. More powerful states intervene in the internal affairs of less powerful states. In an anarchical world there is nothing to prevent a state from exploring all possible foreign policy options" (1995, 229). He goes on to state, "The most powerful explanation for intervention in the international system continues to be state power," rather than liberal commitments to human rights (1995, 246).

Legal practitioners, on the other hand, argue that states that fail to fulfill their responsibilities toward their people should have their sovereignty forfeited; hence, they also support the idea of intervention. According to the ICISS report, "The 'responsibility to protect' implies above all else a responsibility to react to situations of compelling need for human protection. When preventive measures fail to resolve or contain the situation and when a state is unable or unwilling to redress the situation, then intervention measures by other members of the broader community of states may be required. . . . In extreme and exceptional cases, the responsibility to react may involve the need to resort to military action" (2001, 29–31).

Reviewing international interventions in recent years seems to support the claim that power politics plays a key role in the enforcement of human rights. The application of human rights law continues to be uneven, targeting small and weak states much more than large, powerful states. International agreements often see weak states pressured by both stronger states and international organizations like the International Monetary Fund and World Bank to sign on in order to gain full participation in the international community (Waltz 1979; Brysk 1994). International humanitarian military interventions have taken place only in very weak states, such as the Democratic Republic of Congo, Haiti, Sierra Leone, Somalia, the former Yugoslavia, places where, as Donnelly (1995, 115–146) points out, the state had decayed to a point at which sovereignty could no longer be exercised. Even human rights pressure, short of armed intervention, has been quite selective. While states such as Cuba, North Korea, and Uzbekistan have faced international pressures on human rights issues, powerful states like China or strategically significant states like Saudi Arabia are criticized only mildly, while normal diplomatic and trade relations continue. In a number of cases of extreme human rights abuses, as in Cambodia under the Khmer Rouge, Kurdish Iraq in the late 1980s, and Rwanda in 1994, the international community has pointedly failed to intervene to stop mass slaughter. Furthermore, the application of international justice has been particularly selective. International courts have only been set up to deal with human rights abuses in small, weak states like Cambodia, Rwanda, and Sierra Leone, while larger, more powerful states are free from international judicial consequences. All four of the ICC's first investigations have targeted African states, although in fairness one should note that three of these cases were initiated by the state itself. As Call contends, "Individuals from powerful or wealthy countries, especially the United States, enjoy significantly more immunity from international criminal prosecution" (2004, 109).

The influence of human rights issues on U.S. policy is particularly instructive and further illustrates the above. While the Carter administration condemned the Soviet Union and its allies, such as Cuba and Poland, for human rights abuses, American allies such as Indonesia, Israel, and Saudi Arabia remained immune from human rights critiques. The United States actually supported the brutal Khmer Rouge because it considered Vietnam a greater threat (Stoyanov 2005). The practice of selectively emphasizing human rights issues has remained consistent. The U.S. government has worked hard to isolate Cuba, maintaining strict boycotts and harsh diplomatic pressure, while consistently defending Israel from criticism for its abuses of Palestinians and largely ignoring human rights abuses in Saudi Arabia, a major petroleum supplier. Under the Bush administration, human rights concerns were used as one of the justifications for the 2003 invasion of Iraq, despite U.S. support for Saddam Hussein in his fight against Iran during the 1980–1988 Iran-Iraq War, even as his government was committing genocide against the Kurdish population. The United States was among the few countries to label the violence in the Darfur region of Sudan genocide, but it also has no investments in Sudan, due to an embargo, unlike China, France, and Russia, all of which have investments in Sudan's oil sector and, therefore, have been reluctant to criticize its government.

While these observations could lead to a very cynical vision of the role of human rights in international politics, Donnelly argues that in fact human rights enforcement is better left to individual states and that the role of the international community in promoting human rights is rightfully limited. According to Donnelly (2003, 127–154), while the international community can play an important role in the promotion of human rights and even help in their implementation, individual states must ultimately take responsibility for enforcement. In order for human rights to be universal, societies must voluntarily adopt human rights principles and regulate the actions of their own governments, a process that he asserts is already taking place. States enter into treaties voluntarily, and the ratification process of international treaties usually involves time to reconsider and implement necessary changes to domestic law (Dugard 2005, 408), before final notice is given to the international community that a state now considers itself bound (Gardiner 2003, 70). International human rights law seems to serve more as a resource for domestic politics, providing a basis for political parties and civil society groups to hold their own governments accountable. In practice, the international organs set up to enforce human rights have very little power and must rely on the voluntary compliance of member states to abide by their standards or, on rare occasions, to force other members to comply (Donnelly 2003, 127–154).

As a result, at least for now, human rights enforcement remains a predominantly domestic affair, with international intervention limited chiefly to diplomatic pressures. In terms of adherence to human rights, this means that "congruence and internalization emerge as powerful and reinforcing reasons for compliance with international human rights law. . . . Change in international human rights law—especially in terms of its spreading influence—may be explained in terms of a social process centered on elite learning and state socialization" (Armstrong, Farrell, and Lambert 2007, 173).

Explaining Human Rights in International Relations

While we readily concede that human rights regimes pose much less of a threat to sovereignty than many of both their advocates and critics believe, the emergence of human rights as a factor in international affairs has had a significant impact on world politics. As David Forsythe notes, human rights may not be backed up by "hard law," the kind of law that is enforced through coercive means, but "human rights as soft law is important and pervasive" (2006, 25). To illustrate, some success in human rights enforcement involving neither courts nor military intervention has been achieved by less formal legal means, such as the application of diplomatic pressure (as was placed on Turkey by the European Union) and sanctions (for example, the cultural and sports boycott implemented against apartheid South Africa) (Forsythe 2006, 156). As Donnelly observes, "The foreign policy of many states has incorporated a concern for international human rights—as a secondary, but nonetheless real, element" (1995, 145). While countries may make diplomatic decisions based primarily on their economic and security concerns, human rights are now one consideration in foreign policy, and this is a significant point. While military interventions are few, governments do regularly pressure other states to improve their human rights records, using means as limited as public condemnation or as extensive as economic boycotts and arms embargoes.

Before leaving the topic of the impact of human rights on foreign affairs, exploring why countries have increasingly incorporated human rights into their diplomatic policies is worthwhile. As the discussion above suggests, while human rights concerns have sometimes been driven by cynical concerns for security and economic opportunity, criticisms of land seizure in Zimbabwe or a coup d'état in Honduras or fraudulent elections in Kenya or repression of the press in Eritrea cannot be explained exclusively in these terms. Instead, we contend that several factors have helped to propel human rights issues into a more prominent position in international diplomatic discourse.

Human Rights Abuses as a Security Concern

Increasingly, the international community has come to recognize that allowing human rights abuses to go unchecked creates a threat to international security. The idea of human rights as a security concern was key to the inclusion of human rights in the UN Charter, but only in recent years have diplomats embraced this idea more fully. The failure of the world to stop the 1994 genocide in Rwanda created insecurity throughout the region, leading to a decade of war in neighboring Democratic Republic of Congo that involved as many as ten African militaries and directly or indirectly killed several million people. Unchecked civil war in Liberia spread violence into neighboring Côte d'Ivoire, Guinea, Guinea-Bissau, and Sierra Leone. Violence in the Darfur region of Sudan has spilled over into neighboring Chad and the Central African Republic. Even within individual countries, mass atrocities have effects that linger for decades, continuing to destabilize regimes and slowing economic growth.

Human rights disasters have other more direct negative impacts on the international community as well. War-related famines in Ethiopia in the 1980s and Somalia in the 1990s created tens of thousands of refugees whom the international community maintained in refugee camps at considerable expense and many of whom ended up in Europe and North America as political and economic refugees. The international community often spends great amounts on rebuilding countries after civil wars and other human rights atrocities. Human rights activists and diplomats alike are increasingly calling on the UN Security Council to regard massive human rights abuses as "threats to the peace," for which the Security Council can authorize military intervention under Chapter 7 of the UN Charter.

Countries experiencing instability caused by human rights abuses generally see their economies decline sharply, while previous international investment in these countries is often completely lost. In contrast, economic development is much more likely in stable countries. When Ghana was experiencing brutal dictatorship and repeated bloody coups in the 1970s, its economy was a shambles, but since Ghana has achieved political stability and has transitioned to democratic rule, the country has known an impressive rate of economic growth.

In short, if the realists are right in arguing that states act largely out of self-interest, this does not mean that states cannot support human rights. Increasingly, government leaders seem to be recognizing that allowing human rights abuses to go unchecked is ultimately detrimental not simply to the people in the country who suffer directly but also to the region, which is likely to be destabilized, and to the international community as a whole, which faces not just limited opportunities for investment but also high costs for rebuilding states and caring for refugees and other victims of abuses. Support for human rights, thus, does not have to be driven exclusively by idealistic concerns.

International Civil Society

Another major factor contributing to the expansion of support for human rights is the growing influence of international civil society. From the beginning, private citizens have played an important role in pushing for the adoption of human rights treaties, be it Henri Dunant pushing for the Geneva Conventions or Rafael Lempkin leading a drive for the Convention on the Prevention and Punishment of the Crime of Genocide. The growth of human rights organizations over the past several decades and their increasing popular support have transformed the international diplomatic landscape. The work of Amnesty International, Human Rights Watch, and other organizations is driven by a policy of "name and shame" that seeks to expose human rights abuses in order to rally international outrage. These organizations not only investigate and report on abuses but also do extensive advocacy work with the media and with governments (Wiseberg 1992).

As Samantha Power's analysis (2003) of U.S. policy in response to genocide suggests, governments respond to human rights abuses when their constituents demand it, but the public only rarely raises its voice on human rights issues, being more concerned about domestic issues. Nevertheless, concern for human rights has become an increasingly important public issue. The antiapartheid movement was largely driven by popular action in countries such as the United States, with citizens pressuring their governments to take action against South Africa. Public support pushed the U.S. Congress to enact the Comprehensive Antiapartheid Act of 1986 over President Ronald Reagan's veto. A similar widespread movement has arisen in response to the violence in Darfur, as people around the globe have sought to pressure their governments to take action. While government actions have so far been limited and the violence continues, even China has been pressured to revise its approach to Sudan at least somewhat. In a few countries, such as Canada, the Netherlands, and the Scandinavian states, strong human rights movements have pushed their governments to be advocates of human rights. Clearly, while governments may still be motivated primarily by self-interest, citizens are increasingly regarding human rights abuses in foreign places as something that is of concern to them, and they are placing pressure on their governments to act.

Conclusion

In this chapter, we have argued that the emergence of human rights regimes has so far not represented a radical challenge to sovereignty. Human rights regimes remain relatively weak, their enforcement is inconsistent, and individual states play the primary role of enforcing human rights in their own territories. In many ways, the realist perspective that views sovereignty as central and sees the international community as driven by power politics remains an accurate depiction of the world.

Yet, the emergence of human rights as an increasingly important element of international politics is significant. While the Westphalian system remains intact, as Forsythe argues, "State sovereignty is not what it used to be" (2006, 25). Even if states are not using coercive means to enforce human rights, they are nevertheless increasingly including human rights as an issue in diplomatic relations and are using "soft law" to enforce them. More and more, the protection of human rights is being viewed not simply as charitable but as actually in the interest of people outside the state where the abuses are taking place. The growth of international civil society fighting for human rights is having an impact, and if a growing number of people take up human rights as a cause, the changes to the international system may ultimately be much more significant. For now, the trend toward human rights protection can be explained largely by the fact that states themselves are at the heart of this development. While human rights may not be a direct challenge to the principle of sovereignty, as international support for human rights continues to develop, the anarchic nature of the world system appears, gradually, to be diminishing somewhat.

Notes

1. Hans Morgenthau (1948) makes the classic articulation that sovereignty preserves order and is the very basis of international law.

2. The International Covenant on Civil and Political Rights furthermore allows for interstate and individual complaints of human rights abuses, though the latter is optional.

References

Armstrong, D., T. Farrell, and H. Lambert. 2007. *International law and international relations.* Cambridge: Cambridge University Press.

Bassiouni, M. C. 2003. Preface to *State sovereignty and international criminal law: From Versailles to Rome,* ed. J. N. Maogota. Ardsley, NY: Transnational Publishers.

Boutros-Ghali, B. 1992. *An agenda for peace.* New York: United Nations. www.un.org/DOCS/SG/agpeace.html.

Brown, C. 2002. *Sovereignty, rights and justice: International political theory today.* Cambridge, UK: Polity Press.

Brysk, A. 1994. *The politics of human rights in Argentina: Protest, change, and democratization.* Palo Alto, CA: Stanford University Press.

Call, C. T. 2004. Is transitional justice really just? *Brown Journal of World Affairs* 11, no. 1 (summer–fall): 101–113.

Cronin, B. 2007. The tension between sovereignty and intervention in the prevention of genocide. *Human Rights Review* 8, no. 4 (July): 293–305.

Donnelly, J. 2003. *Universal human rights in theory and practice.* Ithaca, NY: Cornell University Press.

———. 1995. State sovereignty and international intervention: The case of human rights. In *Beyond Westphalia? State sovereignty and international intervention,* ed. G. M. Lyons and M. Mastanduno, 115–146. Baltimore: Johns Hopkins University Press.

Dugard, J. 2005. *International law—a South African perspective.* Cape Town, South Africa: Juta.

Forsythe, D. P. 2006. *Human rights in international relations.* 2nd ed. Cambridge: Cambridge University Press.

Gardiner, R. 2003. *International law.* Dorset, UK: Person-Longman.

Gumpert, M. 1938. *Dunant: The story of the Red Cross.* Oxford: Oxford University Press.

Hochschild, A. 2005. *Bury the chains: Prophets and rebels in the fight to free an empire's slaves.* New York: Mariner Books.

International Commission on Intervention and State Sovereignty (ICISS). 2001. *The responsibility to protect.* Report of the International Commission on Intervention and State Sovereignty. Ottawa, Canada: International Development Research Center. Available online at www.iciss.gc.ca.

Ishay, M. R. 2004. *The history of human rights: From ancient times to the globalization era.* Berkeley: University of California Press.

Jacobsen, T., C. Sampford, and R. Thakur, eds. 2008. *Re-envisioning sovereignty: The end of Westphalia?* Surrey, UK: Ashgate Publishing.

Kamminga, M. T. 2001. Lessons learned from the exercise of universal jurisdiction in response to gross human rights offenses. *Human Rights Quarterly* 23, no. 4 (November): 940–974.

Krasner, S. D. 1995. Sovereignty and intervention. In *Beyond Westphalia? State sovereignty and international intervention*, ed. G. M. Lyons and M. Mastanduno, 228–249. Baltimore: Johns Hopkins University Press.

Lawson, L., and D. Rothchild. 2005. Sovereignty reconsidered. *Current History* 104 (May): 223–235.

Loriaux, M. 1992. The realists and Saint Augustine: Skepticism, psychology, and moral action in international relations thought. *International Studies Quarterly* 36 (December): 401–420.

Lyons, G. M., and M. Mastanduno 1995. Introduction: International intervention, state sovereignty, and the future of international society. In *Beyond Westphalia? State sovereignty and international intervention*, ed. G. M. Lyons and M. Mastanduno, 1–20. Baltimore: Johns Hopkins University Press.

Maogoto, J. N. 2008. Westphalian sovereignty in the shadow of international justice? A fresh coat of paint for a tainted concept. In *Re-envisioning sovereignty: The end of Westphalia?* ed. T. Jacobsen, C. Sampford, and R. Thakur, 211–227. Surrey, UK: Ashgate Publishing.

Minow, M. 1998. *Between vengeance and forgiveness: Facing history after genocide and mass violence.* Boston: Beacon Press.

Moravcsik, A. 2000. The origins of human rights regimes: Democratic delegation in postwar Europe. *International Organization* 54, no. 2 (spring): 217–252.

Morgenthau, H. 1948. World politics in the mid-twentieth century. *The Review of Politics* 9 (April): 154–173.

Niebuhr, R. 1932. *Moral man and immoral society: A study in ethics and politics.* New York: Simon and Schuster.

Nill, D. A. 1999. National sovereignty: Must it be sacrificed to the International Criminal Court? *BYU Journal of Public Law* 14 (fall): 119–150.

Power, S. 2003. *A problem from hell: The United States in the age of genocide.* New York: Basic Books.

Roth, K. 2000. Human rights organizations: A new force for social change. In *Realizing human rights: Moving from inspiration to impact*, ed. S. Power and G. Allison, 225–248. New York: St. Martin's Press.

Shepherd, G. W., ed. 1991. *Effective sanctions on South Africa: The cutting edge of economic intervention.* New York: Praeger.

Stoyanov, S. 2005. Moralism as realism: Jimmy Carter's human rights policies. Paper presented at the annual meeting of the Midwest Political Science Association, April 9, Chicago, Illinois.

Vincent, R. J. 1986. *Human rights and international relations.* Cambridge: Cambridge University Press.

Waltz, K. N. 1979. *Theory of international politics.* Reading, MA: Addison-Wesley.

Wiseberg, L. S. 1992. Human rights nongovernmental organizations. In *Human rights in the world community,* ed. R. P. Claude and B. H. Weston, 372–381. Philadelphia: University of Pennsylvania Press.

PART THREE
The Role of Nonstate Actors: Essential or Incidental to Global Governance?

Introduction

JoAnn Fagot Aviel

Because of the globalization of actors, issues, and problems, the international system today cannot be understood without taking into account nonstate actors. The term *nonstate actor* covers a wide variety of parties and includes individuals, research institutes and epistemic communities, terrorist groups and criminal networks, religious groups, multinational corporations, social movements, transnational networks and coalitions, foundations, and nongovernmental organizations (NGOs). Since World War II their growth has been exponential, and their exact number can only be estimated. Margaret Karns and Karen Mingst (2010) estimate that in 2008 there were over 7,500 international NGOs and several million national and indigenous NGOs. This amazing growth and their increasing role and influence in multilateral processes have made nonstate actors essential to global governance.

This part of the book focuses on the growing role of nonstate actors in contemporary international relations. The chapters look at a selection of NGOs and private foundations and reveal a variety of approaches and techniques that have enabled nonstate actors to be effective participants in multilateral efforts on an array of international issues.

Chapter 9 focuses on the role played by humanitarian NGOs in humanitarian emergencies as well as in development. Peter Bell and Sherine Jayawickrama provide a detailed analysis of the key role of nongovernmental humanitarian and development organizations in contemporary multilateral diplomacy. They point out that some of the longest-established and larger NGOs have globalized by developing autonomous affiliates in both industrialized and developing countries that

are organized into international confederations and federations, which are themselves multilateral organizations; furthermore, their annual budgets collectively
often exceed that of the UN agencies engaged in international relief and development. Their size and immense financial resources make these NGOs critical actors
on issues regarding relief and development. Bell and Jayawickrama argue that humanitarian NGOs increased their participation in multilateral diplomacy when
they transformed themselves from simply delivering relief supplies. With a deeper
understanding of the relationship between conflict dynamics and humanitarian
crisis, they developed an appreciation that diverse internal and external stakeholders must be engaged in order to help resolve complex underlying issues.

In Chapter 10 Carroll Bogert analyzes "how and why transnational actors grow
and exercise their influence, from the perspective of a practitioner at Human
Rights Watch [HRW]." With HRW as a case in point, she describes four key factors for increasing and exercising influence—technology, money, the media, and
rigorous research—on national and international human rights issues and illustrates the crucial role HRW played in the Cluster Munitions Coalition, which
produced an international convention to ban cluster munitions. Bogert points
out that HRW's credibility and prestige in the field of human rights is an essential
aspect of the organization's ability to exercise influence.

The role of NGOs in multilateral efforts regarding the global environment is
the focus of Chapter 11. In this chapter Stanley Burgiel presents a case study of
The Nature Conservancy (TNC) and its work relating to global invasive species.
He describes how TNC's Global Invasive Species Program undertook with its
partners to influence the UN Convention on Biological Diversity's negotiations
on invasive species and engage national governments on the issue. Burgiel emphasizes the key importance of building broad alliances with other NGOs, states,
and secretariats before negotiations even begin; he stresses that "decisions remain
so many words on paper, unless there is follow through to see them implemented"
and that NGOs play a crucial role in doing so.

Chapter 12 examines the role of the private sector in multilateral diplomacy
and global governance. Although corporations can be involved in multilateral
diplomacy on their own behalf, they often work through business associations or
in partnership with NGOs. Stephen Jordan and Taryn Bird describe how the
U.S. Chamber of Commerce, the world's largest business association, engages its
members, nonprofit groups, and governments on international issues and problems. They state that the U.S. Chamber of Commerce has worked with broad
coalitions of both public- and private-sector actors in response to the 2004

tsunami and on other problems. According to Jordan and Bird, this rise of multisector multilateralism did not take off until the 1990s. They warn, however, that these initiatives "do not substitute for, and are subsidiary to, the sovereign political powers in the geographies in which they operate." They argue that this "iteration of multisectoral multilateralism" is a work in progress, and as it continues to develop, it will improve "prospects for enhanced global governance."

In the final chapter of this part, Joan Spero analyzes the growing involvement of private foundations around the world in international relations. She points out that private foundations, often established by successful business leaders, have played a key role in funding efforts of governments and nonstate actors to alleviate suffering and improve people's lives and have become quite effective in the arena of multilateral diplomacy. She describes their engagement in cultural diplomacy and human rights as well as foundations' leadership role in the formation of partnerships for global health with NGOs, business, and states. In addition to helping to transform agriculture and being involved with climate diplomacy, foundations have promoted programs to advance peace and security and have engaged in Track II diplomacy with Iran, North Korea, and the Soviet Union. Spero analyzes their particular strengths in dealing with global issues and concludes, "Foundations are well suited to play a role in global diplomacy in the twenty-first century."

The authors in this part of the book conclusively prove the importance of nonstate actors in multilateral diplomacy. Acting alone or with other nonstate actors either in cooperating with states and international secretariats or in confronting them, they are indeed essential actors in global governance today.

Reference

Karns, M. P., and K. A. Mingst. 2010. *International organizations: The politics and processes of global governance.* Boulder, CO: Lynne Rienner.

9

The Role of Humanitarian NGOs in Multilateral Diplomacy

Peter D. Bell and Sherine S. Jayawickrama

Although nation-states may still be the central actors in world politics, the stage on which multilateral diplomacy unfolds is much broader now—and the actors have become considerably more diverse. Major issues that have been the subjects of multilateral consultations, negotiations, and agreements are being shaped, at least in part, by the experience, analysis, and activism of nonstate actors whose missions transcend national borders. In multilateral diplomacy, the roles of nongovernmental organizations (NGOs), particularly international NGOs, have been increasing in volume, complexity, and influence. NGOs are engaging actively on issues ranging from climate change and trade policy to gender equity and poverty reduction at venues like the Group of Twenty, World Trade Organization, World Economic Forum, World Social Forum, and numerous United Nations summits. NGOs have become forces with which governments, multilateral organizations, and global corporations must contend. On many issues, their influence in world politics and multilateral diplomacy has become increasingly salient.

The Importance of Nonstate Actors and Transnational Relations

Nearly forty years ago, Joseph Nye and Robert Keohane broke new ground with their book *Transnational Relations and World Politics* by replacing the state-centered paradigm of world politics with one that recognized the importance of transnational actors. The book shed new light on the political dimension of

NGOs that project action, people, and values across national boundaries. There was a day when most U.S.-based, transnational NGOs, including philanthropies like the Ford Foundation and relief and development organizations like CARE, regarded themselves as apolitical. Indeed, it was a basic tenet of their credos. But most sophisticated NGOs now recognize that clinging to that belief can actually cause harm, however inadvertently.

Over the past two decades, the structure, content, and processes of world politics and policy negotiations have been changing. These changes are due in part to the end of the Cold War, the subsequent decline of the United States as the world's superpower, the rise of the European Union and China as counterbalances, and the increasing influence of developing countries like India and Brazil. But they are also due to the decline of nation-states in a globalized world, advances in communications and information technology, the burgeoning of nationally and globally networked communities, and the activism of these communities to help shape issues on national and global political agendas. The growing political self-consciousness of NGOs—especially the larger international NGOs—and the increasing participation of civil society organizations in national and global policy debates have been part and parcel of these changes.

The Case of CARE

This chapter focuses on the role of CARE, one of the world's largest international relief and development NGOs, within the new dynamics of multilateral diplomacy. It first examines major changes in the organization over the past two decades—some generated internally and others triggered by external forces—with a focus on the changes that have influenced CARE's growing role in policy analysis, advocacy, and multilateral processes. It also explores the key assets that NGOs like CARE bring to the arena of multilateral diplomacy. The chapter draws from several CARE experiences, particularly the roles that CARE and its NGO partners have played in multilateral diplomatic processes related to civil conflicts in developing countries. Finally, the chapter extracts some key lessons learned from CARE's experience in the arena of multilateral diplomacy and identifies limitations to the influence of CARE and similar NGOs on multilateral diplomacy.

In writing the chapter, we have drawn from our decade-long experiences working at CARE and our reviews of various CARE papers and reports. We have also drawn on our recent experience working with the heads of the twelve major U.S.-based international relief and development NGOs who meet semiannually as members of the NGO Leaders Forum.[1] CARE's evolution as an organization, including its role in multilateral diplomacy, is similar in many ways to that of the eleven other NGOs that participate in the forum, especially those that are members of international alliances.

The Evolution of NGOs: Setting the Stage for Engaging in Multilateral Diplomacy

One dimension of the evolution of CARE and other large international NGOs is simply the magnitude of financial, human, and program resources they now bring to the humanitarian and development sphere. In 2008, CARE USA had a budget of more than $700 million and reached some 55 million people in sixty-six countries. With a budget of approximately $1 billion, World Vision U.S. is larger still. Collectively, the organizations represented in the NGO Leaders Forum have a combined annual budget exceeding that of the UN agencies engaged in international relief and development.

Until twenty years ago, most of the NGOs now in the forum, with the notable exception of Oxfam, regarded themselves as manifestly nonpolitical. They were almost exclusively engaged in the relief of human suffering and the amelioration of poverty through the direct delivery of services. Only Oxfam has long embraced a role in policy advocacy and global campaigning. Today, even though they still eschew partisanship, most of these NGOs have come to accept and embrace their political roles. Médicins Sans Frontières, which is strongly committed to upholding the principle of neutrality, might be an exception.

What changed? Most fundamentally, these NGOs now reject the notion that extreme poverty is an inevitable part of the human condition. They believe that the knowledge, technology, and wealth to end extreme poverty already exist in the world. They are no longer satisfied to work on the symptoms of poverty. They want to attack both its proximate causes, such as illiteracy, disease, and malnutrition, and such underlying causes as discrimination, gender inequities, social exclusion, abuse of authority, and even violent conflict.

Once purportedly and proudly apolitical, the leaders of these NGOs now realize that promoting development and reducing poverty must be political in at least three different senses. First, NGOs need to be aware of the distributive aspects of their programs so that they do not unintentionally accentuate inequities and social divisions. They have become more conscious, for example, of the importance of who participates in decisions about the allocation of resources within communities; who benefits from the design, placement, and management of wells, latrines, bridges, schools, access roads, and so forth; and what the local mechanisms for participation and accountability are.

Second, NGOs increasingly understand the reduction of poverty in terms of greater empowerment. Economic growth is necessary but not sufficient. These NGOs aim to increase people's effective control over important decisions in their lives—at the level of the individual, family, community, and beyond. Third, to sustain the changes they want to see in the world, NGOs now seek to influence policies on the part of governments in both developing and industrialized countries. NGOs are increasingly engaged in building the capacity of citizens in poor communities to hold their governments accountable and in building constituencies in wealthy nations to demand effective policies to reduce global poverty. Organizations like CARE, Oxfam, World Vision, and Save the Children employ experts in policy analysis and advocacy not only in Washington, D.C., but also through their international alliances, such as CARE International, in places like Brussels, Geneva, and the United Nations in New York. These NGOs also mobilize citizens to press their lawmakers to take actions to reduce global poverty. For example, in the United States, members of the CARE Action Network send thousands of e-mail messages and make hundreds of phone calls and visits to members of Congress and the executive branch each year.

Observers who formed their view of international NGOs like CARE two decades or more ago will find these organizations almost wholly transformed. They are not just handing out food and relief supplies and delivering other services to people in need. They are no longer "charities" in the traditional sense. They have taken on more of an edge and become cause-related organizations. More of them are taking rights-based approaches to their work and are tackling underlying causes of extreme poverty, giving voice to the aspirations and concerns of poor communities, and advocating and campaigning at the local, national, and global levels.

Over the past two decades, the emphasis of NGOs like CARE has been shifting from direct service delivery to building the capacity of local organizations. Part of that shift has been in heightened attention to developing local management and leadership. For example, of the more than 8,000 CARE staff members, all but a few hundred are from the countries in which CARE has programs. One of CARE's most important contributions is the training and development of these staff so that they rise to senior management responsibilities, often going on to take jobs in government or to lead local NGOs. Moreover, international NGOs increasingly partner with local NGOs and government agencies to help build their governance, management, and implementation capacities and to transfer the delivery of services to them.

Some of the longest established and largest NGOs in their respective countries (including Oxfam and Save the Children in the United Kingdom, World Vision and CARE in the United States, and Médicins Sans Frontières in France) have sought to "globalize" by developing autonomous affiliates within international confederations, federations, and even unitary organizations. Over the last decade, a growing number of these organizations have invested in affiliates not only in industrialized countries but also in developing countries. In a sense, these global alliances are themselves multilateral organizations, and the experience of negotiating among affiliates with diverse interests to fashion joint solutions to shared challenges is useful preparation for engaging in multilateral diplomacy more broadly. Virtually all of the globalizing organizations, ranging up to nearly one hundred affiliates in the case of World Vision, have sought to expand the number of their private and governmental donors and citizen constituents around the world; draw on the particular program expertise of each of their affiliates; establish shared visions, missions, program principles, standards, and systems; and build increasingly global networks for policy advocacy.

Distinctive Assets of NGOs in Influencing Policy and Diplomacy

Large international NGOs bring at least five important assets to bear in attempting to influence politics, diplomacy, and policy. First, they bring a firm commitment to a compelling set of humanitarian values and a vision of a more prosperous, more equitable, and safer world. In this sense, their missions of relief and development are political assets. Surveys of public attitudes indicate that the humanitarian values of the NGOs resonate within much of America and in much of the world (Council on Foreign Relations 2009, 81).

Second, these NGOs have significant experience on the ground in the poorest countries. They work in literally hundreds of thousands of the world's poorest communities. This experience provides firsthand, highly textured information about the conditions of people who live in those communities. With this detailed knowledge, the NGOs are often able to convey the aspirations and concerns of the world's poorest citizens or—even better—to obtain a seat for them at the policy table.

Third, when NGOs work with independence and impartiality on both sides of civil conflicts, it can give them credibility to contribute to peace processes. In countries like Nepal and Sri Lanka, CARE and other NGOs engaged governmental officials and rebel leaders, international organizations, and members of the diplomatic community to bring to light unintended harm and self-defeating practices that caused needless suffering and exacerbated hostilities.

Fourth, NGOs are present not only at the local level in poor countries but also at the national and international levels. Several years ago, for example, during one ten-day period, leaders from the U.S., U.K., Norwegian, German, and French branches of the CARE International confederation spoke, more or less simultaneously, before committees of their own congresses or parliaments about the importance of human security and reconstruction within Afghanistan. NGO leaders often enjoy access at the highest levels of national governments, international and multilateral organizations, and for-profit corporations.

Fifth, these NGOs are large, measured not only by their budgets and staffs but also by the numbers of individual citizens who join their advocacy campaigns or make donations each year. Within CARE alone, nearly 500,000 people in the United States make annual donations totaling well over $100 million. This compares favorably with the amounts that presidential candidates, for example, raise during primary periods and is duly noted by politicians and policy makers. Several hundred volunteers in the CARE Action Network from across the United States now pay their own way to Washington, D.C., each year to take part in advocacy training and make visits to key members of their states' congressional delegations.

The five assets identified here do not guarantee that NGOs will be effective, but such assets help to ensure that their leaders have access to diplomatic and policy processes. Moreover, these particular assets gain in value as national political leaders come to understand that the security of each nation is increasingly linked to the security of all nations and to human security everywhere. Especially since September 11, 2001, the assets of these international NGOs have appreciated.

CARE in the Arena of Multilateral Diplomacy: An Illustrative Example

As CARE and other NGOs have begun to interpret their missions more broadly, they have come to see advocacy as a powerful tool that can be used to effect change at a systemic level. Such advocacy may involve influencing policies and institutions (or governance and peace-making processes) on issues that might have seemed beyond the reach of these NGOs two decades ago.

In the case of CARE, whose origins were in humanitarian relief in response to the threat of famine in Europe and Asia at the end of World War II, a turning point occurred with (1) the recognition that recurrent humanitarian crises in countries like Afghanistan, Angola, El Salvador, Myanmar, Nepal, Sierra Leone, and Sri Lanka were underpinned by long-standing, persistent civil conflicts, and (2) the growing conviction that CARE might contribute to ending such conflicts if it committed itself to trying. This led to a deeper understanding of the relationship between conflict dynamics and humanitarian crises, as well as an appreciation of the diverse internal and external stakeholders that must be engaged to resolve complex underlying issues. In practice, that meant employing policy analysis and advocacy as a key strategy and entering the arena of multilateral diplomacy. CARE's advocacy, however, remained firmly grounded in its core humanitarian and development mission in poor communities because the organization recognized that this "grounding" is critical to the value and credibility of its recommendations.

In one country, where CARE had responded to repeated floods, droughts, epidemics, and famines over two decades, CARE staff became convinced that the underlying cause of these humanitarian disasters was the ongoing civil war. Having witnessed the devastating toll of the war on poor communities on both sides and heard the rising pleas of those communities for a peace settlement, CARE decided that it needed to do something different. CARE was prepared to continue its relief efforts alongside other humanitarian organizations but resolved that it must simultaneously engage in advocacy toward a just and lasting peace.

Over the next several years, CARE staff prepared analyses of the conflict and its effect on people's lives, developed messaging on ways to take positive steps toward peace, hired an advocacy coordinator, and helped build an NGO coalition that could combine diverse strengths and advocate collectively. CARE and its coalition partners also engaged in quiet diplomacy with key actors at opportune moments, with the previously fitful regional peace process, and with the broader international diplomatic, political, and donor community. These NGO efforts shone a light on the connection between the ongoing civil war and humanitarian conditions and encouraged a more unified and consistent approach to peace in the country within the international community.

The NGO advocacy coalition of which CARE was a part proved to be an effective mechanism for unifying the advocacy efforts of the large humanitarian groups working in that country. Standing together, these NGOs could bring to bear on-the-ground experience and could amplify their voice, access, and influence. Their joint effort was supported by the leadership of CARE not only at the CARE International Secretariat (and its liaison to the United Nations in New York) but also by CARE USA. CARE USA's president met with successive U.S. secretaries of state, National Security Council and State Department staff, and key members of Congress. He and the chair and secretary-general of CARE International met with UN Security Council officials and with high-level government officials in the country concerned to urge concerted attention to advancing the peace process—and to including community and humanitarian perspectives within the process, starting with unimpeded access to all people in need.

CARE complemented its meetings with key policy makers with trying to increase media coverage of the conflict. CARE's access to media outlets such as CNN, the BBC, the *New York Times*, and the *Washington Post* helped, as did well-placed op-eds. Combined with CARE's long presence in the country and its strong reputation internationally, increased media attention may well have predisposed some officials to be more attentive to the need for a just peace in this overlooked part of the world.

The NGO advocacy coalition sought to build commitment among key stakeholders to a just peace by underscoring the toll of the war on ordinary citizens, a virtually neglected perspective otherwise. The coalition's advocacy efforts rested on analysis that set out key arguments in compelling briefing documents that were circulated widely. Their first document argued for an end to the civil war in order to stop the enormous suffering. Advocacy efforts targeted not only the combatants but also those responsible for mediating the peace talks, key European and North American governments and donors, and the United Nations. The NGO advocacy coalition strove to be impartial and to convey its messages within a humanitarian frame.

Initially, the government was uncomfortable with CARE's advocacy efforts and accused CARE of having "politicized" its role. Over the next several years, however, CARE gained greater access to, and engagement with, government officials and observed that the NGO advocacy coalition's analyses and publications were being considered with more openness and interest. Relations between CARE and leaders of the rebel movement were also difficult in the first years of the advocacy initiative, but in time the tensions eased to some extent, even if relations with neither the government nor the rebels were ever warm.

CARE USA also invested time and effort in pressing senior officials in the U.S. government to change its approach toward the country of concern—away from isolating that government and toward more constructive engagement in a peace process. In public actions taken—including timely op-ed pieces and principled operational decisions—CARE underscored its strong commitment to the principles of independence and impartiality. This helped position CARE and partner NGOs as credible voices that represented a deep body of experience working alongside communities affected by the war. It also enabled the NGO coalition to press for the inclusion of civil society perspectives in the peace process, arguing in a report that the peace process was too "top-down" and overly focused on high-level government and rebel actors.

CARE played an important role in getting the peace process on the UN Security Council's agenda. It did so by drawing on its experience in helping to organize an earlier meeting of Security Council members in Afghanistan. That had been the first-ever meeting outside of New York to apply the Arria Formula format, which enables a member of the Security Council to invite other members to an informal session held outside the council's chambers (Paul 2003). This format is an option the Security Council can use to hear the views of nonstate actors, which cannot speak formally at Security Council meetings.

Working closely with a key mission to the United Nations to organize this Arria Formula meeting, CARE arranged for several local civil society groups to make presentations. The briefing gave Security Council members greater understanding of the situation of civilians affected by the conflict and increased their openness to consulting with civil society. Engaging the Security Council members in the peace process resulted in strong language—on civilian protection, humanitarian access, and contribution of troops to UN operations—in UN resolutions in support of the eventual peace settlement.

Even before a peace agreement was signed, the NGO advocacy coalition turned its attention to monitoring the implementation of the agreement and to sustaining international attention to the situation. After the signing, CARE conducted a series of focus groups and surveys to gauge community perceptions of the peace process and ascertain how the lives of ordinary citizens had changed. CARE and the coalition focused, in particular, on the issue of refugee returns to help ensure that the international focus on returnees did not stoke local tensions by creating rifts between returnees and the communities in which they resettled.

Over a multiyear period, even while continuing their humanitarian and development work in poor communities, CARE and its NGO partners engaged in multilateral diplomacy to help end this long-running civil war. By bringing to the table otherwise neglected perspectives from local civil society and pressing for concerted international engagement in support of a just peace—and by remaining nonpartisan and grounded in the experience of poor communities—NGOs elevated the issue of peace in this country on the agendas of the UN Security Council, the U.S. government, and various European governments. Playing the role of subject matter expert, policy advocate, and connector to local groups, NGOs were attentive to the shifting landscape of challenges and opportunities related to peace—and acted together to produce analysis, target key stakeholders, and doggedly press for a just peace. In doing so, NGOs helped to advance multilateral diplomacy on the peace agreement.

Although this peace process is far from a neat success story—peace agreements to end long-standing civil conflicts rarely are—it is explored here as an illustration of how NGOs can contribute to multilateral peacemaking, even when the complexities are formidable.

Some Lessons Learned

CARE's experience—on issues ranging from Afghanistan to climate change to food security—points to three major lessons. First, although NGOs have reputations for working in isolation from one another and are sometimes rightly criticized for working at cross-purposes, the major international NGOs have learned that collaboration on advocacy can yield powerful results. This was particularly evident in Afghanistan—in the years after September 11, 2001—where CARE was a member and facilitator of NGO coalitions that stood together on issues ranging from the fulfillment of international commitments on reconstruction assistance to the need for military actors to respect the integrity of humanitarian principles. The Agency Coordinating Body for Afghan Relief, or ACBAR, and InterAction, the major umbrella organization for U.S.-based relief and development NGOs, were the broadest-based coalitions in Afghanistan and the United States, respectively. Working together enhances the credibility of advocacy efforts, expands outreach, amplifies voice, and provides the security of numbers. NGOs have also worked in coalitions and alliances to push for the International Treaty to Ban Landmines, to seek debt relief for the most indebted countries, and, most recently, to press for a fair, ambitious, and binding international treaty on climate change that safeguards the interests of poor communities.

Second, NGOs can impact multilateral diplomatic processes directly and indirectly by leveraging their distinctive capabilities. They contribute directly by engaging governments involved in multilateral decision making and seeking to influence their positions. For example, NGOs draw on their field experience and community relationships to bring local perspectives and knowledge to the negotiating table. NGOs contribute indirectly by impacting the way certain issues get covered in the media or shaping public attitudes on those issues. To make these direct and indirect contributions, NGOs must deploy a range of strategies: meeting with senior policy makers, producing analysis that brings evidence from the field to the policy arena, conveying advocacy messages via influential international media outlets, exposing decision makers to community perspectives and concerns, and encouraging constituents to express outrage at social injustices and press for corrective action.

The professionalism of major international NGOs, their long-term presence in developing countries, their access to policy makers in world capitals, and the transnational nature of their interests, operations, and values position international NGOs to influence multilateral diplomacy. In addition, the standing of key NGO leaders—for example, the chair of CARE International, who was a former British ambassador, and the secretary-general of CARE International, who had led the UN peacekeeping force in Rwanda in 1994—facilitates access to the higher reaches of political power and enhances organizational influence.

Finally, NGOs' influence on multilateral diplomacy is partly shaped by the space that governments and international organizations make available to NGOs to provide their locally grounded, transnational perspective. For example, the UN Security Council has been using the format of Arria Formula meetings more frequently to enable its members to hear from nonstate actors. NGOs like CARE have built relationships of trust with relevant UN officials. On issues like peace and reconstruction in conflict and postconflict settings, these relationships enable NGOs to help organize Arria Formula meetings that have brought previously inaccessible perspectives to Security Council members. Bodies involved in processes of multilateral diplomacy have increasingly created spaces and included the participation of NGOs and other civil society actors.

Limitations of NGOs in the Arena of Multilateral Diplomacy

Although NGOs have become more influential in the arena of world politics and multilateral diplomacy, their influence is still limited. What, then, is constraining the political influence of the larger NGOs? Within the United States and other donor countries, powerful interests have a stake in policies that perpetuate world poverty. NGOs have made few inroads against their well-financed lobbyists. A prime example is the corporate agribusiness lobby that supports the U.S. Farm Bill. By successfully protecting billions of dollars in government subsidies, U.S. agribusiness blocks competition from developing countries in many commodities. NGOs have been able to do very little to reduce those subsidies.

There are times when no level of influence can divert a crusading national leader from his or her course. For example, NGOs had little or no influence on President George W. Bush in the run up to the Iraq War. CARE refused to accept

U.S. government funds for contingency planning for humanitarian relief, and the country director in Iraq, who had been there for fourteen years, tried at the United Nations to make the case against war—but all to no avail. With several NGO colleagues, the president of CARE USA tried repeatedly, but unsuccessfully, to secure a meeting with Secretary of Defense Donald Rumsfeld during this period.

These limitations suggest a deeper weakness in the political influence of most large NGOs. Because (with the notable exception of Oxfam) they depend heavily on government funding, these NGOs can be punished, or at least checkmated, by donor governments that view their advocacy agendas as troublesome. Governments can turn to their own military to deliver "humanitarian" relief, as the Bush administration did in Iraq and Afghanistan. Government funding agencies, such as the U.S. Agency for International Development, can also turn to commercial contractors who "know how to take orders," as a former administrator of the U.S. Agency for International Development put it.

Host governments and rebel militants in developing countries can threaten and punish NGOs that cause them trouble and can curtail the space within which NGOs operate. In crisis settings like Serbia and Zimbabwe, NGOs have had to choose between speaking out on abuses of human rights and carrying out humanitarian activities to save lives and relieve suffering. On occasion, governments offended by NGOs that dare "speak truth to power" or that otherwise provoke their ire have declared NGO country directors as personae non grata, shut down entire organizations, detained their personnel, or sought to intimidate them physically. Rebel militants have also engaged in kidnapping, extortion, and murder to intimidate NGOs. Security has become a major concern for all humanitarian organizations.

Conclusion

Despite real limitations, the direction of movement is clear: International NGOs are gaining political influence. They can effectively contribute to multilateral diplomacy when they can bring their values, their experience, their impartiality, and their access to bear and when their ambitions resonate with their broad constituency. To the extent that they bring vital but neglected perspectives to the table, international NGOs enhance the quality and outcomes of multilateral diplomacy.

While multilateral institutions and diplomatic processes are increasingly recognizing the value of civil society perspectives, they can do more to systematically create space and foster an enabling climate in which the voices of NGOs and civil society groups can be heard. The use of the Arria Formula at the Security Council is a good example of how such a space can be made available and leveraged for obtaining deeply grounded civil society perspectives. Multilateral agencies like the United Nations AIDS Agency have also been deliberate about creating mechanisms for civil society engagement and consultation—as have leaders like James Wolfensohn and Robert Zoellick of the World Bank.

These openings are quite uneven, however; they differ significantly by issue and depend on how leaders of multilateral organizations understand the value that NGOs can bring. There is a need to create some "rules of the road" about civil society and NGO engagement, and these rules must balance a tolerance for diverse perspectives with an expectation of reasonable orderliness. For their part, NGOs and civil society groups must be willing and able to seize the opportunities available and engage meaningfully in processes of multilateral diplomacy. This often requires an investment of resources in staff, relationships, and analytical products—and it demands a high level of commitment by NGO leaders. Most vitally, NGOs must strive to be nonpartisan in processes of multilateral diplomacy and preserve their independence and impartiality as humanitarian actors.

Note

1. The NGO Leaders Forum includes the chief executives of BRAC USA, CARE USA, Catholic Relief Services, Habitat for Humanity, International Medical Corps, International Rescue Committee, Médicins Sans Frontières USA, Mercy Corps, Oxfam America, Plan USA, Save the Children U.S., and World Vision U.S.

References

Council on Foreign Relations. 2009. Public opinion on global issues: A Web-based digest of polling from around the world. November. www.cfr.org/public_opinion.

Lindenberg, M., and C. Bryant. 2001. *Going global: Transforming relief and development NGOs*. Bloomfield, CT: Kumarian Press.

Mathews, J. T. 1997. "Power shift." *Foreign Affairs* 76 (January–February): 50–54.

Nye, J., and R. Keohane. 1972. *Transnational relations and world politics*. Cambridge, MA: Harvard University Press.

Paul, J. 2003. The Arria Formula. Global Policy Forum. October 2003. www.globalpolicy.org/component/content/article/185/40088.html (accessed November 21, 2009).

10

Human Rights Advocacy in Global Governance: A Case Study of Human Rights Watch

Carroll Bogert

This chapter examines the question of how and why transnational actors grow and exercise their influence from the perspective of a practitioner at Human Rights Watch, where I am associate director and have been working since 1998. Certainly Human Rights Watch has benefited from the growing clout of the nongovernmental organization (NGO) sector as a whole, and over the years it has worked in concert with hundreds, perhaps thousands, of NGOs whose professionalism and vigor have helped to give international civil society a good name. Human Rights Watch, as the largest international human rights organization based in the United States and one of only two in the world, along with Amnesty International, to exercise a truly global scope, has itself contributed to the growth in influence of international civil society. The question, again, is how.

NGOs' Growing Influence in the Post–Cold War World

I arrived at Human Rights Watch at the end of the 1990s, after more than a decade as an international correspondent for *Newsweek*, as this growth was already underway. The end of the Cold War had provided new opportunities for NGO engagement in circles of international diplomacy that had previously been the near-exclusive preserve of governments; the United Nations, in particular, became a more meaningful arena after the standoff between Washington and Moscow eased. The 1997 Nobel Peace Prize awarded to the International Campaign to

Ban Landmines, in which Human Rights Watch was a key player, clearly acknowledged the urgent diplomatic relevance of NGOs. The 1990s had also seen the development of the idea of humanitarian intervention and a growing consensus, from NGOs and their allies, that some of the principles they advocated most vociferously were worth putting into operation even when big countries opposed them—simply put, that NGOs could win arguments with powerful states.

Key Factors of Human Rights Watch's Influence: Technology, Money, the Media, and Rigorous Research

The first decade of the twenty-first century—especially unilateral U.S. military action—has considerably frayed the support for humanitarian intervention. But the last ten years have also brought tremendous benefits to the international human rights movement. NGOs deal in the world of information, and revolutions in information technology have enabled organizations on limited budgets to do more, with less. Some techniques have also made it possible to report on "closed" countries to which human rights workers could not get visas. Skype, e-mail (including its encrypted forms), Internet chat rooms, digital photography, satellite imaging, and other technological advances have allowed Human Rights Watch to gather more information in more formats, and to distribute it more quickly and more widely, than ever before.

At the same time, strong economic growth in countries where Human Rights Watch does most of its fund-raising made it possible for the organization, like many others in the NGO sector, to grow extremely quickly. In ten years, Human Rights Watch's budget more than tripled, from about US$14 million in 1998 to more than US$44 million in 2009. That enabled the hiring of more researchers covering more countries and more advocates lobbying more governments. The organization would have been poorly managed indeed if its influence had not grown substantially in this period, along with the size of its staff and resources.

The fund-raising successes of Human Rights Watch enabled the organization to become more influential, but they also were possible because donors increasingly perceived Human Rights Watch as influential. Donors want to see impact. Human Rights Watch offered concrete examples of where it had made an impact—from long-term efforts such as the Land Mines Treaty to immediate policy changes by regimes, such as the Egyptian government's desisting from the entrapment of gay men via the Internet on the day after Human Rights Watch published a report detailing the practice. Donors became persuaded that they were contributing not simply to a single project that might or might not work but to a proven methodology that could reliably produce political change (about which, more below). Their support made such work possible, but it also constituted one of the indices of Human Rights Watch's rising clout. We were increasingly considered influential by people who were themselves influential.

Another measure of Human Rights Watch's growing influence was the number of times it got mentioned in major media. Obtaining reliable data about media mentions would seem a relatively straightforward, even mathematical, exercise. But media search tools today include a variety of non-English publications that were much harder to track ten years ago, meaning that the growth in the number of hits may seem artificially high. At the same time, mentions on radio and television broadcasts remain difficult to track, perhaps keeping those hits low. And the growth of media overall—with the addition of online publications, blogs, and others—means that any organization worth its salt should be able to show an uptick in media mentions.

Notwithstanding those uncertainties of measurement, Human Rights Watch's media mentions have clearly grown fairly steadily since the organization was founded more than thirty years ago, and they grew particularly quickly in the first decade of the twenty-first century. According to the factiva.com media search engine, in 1998 Human Rights Watch was cited in the media 4,792 times, and in 2007, 17,936 times. According to a simple Google search, in 1998 the figure was 2,414, and in 2007 it was 18,970. Although those figures vary fairly widely, they both indicate that Human Rights Watch was at least four times as present in major, predominantly English-language media by the end of this most recent ten-year period than it had been at the beginning. According to the anecdotal impressions of Human Rights Watch researchers, the growth in the organization's coverage by vernacular media in many parts of the world has also been exponential, but this is much harder to measure in any scientific way.

Over the decades, more rigorous research standards have also contributed to the rise of Human Rights Watch's influence. Researchers now come to the organization with more academic expertise and more field expertise than in the past—partly, of course, because both the academic study and the field experience of human rights have grown more extensive in recent years too. The organization has also hired experts in fields ranging beyond human rights—for example, in public health and high-tech weaponry. Their expertise has helped to sharpen Human Rights Watch's research conclusions and recommendations for policy makers. New strategies for reporting on economic, social, and cultural rights have been honed. The vast and complex field of international humanitarian law—the laws of war—has been incorporated into Human Rights Watch's standard tool kit, enabling real-time work in conflict situations, sometimes while the bullets are still flying, as well as *post bellum* analysis.

Once they join Human Rights Watch, researchers undergo longer and more rigorous training than ever before—into research methods, interviewing techniques, and advocacy strategies, among other topics. They also receive libel training, security training for hostile environments, and training in how to handle journalistic interviewers. Every researcher does his or her first mission with an experienced colleague, and a larger staff means that a great deal of research is conducted by teams rather than individuals. The number of reports—some of them full-length books—has doubled in the last decade, from forty in 1998 to ninety-five in 2009. But that does not take into consideration the enormous growth in other documents Human Rights Watch produces, such as letters to government officials, briefing papers, amicus briefs, and formal submissions to UN bodies.

Producing a better research "product" does not mean, necessarily, that Human Rights Watch's influence has grown too, but it does indicate a kind of maturation and professionalization. By publishing reports that reflect greater expertise, Human Rights Watch has demonstrated the authority and capacity to enter into debates and policy discussions with policy makers at the highest levels. Better research skills are part of how it all happened.

Along with a rise in donations, media mentions, and the rigor of its research, Human Rights Watch's greater access to the corridors of power demonstrates its growing influence. This access is difficult to pinpoint numerically. Even in the early years of what became Human Rights Watch, the staff met with high-level policy makers and even heads of state, such as Jose Napoleon Duarte of El Salvador and Vinicio Cerezo of Guatemala. In 2008, Executive Director Kenneth Roth and other advocates and directors at Human Rights Watch probably met with more than a dozen heads of government, from Angela Merkel of Germany to Francois Bozize of the Central African Republic. But often more meaningful, and more substantive, were the discussions with the literally hundreds of government ministers, military commanders, rebel leaders, parliamentarians, ambassadors, UN officials, international criminal investigators, and corporate bigwigs who agreed to meet with Human Rights Watch staffers in dozens of countries around the world.

Some of that growth can be attributed to the fact that Human Rights Watch is simply bigger—leading to more research on more countries. But some of it speaks to a growing appreciation for Human Rights Watch's clout, even among people against whom that clout is sometimes directed. During a round of diplomatic visits to UN missions in September 2006 designed to cement his candidacy for the post of secretary-general, then South Korean foreign minister Ban Ki-moon paid a call on senior staff at Human Rights Watch's headquarters in the Empire State Building. The reason for his visit was patently obvious. The good opinion of Human Rights Watch, as an institution, mattered to Ban in his campaign to become secretary-general of the United Nations. We were an influential transnational actor. As Justice Richard Goldstone, a former judge on the Constitutional Court of South Africa, first chief prosecutor at the Yugoslavia and Rwanda war crimes tribunals, and a former board member of Human Rights Watch put it in a private talk in The Hague in June 2009, "Human Rights Watch is roughly as influential on the world stage as a middle-sized country."

From "Watching" to "Advocating": Human Rights Watch's Journey to Influence

How did this come to pass? Robert Bernstein, the CEO of Random House, convened some famous writers and powerful lawyers around the conference table in his lofty offices in midtown Manhattan in 1975 to discuss, primarily, issues of free expression. Knowing of the group, program officers at the Ford Foundation gave the first grant, to hire staff to help monitor compliance with the human rights provisions of the Helsinki Accords. Thus was born Helsinki Watch. Unlike Amnesty International, the group did not claim to represent a worldwide membership. Born into the world of publishing and information when the Cold War still held the world in its seemingly permanent grip, it focused on "watching"—on tracking the fates of Soviet Bloc dissidents who were bravely challenging their own governments' human rights records. When the companion Americas Watch was founded in 1981, the high-voltage politics of Reagan-era Washington helped to forge a methodology that would sustain Human Rights Watch for decades to come.

The group's first executive director, Aryeh Neier, established its rigorous research standards and sense of strategic moment; the board of directors and early staff brought their own gold-plated political and media connections. The new NGO enjoyed intellectual cachet in high-brow circles, though it was not yet widely known. In the early 1980s, the large amounts of American aid pouring into Central America gave Americas Watch a fulcrum for leveraging influence and a relevance to the hottest foreign policy debates of the time. Helsinki Watch focused on the Soviet Bloc, and Americas Watch kept an eye mostly on U.S. allies, which meant that the canny advocacy of Washington director Holly Burkhalter could not be politically pigeonholed.

Among certain foreign policy circles in the United States, the "watch committees," as they were then known, steadily earned a reputation for treating information as sacred and having trustworthy facts to offer. Solid information thus formed the cornerstone of Human Rights Watch's methodology from the beginning: finding out the facts, revealing the facts, and getting policy changed in light of those facts. Ultimately, those functions would come to be expressed in the organizational structure as the Program Department, the Communications Department, and the Advocacy Department. After the founding of Helsinki Watch and Americas Watch, more regional watch committees were added until all parts of the world were covered. In the 1990s, what was now called the Program Department began adding an even greater number of thematic divisions.[1] To this day, the divisions are responsible for doing extensive field research, including conducting dozens of interviews with victims of human rights abuse, eyewitnesses, family members, lawyers, prison staff, human rights activists, UN staff, and government officials, as well as gathering other forms of evidence and documentation. Each report they produce includes a set of detailed recommendations to relevant policy makers, setting forth the actions that must be taken in order for the abuse to end. Many of the divisions also include an advocate on staff, whose job is to press for those recommendations to be adopted. The Legal and Policy Department reviews all public documents to ensure their consistency across the organization.

At the end of the 1990s, Human Rights Watch started a separate Advocacy Department and began augmenting its Communications Department, ultimately recognizing these two functions as part of a triumvirate, along with the Program Department, that together constituted the organization's unique methodology. The seventy-plus researchers who fall under the purview of the Program Department and conduct the field investigations have responsibilities to speak with the media and to conduct advocacy based upon the reports they write. But in the first decade of the twenty-first century, advocacy and communications developed sophisticated networks of their own to contribute to Human Rights Watch's impact.

The critical change in advocacy was internationalization. Human Rights Watch had had an advocate in Washington since 1982 and added one in Brussels, to engage the European Union, in 1994. By the turn of the century, it was adding advocates in Berlin, Cairo, Geneva, Johannesburg, London, Paris, and Tokyo, with more planned. Such growth was possible only because Human Rights Watch was also diversifying its fund-raising base beyond the United States, and in almost all cases, the new advocates also had to maintain, if not take primary responsibility for, good relations with the local, private donors who funded their operations.[2]

A global fund-raising strategy made this growth possible. But what drove the trend was an appreciation that Human Rights Watch had to pull more levers of power in more places in order to bring about the policy change that once could be achieved, in significant measure, in Washington. New and increasingly influential institutions as diverse as the UN Human Rights Council (HRC), the African Union, the European Court of Human Rights, the International Criminal Court, and the Association of Southeast Asian Nations required Human Rights Watch's attention and engagement. Each had influence that needed to be brought to bear on offending governments in order to get policies changed. And it was clear that, for example, the road to making change in Zimbabwe did not run through Washington; it ran through Johannesburg. To put it positively, many governments and institutions had gained influence on the world stage, and Human Rights Watch clearly needed to be persuading them to use that influence in defense of human rights.

To put it negatively, the United States had lost influence. The U.S. government's reluctance to engage in multilateral human rights diplomacy certainly predated the Bush administration and had done long-term damage to its image as a human rights leader. But after 2000, the U.S. government became more actively hostile to international law and after September 11, 2001, more willing to overlook serious human rights abuses by certain governments as long as they remained close allies in the "war on terror." With the establishment of detention facilities at Guantánamo Bay and the revelation of torture photographs from Abu Ghraib, it became clear that Washington was not just fighting a messy war in Iraq but becoming an increasingly reluctant partner in making human rights progress around the world. It was, itself, a high-visibility violator of human rights. After the invasion of Iraq, to have the U.S. government publicly embrace a human rights cause was, in certain parts of the world, to doom it to failure. The loss of credibility was not complete, but it was precipitous.

To maintain and expand its ability to influence governments to protect human rights, Human Rights Watch had to grow internationally. Concomitant with that trend, in the first decade of the twenty-first century the organization also had to respond to the financial woes of an important partner: the media, particularly American newspapers. Publicizing human rights violations—"naming and shaming"—had been the primary tool of the human rights movement since its inception. Without publicity for the abuse of power, without its revelation, the pressure for change in many cases dwindled sharply. For more than two decades, Human Rights Watch had built relationships with a core group of foreign correspondents for elite American and European newspapers. Now those newspapers were paring back their budgets, especially their foreign news budgets, in response to falling revenues.

The source of the newspapers' problem also constituted Human Rights Watch's partial solution to it: the Internet. Newspapers were losing readers, and therefore advertisers, to this new medium. But via its own website, Human Rights Watch could now communicate directly with policy makers, donors, and the concerned public. With approximately 25,000 unique visitors per day in 2009, Human Rights Watch could not command anything like the audience of a major American daily such as the *New York Times*. Moreover, only people with a predetermined interest in human rights visited www.hrw.org, while being quoted in the newspaper offered the possibility of reaching the uninitiated and the unpersuaded. At the same time, however, on its own website, Human Rights Watch could be more than a simple quote in a story; it had the opportunity instead to tell its own story.

The problem was that Human Rights Watch's relatively dense, legalistic, and lengthy reports did not tell the story in a way that most people were inclined to listen to. That required journalistic storytelling skills, as well as visual elements to make the website lively and attractive. So a new multimedia department began creating pieces of electronic journalism to go along with the report and the press release on the Web. A photo editor assigned photographers and videographers— sometimes very well-known ones who were no longer getting assignments from the financially strapped mainstream media—to go into the field. A radio producer was hired to teach researchers how to gather sound in the field, as well as to assign radio producers to accompany those researchers, help record their interviews, and produce ambient, or "b-roll," sound. Human Rights Watch began a weekly podcast.

This journalistic content did not, on its own, produce policy change—the stated mission of Human Rights Watch. That required the two other elements of the methodology: hard-hitting research and advocacy. But Human Rights Watch's relatively high media profile made policy makers feel they could not afford not to listen. It made Human Rights Watch seem bigger than it was. It made Human Rights Watch seem more influential than perhaps it really was.

And influence is also a matter of perception, so it also made Human Rights Watch more influential.

Human Rights Watch and the Campaign to Ban Cluster Munitions

Academic analysts have written about the participation of NGOs in the International Campaign to Ban Landmines, which won the Nobel Peace Prize in 1997 and marked a new era of civil society participation in international diplomacy. It may also be instructive to look briefly at the Cluster Munitions Coalition (CMC), which produced an international convention to ban cluster munitions almost exactly a decade later. The negotiations demonstrated a solidification of the position of NGOs as diplomatic partners ten years on and made clear that their involvement would likely be permanent. Human Rights Watch participated in both campaigns. Indeed, many of the NGO experts were the same people, and even some of the professional diplomats representing their countries were the same. In both cases, a weapons expert and former grassroots campaigner named Steve Goose led Human Rights Watch's delegations in his capacity as director of the Arms Division. Cluster munitions are bombs or rocket- and artillery-launched munitions that open in the air, sending dozens or even hundreds of bomblets to explode over an area that may be as big as a football field. When used in a populated area, they cannot discriminate between combatants and civilians. That makes their use a violation of international humanitarian law. A certain percentage of them fail to explode and instead lodge in the ground, or even in trees or bushes, where they act like landmines, exploding if a person touches them—whether that person is a soldier, and a legitimate target in war, or a child playing in the area long after the war is over.

Human Rights Watch had been researching, publicizing, and advocating on cluster munitions for a decade by the time the treaty was signed in December 2008. Its focus on the weapon began in 1999, when the North Atlantic Treaty Organization (NATO) dropped cluster bombs against military targets in populated areas of Serbia in its effort to get Yugoslav president Slobodan Milošević to pull his troops out of Kosovo. The U.S. Air Force could not get access to the areas it had targeted because Milošević remained in power. Nor could the Yugoslav government be trusted to provide an accurate accounting of the civilian deaths and damage to civilian infrastructure from cluster bombs. If reasonable precautions could have been taken to avoid such destruction, the U.S. government might reasonably be accused of having violated international humanitarian law, or the laws of war.

Human Rights Watch thus hired a military consultant with extensive expertise in assessing bomb damage to visit each site in Serbia where cluster bombs had been dropped, together with the organization's Yugoslavia researcher. They produced the first reliable study on cluster bomb damage—and they did in fact conclude that the Pentagon's use of clusters had caused unnecessary and unacceptable civilian death and suffering. The report received moderate coverage in the media, but its conclusions were compelling enough (and valuable enough to a Pentagon that could not make on-the-ground, postconflict weapons assessments of its own) to win Human Rights Watch an audience with relatively high-ranking Air Force lawyers. Rather than disputing the report's conclusions (which is certainly the most common experience that Human Rights Watch has in advocacy meetings with government officials), the Air Force appeared to take Human Rights Watch's recommendations on board. In Afghanistan in 2001 and 2002, and in Iraq in 2003, it generally avoided using cluster bombs in populated areas. In Iraq, however, the U.S. Army availed itself of ground rocket- and artillery-launched cluster munitions, causing substantial civilian casualties, and in August 2006, the Israeli Defense Forces subjected southern Lebanon to a withering barrage of cluster bombs. In August 2008, both Russian and Georgian forces used cluster munitions in their war over the disputed Georgian region of South Ossetia. Human Rights Watch reported on the use of clusters in all these conflicts. It had meetings with government officials in Georgia, Israel, Russia, and the United States to discuss its findings. Most importantly, its reports established the substantial humanitarian harm that cluster munitions were causing—which had previously been a matter of some debate. The reports also established Human Rights Watch's own expertise on the clusters issue, as well as that of other NGOs. That credibility would prove crucial in the process of drafting and negotiating the treaty.

Sometimes the reports on clusters had quite immediate impact, such as in the conflict over South Ossetia, where it was ultimately determined that both Russian and Georgian forces had used clusters. Human Rights Watch's initial documentation of Russia's use of cluster munitions received wide media coverage.[3] In a relatively small country like Georgia, which felt its very existence depended on international perceptions that it was the victim in the war, Human Rights Watch immediately obtained meetings with high-level Defense Ministry officials, including the minister of defense himself, to warn that unexploded Russian ordnance posed an immediate threat to a number of Georgian villages. The Georgian government responded by circulating leaflets to the population and running public-education campaigns on television. When Human Rights Watch published its report on Georgia's use of cluster munitions (and other violations of international humanitarian law) four months after the war ended, the Georgian government received the delegation at the highest levels. President Mikheil Saakashvili, as well as the defense minister, national security adviser, and a number of officials from the Foreign and Interior ministries, did not dispute the report's findings but insisted that the use of cluster munitions had helped to keep Russian forces at bay for nearly three days and staved off the destruction of some villages.[4] The report received wide media coverage inside Georgia, and the Human Rights Watch delegation met with more than a dozen European Union ambassadors who professed support for the idea that the Georgian government should not use cluster munitions. But it was also clear that the most powerful influence on the Georgian government's behavior at that time was the United States. In the waning days of the Bush administration, Washington was unlikely to press Tbilisi to renounce the weapon.

That was particularly true because Washington had clearly demonstrated its hostility to an international effort to ban cluster munitions entirely. As with landmines, a handful of medium-sized states had taken the lead in drafting a new treaty. Like Human Rights Watch, they had grown tired of obfuscation and filibustering at the Geneva-based Convention on Conventional Weapons (CCW), the initial locus of diplomatic conversation about the weapon. Since the CCW operated by consensus, any government that opposed limits on cluster munitions could block progress. In November 2006, Austria, Ireland, New Zealand, Norway, Mexico, and the Holy See initiated an "outside the CCW" negotiation on clusters with a treaty ban as its goal. The United States did not participate. Indeed, it actively lobbied against the treaty in NATO capitals. It reportedly discouraged the government of Afghanistan, whose territory had been sorely affected by cluster munitions over many decades of war, from participating.

The CMC, which was cochaired by Steve Goose of Human Rights Watch, Simon Conway of Landmine Action, and Grethe Ostern of Norwegian People's Aid, comprised hundreds of NGOs from around the world. It fielded experts at each round of diplomatic negotiations, prepared position papers, drafted language, met with and badgered delegates, and, of course, distributed fact-based research on the nefarious effects of the weapon. But the NGO representatives were not just bird dogs. They did more than hector and lobby. They acted as a repository of expertise for some of the very governments who were leading the process. "I know there is often a perception that, you know, governments are omnipotent and even smaller governments like mine have a huge reservoir of knowledge to draw on," Don McKay, the chief delegate for New Zealand, said in Dublin in May 2008.

> But that's not always the case. . . . We don't actually have cluster munitions ourselves. . . . So what this means is that I don't have a particular expert on cluster munitions in the Ministry of Defense or the New Zealand Defense Forces back in Wellington. . . . We don't have people who actually know the technical characteristics of a weapon we don't have. . . . I've been constantly referring back to the CMC, to Steve, to Marc [Garlasco, another Human Rights Watch weapons expert], in terms of the technical characteristics of weapons.[5]

The so-called Oslo process moved quickly. Within fifteen months, the treaty was drafted, negotiated, and adopted—near-lightning speed for a new piece of international law. The United States remained aloof from the treaty, and some of the world's other major producers, such as China, Israel, and Russia, also made it clear they would not sign. While this rightfully raised questions about how effective the new treaty would be, experience with the landmines convention suggested that the most important effect of the new convention would be to stigmatize the weapon. Although the United States still has not signed the landmines treaty, it has largely abided by its provisions ever since the treaty went into effect. Landmines became a virtually unusable weapon. Human Rights Watch and the representatives of small states that could not tie the Gullivers down still felt the treaty would ultimately attain its objective of ending the use of clusters. The new treaty also solidified an important partnership between civil society and smaller, progressive states that sought to create new pieces of international law to protect human rights. "I think the best way in which things have changed is that civil society tends to be the opinion leader on innovation," McKay said. "Governments are not. Governments, for the most part, tend to be reactive. And certainly, over the last sort of ten or fifteen years . . . risk-averse."

Conclusion

Despite the growth of Human Rights Watch and the increasing influence of the human rights movement as a whole, significant flaws in the international architecture of human rights still impede progress. Perhaps the most salient example is the UN Human Rights Council, which, since its establishment in 2006, has performed poorly on a host of issues. The number of country-specific experts appointed by the Council has shrunk from sixteen to eight, and the work of human rights experts appointed by the HRC has been threatened. The HRC has also adopted numerous one-sided resolutions on human rights violations by Israel while failing to address the roles and responsibilities of other parties to the conflict, as well as resolutions on defamation of religions that undermine freedom of expression. Moreover, the HRC has failed to address human rights violations in numerous situations warranting its attention, while offering only weak resolutions on some of the country situations it has taken up. A group of states dedicated to undermining human rights protections at the HRC have proven to be both very focused and well resourced. States such as China, Egypt, and Pakistan (the "spoilers") have made a concerted effort to weaken the UN human rights system and been able to use the divide between northern and southern states, as well as polarization between the Muslim and non-Muslim world, to forge alliances to forward their aims and gain support for their proposals.

Despite those significant problems, the HRC remains an indispensible tool for addressing human rights violations. In particular, it continues to have an important impact on human rights violations through the work of the thematic and country-specific rapporteurs that it appoints, through the Universal Periodic Review that examines the human rights records of each and every nation over time, and through engagement on particular issues at its general and special sessions. The Council's problems are not primarily the result of a design flaw—both its membership and its mechanisms allow for a much more effective human rights body than the old, discredited UN Human Rights Commission that preceded it. Its shortcomings to date have resulted mostly from the failure of moderate states with relatively progressive views on human rights to live up to those principles at the Council. Part of the role of NGOs, including Human Rights Watch, in such an environment is to publicize these failures and pressure governments to do a better job in Geneva. With the United States joining the HRC as a member in June 2009 and several positive developments in African, EU, and Latin American engagement at the HRC, there were real opportunities to put the Council on a better track.

Human Rights Watch is only one of many nonstate actors exercising influence in international diplomacy today. Commercial entities also play a significant role, from private security businesses and mercenaries who engage directly in conflict on behalf of governments, to multinational corporations whose revenues exceed some national budgets and whose lobbying efforts dwarf those of smaller states.

Even within the nonprofit sector, outside the field of human rights in areas such as the environment or international development, big international NGOs operate with budgets much larger than Human Rights Watch's. Greenpeace and Oxfam are household names in many countries around the world. Their growth in recent decades may stem from some trends that are unique to their field of endeavor. But all NGOs are sharing in a recent wave of public trust and approval. According to a fairly extensive survey conducted annually by an international public relations agency, the 2009 Edelman Trust Barometer, NGOs enjoy greater public confidence than business, media, or government among "informed publics" aged thirty-five to sixty-four in twenty countries. The NGO sector is, in fact, the only institution trusted by more than 50 percent of the global public (Edelman 2009, 8, fig. 8). Trust in NGOs is significantly higher in Latin America and relatively lower in Asia, for reasons the survey does not fully explain. This means that while Human Rights Watch continues to use levers of influence wherever possible—enlisting governments around the world, the United Nations, and a range of other state and nonstate actors to adopt human rights–friendly positions—it also relies on its own credibility and prestige to exercise influence. Human Rights Watch has become a force in its own right rather than merely a force pushing others to act.

Notes

1. Children's Rights; Women's Rights; Arms; Refugees; International Justice; Terrorism and Counterterrorism; Health and Human Rights; Lesbian, Gay, Bisexual, and Transgender Rights; Emergencies; and Business and Human Rights.

2. Human Rights Watch accepts no funds from any government.

3. The death of a Dutch journalist in one Russian cluster bomb attack also generated a great deal of international attention. But Human Rights Watch's military experts on the ground during the war gave independent confirmation of cluster use to journalists who were then able to run with the story.

4. A number of Georgian cluster bombs actually misfired and fell on Georgian territory.

5. Video of McKay's remarks are on file at Human Rights Watch.

Reference

Edelman. 2009. Edelman Trust Barometer. Edelman. www.edelman.com/trust/2009/docs/Trust_Book_Final_2.pdf.

11

Seven Steps to Influencing Multilateral Environmental Negotiations: A Case Study on Invasive Species and the Convention on Biological Diversity

Stanley W. Burgiel

Invasive species are one of the critical drivers of biodiversity loss and threaten economic development and public health through their role as agricultural pests, livestock diseases, and vectors for the transmission of pathogens and other viruses. Despite their significant impacts, the international community generally lacks the consolidated approach and mobilized constituency necessary to address the magnitude of the issue across environmental, economic, health, and other sectors. This chapter describes the role that The Nature Conservancy (TNC), the Global Invasive Species Program (GISP), and their partners played in multilateral negotiations on invasive species under the Convention on Biological Diversity (CBD) from 2006 to 2008. During this period, I served as TNC's senior policy advisor on invasive species as well as GISP's policy director, so the description and analysis of events comes from firsthand experience. While personal involvement can result in subjective bias, its greater value is the opportunity it provides to illustrate the step-by-step approach used in the planning and execution of this "campaign" on invasive species.

Role of TNC and GISP

As mentioned the primary drivers of this effort included TNC, GISP, and a range of institutional and country partners. TNC is one of the world's largest conservation organizations with offices in all fifty U.S. states and in more than thirty countries. The organization maintained an invasive-species unit, which supported both management and policy efforts within its site-based programs. TNC is also one of the members of GISP, which is one of the leading international organizations providing technical advice on invasive-species policy issues. Other GISP members include the International Union for the Conservation of Nature and Natural Resources (or World Conservation Union), Commonwealth Agricultural Bureaux International, and the South African National Biodiversity Institute, which are all either intergovernmental or governmental agencies. It is critical to note that TNC is one of the only nongovernmental organizations (NGOs) working on environmental aspects of invasive species at the international level.

In 2005, TNC's invasive-species program brought on board policy expertise with the rationale that leveraging policy frameworks and respective changes in budgets, departmental priorities, and political awareness could create change at a larger scale than existing site-based activities. An improved policy environment would thereby provide a supportive context for work on the ground and in the water.

The Challenge

Invasive species are those plants, animals, and microorganisms whose introduction or spread beyond their natural distribution threatens biodiversity. Invasive species are found across taxonomic groups and are commonly regarded as one of the top three drivers of biodiversity loss. Increased trade, travel, and tourism have facilitated the movement of invasive species, increasing their potential range and rates of introduction with significant consequences in all major ecosystem types and sectors.

At the ecological level, invasive species can change ecosystem structures by impacting ecological services and species compositions. In economic terms, some experts estimate the global cost of invasive species at US$1.4 trillion annually (Pimentel et al. 2001). Their movement and spread are also linked to other drivers of global change, such as climate change, desertification, fire, and so forth. Despite their relevance across a spectrum of environmental issues, their political profile is relatively low compared to other environmental concerns, such as climate change, protected areas, and species conservation. This is particularly important at the national level, where political and fiscal decisions determine which priorities will be implemented. Recognizing that invasive species are interrelated with these other environmental issues and also intersect with trade, transport, and public health sectors, we thought it necessary to raise the profile of invasive species to focus the international community on this problem.

At the international level, TNC, working with GISP, targeted the UN Convention on Biological Diversity, which entered into force in 1994. Its core objectives include the conservation and sustainable use of biodiversity, as well as the fair, equitable sharing of its benefits. The agreement covers a broad array of concerns that span all major ecosystem types as well as a number of cross-cutting issues. The main reasons for concentrating on the CBD include the following:

- Invasive species are formally recognized as a cross-cutting issue on the CBD's rolling list of agenda items.
- The CBD includes over 190 country members, known as parties, thereby serving as a truly global platform.
- Through its intergovernmental linkages and secretariat, the CBD can provide entrée into a range of other relevant international institutions, including environmental, agricultural, transport, financing, and trade agreements.

Negotiating Strategies of NGOs

The following section outlines the work that TNC and GISP undertook to influence the CBD's negotiations on invasive species and to engage national governments in building their efforts to address this threat. The underlying strategy includes seven main elements that are loosely based on experience with other environmental campaigns on issues such as protected areas, island biodiversity, and forests. It is also essential to note at the start that this effort largely engaged in "insider politics" where NGOs seek to induce change internally by working with governments and other institutions to influence negotiated outcomes. In contrast, "outsider politics" involve a more media-oriented strategy of shame, blame, praise, or a combination of the three, along with external public pressure to induce change in government positions. Both styles are equally valid forms of advocacy and can often be complementary (Burgiel 2008, 83). In this case, TNC, GISP, and their partners presumed that more could be gained by taking a supporting role using their familiarity with the issue, technical expertise, and other resources to influence the process.

1. Platform   A basic first step in advocacy work is to find a hook for why an issue is relevant and the appropriate rationale for changing the status quo. Without a hook, whether it be an agenda item at an official meeting or a recent environmental calamity, one's ability is severely limited in getting governments to consider the issue.

As previously mentioned, the CBD already had a track record on invasive species, which started in the late 1990s. These formal discussions resulted in the adoption by the CBD's Sixth Conference of the Parties (COP) at The Hague in 2002 of voluntary guiding principles for how countries could address the threat of invasive species. Despite being relatively abstract, the guiding principles suffered from political contention over linkages to trade issues as well as controversy over the actual process of their adoption. The longer-term result was a chilling effect and reluctance by countries and other intergovernmental processes to address invasive species or the CBD's guiding principles in detail. This had significant impacts on the profile that the issue took on many national agendas, particularly in countries dependent on bilateral assistance or funds from the international community to implement their international environmental commitments.

The CBD's Ninth Conference of the Parties (COP9) at Bonn in 2008 was scheduled to take up the issue of invasive species again through a review of country efforts to implement relevant CBD decisions to date. Our concern was that the issue would be quietly pushed aside as a pro forma exercise if significant pressure was not put on governments and the CBD process to examine the issue seriously. From a self-serving perspective, TNC and GISP were also significantly interested in advancing the process, as "success" would create a more supportive platform for future work, particularly if the debate could be moved beyond awareness raising to a focus on policy development and capacity building. Failure would only worsen the current struggle to put invasive species on the political agenda at all levels.

2. Champions and Detractors   Another basic step in advocacy is identifying those countries or institutions that are the best allies and those that could present the most problems. The broader the alliance supporting a position, the better the chances of moving it through formal negotiating channels. This alliance needs to include governments, ideally early on in the campaign, as they are the actors with a seat at the table and the ability to take the floor during formal negotiations. Geographic and geopolitical considerations are critical in identifying key supporters. Identifying lead countries in the United Nations' major geographic regions and political blocs is ideal, yet often times unrealistic, given regional interests and politics.

The benefit of working with an organization like TNC and the other GISP members is that they have country programs with existing connections to government agencies. Our campaign thereby targeted outreach to Africa, the Caribbean, China, Mexico, Pacific Island countries, and South America. We also identified Europe as a key region, given that it would serve as host to COP9 and European countries would play a major role in the CBD negotiation process. We even went so far as to engage a well-regarded German environmental organization/ think tank in furthering our European strategy. Within these regions, we targeted key countries based on existing relations or their political roles regionally or in official CBD bodies in the hope that they could serve as champions for pushing common priorities.

Outside of governments we sought other partners in our campaign. Unlike protected areas and forests, invasive species is not a common focus of most environmental organizations. This foreclosed the possibility of a broad-based NGO coalition (which had proved very successful around protected areas and islands). This lack of partners among our "peers" forced more selective engagement with regional and other technical agencies involved in work on invasive species. For example, the Inter-American Biodiversity Information Network, the South Pacific Regional Environment Program, and regional invasive-species project coordinators became key players for identifying priorities, liaising with countries, and moving the debate forward. As regional governmental bodies, many of these partners had better access to governmental decision makers than an NGO normally would. The key lesson here is to diversify as best possible those supporting your cause with a key focus on governmental partners and other types of regional, nongovernmental, and intergovernmental bodies.

A final partner in this process was the CBD Secretariat itself. The secretariat is a neutral body tasked with undertaking intersessional activities and preparing documentation for official CBD meetings. It is therefore not a body to be influenced by overt lobbying. As in many other institutions, however, overworked staff often welcome assistance in completing their mandate. Thereby, through GISP, which is recognized in a number of past CBD decisions, we worked to solicit information from countries regarding their implementation efforts and to compile the data so that capacity and policy priorities were easily identifiable. This collaborative role with the secretariat and corresponding outreach to countries on their priorities helped frame us as supporting the process rather than solely pursuing our own agenda.

Beyond allies, one also needs to consider potential "enemies," or detractors from your cause. A government or other NGO might oppose your interests for reasons ranging from conflicting political or economic views, concerns about the process, or even the personal baggage of negotiators with a past history on the issue. Ignoring these factors in the hope that they will go away is probably the worst strategy. Without an idea of how these actors might behave within the formal negotiations, one cannot seek areas of compromise or devise counterstrategies. This can leave a well-developed campaign vulnerable to a single objection from the floor. Despite a heavy focus on due process in the negotiation of environmental treaties and decisions, deliberations are still subject to a high degree of unpredictability, which can ultimately come down to who is in the room when discussions start, how the chair chooses to address the issue, and other seemingly trivial items, such as illness of a negotiator, morning traffic, or more "important" negotiations in the next room.

Given the past contention over the adoption of the CBD's guiding principles, we sought information from key countries that had a stake in those discussions, including Argentina, Australia, Brazil, the European Community, and the United States (despite its not being a party to the CBD). Our general approach was to argue the need for continuing work on the substance, combined with the veiled suggestion that continued grandstanding on these process issues could torpedo any substantive work on invasive species for the foreseeable future. While these issues did arise during COP9 and were not resolved, they were successfully segregated from the more substantive deliberations and the meeting's corresponding decision.

3. Substance   Aside from identifying the procedural hook for raising concerns, one needs to detail fully the expected outcomes from a COP or particular countries. Generally, the parameters for what can reasonably be advocated are set by

- past discourse and decisions under convention bodies
- the issue's presentation in the agenda by the secretariat and then, more specifically, its spelling out in annotated drafts and background documents
- opportunities presented by major environmental events or other changes occurring outside of the convention process

The CBD's in-depth review on invasive species presented a broad range of possible opportunities. The real concern was making sure that the secretariat's effort was not simply a historical review but instead was framed to raise the profile of the issue and present a suite of priorities for future work.

TNC and GISP worked to frame the discussion at three levels: the national, the regional, and the international. At the national level, we worked to solicit inputs from countries on their work to date as well as on their capacity needs and near-term priorities. This input, combined with our previous experience in other venues, allowed us to develop a phased-approach model of implementation. Given that CBD decisions in the past had been relatively piecemeal in their focus, this model also provided a framework that helped organize components of a national invasive-species system into beginning, intermediate, and advanced steps, while allowing enough flexibility for countries to pick and choose the elements most relevant to them. The breadth of such a framework also served to recognize the priorities that countries had put forward to give them a sense of ownership over the process.

At the regional level, we highlighted the role of regional organizations particularly in the area of supporting implementation, developing information systems, and sharing experiences across countries. Emphasizing such groups was also a tactical choice, given that they were key allies of ours and that there are constraints on their ability to lobby for their own cause. Such work solidified positive relations with these regional groups, thereby opening opportunities for future collaboration.

Finally, at the international level, we identified several gaps, particularly in the area of pathways for the movement of invasive species, which required guidance for countries. Past discussions under the CBD had identified approximately fifteen major areas for work at the international level but did not set out a plan or a set of priorities on which to start work. This past dialogue provided the opportunity to advocate for a refined set of priorities for more immediate focus. We made sure that the list of three or four pathways that we chose to promote had support among countries and relevant intergovernmental institutions and also accorded with our own programmatic priorities.

4. Prenegotiations   Moving an issue within international environmental law requires a long-term investment of time and energy. An NGO cannot show up at a COP and reasonably expect to insert its lobbying points into the meeting's final decisions, as the work to frame those outcomes will have started months if not years beforehand. This requires attention to the full schedule of official CBD meetings, informal meetings of expert groups, and the ongoing work of the secretariat.

As a general rule, the CBD's Scientific Body on Scientific, Technical and Technological Advice (SBSTTA) is charged with conducting preliminary discussions on an agenda item and forwarding a set of recommendations for review by the

CBD's decision-making organ—the COP. Thus, the general approach outlined here can be conducted on a smaller scale to influence the inputs and outputs of the scientific body as a necessary step in ultimately influencing the COP. In the case of invasive species, a decision had been made very early on not to put the issue on SBSTTA's agenda. This represents one of the unpredictable twists and turns that negotiations can take.

In this instance, an intervention by the representative of a major regional group at a late-night negotiating session in an earlier COP took the issue off SBSTTA's agenda. Ironically, several countries from that region later voiced their displeasure with that approach, while the issue went unobserved and unrecognized by many other countries. Removal of invasive species from SBSTTA's agenda was a significant obstacle as it eliminated an obvious point to focus countries on the issue and to provide input from their own national experiences. We therefore had to work extra hard to reach out to countries prior to the COP to keep them apprised of the review and the need to focus on it prior to and at COP9 itself. This setback also created an opportunity to provide support to the secretariat, which was working without the benefit of input from the parties as to what should be included in the recommendations being forwarded to the COP. This way of progressing was certainly riskier but clearly illustrates how one's strategy can be dictated by procedural matters.

The other important aspect of the prenegotiation period is working directly with countries in their preparations. Through GISP, we sent notices and follow-up communications to all of the national CBD focal points informing them of the in-depth review and the opportunities it presented for them. In countries where the different GISP members had relations, we worked in more detail to identify their priorities and to distribute position papers that could serve as background for their internal discussions and provide possible elements for interventions they might make at the COP. Sometimes groups including the Pacific Islands, Africa, the European Community, and parts of Latin America and the Caribbean hold regional meetings to identify common positions. Given sufficient capacity, time, and relations, these are excellent forums to test concepts and gain broader buy in. We were able to distribute some information to key colleagues prior to a few of these meetings but did not have the resources to engage directly at these sessions.

5. Negotiations By this time, the negotiations are often anticlimactic. If all of the legwork has been done to prepare the groundwork and secure champions on the floor, it almost becomes a matter of shepherding the process through. It is rarely that easy, but there are clear advantages to having set the stage prior to arriving at the COP.

For invasive species at COP9, despite all of our outreach there was still uncertainty as to how the recommendations from the secretariat would be received and whether there were any outlier countries that we had not canvassed. Usually, one can foresee what the big political issues for a COP will be and which issues will take a lesser profile. However, even seemingly benign issues can blow up into larger debates for any number of unpredictable reasons.

So, we continued to work with our allies and to talk with the secretariat and other major countries to get a feeling for how the formal negotiations would proceed. The first round of discussions within a broader working group went well, and there were voices of support for many ideas that we were championing, which set the stage for a positive outcome. The key would be to ensure that such ideas were incorporated into subsequent draft decision texts by the secretariat for continued discussions over the course of rest of the meeting.

While the first revised draft we received was promising, there were still items of concern and language that we thought should be tweaked. We therefore went back to our key champions and regional groups, mostly Caribbean and Pacific countries, to make suggestions and help them prepare. The reality of COPs is that the large number of ongoing discussions frequently requires small delegations to make strategic choices about the issues that they will follow. It is therefore not enough to identify countries that will support a position, as one needs to make sure that they are in the room at the time that an issue is discussed for a second, third, or fourth time. This can be a process of attrition as small delegations are increasingly scattered (and fatigued), while the larger delegations (usually from developed countries) remain in the room to make the final amendments.

With invasive species, we were able to secure inputs from key allies in the second round of discussions but largely lost traction in the final review of the recommended decision as our key country negotiators were not available. While we did not lose any of our major substantive points, we did lose some opportunities to achieve more favorable language on funding and identify concrete steps for future work on the issue.

6. Publicity Alongside the formal negotiations at COP9, we worked to highlight the issue of invasive species through a display booth, several publications, and a number of events. The booth and printed materials served as a base for outreach to countries and other participants, as well as an informal place to provide input on a range of invasive-species concerns (from policy to management questions).

The materials we provided included a range of technical guidance on regulation of pathways, development of indicator and monitoring systems, and other issue-specific pieces, such as biofuels.

In the run-up to COP9, we also worked with a number of countries to persuade them to make public commitments at the COP on the work that they would do around invasive species. We were able to secure such commitments from twelve countries and U.S. territories, including places like Brazil, China, Croatia, New Zealand, Peru, the United Kingdom, and the countries and U.S. territories of Micronesia. We held an event specifically to highlight these commitments and recognize the work of these countries, which helped further secure their interest in the outcomes of the COP's decision on invasive species.

A separate event we hosted at the very beginning of COP9 highlighted our overall policy recommendations and served as a more technical forum for reviewing some elements of the draft COP decision on invasive species. Finally, we launched a technical report on biofuels and invasive species, which, while slightly outside the COP's deliberations on invasive species, was a very attractive and controversial issue that appealed to the media. Working in tandem with the communications teams of the GISP members, we hosted a press briefing that received coverage in a wide range of international press outlets, including the *New York Times* and *Herald Tribune*. Such media coverage helped to build awareness around invasive species and gave GISP some additional publicity.

Side events, dinners, and other opportunities to highlight an issue are a valuable means of developing relations with countries and other organizations and of securing a network of individuals willing to work on an issue. Getting a country to make a statement to the media or in a more public venue can go a long way toward getting them to support related issues in the formal negotiations.

7. Follow-Up Ultimately, COP decisions remain so many words on paper, unless there is follow-through to see them implemented. The end is just the beginning as the outcomes of the COP signal the start of a new phase of ensuring that work is done on the ground. This is especially true with the CBD, which is essentially soft law. There is no strict enforcement mechanism, and countries often implement work around their priorities and in accord with their capacity. Ensuring action frequently requires the ongoing provision of technical advice and guidance, as well as assistance in securing funds through donor funding or private means.

At COP9, we secured most of our objectives in the formal decision while also securing the aforementioned public commitments from a number of countries. More specifically, the decision included references to the following:

- support for regional work and institutions, particularly relating to islands
- priority focus on key pathways, including animal invasive species, civil aviation, hull fouling, tourism, and development projects funded by international aid
- reference to GISP collaboration with the CBD Secretariat on a number of substantive issues to assist with national implementation

Until the next COP, this will serve as the framework for continued engagement with countries and intergovernmental organizations on invasive species. Then for the CBD's Tenth COP (Nagano, October 2010) the process will start all over again, while building on the gains and hard work of the past.

Conclusion

This section will review the efforts of the campaign on invasive species described above in the context of five key questions about the broader role of nonstate actors in multilateral diplomacy. The discussion below builds on the specific efforts around CBD COP9, while recognizing the broader context of related issues in international environmental law.

1. Role and Effectiveness of TNC and GISP   As noted above, the primary approach taken toward influencing COP9 was one of insider politics. Based on an analysis of the existing political context, TNC and GISP chose to work with governments, the CBD Secretariat, and other partners to provide technical input into the deliberations to shape outcomes supportive of existing efforts to build capacity and longer-term work to develop additional policy guidance. By serving as a broker to channel information developed at the national and regional levels, TNC and GISP could provide additional value by framing it for maximum impact within the international discussions. While the ultimate goals were reshaped over the course of this dialogue, the ability to adjust to and incorporate the priorities of other actors helped to create greater buy in. In the end, the CBD's in-depth review was more than a simple exercise on paper, which lent political support to most of the key priorities promoted by TNC and GISP.

2. Nonstate Actors in Multilateral Diplomacy   Nonstate actors are crucial in two regards. First, they are critical in thinking through longer-term strategic issues. Many countries are either too overwhelmed to think beyond the next meeting or are constrained by the priorities of the current political regime in power. The result can be a series of discussions that revisit the same issues or that are not strategically developed. In the case of invasive species, capacity building and the development of technical guidance are processes that take years. By focusing on the process of building national biosecurity systems and prioritizing areas for new guidance, TNC and GISP sought to instill a multiyear framework into the CBD's work on invasive species.

Nonstate actors are also helpful in the short-term, when they can bring emerging environmental issues to the fore. At COP9, TNC and GISP highlighted invasive-species issues around the topic of biofuels. The media attention helped to raise the overall profile of invasive species at the meeting and around the world. Capitalizing on these up-and-coming opportunities requires having an existing investment in the ongoing policy process through which to focus public attention and pressure.

3. Comparative Advantage of Nonstate Actors   Within the CBD's deliberations, the comparative advantage of TNC, GISP, and its partners was the ability to gather and process technical information into a strategic set of policy priorities. Transnational NGOs (often referred to as BINGOs, or big international NGOs) have networks that extend across a range of countries as well as issue-specific programs. This combination provides enhanced levels of expertise with a broader context in national experience than most individual governments can provide. Furthermore, the ability to draw from on-the-ground experience and existing relations with national governments lends additional credibility to organizations like TNC at major intergovernmental meetings. The aim is to speak with the voice of experience, while acknowledging the role and importance of national partners. This is not to downplay the role of smaller NGOs as they, too, may have particular expertise or contacts with a single country that can prove instrumental in moving multilateral diplomacy.

4. Nonstate Actors and the Changing Nature of Global Governance   The seven steps for advocacy described above are essential for setting the stage in any comprehensive lobbying effort at the international level. This is a time- and resource-intensive activity. Those engaged need to be committed for the longer term as movement from concept to policy language to implementation can sometimes span years. The value therein is being able to establish underlying policy frameworks that will leverage national action far greater than would be possible if approaching the issue country by country or site by site.

The world of global environmental politics is becoming increasingly complicated as more problems arise, their severity increases, and additional scientific implications come to light. Issues like invasive species and climate change span a
broad range of issue areas and sectors. This means that efforts to address them
within the context of one agreement such as the CBD or the UN Framework
Convention on Climate Change run the risk of overloading those agreements
while reducing the scope of discussion to a select few areas. As this occurs, nonstate
actors will be critical for identifying the linkages across sectors and agreements.
Governments are recognizing these connections but are frequently more hampered by existing agency structures or overstretched capacity.

5. International Organizations and Today's Global Issues   The proliferation and
the complexity of issues on the global environmental agenda mentioned above
are not commensurate with the plodding pace of intergovernmental policy making. Almost two decades of international climate discussions have done little to
reduce greenhouse-gas emissions, and similarly there has been no decrease in the
rate of invasive-species introductions over that time. Experience in the field is increasingly informed by processes of adaptive management that adjust management
actions to positive and negative indicators on a regular basis. Such practices are
making some inroads into national policy discussions but are revealing the weakness in the international environmental community's ability to respond in real
time to the latest news and data.

In many cases, nonstate actors are the ones highlighting the inadequacies of the
multilateral system to adequately address the growing number of interrelated environmental issues. The United Nations has taken steps to integrate these voices,
most notably through the Commission on Sustainable Development and its work
with "major groups" (e.g., indigenous peoples, women, youth, and industry).
However, the ability to speak within international fora is not equivalent to being
heard. Disaffected groups that once supported internationalism in the search for
global justice (whether environmental, economic, social, or otherwise) have often
put their resources and efforts into other areas with more tangible impact.

While the United Nations and multilateral diplomacy originated with, and are
dominated by, relations between states, nonstate actors increasingly have the ability to bring new science, perspectives, and significant funding resources to global
issues. This energy is critical for solving global problems, particularly those requiring broader public input and acceptance. Ongoing climate-change discussions have clearly shown a lack of capacity and arguably interest to incorporate

a large number of views, technical input, and links to other environmental and social problems. Systemic change needs to happen around such issues that are major drivers of global change and are intrinsically related to multiple other issues.

One possible way forward is to allow governments to set the broad framework of national responsibilities within multilateral negotiations, while delineating areas requiring technical input, development of methodologies, and proof of concept through implementation of projects. For invasive species, this has happened in a few specific areas under the CBD. However, a happy medium remains to be found on how to balance such requests to nonstate actors with provision of resources and ultimate acceptance of results by the multilateral system. Refining our practice in areas such as invasive species may yield positive experiences that can be mainstreamed in other sectors of international environmental diplomacy.

Not all is doom and gloom, as the international community has shown its ability to act quickly and to collaborate in other sectors, such as public health and the circulation of avian flu and other highly pathogenic viruses. Underpinning that readiness to act is a value structure that rightfully sets a high priority on human life. Until the environmental community can instill a similar imperative to mobilize political will that furthers its own engagement, multilateral diplomacy and its associated international organizations will continue to play catch-up in addressing the impacts and causes of today's major ecological issues.

Invasive species are not a new issue, and we have yet to address fully the significant impacts of those already inside national borders, let alone those that might enter in the future. In our advocacy activities, TNC and GISP therefore look to a broader strategy for engagement that addresses the impacts here and now, while also setting forth the steps to develop the technical guidance and mechanisms that will prevent new introductions in the future. Hopefully, we will be able to bring the rest of the world along with us as well.

References

Burgiel, S. W. 2008. Non-state actors and the Cartagena Protocol on Biosafety. In *NGO diplomacy: The influence of nongovernmental organizations in international environmental negotiations*, ed. M. M. Betsill and E. Corell, 67–100. Cambridge, MA: MIT Press.

Pimentel, D., S. McNair, J. Janecka, J. Wightman, C. Simmonds, C. O'Connell, E. Wong, et al. 2001. "Economic and environmental threats of alien plant, animal and microbe invasions." *Agriculture, Ecosystems and Environment* 84, no. 1: 1–20.

The Private Sector and the Business of Global Governance

Stephen Jordan and Taryn Bird

Nonstate actors have become increasingly prominent in international affairs over the past twenty years as organizations, issues, and channels of communication have multiplied and diversified. Nonstate actors, especially business and nonprofit organizations, operate across the spectrum of multilateral diplomacy and governance issues today. Some of these actors are trying to influence the standards, while others are creating them. Some see themselves in a watchdog role, while others have more of a client-service attitude. Others see themselves as giving voice to constituencies that are "outside" the official diplomatic and governance channels. International organizations like the United Nations and the World Bank have sought to become more inclusive and created more space and openness for the private sector and nonprofit groups to work with them. Below, we offer a private-sector perspective on the increasingly important role of nonstate actors in multilateral diplomacy and global governance.

Roles of the U.S. Chamber of Commerce

The U.S. Chamber of Commerce represents over 3,000 state and local chambers of commerce in the United States, over 100 American chambers overseas, and over 800 business associations, with a total "footprint" of over 3 million members. The U.S. Chamber, with the motto "Fighting for your business," takes its role as an advocate for the business community very seriously, often ranking as the top lobbyist for business on an annual basis. The U.S. Chamber covers a wide range of issues for the business community, including trade, taxes, intellectual property rights, environmental and energy policy, immigration, labor practices, health care, education and workforce development, procurement, regulatory and capital-markets reform, and so forth. Many of these issues have both domestic and international ramifications. The U.S. Chamber does not just invest in direct lobbying but has a significant "bully pulpit" as well. It boasts some of the finest conference facilities in Washington, D.C., and produces periodicals, reports, studies, newsletters, white papers, websites, tool kits, and a host of other communications tools in a variety of media. For all of these reasons, the U.S. Chamber plays a number of roles in multilateral diplomacy and global governance, including the following.

- *Convener:* For example, the Chamber's Energy Institute hosted the Major Economies Business Forum on Energy Security and Climate Change at the U.S. Chamber of Commerce building on September 21 to 22, 2009. This event facilitated a dialogue among global business groups in major developed and developing nations ahead of the UN climate-change negotiations that took place in December 2009 in Copenhagen, Denmark.
- *Facilitator:* The Business Civic Leadership Center (BCLC), a 501(c)(3) affiliate of the U.S. Chamber, often arranges meetings and connections between government agencies and nonprofit organizations and companies that are interested in partnerships for emerging-market development. On April 8, 2010, BCLC partnered with the United Nations to host a meeting to discuss the role of the private sector in addressing the Millennium Development Goals.
- *Advocate:* The U.S. Chamber has rallied support for a number of multilateral trade and investment initiatives, including the North American Free Trade Agreement (NAFTA), the World Trade Organization (WTO), and more specialized initiatives in the realm of intellectual property rights, counterfeiting, dumping, standards, nontariff trade barriers, and others.
- *Information provider:* The U.S. Chamber and its Center for International Private Enterprise affiliate frequently survey companies and stakeholders and conduct other kinds of research regarding corporate attitudes toward multilateral initiatives and global governance, then make this information available through various channels.
- *Negotiator:* U.S. Chamber representatives are frequently consulted about business attitudes regarding particular issues and often work closely with

government officials to reach mutually agreeable outcomes for their respective constituencies.

- *Watchdog:* The U.S. Chamber both monitors agreements and coordinates with American chambers overseas and raises awareness about compliance and noncompliance factors and issues.

The U.S. Chamber has been very effective in conveying its agenda and winning significant policy battles in the past decade—the most notable being the passage of NAFTA and the acceptance of China into the WTO. However, outside of the areas of economics, trade, and investment, the U.S. Chamber has played a much more subdued role in multilateral activities. It did not participate in the development of the UN Global Compact or the formulation of the Millennium Development Goals, and the farther away an issue is from its core business focus, the less involved the U.S. Chamber is.

That being said, the Business Civic Leadership Center, which works with corporate foundations and corporate citizenship programs, has engaged with the United Nations, the World Bank, the Organization for Economic Cooperation and Development, the European Union, the One Campaign, the Global Business Council on HIV/AIDS, Inter Action, the International Red Cross, and a number of other groups on an operational level, particularly around humanitarian crises and disasters such as the 2004 Southeast Asian tsunami, the earthquakes in Peru and China, the Pakistan refugee crisis, and other disasters.

In addition, BCLC works with the local American chambers of commerce and respective U.S. relief agencies following natural disasters. BCLC fosters best-practice sharing among American chambers that have experienced disasters both in the United States and abroad. For example, during an earthquake in Indonesia and a tsunami in Samoa, BCLC hosted a coordination conference call to help connect companies that wanted to give with organizations that were helping to rebuild those countries. The BCLC role was to raise awareness of the humanitarian need and to help connect donors to organizations that were working to meet it. BCLC has also worked with the Caux Roundtable, the Center for International Private Enterprise, and other groups on ethics, trust, and governance-related issues in the international arena.

The Rise of Multisector Multilateralism

Multisector multilateralism—defined as arrangements that incorporate not just public-sector actors from multiple states but also private and nonprofit entities—

is a relatively new phenomenon that did not really start to take off until the 1990s. The most promising area for multisector multilateralism is probably encompassed in the fields of humanitarian assistance and global development. BCLC and the U.S. Chamber worked with broad coalitions of both public- and private-sector actors in the response to the 2004 tsunami. Organizations like the World Health Organization and the World Food Program have created mechanisms for leveraging private and nonprofit expertise and capacities. Programs like the U.S. Agency for International Development's (USAID) Global Development Alliance and the Millennium Challenge Corporation actively promote public-private partnerships in the fields of water purification; refugee assistance; disease prevention, treatment, and mitigation; and other humanitarian and developmental areas.

In fact, numerous public agencies have programs to leverage private-sector investment and international corporate social-responsibility programs. BCLC released a report titled *Partnering for Global Development: The Evolving Links Between Business and International Development Agencies*, which examined how and why public institutions work with private-sector companies to further respective global development programs. While USAID and the German Gesellschaft für Technische Zusammenarbeit were among the first international development agencies to establish solidified programs to work with the private sector, this trend has grown significantly over the past ten years. In addition to the Americans and the Germans, the British, Canadian, Dutch, French, Japanese, Spanish, Swedish, and Swiss aid agencies have begun to develop their private-sector outreach capabilities.

This outreach has also manifested itself from the private-sector side as well. Companies like Chevron, Cisco, IBM, Intel, Microsoft, Shell, and others have produced very positive results in collaboration with development agencies and in their own right. Cisco's Networking Academy has trained thousands of people around the world in information and communications technology. Intel has provided support for teachers in classrooms from Costa Rica to the Philippines. IBM has helped promote entrepreneurship and business development through its SME Toolkit. Microsoft has entered into relationships with the Clinton Global Initiative, Millennium Challenge Corporation, and USAID's Global Development Alliance initiative. The Shell Foundation has created and funded initiatives aimed at promoting African investment, smarter urban planning in developing countries, and rural agribusiness formation. Chevron partnered with USAID to help accelerate the rebuilding of Indonesia in the aftermath of the December 26, 2004, tsunami that rocked Southeast Asia.

There is also significant cause for optimism about this strategy with regard to crime and corruption. Slave trafficking, counterfeiting, money laundering, and corruption have all been tackled by public- and private-sector consortia. The issues that lend themselves to success in this arena have a number of characteristics. They frequently achieve "win-wins," delivering economic and social benefits. They require a broad range of competencies that lend themselves to division of labor. They have a moral clarity, and the ability to gauge progress or failure is easy to measure. The institutional sectors treat each other with mutual respect. CEOs, nonprofit leaders, and government officials are given equal dignity and understand that their perspectives matter and are appreciated by each other. There is a sharp sense of the differentiation of each of the sectors and appreciation that each has a point of view that encompasses aspects that representatives from the other sectors might not see. There is a respect for each other's competencies, as well as a willingness to listen, to share information, and to give participants from the other sectors the benefit of the doubt. The biggest problem with most development projects is that the goals are unclear while the strategies are rigidly defined. The most successful projects have extremely clear goals and objectives, but the implementers are given flexibility about how to achieve them.

We find that attitudes between the three sectors (public, private, and civil society) have changed dramatically over the past two decades. In previous eras there was more of a climate of suspicion. Private-sector actors tended to think of civil society organizations as irresponsible, disorganized, and impractical. Public-sector agencies were viewed as inefficient, bureaucratic, and slow. Conversely, private-sector companies were viewed with suspicion as being greedy, self-interested, and "cold." While these stereotypes can still be found, the past two decades have seen a movement toward a greater willingness to work together and to view each type of organization as having its own constraints and competencies, liabilities and assets. In other words, a more realistic view that gets beyond stereotypes and ideological abstractions is starting to prevail, and this has been very helpful in promoting enhanced communication, coordination, collaboration, and cooperation across the different sectors.

Contributing Factors to Multisector Multilateralism

There are several reasons for the rise of multisectoral multilateralism. The first has to be the extraordinary explosion in national, sectoral, and organizational diversity that has taken place over the last forty years. The *CIA World Factbook* currently lists 265 nations, dependencies, and other politically administrated entities, driven by the fragmentation of the Soviet Union and former Yugoslavia and the creation or expansion of new political arrangements like Mercosur and the European Union.

But the fragmentation of the political sphere is nothing compared to that in the business and civil society sectors. USAID set up its Global Development Alliance office in part because in the 1970s, 70 percent of all overseas capital flows were driven by the public sector, whereas today over 80 percent derives from the private sector. There are currently over 60,000 multinational companies with 800,000 affiliates. In 1980, there were 250,000 registered nonprofits in the United States, and perhaps 1 percent of them had some kind of international profile. Today, there are over 1.5 million nonprofit organizations in the United States alone, and over 30,000 international nonprofits. Nor do these figures take into account the extraordinary rise of the "fourth sector," or "fourth estate"—the media in all of its modern, technology-based applications. Over 1.7 billion people, a quarter of the earth's population, now use the Internet, transcending national borders and mobilizing communication tools in an unprecedented way.

But the sheer numbers of the other sectors would not guarantee them a seat at the table if general attitudes about the role of government and the state had not changed as well. The tipping point in the demise of the myth of the state's universal competence may be debated: Whether Margaret Thatcher and Ronald Reagan ushered it in or it died either with the fall of the Soviet Union in 1990 or when Bill Clinton famously said that "the era of big government is over" is a question for academia. Regardless, the last fifteen years have witnessed an extraordinary opening up by the public sector to nonprofit and private-sector organizations. Numerous UN officials from Kofi Annan and Ban Ki-Moon on down have reflected this change. As one UN official put it at a 2005 conference in Vienna, "Ten years ago, we thought of the private sector as part of the problem. Now we look at it as part of the solution."

It is a question not just of resource flows but of complexity and expertise. Our copy of NAFTA runs close to 1,000 pages, not including appendixes and supplements. There are sections about tariff barriers by industry, nontariff barriers, standards, inspections, arbitration, investments, and so on. Each of these issues has a number of subissues affecting different geographies, industries, and socioeconomic and environmental systems. Even further increasing the complexity, different kinds of trade patterns may have impacts on demographics, immigration, workplace standards, workforce development, infrastructure, traffic congestion, sprawl, pollution, conservation, and water usage, in addition to a number of other unintended and unforeseen consequences.

It is unreasonable to think that any single organization would have the skills and resources to comprehend fully all of the ramifications of linking three sovereign countries comprising more than 450 million people together more closely, and recognition of the need to address complexity and leverage subject matter expertise has increased even more over the last fifteen years since NAFTA was passed. We are seeing a new kind of "concurrent majority" concept coming together as lawmakers and political actors welcome expert perspectives and stakeholder views from businesses, education experts, labor unions, environmentalists, and impacted communities, reflecting the different dimensions of human experience.

Indeed, the separation and differentiation of political, economic, environmental, and social space are other important drivers of multilateralism. Many political boundaries dating back hundreds of years would probably not be the same if they were demarcated now. In the United States, for example, many state boundaries were set by the British during the colonial era and might differ if they were drawn from scratch today. Similar arbitrary boundary examples can be seen in the political boundaries of South America, sub-Saharan Africa, and even within Europe itself. Economically, it makes more sense to address Central America as a market or to look at East Africa as a regional market. Supply chains can stretch globally, with a single T-shirt receiving inputs from four different continents before reaching a fifth to be sold at market. The environment does not respect political boundaries either. The 2004 Southeast Asian tsunami affected eleven different countries. Global climate-change advocates argue that the entire world community needs to change fundamentally in order to reduce the prospect of harmful climactic changes.

A related issue contributing to multilateralism is a growing appreciation that not all states have the same resources available to them. Weak and failed states have incubated terrorism, genocide, narcotics trafficking, human trafficking, and slavery, or they have not been up to the task of dealing with natural disasters, extreme health-care issues, famine, and drought.

What is particularly refreshing about the changes that have enabled multisectoral multilateral efforts to become more effective is that the old state-versus-market debate has been put to rest. As Daniel Yergin (2002) wrote, one can look at the twentieth century as a clash between ideologues who held that the state was the proper vehicle for all social and economic advancement and those who held that unfettered markets were the solution, with the rise and fall of the Soviet Union bookending the era. In multisectoral, multilateral settings, there is no sense that either markets or governments are good or evil; rather there is an evaluation of whether or not they function well or poorly and a capacity to look beyond the deeds of a particular entity when judging the functionality and contributions of the sector as a whole. Just as you would not do away with all government because some have produced a Hitler or Stalin, you would not do away with the private sector because it produced an Enron or a Bernie Madoff. This transition from a normative to a more instrumental approach has been very helpful in terms of improving the capability and capacity of the three sectors to work together.

At the same time, multilateralism has also brought about its share of problems and frustrations. People and advocacy organizations wonder and worry about the efficacy of organizations like the WTO, International Monetary Fund, and World Bank all the time. With over 1,000 codes of conduct and a dizzying array of socially responsible investment screens, social-media watchdog groups, and cross-cultural conditions to contend with, many companies struggle to navigate all of the competing interests and claims. Do multilateral standards represent floors or ceilings, compulsions or aspirations? What can participants in multilateral initiatives do to protect themselves from free riders and nonparticipants? How can small and medium-sized businesses and organizations avoid being compelled to join initiatives that might sap their resources and hurt their competitiveness? On the other hand, how can other groups join various multilateral efforts and keep from being locked out?

A particularly important part of this conversation relates to the legitimacy and authority of these initiatives. Private-sector and civil society organizations are, by definition, not public authorities. As dreams of global government segue to more prosaic concepts of global governance, legitimacy and authority should not be imputed to nonpublic actors just because they help political entities deliver public goods more effectively and efficiently. Their public responsibilities and liabilities are delimited by the boundaries of the projects in which they participate. In this regard, it is important not to overstate the importance of multisectoral multilateral initiatives. They do not substitute for, and are subsidiary to, the sovereign political powers in the geographies in which they operate.

Key Challenges

In the old image of diplomacy up to the Treaty of Versailles, a small group of elegantly dressed men negotiated with each other behind the closed doors of smoke-filled rooms, hammered out positions, and then presented them to the world at large.

The twentieth century saw a steady rise in the professionalization and bureaucratization of diplomatic practice, which was still hierarchical, still relatively elitist, and no doubt heavily informed by the experience of World War II and the Cold War.

The new diplomacy that emerged after the fall of the Soviet Union retained some of the bureaucratic elements of the old diplomacy, such as the interminable length of negotiating rounds, but in many ways, governments opened up the diplomatic process. Multilateral meetings around specific issues like the environment, trade, human rights, and poverty reduction have been increasingly opened up to civil society and private-sector participation. The Group of Eight, the Summit of the Americas, and United Nations–sponsored events have all increasingly welcomed nongovernmental companion events. At the same time, diplomatic initiatives that have tried to keep nonstate actors at bay have found their agendas significantly impacted. The WTO talks of November 1999 will be remembered for "the Battle in Seattle."

So, it seems there have been some trade-offs. Fewer actors participating in more secretive discussions negotiated more quickly, and while sweeping, the agreements they reached were not nearly as complex as those our negotiators reach today. Now, with greater participation and transparency, the result is much more complexity fraught with greater potential for delay.

Sometimes organizations take on a form of self-regulation that serves as a proxy for agreements with state authority behind them. There are over 1,000 "codes of conduct" or variations known as statements of principles or ideals. They range from the UN Global Compact to the Sullivan Principles to industry-specific codes for apparel, manufacturing, extractive industries, and finance. These codes of conduct can impact the way that particular issues, such as supply-chain management, labor, environment, and human rights, are negotiated in state-sponsored forums.

They can also create competing frameworks that address particular stakeholder claims and issues. The Fair Labor Association and the Worldwide Responsible Accredited Production programs both appeal to apparel and footwear manufacturers concerned about global sourcing issues, but they come at these issues from different perspectives. Paradoxically, therefore, the proliferation of nonstate actors in the standard-setting and governance space has led to compliance and stakeholder relationship challenges as entities have tried to balance the competing interests and priorities. On a personal note, we heard stories about Central American factories that had put their overhead lighting systems on pulleys because different inspection groups had different standards regarding the distance lights should be from the workspace.

From the private sector's perspective, working with multilateral and international nongovernmental organizations is still very much a work in progress. Companies often find the bureaucracies of various government agencies to be impenetrable. "I wish there was a one-stop shop or a help desk to help me find the right person" is a refrain we often hear. At one conference we organized at the UN headquarters, a UN representative responded to this exact statement by saying, "Keep trying. You should find the right person by the fifth or sixth call."

Another challenge is the lack of information about who is doing what. Often several multilateral organizations will be working in a given country, but their geographies, duties, and resources will not clearly be understood or defined. This makes it hard for private companies to work with international organizations in diplomatic settings because they do not know how the operations on the ground translate at the policy level and vice versa.

Besides the challenges stemming from bureaucracy, information flow, and institutional efficacy, there is also often a cultural challenge. An old joke says that America and England are divided by the same language, and the same can often be said of companies, government agencies, and nongovernmental organizations. We may think we are saying the same things, but our various organizations' expectations and understandings are often very different after the fact. Many companies wish that their sectoral counterparts had "profit and loss" experience, while government agencies wish that the other sectors had a better understanding of the laws, rules, and regulations they have to conform to, and the nonprofit sector wishes the other two sectors had a better understanding of their particular cause and its ramifications.

The universality of multilateral arrangements is also a cause for concern. Some actors and countries view multilateral arrangements as aspirational, while others with more litigious cultures worry about them as sources of liability. As a result, multilateral arrangements are sometimes seen as causing a competitive disadvantage for companies in more litigious countries. Liability reform in litigious countries would be a key element for enabling the expansion of multilateral arrangements.

In short, the modern iteration of multisectoral multilateralism is a relatively new phenomenon and definitely a work in progress. The U.S. Chamber and the business community writ large are playing key roles in economically related multilateral arrangements, but their influence and participation ebb as the issue becomes less economically related. Increased communication, transparency, and institutional efficacy will continue to enhance the development of this diplomatic approach and prospects for enhanced global governance.

Reference

Yergin, D. 2002. *The commanding height: The battle for the world economy.* New York: Touchstone.

13

Private Foundations and Multilateral Diplomacy

Joan E. Spero

Since their founding at the beginning of the twentieth century, private foundations—nonprofit organizations that have endowments, make grants, and serve the public good—have been active internationally.[1] Andrew Carnegie supported libraries and education in Scotland and the United Kingdom and established the Carnegie Endowment for International Peace to "hasten the abolition of war." John D. Rockefeller funded public health, medicine, and agriculture in Asia, Europe, and Latin America. Early foundation representatives worked with government officials and sometimes established offices abroad. International work accelerated during the Cold War as private foundations established foreign offices, interacted with governments and multilateral organizations, and spent ever larger sums abroad (Rosenberg 2003; Kiger 2008).

In the last two decades, private foundations have grown in number and wealth and become more active around the world. Between 1990 and 2008, the assets of U.S. foundations increased threefold from $143 billion to an estimated $533 billion, and their giving quintupled from $8.7 billion to $45.6 billion. International giving by the largest American foundations rose from $680 million in 1994 to $4.2 billion in 2006, and international grants came to represent 22 percent of all grants by large U.S. foundations.[2] That $4.2 billion is even more significant when compared with total U.S. government overseas development assistance in 2006, which was $22.8 billion.[3]

Due to the size of the economy, a political culture that favors private support for public services, and favorable tax laws, U.S. private foundations have long been the dominant foundation players in number, size, and international activities. Outside the United States, citizens look primarily to government to provide public goods, and tax laws have not been conducive to private foundations. Legal definitions of the word "foundation" and the nature of their activities vary widely around the world, and data about private foundations is sketchy and not comparable across countries.[4] Evidence suggests, however, that foundations are on the rise around the world due to the accumulation of new wealth, changing social norms, financial limits of governments, and changes in laws and policies to promote the private use of wealth for public purposes (OECD 2003, 57–78; European Foundation Center 2005).

Although most non-American foundations focus on local philanthropy, some have a global mission. Japan's Sasakawa Peace Foundation fosters international understanding, exchange, and cooperation. The United Kingdom's Wellcome Trust, which funds biomedical research, supports projects in Africa and Southeast Asia. The Children's Investment Fund Foundation, also based in the United Kingdom, works in Africa and India to improve the lives of poor children living in developing countries. The Oak Foundation, headquartered in Switzerland, funds international programs on topics including climate change, human rights, and women's issues. The Aga Khan Foundation, also headquartered in Switzerland, supports education, health, and economic development globally. Several new foundations based on wealth from oil and natural gas address the problems of Islamic countries. One is the Qatar Foundation, which seeks to build human capital in the Middle East.

While they want to help people in need and alleviate suffering, the objective of large, internationally active foundations is not charity but social change. Their goal is to improve the human condition by addressing the root causes of social, political, and economic problems.[5] Today, for example, foundations are trying to build democracy around the world, transform health care and agriculture in poor countries, advance policies to prevent climate change, and prevent nuclear proliferation. In their work, foundations deal directly or through their grantees with individuals, media, and civil society groups around the world; engage official and unofficial representatives of governments and multilateral organizations; establish partnerships with nongovernmental organizations (NGOs), governments, international organizations, and businesses; and, not infrequently, sit at the policy table with all of these players. Several examples reveal the scope of foundation diplomacy.

Cultural Diplomacy

During the Cold War, the overriding international concerns of the United States and its allies were the physical and economic decimation of Europe and Japan, the collapse of colonial empires, and the threat of Communist expansion. During this period, the international grants of foundations complemented and aligned closely with government policy. Foundations focused on promoting democratic societies and free market economies around the world. One of their principal tools was cultural diplomacy.

In Japan, foundations helped rebuild educational systems, create civil society organizations, promote Western-oriented elites, and generate a network of ties among private citizens and government officials on both sides of the Pacific. This private diplomacy, which continued into the 1970s, helped to shape the democratic and free market orientation of Japan's intellectual and political elites and contributed to close relations between the two countries[6] (Iokibe 2006, 61–98). As the U.S. government helped rebuild Western Europe's economic and political infrastructure, American foundations helped restore its intellectual infrastructure by funding universities, libraries, research centers, and scholars. Throughout the Cold War, foundations financed exchanges among leaders on both sides of the Atlantic in order to build enduring transatlantic networks and counter the threat of Communist expansion (Gemelli and MacLeod 2003). When the Cold War moved to the developing world, foundations turned to Africa, Asia, and Latin America. They funded scholars, teachers, economists, agronomists, and public officials; established universities and research centers; and financed expatriate experts such as agronomists and demographers who worked in developing-country governments (Berman 1981).

While private cultural diplomacy was closely aligned with government efforts, human rights diplomacy at times conflicted with official policy. In the 1970s, for example, the U.S. government supported repressive but anti-Communist regimes in Latin America, while foundations protected scholars, intellectuals, and individuals threatened by their governments and funded human rights organizations that monitored, documented, and publicized human rights abuses (Korey 2007, 25–68). At a time when the U.S. government treated apartheid South Africa as a bulwark against communism, opposed UN resolutions calling for sanctions against the regime, and pursued a policy of "constructive engagement," foundations funded South African academic institutions and civil society organizations that brought court cases, publicized repressive practices, and advocated against discriminatory practices with regulatory and administrative authorities (Golub 2000).

Foundation support for human rights behind the Iron Curtain did align with government policy. In 1978, for example, the Ford Foundation created U.S. Helsinki Watch, a human rights organization that established links with incipient human rights groups in the Soviet Union and Eastern Europe, publicized human rights abuses behind the Iron Curtain, lobbied Western governments to address human rights violations in intergovernmental forums, and participated in meetings of international organizations, especially the Conference on Security and Cooperation in Europe (Korey 2007, 89–117). In the 1980s, George Soros's foundations supported Eastern European intellectuals and dissident groups, including the Polish labor union Solidarity and the Czech human rights group Charta 77 (Kohler 2007d, 156–162).

After the collapse of communism in 1989, American and Western European foundations moved rapidly to support the transition from communism to democracy and free markets in Eastern Europe. Although Western government assistance far outweighed philanthropic funds, government money primarily supported political and economic reforms and was directed through other governments. Foundations, however, focused on building democracy and market economies at the grass roots. American and Western European foundations funded higher education and research in Eastern Europe and helped rebuild or build universities and libraries to train scholars, scientists, experts, and leaders in market economics, Western science and scientific systems, social sciences, and management. Foundations also supported civil society organizations by helping to design the legal infrastructure for nonprofit organizations and providing training, leadership development, and technical assistance for nonprofits (Quigley 1997, 21–23, 97–99; Kohler 2007a, 212–217; Quandt 2002; Kohler 2007b, 228–231).

Today, foundations continue their cultural diplomacy with increasing emphasis on social justice and empowerment of disenfranchised members of society. Foundations provide fellowships and scholarships for individuals in developing countries, particularly those from disadvantaged groups; support universities, academic centers, libraries, research institutes, publications, and academic meetings; fund civil society organizations in former Communist countries, China, the Middle East, South Africa, and Vietnam; and support the development of international human rights law and its application by judges, courts, and law enforcement agencies.

The impact of cultural diplomacy is difficult to evaluate. Programs to build civil society, educate leaders, develop human rights, and empower the disadvantaged are long-term, experimental, risky, and difficult to measure—even in the long term. Some programs have had an impact, and some have not. Success depends far more on local capabilities, values, and initiatives than on external support. Foundations have been criticized for exaggerating their impact, operating through Western intermediaries, not taking into account the long-term sustainability of new civil society organizations, or imposing a Western-centric view of civil society. Yet, the record suggests that foundations played a meaningful supporting role in protecting human rights in Eastern Europe, Latin America, and South Africa and facilitating the transition to democracy and free markets in Eastern Europe.[7]

Partnerships for Global Health

Inadequate access to health care in developing countries is not only a danger to global health but also a barrier to economic development and a threat to global security (WHO 2001; United Nations 2001). Today, health is the largest area of international funding by foundations. A significant share of that funding goes to address the HIV/AIDS crisis—to finance drug and clinical research, pilot programs for the delivery of AIDS treatments and improving public health systems, civil society organizations that advocate on behalf of people living with AIDS, and public education about prevention. Because the cost of health-care programs is so great and health-care delivery in developing countries is so complicated, foundations have frequently leveraged their funding, expertise, and political influence through international public-private partnerships.

Several partnerships address the dearth of research on drugs for use in poor countries. One of the earliest was the International AIDS Vaccine Initiative (IAVI), created by the Rockefeller Foundation in 1996 with support from American and European private and corporate foundations, nonprofit organizations, and the World Bank (IAVI 2006). IAVI began as an effort to raise political awareness about the need for an HIV vaccine targeted at developing countries, where the subtype of the virus is different from that in developed countries. It evolved into an international organization that supports vaccine trials and prepares for the eventual marketing and distribution of an AIDS vaccine in developing countries. Three-quarters of IAVI's budget is devoted to research and development and particularly to clinical trials of HIV/AIDS vaccines, which it conducts and coordinates, working with governments, universities, and pharmaceutical companies. IAVI funders now include many private foundations, governments, international organizations, pharmaceutical companies, and other businesses.

The Global Alliance for Vaccines and Immunization (GAVI), created in 2000, is another partnership of foundations, civil society organizations, businesses, pharmaceutical companies, governments, and international organizations. It aims to bring existing and new vaccines and immunization technologies to developing countries and to strengthen their health and immunization systems. GAVI began by distributing existing vaccines for influenza, yellow fever, and hepatitis and now also supports the development of newer vaccines for pneumonia and diarrhea. If and when an HIV/AIDS vaccine is developed, GAVI will likely play a role in its delivery.

The main goal of the African Comprehensive HIV/AIDS Partnership (ACHAP) is to deliver antiretroviral treatment (ART) in Botswana. In the 1990s, antiretroviral therapy revolutionized AIDS treatment in the developed world. Although it did not cure the disease, ART turned HIV/AIDS into a chronic disease and saved countless lives. Many experts believed that ART could not be implemented in developing countries due to the cost of the medicines and the complexity of administering them. But in the late 1990s, Partners in Health, a Harvard-based organization under the leadership of Dr. Paul Farmer, demonstrated in Haiti that ART could be delivered effectively in a low-resource setting (Kidder 2003).

In 2000, the Gates Foundation, the pharmaceutical company Merck, and the government of Botswana created ACHAP with the goal of eventually providing free ART treatment to all citizens of Botswana, whose president committed his government to the project. Merck agreed to provide drugs at no cost, and Merck and Gates each committed to fund a five-year pilot project.[8] Despite strong support, the partnership had to address numerous problems. Although wealthy by African standards, Botswana had a shortage of health workers and inadequate medical facilities. While the government of Botswana committed to the project at the highest level, responsibility was divided among several ministries, complicating decision making and coordination. Furthermore, the relevant ministries were thinly staffed and inundated with requests from numerous other donors wanting to help. The ACHAP partners did not have experience working together and naturally had different perspectives and expectations. Other donors working on HIV/AIDS in Botswana—the World Bank, the U.S. and other governments, and private donors—had their own perspectives, plans, standards, and requirements and proceeded on their own with little coordination. Thus, ACHAP's original five-year time frame proved too ambitious.

By 2007, ACHAP was functioning effectively. The three partners had developed their policies and procedures more fully and learned how to coordinate with each other. ACHAP had trained 5,000 new health-care workers on ART, and thirty-one ACHAP ART clinics were up and running, providing free treatment to 83,000 people in Botswana. The donors agreed to extend the project until 2009 and to increase their financial support (ACHAP 2007). Nevertheless, the issue of long-term sustainability, particularly long-term sources of funding from the government and international organizations, remained unresolved.

The African Health Care Initiative of the Doris Duke Charitable Foundation represents a different partnership model. The initiative addresses two problems encountered by ACHAP: fragile health systems and the dire shortage of health-care workers in Africa. In the last decade, there has been an unprecedented growth in health funding in Africa—from foundations, NGOs, governments, international organizations, and individuals. Yet, public health systems in Africa—the delivery system for basic health services, drugs, and treatments—are unable to cope with the most basic health needs, let alone epidemics such as HIV.[9]

The Duke Foundation is supporting four pilot projects called Population Health Improvement and Training Partnerships, whose goal is to learn how best to deliver primary, integrated health care in poor countries. The partnerships include various players—universities and academic centers, Western and African scientists, and African public health officials—with a long record of working effectively together. They provide health care in different African countries and research and document their work in order to learn how best to improve the physical and information infrastructure, management tools and systems, and workforce required to deliver health care in severely resource-constrained sites. The objective is that the research findings will eventually be put into practice by governments, international organizations, and private funders.[10]

Transforming Agriculture

Foundations were leaders in economic development long before governments and international organizations. The Green Revolution began in 1941, when U.S. Vice President Henry Wallace told the president of the Rockefeller Foundation about the problems of nutrition in Mexico and suggested that an improvement in crop yields would be the single-most effective contribution to that country's welfare. In 1943, Rockefeller and Mexico's Department of Agriculture signed an agreement for a program to modernize Mexican agriculture that would be run by the foundation. In the coming years, Rockefeller and Mexican scientists developed new disease-resistant, high-yield varieties of corn, wheat, and other crops; designed new farming methods, including the use of fertilizers, insecticides, and irrigation; took these seeds and practices into the field; and trained Mexican agronomists and other professionals to carry on the work (Fosdick 1952, 184–191).

Over the following decades, the Ford and Kellogg foundations became supporters of the Green Revolution's work with governments in Africa, Asia, and Latin America. Foundations financed research, development, and use of new seeds, irrigation, and pesticides that dramatically increased agricultural production in many developing countries and had a significant impact on the economies, societies, and polities of many countries in the developing world. The Green Revolution became a model for foundations working closely with governments and applying scientific methods to solve economic and social problems. The program was criticized later for its technological approach, especially the emphasis on chemical fertilizers and pesticides as well as energy-intensive and irrigation-based farming methods, and for its failure to help the poorest farmers. Nevertheless, it transformed agriculture, dramatically increased food production, improved nutrition, and benefitted many countries in Asia and Latin America (Kohler 2007d, 51–58).

Today, the Gates and Rockefeller foundations are trying to create a second Green Revolution in Africa. Despite its success in Asia and Latin America, the Green Revolution did not transform agriculture in sub-Saharan Africa. Food production there has declined in the last thirty years, and countries that once were food sufficient or food exporters now rely on imports and food aid. The vast majority of Africans depends on subsistence farming, whose productivity is limited by harsh environments, frequent droughts, poor soil quality, diverse soils, environments requiring varied products and seed types, a lack of infrastructure like roads and irrigation, and poorly developed and distorted agricultural markets. Food production has also suffered from the development policies of African governments, which have focused on industrial, not rural, development and from declining international aid for agricultural development (Bell and Milder 2008, 3–5).

The Gates and Rockefeller foundations are now experimenting with a comprehensive approach to this complex set of problems. In 2006, they created and funded the Alliance for a Green Revolution in Africa (AGRA), which aims to increase food production and agricultural sustainability in Africa and to improve the plight of small farmers. The new organization is based in Nairobi, Kenya, and its board is chaired by former UN Secretary-General Kofi Annan. Since its founding, AGRA has received funding from, and cooperated with, private foundations, African and developed-country governments, and multilateral organizations, including the African Development Bank, the Food and Agricultural Organization, the International Fund for Agricultural Development, and the World Food Program.

AGRA targets countries with pressing food-security needs and a supportive national government willing to invest in the program. Its ambitious strategy is to improve the availability and variety of seeds that can produce higher and more stable crop yields; improve soil fertility through better management and access to fertilizers; increase access to, and develop efficient means of using, water; train experts in agricultural research and production; improve markets, transportation, and finance for agricultural inputs and food products; and assure sustainability of agricultural methods. AGRA began with a program designed to develop new seed varieties and stimulate private markets at the local level to distribute the new seeds to farmers (Bell and Milder 2008, 10–14).

It is far too early to judge the impact of AGRA. Supporters praise its integrated approach to agricultural production, cooperation with governments and the United Nations, and emphasis on sustainability, as well as the attention it has brought to the problems of subsistence agriculture in Africa. Critics raise the same concerns that they had about the original Green Revolution: they wonder whether the program will rely on inorganic fertilizers, pesticides, and herbicides as well as hybrid seeds and irrigation. Some critics have expressed concerns about the role of large American foundations and the privatization of foreign aid. Finally, like other foundation programs and partnerships, AGRA must eventually face the question of long-term sustainability: Will its programs be adopted and taken to scale by local governments, foreign funders, or both?

Climate Diplomacy

For nearly two decades, American foundations have funded scientific research, policy development, and public advocacy in an effort to change U.S. policies to address climate change. More recently, foundations have taken these efforts abroad.

One of the key global players has been the Energy Foundation, created in 1991 by the MacArthur, Pew, and Rockefeller foundations with the goal of improving the environment by changing U.S. energy policy and reducing the use of fossil fuels and carbon emissions. In the United States, the Energy Foundation has helped design government standards for renewable energy, efficient appliances, and utility efficiency; developed regulations for vehicle emissions and energy-efficient building codes; and helped build coalitions to press for the implementation of these standards and codes (Wei-Skillern and Berkley Wagonfeld 2008).

In 1999, with support from the Packard Foundation, the Energy Foundation launched the China Sustainable Energy Project (CSEP). Based in Beijing and staffed by Chinese nationals, CSEP aims to bring best international energy and climate practices to China. It supports the design, development, and implementation of new sustainable energy standards and policies by making grants to Chinese research institutes and international NGOs, commissioning research, and convening experts from around the world to inform Chinese researchers, analysts, and government officials. A number of the standards developed by CSEP grantees have been adopted by the central Chinese government, and CSEP is now also working to assure that those policies are put into practice.[11]

U.S. and European foundations are now taking the Energy Foundation model to other countries. In 2008, several foundations launched a global initiative called Climate Works, whose goal is to reduce greenhouse-gas emissions. Climate Works supports the design of, and advocates for, sustainable energy policies in key countries and regions around the world (California Environmental Associates 2007). It operates through a network of international climate-change organizations that share best practices regarding, collaborate on, and coordinate national and international climate strategies and policies.

The Energy Foundation is a member of the network, as is the European Climate Foundation (ECF), created in 2008 by several European foundations, including the Oak, Arcadia, and Children's Investment Fund foundations, as well as the McCall McBain Foundation of Canada. It received both financial and technical support from U.S. foundations, including the Energy and Hewlett foundations. Led and staffed by Europeans, the ECF strives to promote policies that reduce Europe's greenhouse-gas emissions and strengthen European international leadership on mitigating climate change. It supports programs on energy efficiency, power, transportation, climate policies, and diplomacy.

Climate Works has also created an initiative called Project Catalyst to support and advance international climate-change negotiations. The project provides technical support to climate-change advocates in a variety of countries and, through them, to their government officials engaged in international climate-change negotiations. It helps analyze and measure policy options for reducing national carbon emissions and broader standards and requirements needed for an international regime.[12]

Track II Diplomacy

Since the days of Andrew Carnegie, U.S. foundations have supported programs to promote peace and security. Often, that has meant supporting scholars and analysts at academic and public-policy institutions to study international law, crisis prevention, conflict resolution, and arms control.[13] Foundations have also funded and helped to organize private diplomacy. During the Cold War, such diplomacy consisted of meetings of scientists, academics, experts, and government officials on both sides of the Iron Curtain intended to build mutual trust and understanding.

During the Cold War, private diplomacy focused on improving relations between the West and the Communist world. The Pugwash Conferences on Science and World Affairs, which began in 1957, convened distinguished scientists from around the world to discuss, and warn the world about, the threat of nuclear war. Pugwash, which was awarded the Nobel Peace Prize for its contributions to controlling nuclear weapons, was initially sponsored by Cyrus Eaton, a wealthy Canadian industrialist. After 1959, it received support from other foundations, including Ford. The Dartmouth Conferences, which began in 1960, convened American and Soviet intellectuals to discuss options for encouraging peace between the superpowers. The meetings were funded initially by Ford and other foundations and were said to have been encouraged by President Dwight D. Eisenhower. While participants on both sides were private citizens, they regularly briefed their governments on their discussions.

In the 1980s, the Carnegie Corporation supported the U.S. National Academy of Sciences and the Soviet Academy of Sciences in organizing meetings of scientists to study arms control, crisis prevention, conflict resolution, and regional conflicts. Carnegie also sponsored Aspen Institute meetings between members of Congress and the Russian Duma and between U.S. and Soviet military leaders. Through this private diplomacy, Carnegie president David Hamburg met Mikhail Gorbachev, who became the general secretary of the Communist Party of the Soviet Union in 1985. Hamburg, encouraged by members of the Reagan administration wanting to improve relations with the new Russian government, engaged in a two-year private dialogue with Gorbachev that covered issues such as the dangers of nuclear weapons and the need for the United States and the Soviet

Union to engage with each other to prevent nuclear war. Hamburg regularly informed administration officials about the meetings.[14]

Such dialogues have come to be known as Track II diplomacy. Unlike government-to-government, or Track I, diplomacy, Track II involves unofficial and informal contacts among private individuals whose purpose is to open communication, build confidence, or explore solutions in adversarial situations. Track II establishes contact and discussion when governments are in serious conflict or do not have official relations. It provides an alternative diplomatic channel that has no official standing and can make no official commitments but might contribute to problem solving. The participants are usually influential private-sector leaders and often include former government officials acting in a personal capacity. Participants inform their governments about their discussions, and governments may informally support such meetings and use them to learn about the other side, test ideas, or send messages to foreign governments. Sometimes government officials participate in this private diplomacy, then known informally as Track I and 1/2. Track II initiatives are privately funded, may take place over long periods, and may lead nowhere (Zuckerman 2005; Schweitzer 2004; Saunders 2001; Fisher 1997).

Two more recent Track II initiatives have addressed the threat of nuclear proliferation posed by North Korea and Iran. From 2003 to 2005, the Carnegie, MacArthur, and Korea foundations supported a Track II dialogue run by the National Committee on American Foreign Policy that paralleled the six-party official talks addressing North Korea's nuclear program. Its goals were "to explore and build support for cooperative multilateral means of assuring a denuclearized Korean Peninsula, developing an appropriate verification regime, and integrating North Korea into the global community."[15] Former U.S. government officials, American experts, and Carnegie Corporation officials participated in the talks at various points along with North Korean representatives, including that country's ambassador to the United Nations.[16]

A Track II dialogue with Iran, initiated by the Rockefeller Brothers Fund (RBF) under the auspices of the United Nations Association of the United States, met fourteen times between 2002 and 2008. It aimed to open communications; build mutual knowledge, communication, and trust; and develop ideas for improving relations. U.S. participants included the president of RBF, the president of the United Nations Association, who is a former senior State Department official, and other former senior U.S. government officials and arms-control experts. Members of Congress occasionally attended meetings. Iranian representatives included academics and policy advisors from reform groups in Iran. Although the U.S. side met regularly with high-level government officials, the Iranian side did not have similar access to its government, especially after the 2005 election of hard-line president Mahmoud Ahmadinejad.

The agenda of the Iran-U.S. dialogue included the domestic context in each country, regional issues, terrorism, and Iran's nuclear program.[17] In 2006, after extensive negotiation, the group agreed on a joint paper that identified both common ground and areas of difference between the two countries and suggested options for improving the relationship, including government-to-government negotiations. The proposal for official negotiations was resisted by conservatives in both governments, especially after the 2005 election in Iran, and there have been no meetings since 2008.[18]

Foundations and the Global System

Foundations have particular strengths in today's global system. Because they have their own resources, foundations do not have to contend with legislative processes or government bureaucracies. They can take financial risks with their own funds, for example, by supporting new approaches to the HIV/AIDS pandemic and creating new climate-change organizations. They can also take political risks that governments cannot or will not take—supporting human rights and civil society abroad, advocating for an international climate regime, or engaging in dialogue with nuclear proliferators.

Foundations can be more nimble and act more quickly than governments. They moved rapidly into Eastern and Central Europe after 1989 to support scientists and intellectuals and help build civil society. Foundations are also free to take the long view and can be patient funders. They have financed civil society and human rights and battled global warming despite little promise of early returns on their investments. Foundations are able to reach inside foreign societies and polities, where it is often inappropriate, difficult, or impossible for government to go. While governments and international organizations must work through other governments, foundations or their grantees can work directly with civil society organizations and individuals abroad.

Foundations work flexibly with governments, international organizations, nonprofits, businesses, and individuals. Sometimes, they are closely involved with foreign governments, as in Eastern Europe after 1989 or as in Africa with ACHAP today. Sometimes foundations bypass local governments or support groups that challenge or oppose governments, as in Communist Eastern Europe and apartheid South Africa and, more recently, in advocating for HIV/AIDS in South Africa.

Foundations have also experimented with new models of international cooperation. They have created new entities and acted as catalysts for multinational and multisector cooperation on global issues, as they did with IAVI, AGRA, and the Energy Foundation. With Track II diplomacy, they foster and participate in private international networks of experts to address conflicts, build trust, and even advance solutions to thorny problems.

While foundations are increasingly active and important players, they cannot change the world. Most of the problems that they address are difficult, long-term, and resistant to change. Foundation resources cannot match those of governments, international organizations, and businesses. They do not always use their resources effectively, and their programs are not always successful. Even successful programs may not be sustainable over the long term.

However, at their best, foundations can be strategic and can identify gaps, needs, and niches where their resources can contribute to change. They can leverage their funds and knowledge with those of other foundations, governments, and businesses to maximize their impact. Like venture capitalists, foundations can support innovative ideas and solutions to global issues that, if successful, can be adopted by governments, multilateral organizations, or other funders. In the long run, the effectiveness of foundation diplomacy must be measured by its impact on social, economic, and political change.

Conclusion

Foundations are well suited to play a role in global diplomacy in the twenty-first century. Contemporary international issues requiring collective action have expanded to include global challenges, such as addressing health inequities, preventing climate change, and halting nuclear proliferation. Like other civil society organizations, foundations have become increasingly aware of the global nature of many contemporary social, economic, and political problems and have devoted greater attention and resources to international programs. They and other nonstate actors have joined governments and intergovernmental organizations as funders, policy makers, advocates, and diplomats.

As we have seen, foundations use various forms of private diplomacy to address global problems: interacting directly with civil society organizations in other countries, forming partnerships and cooperating with governments and international organizations, and engaging in bilateral or multilateral networks of private and sometimes public individuals. Foundations are helping to establish new global norms, devise and advocate for new national and multilateral policies and regimes, create new public-private alliances and networks to address complex global issues, conduct bilateral dialogues, and thereby influence the context for traditional multilateral diplomacy. Thus, private foundations have become part of the dense web of globalization and of efforts to govern that globalization. The road to more effective and democratic global governance is long and difficult and will involve many traditional and nontraditional players. Foundations have the potential to make important contributions to the journey.

Notes

1. The definition used here is based on U.S. law. However, the term *foundation* is commonly used for many types of organizations. Some organizations called foundations such as the Carter, Clinton, and United Nations foundations have a different legal status in the United States as "public charities." They and many of their counterparts abroad make grants and serve the public good, but they raise funds from other sources, including the public, private foundations, corporations, or governments and do not rely on their own endowments. Corporations also have "foundations" that are usually not endowed and are funded from company resources.

2. These are Foundation Center statistics. Major private American foundations active abroad include Carnegie, Ford, Gates, Hewlett, Kellogg, MacArthur, Moore, Mellon, Mott, Open Society Institute (Soros), Packard, Rockefeller, and Rockefeller Brothers Fund.

3. These are Organization for Economic Cooperation and Development, Development Assistance Committee statistics.

4. Private giving has deep roots around the world, reflecting different local religions, cultures, and histories. However, the organized private foundation that focuses on social change has most often been associated with American foundations. Public law and policy in Europe (with the exception of the United Kingdom) and Japan, for example, have not favored private foundations, and for the most part, those foundations that existed there have only rarely engaged in international work. See L. Tayart de Borms et al. (2001) and OECD (2003, 30–36, 57–74).

5. For a history of the concepts of charity and philanthropy, see R. A. Gross (2003).

6. This effort was due, in part, to John Foster Dulles, the principal negotiator of the peace treaty between the United States and Japan, a member of the Rockefeller Foundation board, and a future secretary of state. In 1951, Dulles asked John D. Rockefeller III to visit Japan to study what private philanthropy could do to establish close relations between the two countries.

7. For the case in favor of funding for civil society, see M. Edwards (2008).

8. Approved by the government in 2001, the plan laid out a five-year agenda for implementing an ART program, including priority groups to receive treatment,

recruitment and training of health-care workers and other staff, creation of clinics and laboratories, public education, monitoring, evaluation, and operations research.

9. See, for example, L. Garrett (2007).

10. This information is based on Doris Duke Charitable Foundation papers and interviews with foundation staff.

11. See "Energy in China: The Myths, Reality, and Challenges," 2007 Energy Foundation Annual Report, Energy Foundation, www.ef.org/documents/2007_EF _Annual_Report.pdf.

12. Discussion of Catalyst, Climate Works, CSEP, the Energy Foundation, and the European Climate Foundation is also based on interviews with Andrew Bowman, director of climate change, Doris Duke Charitable Foundation; Eric Heitz, executive director, Energy Foundation; Paul Brest, president, Hewlett Foundation; Susan Bell, vice president, Hewlett Foundation; Carol Larsen, president, Packard Foundation; and Bradford Smith, president, Foundation Center, and former president of Oak Foundation.

13. During the Cold War, foundations funded studies of Cold War conflicts, military strategy, arms control, and foreign policy. They also helped create regional area studies at American universities to prepare a new generation of foreign policy experts and leaders. Since the end of the Cold War, foundations have funded studies of new security threats: nuclear proliferation, ethnic and religious conflict, biological and chemical weapons, bioterrorism and cyberterrorism, and arms races in space.

14. This information is based on an interview with and the papers of David Hamburg.

15. See www.ncafp.org/projects_northeastasia.html. With support from the Ford, Luce, and MacArthur foundations, the National Committee on American Foreign Policy also runs Track II dialogues among Americans, Chinese, and Taiwanese in an effort to ease tensions across the Taiwan Strait.

16. This information is based on an interview with Wendy Sherman, a dialogue participant. See "The U.S. and North Korea: A Track II Meeting Brings Results," *Carnegie Reporter* 3, no. 3 (fall 2005): 11.

17. This information is based on an interview with Stephen Heintz and Rockefeller Brothers Fund documents.

18. In 2008, the American side went public with its proposal for addressing the U.S.-Iran nuclear standoff. Coauthored by dialogue members and endorsed by former senior officials in both Democratic and Republican administrations, the proposal analyzed Iran's nuclear program, offered a new multilateral approach to solving the nuclear problem, and proposed an agenda for a new American policy of engagement with Iran (Luers, Pickering, and Walsh 2008).

References

African Comprehensive HIV/AIDS Partnership (ACHAP). 2007. Annual report. ACHAP. www.achap.org/doc/annual_reports/achap_annual_report_2007.pdf.

Bell, D. E., and B. Milder. 2008. Alliance for a green revolution in Africa (AGRA). Case Study, Product 509007. Cambridge, MA: Harvard Business School Publishing.

Berman, E. H. 1981. *The influence of the Carnegie, Ford, and Rockefeller foundations on American foreign policy: The ideology of philanthropy.* Albany: State University of New York Press.

California Environmental Associates. 2007. *Design to win: Philanthropy's role in the fight against global warming.* San Francisco, CA: California Environmental Associates. Available at www.ceaconsulting.com/CaseStudyFiles/DesignToWin_FinalReport.pdf.

Edwards, M. 2008. *Just another emperor? The myths and realities of philanthrocapitalism.* New York: Demos.

European Foundation Center. 2005. Foundation facts and figures across the EU—associating private wealth for public benefit. European Foundation Center. April. www.efc.be/NewsKnowledge/Documents/Facts_Figs_publication.pdf.

Fisher, R. J. 1997. *Interactive conflict resolution.* Syracuse, NY: Syracuse University Press.

Fleischman, J., J. S. Kohler, and S. Schindler. 2007. *Casebook for the foundation: A great American secret.* New York: Public Affairs.

Fosdick, R. B. 1952. *The story of the Rockefeller foundation.* New York: Harper & Brothers.

Friedman, L. J., and M. D. McGarvie, eds. 2003. *Charity, philanthropy, and civility in American history.* Cambridge: Cambridge University Press.

Garrett, L. 2007. The challenge of global health. *Foreign Affairs* 86, no. 1: 14–38.

Gemelli, G., and R. MacLeod, eds. 2003. *American foundations in Europe: Grant-giving policies, cultural diplomacy, and trans-Atlantic relations, 1920–1980.* Brussels and New York: P. I. E.–Peter Lang.

Golub, S. 2000. Battling apartheid, building a new South Africa. In *Many roads to justice: The law-related work of Ford foundation grantees around the world*, ed. M. McClymont and S. Golub, 19–54. New York: Ford Foundation.

Gross, R. A. 2003. Giving in America: From charity to philanthropy. In *Charity, philanthropy, and civility in American history*, ed. L. J. Friedman and M. D. McGarvie, 29–48. Cambridge: Cambridge University Press.

International AIDS Vaccine Initiative (IAVI). 2006. *Imagining a world without AIDS: A history of the International AIDS Vaccine Initiative.* IAVI. www.iavi.org/Lists/IAVIPublications/attachments/824ab6b0-57f4-44ac-a844-26a7b95cf5e8/IAVI_Ten_Year_Timeline_2006_ENG.pdf.

Iokibe, M. 2006. U.S.-Japan intellectual exchange: The relationship between government and private foundations. In *Philanthropy and reconciliation: Rebuilding postwar U.S.-Japan relations*, ed. T. Yamamoto, A. Iriye, and M. Iokibe, 61–98. Tokyo: Japan Center for International Exchange.

Kidder, T. 2003. *Mountain beyond mountain: The quest of Dr. Paul Farmer, the man who would cure the world.* New York: Random House.

Kiger, J. C. 2008. *Philanthropists and foundation globalization.* New Brunswick, NJ: Transaction Publishers.

Kohler, S. 2007a. Central European University. In *Casebook for the foundation: A great American secret*, ed. J. Fleischman, J. S. Kohler, and S. Schindler, 215–216. New York: Public Affairs.

———. 2007b. International Science Foundation. In *Casebook for the foundation: A great American secret*, ed. J. Fleischman, J. S. Kohler, and S. Schindler, 228–230. New York: Public Affairs.

———. 2007c. Support of democratization and civil societies in central and eastern Europe: Open Society Institute and the Soros Foundation Network. In *Casebook for the foundation: A great American secret*, ed. J. Fleischman, J. S. Kohler, and S. Schindler, 156–161. New York: Public Affairs.

———. 2007d. The green revolution. In *Casebook for the foundation: A great American secret*, ed. J. Fleischman, J. S. Kohler, and S. Schindler, 51–57. New York: Public Affairs.

Korey, W. 2007. *Taking on the world's repressive regimes: The Ford Foundation's international human rights policies and practices.* New York: Palgrave Macmillan.

Luers, W., T. R. Pickering, and J. Walsh. 2008. A solution for the U.S.-Iran nuclear standoff. *New York Review of Books* 55, no. 4 (March 20): 19–22.

McClymont, M., and S. Golub, eds. 2000. *Many roads to justice: The law-related work of Ford Foundation grantees around the world.* New York: Ford Foundation.

Organization for Economic Cooperation and Development (OECD), Development Assistance Committee. 2003. Philanthropic foundations and development cooperation. *DAC Journal* 4, no. 3. www.oecd.org/dataoecd/23/4/22272860.pdf.

Quandt, R. E. 2002. *The changing landscape in eastern Europe: A personal perspective on philanthropy and technology transfer.* Oxford: Oxford University Press.

Quigley, K. F. F. 1997. *For democracy's sake.* Baltimore: John Hopkins University Press.

Rosenberg, E. S. 2003. Missions to the world: Philanthropy abroad. In *Charity, philanthropy, and civility in American history*, ed. L. J. Friedman and M. D. McGarvie, 241–257. Cambridge: Cambridge University Press.

Saunders, H. H. 2001. *A public peace process: Sustained dialogue to transform racial and ethnic conflicts.* New York: Palgrave Macmillan.

Schweitzer, G. E. 2004. *Scientists, engineers and track II diplomacy: A half-century of U.S.-Russian inter-academy cooperation.* Washington, DC: National Research Council of the National Academies.

Tayart de Borms, L., A. Schluter, V. Then, and P. Walkenhorst, eds. 2001. *Foundations in Europe: Society, management, and law.* London: Directory of Social Change.

United Nations. 2001. Declaration of commitment on HIV/AIDS. General Assembly Resolution A/Res/S-26/2. United Nations. www.un.org/ga/aids/docs/aress262.pdf.

Wei-Skillern, J., and A. Berkley Wagonfeld. 2008. The Energy Foundation. Case Study, Product 308078. Cambridge, MA: Harvard Business School Publishing.

World Health Organization (WHO). 2001. *Macroeconomics and health: Investing in health for economic development.* Report of the Commission on Macroeconomics and Health. Geneva: WHO.

Yamamoto, T., A. Iriye, and M. Iokibe, eds. 2006. *Philanthropy and reconciliation: Rebuilding postwar U.S.-Japan relations.* Tokyo: Japan Center for International Exchange.

Zuckerman, M. J. 2005. Track II diplomacy: Can unofficial talks avert disaster. *Carnegie Reporter* 3, no. 3: 3–11.

PART FOUR
The Role of International Secretariats

Introduction

Earl Sullivan

In many ways the arena for international politics has changed dramatically over the last century, and these changes have had a major impact on the way diplomacy is conducted. The number of states has increased markedly, although states are not the only significant actors in international affairs, as multinational actors of many kinds have increased in number as well as in political salience; more weapons of war have been created, and their ability to kill and maim has increased; the ability to travel and to communicate across borders has transformed the ability of leaders as well as of ordinary citizens to react more rapidly to events anywhere and at any time; ideas, as well as diseases, can move relatively rapidly and unimpeded across borders in ways that were not possible until recently; and the number and importance of international organizations (IOs) and other venues for multilateral diplomacy have increased to an astonishing degree.

In light of all this change, it is remarkable that most of the major issues regarding the secretariats of IOs were identified early in the history of IOs and have remained constant over many decades. The first secretary-general of the League of Nations, Sir Eric Drummond, established one paradigm for subsequent secretariats: He was "a British civil servant by temperament and conviction . . . [and was] efficient and unobtrusive" (Claude 1971, 193). By contrast, Albert Thomas, the first director of the International Labor Office, presented an example of "articulate and dynamic leadership in matters of policy" (Claude 1971, 194). Thus, from the early days of the twentieth century until now, one of the major questions for the leaders of IOs and the staff of their secretariats has been clear: Is their role primarily to manage the affairs of the organization, or are they also expected to provide leadership? The covenant of the League of Nations said very little about the secretariat—see Article 6—and the implication was clear: The secretary-general and his staff were expected to function as efficient civil servants and managers of the collective will of the organization. The UN Charter was more elaborate and also specified in Article 97 that the secretary-general "shall be the chief administrative officer of the Organization." However, the charter did envisage a more activist role for the secretary-general with Article 99, which authorizes the secretary-general to "bring to the attention of the Security Council any matter which in his opinion may threaten the maintenance of international peace and security." While the charter implied that the secretary-general could act independently of an a priori declaration of policy by the Security Council, history demonstrates that the major powers did not always support an activist secretary-general, and the chief executive officer of the organization was in an exceptionally precarious position when he perceived that a threat to the peace emanated from a great power.

However one views this issue, one thing is clear. As Inis L. Claude Jr. pointed out many years ago, the secretariat staff of an IO "*is* the organization" (1971, 191). The secretariat, and particularly the secretary-general or other top executive, is the chief representative and leading symbol of the organization itself. Consequently, criticism of the organization typically takes the form of criticism of the secretary-general or other chief executive of the institution. There are three core issues to what Claude called "the problem of the international secretariat": (1) bureaucratic efficiency, (2) allegiance, and (3) political initiative (1971, 199–211). Typically, the secretariat of an organization consists of officials from many nations, perhaps containing citizens of all member states. Can such a group function efficiently? Where does its members' allegiance lie, to the organization or to their home state or territory? Finally, can the secretariat, particularly the chief executive, however named, exercise leadership or is his or her role more that of a "secretary" than that of a "general" (Chesterman 2007)?

A major problem facing IOs such as the United Nations and other institutions discussed in this book is "the contradiction between national sovereignty and the effectiveness of an international organization" (Morgenthau 1973, 467). States seldom, if ever, are willing to yield enough independence and authority to an international organization to enable it to address effectively the issues it has been created to address. Furthermore, as the secretary-general or other top executive of the organization is charged with implementing its policies, opposition to the policy typically takes the form of opposition to the secretariat and its leadership. States that object to an IO's actions have historically thwarted the policies of that organization in a number of ways, including by withdrawing, refusing to pay dues, supporting alternative leadership, and taking other actions that need not be repeated here. (For a discussion of some of the early efforts in this regard, see Morgenthau 1973, 455–473.)

In an extremely statecentric vision of international relations, international organizations are merely venues or platforms for the actions of states in the international arena. A more realistic perspective, however, recognizes that IOs are actors in international relations, often with considerable freedom of action. Ultranationalists may abhor this fact, while many internationalists may celebrate it, but regardless of the ideological perspective one adopts, IOs are major actors in international politics in the contemporary world, and those who lead them are politically significant in their own right. Leading officials of contemporary IOs, especially the chief executive officers, often have a significant impact on the policies and practices of states in addition to the impact they have on the policies and practices of the organizations they lead. International organizations function both as important venues for, and meaningful actors in, international relations. The political salience of both roles—venue and actor—is likely to increase as states find that the problems they must address cannot be solved by states acting alone. International organizations and their leaders are thus likely to be more visible and more relevant in international relations, not less so, and the quality of leadership in these increasingly essential institutions will likely become even more important than has been the case in the past.

Many international organizations have been discussed in this book, and this part of the book will focus on a selected sample of them. John Mathiason, a leading authority on international secretariats, provides an overview of the status of the issues facing the leaders of IOs in the early twenty-first century. In a highly focused, yet wide ranging chapter, "International Secretariats: Diplomats or Civil Servants?" he makes it abundantly clear that the secretariats of the major IOs serve as international civil servants and as diplomats in their own right. Drawing on examples from such organizations as the World Trade Organization, the World Health Organization (WHO), the Office of the United Nations High Commissioner for Refugees, the International Atomic Energy Agency (IAEA), the United Nations Relief and Works Agency, the World Bank, and others, he demonstrates that international secretariats are engaged in three major functional areas: (1) regime creation, (2) norm enforcement, and (3) direct provision of services. As he points out, as international secretariats participate in the process of regime creation, they "are political actors in the process with somewhat more independence than state negotiators, who are constrained by national positions." This is also true for their roles in norm enforcement and especially in the critical role of providing services to people in various countries, including places such as Haiti, Kosovo, Liberia, and Timor Leste, in which the United Nations itself has taken over the responsibility for providing services that under normal circumstances would only be provided by governments.

The record makes clear that international secretariats are able to take initiatives in dealing with many critical issues, and they are not merely functioning as civil servants carrying out the orders and collective will of the members of the various organizations they lead. Conventional analysts posed a false dichotomy, asking if international secretariats were *either* diplomats *or* civil servants: The leaders of IOs are both diplomats and international civil servants, and there is no essential contradiction in terms involved as they perform their roles.

Ramesh Thakur's chapter, "Multilateral Diplomacy and the United Nations: Global Governance Venue or Actor," takes up the issue of whether international organizations are merely venues for state action or are actors in their own right. Like John Mathiason, he demonstrates that this is a false, and indeed artificial, distinction that prevents us from developing an accurate understanding of the roles and functions of IOs in contemporary international politics. International organizations are simultaneously actors and venues for action, and the two roles are mutually supportive rather than contradictory. This very data-rich chapter discusses a number of important topics, but from a substantive perspective; the central themes are illustrated by detailed discussions of arms control and disarmament and an especially rich and nuanced analysis of the genesis of the responsibility to protect norm, typically referred to as R2P. It is worth noting that, while in this chapter Thakur serves as an analyst, he was also a participant as a secretariat official in dealing with the issues he discusses. This is true especially of R2P, and his observations as a participant make this chapter particularly worthy of careful study.

As one of the purposes of this introduction is to encourage readers to study the chapters in this part of the book carefully, I will not elaborate a great deal in describing them here. However, it is important to explain what R2P is and is not. The responsibility to protect can be distilled down to two basic principles:

A. State sovereignty implies responsibility, and the primary responsibility for the protection of its people lies with the state itself.

B. Where a population is suffering serious harm, as a result of internal war, insurgency, repression or state failure, and the state in question is unwilling or unable to halt or avert it, the principle of non-intervention yields to the international responsibility to protect. (Center for NTS Studies 2009, 2)

R2P does not authorize powerful states of the global North to engage in unilateral humanitarian intervention in troubled states of the global South.

The core idea of the R2P, according to [Gareth] Evans, [one of the principal actors in the creation of the R2P norm] is simple: It is to turn the notion of the "right to intervene" upside down, and emphasize instead the responsibility of all states to protect their own people from mass atrocity crimes, as well as to help others to do so. The focus is thus on protection and not intervention, and we should look at the whole issue from the perspective of the victims. Further, the "responsibility" in question is that of preventing mass atrocities, with the question of reaction through various means arising only if prevention failed. The reflexive response towards mass atrocity crimes should not be one of whether states and the international community should act—but rather how and when to prevent or respond, using what means, and by whom. (Center for NTS Studies 2009, 6)

In "Multilateral Diplomacy and the United Nations," Ramesh Thakur demonstrates how the R2P norm was developed, and I will leave it to him to tell that important story.

One of the most interesting aspects of Thakur's chapter is his use of three novel concepts drawn from the work of Margaret Joan Anstee. Referring to the record of diplomacy in the broad issue of arms control and disarmament, he argues that the United Nations has functioned as

- a funnel for processing ideas into norms and policies and for transmitting information from national sources to the international community
- a forum for discussion and negotiation of common international positions, policies, conventions, and regimes
- a font of international legitimacy for the authoritative promulgation of international norms, appeals for adherence to global norms and regimes, and coercive measures to enforce compliance with them

Most analysts will probably conclude that these three concepts can also be applied to the record of the United Nations, as well as of several other international organizations in many fields, not just arms control and disarmament. Furthermore, as Thakur makes clear, the role of the secretariat has been central to the process, as the United Nations' role as funnel, forum, and font has been played out. While serving as a forum is a traditional role for IOs, the twin roles of funnel and font are highly suggestive of an activist role as a significant and somewhat independent political actor for IOs and their secretariats.

In "The Diplomacy of Specialized Agencies: High Food Prices and the World Food Program," Hank-Jan Brinkman and Masood Hyder deal with one of the most important topics addressed by multilateral diplomacy in recent years. The substantive focus of this chapter is on the world's response to the global food crisis created by rapidly rising food prices in the early years of the twenty-first century. As both authors participated in the debates that took place, their analysis of the process is especially informative and worthwhile.

While the United Nations is the subject of most books and articles dealing with international organizations, much of the work of multilateral diplomacy takes place in specialized, or functional, agencies such as the World Health Organization, the Food and Agricultural Organization, the International Labor Organization, and other similar institutions. David Mitrany, a Romanian scholar-activist, developed the theory behind what came to be known as functionalism in the 1940s. As he stated in his most seminal work, "The problem of our time is not how to keep the nations peacefully apart but how to bring them actively together" (1943, 28). Mitrany envisaged the development of a growing network of specialized IOs that would concentrate on what he thought of as the welfare functions of states, particularly those that states acting alone cannot address satisfactorily. To him, these functional agencies should be thought of as nonpolitical and could therefore serve as forums for all states, friends and foes alike, to work together to solve specific problems common to them all.[1]

This is not the place for a full-blown exposition of the theory of functionalism, but the record of global politics in recent decades illustrates that contemporary international politics leaves very little room for nonpolitical action. Indeed, virtually everything has been politicized to some degree. However, specialized international agencies have played growing and important roles in international affairs and the theory of functionalism "has the great merit of appealing both to humanitarian idealism and to national self-interest" (Claude 1971, 386). States can address specific global issues such as the food crisis or pandemics of flu or other diseases through the medium of international organizations and at the same time claim to be serving the national interest. It is not surprising, therefore, that functional IOs that specialize in specific global issues have grown in number and significance in the years since Mitrany developed his theories. One of the most successful of such institutions is the World Food Program (WFP), which is the principal IO discussed by Brinkman and Hyder.

As demonstrated by Ramesh Thakur, the heads of IOs and the secretariat officials that serve with them play an important, and often proactive, role in developing and implementing policies and programs even in such highly sensitive arenas as arms control, disarmament, and the development and legitimacy of the R2P norm. It should come as no surprise to learn, therefore, that similar officials have an even greater role to play in creating policies and programs in the functional arenas of global politics and diplomacy, especially in times of crisis, when IOs such as the WFP are deemed essential actors in the efforts to ameliorate the effects of a calamity such as the global food crisis.

In addition to participating in summit meetings and in discussions in a variety of international forums, secretariat officials from the WFP also engaged in bilateral diplomacy between individual states and the WFP. These diplomatic ventures typically focused on issues related to the implementation of decisions and recommendations made in multilateral venues, and, as the authors point out, "bilateral diplomacy is quieter, more focused and more businesslike" than the diplomacy that usually occurs in traditional multilateral sessions. Similarly, diplomacy takes place between international agencies, both public and nongovernmental, on topics dealing both with the development of principles and norms and with the implementation of decisions taken in multilateral venues.

Secretariat officials also engage in public diplomacy. During the global food crisis, for example, "Josette Sheeran, the Executive Director of WFP, did a remarkable job of calling attention to the plight of the hungry." She was seen on television in the United States and around the world, as well as in videos on YouTube and on blogs; she testified in legislative bodies and in general was a very public presence in the global debate on the need for urgent action to address a serious global crisis. In so doing she did not merely represent the WFP and present the case for policies and procedures that had already been settled by the membership. She also served as an advocate for specific policies and actions that had yet to be decided. This is not the role of a traditional civil servant, quietly carrying out the decisions taken by states in various domestic and multilateral settings.

As important as public diplomacy by the WFP may have been, the success of the organization in this field was largely explained by its well-founded reputation for what Brinkman and Hyder call "operational excellence." The WFP and its staff developed a strong reputation for credibility. As a result, when they said there was a crisis, they were believed; when they made proposals for addressing it, they had a ready audience. Although WFP diplomacy did not carry the day on all issues, the secretariat officials who participated in the public and more traditional diplomatic venues were respected participants, in many ways equal in status to their counterparts who represented states.

Brinkman and Hyder make a compelling case on behalf of the diplomatic efficacy of the WFP in the world food crisis of the early years of the twenty-first century. However, in the process of doing so, they also acknowledge that the commendable effort in terms of interagency collaboration has led to quite modest results, in terms of fund-raising, policy reforms, joint actions, or improving assistance to smallholder farmers. Nevertheless, their realistic, honest, and detailed assessment of the events illustrates clearly that international secretariats are international diplomats as well as international civil servants. Arguments to the contrary are more ideological than based on facts and empirical reality and should be recognized as such.

It is clear from the record that public international organizations serve as both platforms and venues for multilateral diplomacy and as actors in their own right. Similarly, the top executives and secretariats of these organizations are actively engaged in diplomacy, sometimes with more flexibility in negotiations than diplomats representing states. They are active participants in regime creation and norm enforcement and, perhaps most notably, in the direct provision of services in times of emergencies and especially when they are invited into failed states to act *as if* the IO is the government of the state in question.

At the outset of this introduction, I wrote that "it is remarkable that most of the major issues regarding the secretariats of international organizations were identified early in the history of IOs and have remained constant over many decades." Some of the questions that have animated commentary on this subject are no longer as valid as they once were. For example, it is abundantly clear that the old issue of whether the secretary-general or other top executive of international organizations is more a secretary than a general should finally be put to rest. It is not an either-or situation. Top executives of public IOs function as both leaders and managers, as civil servants and high-level diplomats, and there is no inherent contradiction in having them perform both roles. Indeed, they must excel in both capacities if they are to succeed.

If the leaders of such institutions were primarily civil servants, then technical skills would be the primary requirements for filling most positions. However, as Boutros Boutros-Ghali, former secretary-general of the United Nations, argued some years ago, diplomatic skills are crucial in these positions (1995, 14). Although he was referring specifically to the necessity of recruiting people for senior positions in preventive diplomacy and other high-stakes activities who have both technical background and high-level diplomatic skills, the point is likely to be valid in most, if not all other fields. For example, a talented physician who heads the WHO will fail unless he or she also possesses considerable diplomatic finesse.

In the early years of the Cold War, the leaders of international organizations had to be very careful about what they said and did on matters of public policy, and it was dangerous for them to disagree in a serious way with the positions taken by leading states, especially the two superpowers. The examples of the first two secretaries-general of the United Nations are illustrative of this point. Trygve Lie audaciously opposed what was commonly regarded as aggression by a super-power in Korea and "soon found himself encumbered by the excessively affec-tionate embrace of the United States, which would not recognize the right of his term to expire, and the inexorable hostility of the Soviet Union, which would not recognize his continued existence" (Claude 1971, 208). When his eventual suc-cessor as secretary-general, Dag Hammarskjöld of Sweden, opposed Soviet policies and actions in the Congo, the leaders of the Soviet Union at the time argued that he was not acting properly as an objective international civil servant but was a tool of the West. His death, under suspicious circumstances and possibly at the hands of the Soviet Union, averted a crisis of leadership but also served as a potent reminder to subsequent leaders of the United Nations and other IOs that taking positions favored by the majority, but strongly opposed by a superpower, was likely to put them and the organizations they led in great danger. There is some evidence, however, that this potent lesson from the past may no longer apply in all cases in the early years of the twenty-first century, at least for leaders of some of the technical agencies.

Many international organizations, perhaps especially those of a technical na-ture, have a reputation for what Brinkman and Hyder call "operational excel-lence," and this provides their leaders the ability to participate in debates about controversial global issues with a great deal of confidence that their views will be respected, even if they disagree with the positions and preferences of major states. For example, in times of financial crisis, the views of the heads of the International Monetary Fund and the World Bank are listened to carefully, and their words are often regarded as authoritative, supported by the reputation for independent and accurate analysis of the organizations they lead. Furthermore, when they speak publicly, even on sensitive topics, they do so not as representatives of the country whose nationality they hold; indeed, they sometimes speak at variance to the views of their own countries. Similarly, the views of the director-general of the World Health Organization and of other senior officials at WHO are often sought out in times of epidemic or pandemic diseases such as H1N1, and these individuals are not averse to providing advice on how governments should act in such circumstances. Perhaps the critical diplomatic role of secretariats in IOs is best illustrated by the case of Mohamed El Baradei, the director-general of the International Atomic Energy Agency. As John Mathiason has pointed out in his chapter on international secretariats, in 2002, El Baradei, speaking on behalf of the IAEA, disputed the presence of weapons of mass destruction in Iraq, directly contradicting the strongly held position of the U.S. government. Hell hath no fury like a superpower scorned, and as a direct result of his refusal to support the position of the White House, the George W. Bush administration attempted to prevent El Baradei from being reelected as director-general of the IAEA. The campaign against El Baradei by the world's leading power failed. As Mathiason states, the United States "was the only country to do so and had to accept El Baradei's reelection." The fact that the leader of an IO could publicly stand against the adamant wishes of the most powerful country in the world on an issue of major importance provides a telling example of how far we have come since the days of the early years of the League of Nations and the United Nations. It also serves as an important indicator of the growing salience of international technical organizations in contemporary international politics, based on the reputation for "operational excellence" they have earned.

Note

1. To cite two simple examples, no state acting alone, no matter how powerful, can insure that there will be a fully functional global system for insuring that global telecommunications will function effectively or that the mail can be delivered across all borders. Thus, the International Telecommunication Union (ITU) and the Universal Postal Union (UPU) were created.

References

Boutros-Ghali, B. 1995. *An agenda for peace*. New York: United Nations.
Center for NTS Studies. 2009. The responsibility to protect: Conceptual misunderstandings and challenges of application. NTS Alert. April 1. www.rsis.edu.sg/nts/resources/nts-alert/NTS%20Alert%20April%200109.pdf.
Chesterman, S., ed. 2007. *Secretary or general? The UN secretary-general in world politics*. Cambridge: Cambridge University Press.
Claude, I. L. 1971. *Swords into plowshares: The problems and progress of international organization*. 4th ed. New York: Random House.
Mitrany, D. 1943. *A working peace system*. Chicago: Quadrangle Books.
Morgenthau, H. J. 1973. *Politics among nations: The struggle for power and peace*. 5th ed. New York: Alfred A. Knopf.

14

International Secretariats:
Diplomats or Civil Servants?

John Mathiason

The answer to the question posed in the title of the chapter is, as is often the case with international organizations, yes. International secretariats are both. They are clearly civil servants, whose rules, regulations, and organizational cultures are based on the classic American, British, and French civil services. But they are also diplomats because, in order to function effectively, they must navigate a complex environment in which an ability to negotiate is critical and an avoidance of conflict is essential.

When the current international system was established over sixty years ago, the role of secretariats was seen as essentially to support intergovernmental negotiations. Now, in the early twenty-first century, the exponential growth of an international public sector has changed that role into one of management, but in a context that civil servants of the former times would have found astounding.

Functions to Be Performed
by International Secretariats

It can be argued that international secretariats perform three functions (Mathiason 2007a). Functional analysis, which is derived from anthropology, observes those elements in a society that hold it together. The international system can be seen in these terms. The three functions—regime creation, norm enforcement, and direct service provision—describe what the secretariats do. Of those, only the first, regime creation, is a traditional function for international secretariats.

Regime Creation: Building the Basis for Multilateral Diplomacy

The international system can be described as a set of overlapping regimes, where regimes are defined, using the classic definition set out by Stephen Krasner, as "sets of implicit or explicit principles, norms, rules, and decision-making procedures around which actors' expectations converge in a given area of international relations" (1983, 2). Put more clearly, whenever there is an issue that states determine cannot be solved by bilateral relations or by the "magic of the marketplace," they can create a regime whose purpose is to maintain, or in some cases establish, order. How the regime will work is one of the elements being negotiated. There are a large number of international regimes on issues as diverse as human rights, law of the sea, control and elimination of weapons of mass destruction (WMDs), trade regulation, food safety, telecommunications connectivity, refugee management, international financial transactions, and climate change. The number and scope of these regimes, which evolve over time, are clearly growing.

Among the main roles of multilateral negotiation is to create these regimes. One of the innovations of the early twentieth century was to establish international secretariats to support these negotiations. Previously, host countries of the negotiations would provide the secretariats. With the creation of the League of Nations, it became the role of permanent secretariats to organize, support, and follow up on negotiations. These career civil servants have become essential for multilateral diplomacy to function over time.

These secretariats maintain low visibility since the global system is still based on national sovereignty. At a primitive level, they ensure that there are meeting halls, translation and interpretation into agreed official languages, and publication of results. In this sense, they provide a nineteenth-century kind of service. Increasingly, however, the international civil servants drive the negotiation process by providing institutional memory, setting agendas and procedures based on experience, structuring information, channeling input from nonstate actors, and identifying potential paths to consensus.

The typical role of secretariat officials is to sit in on the informal negotiations—out of sight and off the record—that states use to achieve consensus and subtly help move the negotiations to closure. Consensus is the dominant mode of decision making at the international level and essentially involves creating a package of agreements in which the whole is sufficiently valuable to all that it offsets problems each may have with specific elements. Secretariats contribute to this by preparing, based on a sense of the possible, starting negotiating texts by intervening in discussions to note past linkages of issues and agreements that have already been made, thus do not need to be revisited, and even some new approaches that may have been suggested by experience. They are also able to state cases in which the secretariats would be unable to implement an agreement, were it to be reached, or other cases in which, if given new roles and functions, the secretariats could provide the basis for an agreement. In this sense, secretariats are political actors in the process with somewhat more independence than state negotiators, who are constrained by national positions.

The fact that the secretariats are permanent defines the parameters of this function. Most multilateral negotiations to create a regime take many years. For example, the negotiations to create the General Agreement on Trade and Tariffs (GATT), now embodied in the World Trade Organization (WTO), took over forty years. The GATT secretariat, which was considered temporary for most of that period, provided consistency in the negotiations and has now become the permanent secretariat of the WTO. The negotiations to create a regime to manage climate change began through the World Meteorological Organization and United Nations Environment Program in the 1970s, were taken over by the UN Secretariat in the late 1980s, and led to the agreement on the UN Framework Convention on Climate Change (UNFCCC) with its own permanent secretariat, a history well described by Matthew Paterson (1996). That secretariat has managed negotiations on implementation agreements like the Kyoto Protocol and its successor.

Regime creation is a complex process, but the role played by the secretariats has not been examined well, in part because secretariats themselves do not analyze their work, and this work is not accessible to outside scholars since it occurs behind the scenes. I have described some of these roles in an analysis of the preparations for the Fourth World Conference on Women in Beijing in 1995, which could be said to have started in 1946 (Mathiason 2001). These roles or functions included the work of a standing intergovernmental commission, a sequence of world conferences, and, in between, a large number of expert groups and seminars run by the secretariat that led to agreements on facts and norms. In the final stage, from 1985 to the Beijing conference, the secretariat organized some twenty-four expert groups and seminars on specific issue areas. The secretariat contracted recognized experts to prepare papers, presented its own analytical studies, and helped focus the discussions of each meeting. Subsequently, it ensured that the results would be transmitted to the Commission on the Status of Women, where a consensus among government representatives could be reached. In consequence, many key issues were resolved before Beijing, and about 80 percent of the final text could be traced back to these preparations.

The incredibly complex negotiations to replace the Kyoto Protocol to the UNFCCC have been guided by its secretariat. This has involved, since 2007, at least four preparatory activities per year, plus a conference of the parties. A critical role of the secretariat has been to prepare negotiation texts from the highly varied submissions of individual states and groups of states. This has involved knowing when texts were similar even though they sounded different or different even though they sounded similar. There has also been at least one strategic overlap between secretariats and government negotiators in that one of the key governmental representatives, Ambassador Michael Zammit Cutajar of Malta, chairing the central working group on the post-Kyoto agreement, is the retired former head of the UNFCCC Secretariat. He publicly reflects clearly the role of secretariats as civil servants and as diplomats. The current head of the secretariat, Ivo de Boer, was previously in the Dutch diplomatic service.

Important as their support of regime creation is, the other functions performed by international civil servants are becoming more important. Once a regime is created, the next issue is how to manage it. Very often the details of the implementation organization are the last—and most contentious—to be agreed on in multilateral negotiations, both because of their increased cost to governments and because the institution inevitably sets a precedent. Once the institution is established, its job is usually a combination of norm enforcement, provision of information, and delivery of direct services. These functions are mostly performed by international civil servants. How they perform the functions depends on what have been defined as their tasks.

Norm Enforcement: Holding States Accountable Without Ruffling Their Feathers

Norm enforcement is usually seen as the process of verifying that states are complying with the obligations that they have accepted under the agreements that they have reached. In the Westphalian system, international agreements are supposed to be self-enforcing in that states are assumed to be serious about their obligations. But most international conventions establish procedures that will permit verification of compliance. Usually, although not always, this involves giving an international secretariat the role of assembling information that will show the extent of compliance or noncompliance.

One of the earliest regimes to do this was the human rights system of the United Nations. Monitoring of compliance with treaty obligations is given over to a system of review committees, whose members are formally elected by states parties in their individual capacity, as well as by a system of special rapporteurs, also appointed in their individual capacities. The Office of the High Commissioner for Human Rights manages the system. The civil servants work with the committees and rapporteurs, ensuring consistency and the credibility of the conclusions drawn. For example, the reports of the Committee on the Elimination of Discrimination Against Women, which was supported until recently by the Division for the Advancement of Women, were in large measure based on the notes taken by secretariat staff concerning the constructive dialogue between the committee experts and the states parties who were presenting their periodic reports.

In the human rights regime, the work of the secretariats is essentially supportive. In the regime to eliminate WMDs, their role is much more direct and intrusive. The International Atomic Energy Agency (IAEA) and the Organization for the Prohibition of Chemical Weapons both send inspectors to states parties of the Nonproliferation Treaty and the Chemical Weapons Convention, respectively. These inspection organizations (which also undertake research, trade monitoring, and other information-collection activities) certify whether states are in compliance with their obligations. The effectiveness of the IAEA inspectors was demonstrated in 2002, when their inspections showed that there were no nuclear weapons in Iraq, a fact reported to the UN Security Council that undercut U.S. efforts to obtain a resolution justifying its invasion of that country. The IAEA conclusions presented by its director-general, Mohamed El Baradei, were phrased in the usual careful way that international secretariats address states: "We have no evidence that . . ." The acceptance by most of the conclusions was based on the credibility that the IAEA has with its members, deriving from the technical quality and neutrality of its work. The importance of this credibility was demonstrated when the United States, reacting to El Baradei's position on WMDs in Iraq, sought to block his reelection. It was the only country to do so and had to accept El Baradei's reelection. While the inspectors are clearly civil servants, in undertaking their work they also need to be diplomats. A critical element for success in their inspections is to obtain access to sites, and that, very often, requires remarkable tact.

Other organizations have begun to take on enforcement functions to ensure international order. The World Health Organization, for example, has used its oversight authority to encourage states to take actions to reduce the possibilities of global pandemics such as SARS and avian influenza. An area of significant growth in the WTO is its dispute-resolution mechanism, which allows orderly arbitration of cases in which one state accuses another of not living up to obligations under GATT. In this, the role of the WTO Secretariat in establishing a credible procedure is critical.

Direct Service Delivery: Running Things Without Seeming To

The area of greatest growth, however, is in the delivery of basic services that governments are unable or unwilling to perform themselves but consider essential to ensure relative stability in the international system. While the large growth of service-delivery organizations is new, the function itself is not. After World War I, the refugee program of the League of Nations was one of the first international programs established. This was because there was a need for some impartial body to determine refugee status and facilitate relocation. This was reflected, eventually, in the Geneva refugee conventions. The secretariat of the refugee program was largely staffed by lawyers, who could determine the validity of a refugee's claim of "well-founded fear of persecution." Most refugees were in Europe, and the host governments were willing to provide basic services while a durable solution could be found. In the late twentieth century, the nature of refugee situations changed; refugees were largely located in developing countries where the host countries were unwilling or unable to provide services. As a result, international secretariats like that of the Office of the High Commissioner for Refugees have had to provide basic services through camps to the refugee population. In effect, they have become the government of the stateless.

This has changed the role of the civil servants in the refugee programs from being legal arbiters (although that role continues) to being service managers through contracting services and managing camps. Because the programs are located in sovereign states, the civil servants must function, in many ways, like diplomats. The complexity of this role is illustrated by the United Nations Relief and Works Agency for Palestine Refugees (UNRWA), which has been maintaining camps now for sixty years, providing basic social services to that population, but also has to negotiate with the Israeli authorities, the Palestinian Authority, and other host-country governments. UNRWA staff must ensure that they convince donor countries (since UNRWA is mostly funded by voluntary contributions) that they are neutral but effective service providers. They have to find a middle position among the various national authorities that do not, in fact, agree on many issues of concern.

A second area in which the international public sector as a service provider has expanded is humanitarian assistance in the context of natural and man-made disasters. The problems of organizing assistance in the wake of a natural disaster have grown as the capacity of national governments to respond has declined. The traditional means of rapid response, through the International Red Cross and its national affiliates, did not provide the medium-term relief necessary to recover from disasters. As a result, an international service to plan, organize, and fund-raise for disasters, the UN Office for the Coordination of Humanitarian Assistance, was created. In addition, recent history has witnessed the development of humanitarian-relief programs within development-assistance organizations like the World Food Program and the United Nations Children's Fund. Relief coordination, because of logistical and other complexities, has become a profession in itself. Again, the civil service function is reflected in planning and coordination, but since the relief takes place in national contexts, the officials must know how to interact with sovereign authorities, whose interests may not correspond. A clear case was the need for UN officials to put significant pressure on the government of Myanmar to permit the provision of relief to areas affected by Typhoon Nargis in 2008.

Without a doubt, however, the largest amount of growth in service delivery has taken place in the context of postconflict resolution. In the late twentieth century, the number of failed states subject to internal conflicts increased dramatically. The United Nations and some regional intergovernmental organizations have been providing peacekeeping troops to help resolve armed conflicts since 1948, but these largely assumed that the conflicts were between states rather than internal. Secretariat work in this context focused on arranging for the provision of national troop contingents. There was also a diplomatic dimension to this in that it was the custom to appoint a secretary-general's representative to act as mediator as well as political head of the peacekeeping operations. Over time, the United Nations became very efficient in providing this service, and indeed some of the operations have been ongoing for over sixty years (i.e., the UN Truce Supervision Organization between Israel and its neighbors and the UN Military Observer Group in India and Pakistan).

By the end of the twentieth century, the majority of conflict interventions labeled as "peacekeeping" have been internal: States have apparently failed and the international community has had to step in to find solutions to the problems. The military side of peacekeeping has increasingly been accompanied by a civilian component. Precedents existed in the form of the Congo operation of the 1960s, but the scale has become much greater and requires staff trained to work in complex conflict and reconstruction situations. One calculation showed that about half of UN staff in 2007 was assigned to these kinds of field missions (Mathiason 2008b).

The United Nations and the rest of the international system have been called upon to find ways to provide services for reconstruction that the states cannot provide. Beyond the contracting of services, this has included functioning as de facto governments in some sectors, like health, education, and public order, in places as diverse as Haiti, Kosovo, Liberia, and Timor Leste. In providing the services, the international staff function as civil servants, but since they are not of the country where they are serving, they need to be diplomatic. One of the largest and most dramatic missions was a sequence of missions in Timor Leste. Here, intervening first to prevent violence, the United Nations undertook most governmental functions until a functioning national government could be established. At a critical stage, the secretary-general's representative was Sergio Vieira de Mello, whose work was documented in Samantha Power's *Chasing the Flame* (2008). Vieira de Mello, like Kofi Annan, exemplified the dual role of secretariat officials, having joined the United Nations as a civil servant and later been recognized as an accomplished diplomat.

While conflict and humanitarian activities have been a major source of growth of the international public sector in the late twentieth century, the likely growth in the twenty-first will be in more positive areas. These will require an even more nuanced international civil service. Three areas in which this is clearly emerging are international finance, Internet management, and climate change. In each of these, emerging international public-sector organizations, built on international secretariats, will provide direct governance functions that could not be realistically provided by individual states or left to the vagaries of the market.

International finance involves a range of functions including banking, investment, and maintenance of a stable system for transnational transactions. The original role of the international public sector in managing the international financial system was reflected in the Bretton Woods institutions, the World Bank Group and the International Monetary Fund (IMF). They originally had specific tasks (reconstruction investment and maintenance of currency trade) that, over time, have evolved. The collapse of the private international financial system during the 2008–2009 recession has led to a rethinking of the IMF's role in which it will play a greater part in regulation and oversight. The civil servants in these institutions have traditionally been economists, whose responsibility was largely to research economic phenomena so as to provide a basis for lending and economic policies. In the future, their role will become more active, involving oversight functions, use of funding to leverage reforms, and provision of normative rules for organizing financial markets. This will be a civil servant function but, again, will require staff able to work, diplomatically, with national and private-sector counterparts. There will be remarkable interaction between the secretariats and national financial institutions facilitated by the fact that many national officials at one point worked in international organizations, just as many international officials have worked in national governments.

The Internet has become a significant tool for international communication. It was developed by a diverse set of actors, some private, some public. The regulation of its use has yet to be determined. The basic architecture of the Internet is managed by the Internet Corporation for Assigned Names and Numbers (ICANN), an evolving secretariat that is formally nongovernmental but working under a contract with the U.S. government. Other governments and nongovernmental organizations have criticized this arrangement. The future of the Internet is currently being debated in a multistakeholder forum (the Internet Governance Forum) that constitutes a new approach to defining international functions (Mathiason 2008a). It has included debate on the future of ICANN. Its secretariat has been drawn from persons who were involved in the negotiation of agreements at the World Summit for the Information Society, who are therefore well equipped in the area of regime creation. The secretariats of these bodies have to navigate a complex set of stakeholders, many of whom are technicians and will need management, technical, and diplomatic skills as they take on the new regulatory functions.

Climate change has emerged at the end of the twentieth century as a dominant issue, given its universality, its borderless character, and the need to act in areas that cut across traditional boundaries. It is leading to the creation of a new set of institutions that will manage global responses to the problem. Some of these will build on existing organizations such as the UN Development Program and the UN Environment Program, which have worked on development issues. Others will be new, involving services that the international public sector has never before performed. Two of the approaches set up under the Kyoto Protocol foreshadow these new institutions. One will have to do with the regulation of emissions trading, where market mechanisms will need to be maintained under scrutiny. The other is the Clean Development Mechanism, an institution designed to develop means of transferring investment resources to developing countries in exchange for the creation of emissions credits. The role of the secretariats is, in many ways, verification of the extent to which the stakeholders who use these institutions are complying with the rules. In some respects this expands the function performed by the IAEA and the Organization for the Prohibition of Chemical Weapons in their verification work, but it involves a different set of issues to which techniques will apply.

Changing Multilateral Diplomacy and Secretariat Challenges

The changing nature of the international public sector will have implications for multilateral diplomacy. The focus will have to move from negotiations about new regimes to ensuring oversight over the new norm-enforcement and service-providing secretariats. Diplomats will have to understand how the institutions function, the results they are expected to induce, and how to hold them accountable. This requires a different approach to training, one more akin to public administration than to negotiation. They will have to understand what is now called results-based management (RBM), an approach to planning, implementation, and evaluation that is particularly applicable to the international public sector. The ability to do this successfully will become one of the means of determining the effectiveness of foreign ministries (Mathiason 2007b).

The new challenges of the international public sector will require that efforts to institute RBM throughout the international secretariats be successful. While international organizations have been under pressure from major contributors to institute RBM since the mid-1990s, the application has been uneven at best. Some secretariats, like the IAEA, have been successful in implementing the approach, but others, including the United Nations itself, have been far less so. There seems to be two reasons for this: Secretariat officials have resisted being held accountable for results outside their control, and governments have not used performance data to evaluate proposed plans and budgets (Mathiason 2004). While RBM is seen as an accountability tool, it is probably more important in managing programs, and civil servants who practice it will be more effective than those who do not.

For the international secretariats, the problem will be to train international civil servants to be effective in a changing environment. Over the first sixty years of the current career civil service, training was not considered a major need. The assumption was that new civil servants would "learn by doing," mentored by their predecessors. This method, however, was contingent on relative stability of functions and slow growth. Neither condition applies in the twenty-first century. The functions performed are evolving very quickly, and a combination of retirements and expanded recruitment means that mentoring systems no longer work. If we are to have effective international secretariats, a new approach to in-service and induction training will have to be put in place, emphasizing the skills necessary to be both effective civil servants and diplomats.

For this to be effective, there will need to be much more research into international public management so that the quality of both the content of training and the structure of oversight can be assured. This is not currently performed by any international institution, including the United Nations Institute for Training and Research or the United Nations Staff College. It will need continual research to note changes in international public functions so that as the international public sector evolves over the twenty-first century, it can be monitored and approved.

References

Krasner, S. D., ed. 1983. *International regimes.* Ithaca, NY: Cornell University Press.

Mathiason, J. 2008a. *Internet governance: The new frontier of global institutions.* London: Routledge.

———. 2008b. What kind of international public service do we need for the 21st century? *Global Governance* 14, no. 2 (April–June): 127–133.

———. 2007a. *Invisible governance: International secretariats in global politics.* Bloomfield, CT: Kumarian Press.

———. 2007b. Linking diplomatic performance assessment to international results-based management. In *Foreign ministries: Managing diplomatic networks and optimizing value,* ed. K. S. Rana and J. Kurbalija. Geneva: DiploFoundation.

———. 2004. Who controls the machine, III: Accountability in the results-based revolution. *Public Administration and Development* 24 (February): 61–73.

———. 2001. *The Vienna years.* Vol. 1 of *The long march to Beijing: The United Nations and the women's revolution.* Mt. Temper, NY: AIMS.

Paterson, M. 1996. *Global warming and global politics (environmental politics).* London: Brunner-Routledge.

Power, S. 2008. *Chasing the flame: Sergio Vieira de Mello and the fight to save the world.* New York: Penguin Press.

Multilateral Diplomacy and the United Nations: Global Governance Venue or Actor?

Ramesh Thakur

In 2002 and 2003, the Bush administration warned the United Nations of its future irrelevance if it failed to support the looming war in Iraq. Many other countries acknowledged the need to confront Saddam Hussein but ruled out acting without UN authorization. From a test of UN relevance, the agenda shifted to being a test of the legitimacy of U.S. action. Imperceptibly and subtly, the issue had metamorphosed into a question of what sort of world we wish to live in, by whom we wish to be ruled, and if we wish to live by rules and laws or by the force of arms (Thakur 2007). The United Nations found itself front and center in the debate, the focus of hopes, fears, and the media's most pressing attention.

This chapter explores whether the United Nations is merely the principal site for engaging with the great debates and controversies of the day, as over Iraq in 2003, or is also an actor in its own right, with the whole—the international community collectively—being greater than the sum of the parts, the member states individually. It begins with a discussion of whether there is any such thing as "UN policy" within the larger context of global governance. The argument is then illustrated with two substantive examples: the issue of arms control and disarmament and the responsibility to protect (R2P) norm.

Global Governance, "UN Policy," and the Principal-Agent Problem

Whether as site or actor, the United Nations' role in world affairs is made possible by the reality of being at the center of global governance—the sum of laws, norms, policies, and institutions that define, constitute, and mediate relations between citizens, societies, markets, and states on the world stage, the wielders and objects of the exercise of international public power.

Global governance faces a fundamental paradox. The policy authority for tackling global problems and mobilizing the necessary resources is principally vested at the country level, in states, while the source and scale of the problems and potential solutions to them are transnational, regional, and global. One result of this situation is that states have the capacity to disable decision making and policy implementation by global bodies like the United Nations but often lack the vision and will to empower and enable their own global problem solving on issues such as climate change, human trafficking, terrorism, and nuclear weapons.

The United Nations was conceived of, fashioned, and negotiated by national leaders dissatisfied with the lack of adequate mechanisms of global governance both for muting conflict and promoting collaboration among sovereign states. There has been a threefold change in the world of diplomacy and diplomats since 1945:

1. in the *levels* of diplomatic activity, from the local, through the domestic-national, to the bilateral, regional, and global
2. in the *domain and scope* of the subject matter or content, expanding rapidly to a very broad array of the different sectors of public-policy and government activity
3. in the rapidly expanding *numbers and types of actors*, from governments to national private-sector firms, multinational corporations, nongovernmental organizations (NGOs), and regional and international organizations

The business of the world has changed almost beyond recognition over the last century. Four decades ago the influential French theorist Raymond Aron argued that "the ambassador and the soldier *live* and *symbolize* international relations which, insofar as they are inter-state relations, concern diplomacy and war" (1967, 5). Today, alongside the horde of diplomats and soldiers, the international lawyer, multinational merchant, cross-border financier, World Bank technocrat, UN peacekeeper, NGO humanitarian worker, and antiglobalization dissenter jostle for space on the increasingly congested international stage.

In the UN context there is a dynamic and symbiotic relationship between national foreign policies and international diplomacy. Its universality provides unique legitimacy in formulating global public policy but raises the principal-agent problem: Who are the actors—the relevant policy makers—in the UN system

(Thakur and Weiss 2009)? Is "international" policy made and implemented by international organizations (IOs) or by national authorities meeting and interacting in international forums? The former would imply IOs are actors, but the latter restricts them to being the venues for state actors. That several actors occupy the stage of international relations has become so commonplace an observation as to be trite. Actors have policies. IOs are one type of the numerous actors playing diverse roles in world affairs, and the United Nations is a key IO actor.

For realists, IOs like the United Nations are creations and tools of sovereign states, not independent actors. For liberal institutionalists, the United Nations is an arena in which interactions among its member states take place and cooperation can be agreed on. For principal-agent theorists, states are the principals, and UN secretariats are the agents. Thus, the notion of a "UN policy" independent of the preferences and interests of the states does not seem to make any sense. Yet, recent works using a revised and more nuanced version of principal-agent theory and constructivism suggest that IOs, including UN specialized agencies, have significant (although incomplete) autonomy vis-à-vis their principals (Barnett and Finnemore 2004). With the retreat of the state in an age of globalization, there is more "space" available for the UN organizations because "a principal-agent relationship looks somewhat like domestic public-private and public-voluntary partnerships. . . . States no longer row, they steer" (Stein 2008, 127). Moreover, there are multiple sources of funding for activities by UN organizations so that the "agents" can go "principal shopping" in order to evade or dilute control by a particular principal.

Finally and importantly, there are "three UNs" playing complementary but essential roles in contemporary policy formulation by the world organization. The first consists of member states, a second of the secretariats, and a third of actors closely associated with the United Nations but not formally part of it (Weiss, Carayannis, and Jolly 2009). This "outside-insider" UN includes NGOs, academics, consultants, experts, independent commissions, and other groups of individuals (Thakur, Cooper, and English 2005). These informal networks often help to affect shifts in ideas, policies, priorities, and practices that are initially seen as undesirable or problematic by state principals and even international secretariats.

According to standard references, a policy is not only a governing principle but also entails "the decision to embark upon certain programs of action (or inaction) in order to achieve desired goals" (Evans and Newnham 1998, 440). It is an intended course of action or inaction in light of a particular problem (Birkland 2005, 17–18). This entails both agency and purposive action. State actors are policy makers. But for states, public policy is usually distinguished from foreign policy, implying a boundary-based, domestic/external separation between the two activities. "The policy-makers and the policy system therefore stand at these junction points and seek to mediate between the various milieux" (Evans and Newnham 1998,179). By contrast, "the UN, through its organs such as the Security Council or the General Assembly, makes policy" (Evans and Newnham 1998, 440). But it cannot be said to make foreign policy: Neither the policy makers nor the policy system of the United Nations is engaged in boundary activities. By definition the world is their stage.

The civil service may shape and influence policy, but it is not normally considered a policy maker. That is the domain of the political heads of civil service departments, cabinet ministers individually, and the legislature and political executive collectively. Likewise, the UN Secretariat and its staff members—international civil servants—may influence policy, but they cannot be described as policy makers. To the extent that in important respects the secretary-general and other senior officials can be called independent actors in their own right, they may on some occasions be classified as peripatetic policy makers (Thakur 2006, 320–342; Ramcharan 2008). Thus, UN "policy makers" are indeed the principal political organs—the Security Council and the General Assembly—and the member states collectively. But all of these are intergovernmental forums. The people—agents—making the decisions by adopting resolutions that set out new governing principles, articulate goals, and authorize programs to achieve those goals do so as national delegates, acting within the governing framework of their national foreign policies and under strict and narrow instructions from capitals. Or member states may make the policy choices directly themselves, for example, at summit conferences.

At the national level, policy can be used to refer holistically to "the entire package of actions and attitudes" (Hill 2001, 290), for instance, Indian or U.S. policy. Alternatively, it can also be applied to specific policies toward particular issues and problems in the international realm (e.g., Indian or U.S. policy toward Israel-Palestinian relations, the International Criminal Court (ICC), or nuclear proliferation) or in domestic affairs (e.g., Indian or U.S. policy on the death penalty, intellectual property, or immigration).

Policy may also be broken down sequentially into three separate phases: formulation, adoption, and implementation. And its object varies: to regulate services like transport, telecommunications, and public utilities; to allocate public resources like housing, employment, and scholarships; and to redress social inequality through social welfare programs (Morris 2001, 703). As distinct from state actors, the responsibility for implementation of most UN policy does not rest primarily with the United Nations itself but with its member states. But even UN policy, in the form of policy resolutions and actions adopted and authorized by the Security Council and the General Assembly or summit decisions made by member states directly, may exhibit regulative, distributive, and redistributive characteristics.

Based on these considerations, resolutions adopted by the General Assembly, though not legally binding, are the equivalent of policy declarations if they articulate broad principles and goals, sometimes with programs of action to attain these goals.[1] One of the clearest examples is General Assembly Resolution 2922 (1972) reaffirming apartheid as a crime against humanity. The phrase became a staple of UN resolutions over many years until the liberation of South Africa and the replacement of the apartheid regime with an elected black-majority government formed by the African National Congress with Nelson Mandela as the first president. Other examples would be General Assembly Resolution 1514 (December 14, 1960), the Declaration on the Granting of Independence to Colonial Countries and Peoples, and similar broad and sweeping declarations delegitimizing racism in general.

A second set of UN policy documents takes the form of goals, plans of action, and desirable codes of conduct embedded in international treaties and conventions. Good examples include the 1948 Genocide Convention, the 1948 Universal Declaration of Human Rights, the 1982 UN Convention on the Law of the Sea, the 1997 Kyoto Protocol, the 1968 Nuclear Nonproliferation Treaty (NPT), and the 1996 Comprehensive Test Ban Treaty (CTBT). (The CTBT—which has yet to enter into force because of nonsignatures or nonratifications by key states like India and the United States, but whose provisions have been respected to date since it was signed over a decade ago—is a good example of an international security policy being integrated into national security policies.)

Arms Control and Disarmament

On the issue of arms control and disarmament, the United Nations has played three linked but analytically distinct roles as a funnel, forum, and font[2]:

- a funnel for processing ideas into norms and policies and for transmitting information from national sources to the international community
- a forum for discussion and negotiation of common international positions, policies, conventions, and regimes
- a font of international legitimacy for the authoritative promulgation of international norms, appeals for adherence to global norms and regimes, and coercive measures to enforce compliance with them

The United Nations As a Funnel

From one point of view, it could be argued that the United Nations has not been the chief architect of arms control and disarmament. Most of the key treaties and regimes—bilateral treaties signed by Moscow and Washington during the Cold War on intermediate range and strategic forces, as well as multilateral regimes like the NPT (Boulden, Thakur, and Weiss 2009), the Chemical Weapons Convention (Thakur and Haru, 2006), the Biological Weapons Convention, and the various regional nuclear-weapons-free zones (Thakur 1998)—were negotiated outside the UN framework. The UN Charter downgraded the disarmament clauses as a path to peace compared to disarmament's central importance in the schema of the League of Nations. This reflected the apparent lesson of the interwar period that arms in themselves are not a problem; having weapons in the wrong hands, or not enough in the right ones, is the problem.

Yet, the ideas behind many of the existing regimes were often first funneled through the UN system. A proposal for the cessation of nuclear testing came from India in the General Assembly in December 1954 (Pande 1996, 25). In 1957, the United States submitted a five-point plan to the General Assembly proposing an end to the production of nuclear weapons and testing. Throughout the 1980s and the mid-1990s, pressure for a comprehensive test ban was funneled through the General Assembly. Similarly, the idea of negotiating a South Pacific nuclear-weapons-free zone was submitted to the General Assembly for endorsement in 1975 by Fiji, New Zealand, and Papua New Guinea, and the 1985 treaty links the regional verification system for the South Pacific to the global International Atomic Energy Agency (IAEA) inspections regime within the UN system (Thakur 1987, 23–45).

The United Nations has thus historically been the funnel for processing arms-control and disarmament proposals, and this role continues today. The New Agenda coalition, building on the Eight Nation (Brazil, Egypt, Ireland, Mexico, New Zealand, Slovenia, South Africa, and Sweden) initiative of June 1998 (following the nuclear tests by India and Pakistan in May), has used the United Nations essentially as the funnel through which to advance the twin agenda of nonproliferation and disarmament. The basic policy positions are agreed to among coalition countries directly, then taken to the international community through UN structures. As with many other examples in the past, any resulting treaty may well be negotiated in forums outside the United Nations. This should not take due credit away from the organization for its invaluable funnel role.

The United Nations As a Forum

The General Assembly, with universal membership, houses the divided fragments of humanity and, when united, speaks with the collective voice of the international community. As such, it is the custodian of the world's conscience. This makes it the unique forum of choice for articulating global values and norms and the arena in which contested norms can be debated and reconciled. Such a role was true historically in delegitimizing colonialism, even though decolonization resulted from policy decisions taken in the national capitals of the colonial powers. It was the United Nations more than any other institution or organization that proclaimed racial equality as a global norm and delegitimized apartheid as an ideology and system of government. The organization has been at the forefront of the universalization of the human rights norm and the internationalization of the human conscience. It is to the General Assembly that civil society actors look and member states go to proclaim and reaffirm arms-control and disarmament norms. This is the chief explanation for why so many declarations and resolutions are adopted in the United Nations before producing conventions and treaties—norms followed by laws—in UN as well as non-UN forums.

A recent example of the use of the United Nations as a forum came in September 2009 when Barack Obama became the first U.S. president to chair a Security Council meeting. On September 24 the Council unanimously adopted the U.S.-sponsored Resolution 1887 reaffirming the goal of nuclear abolition and calling on all states to sign and abide by the NPT, to refrain from testing and sign the CTBT, and to ensure safeguards against and prevent trafficking in nuclear material. It also called on the Conference on Disarmament to negotiate a treaty banning the production of fissile material for nuclear weapons.

The United Nations As a Font

Washington took the Security Council route in 2009 because there is still no substitute for the United Nations as a font of international authority and legitimacy. This was reflected also by the manner in which the campaign to ban landmines was careful to keep in touch with the UN system. The October 1996 Ottawa conference developed a resolution that was adopted by the General Assembly in December by 156–0 votes. In the final conference a year later, negotiators were careful not to quarantine themselves from the international organization, integrating their process with the UN system on review, reporting, and depositary functions.

Calling on UN moral authority to seek compliance with global norms is especially relevant when behavior considered unacceptable is not in fact proscribed by any treaty to which a state may be party. In May 1998, India and Pakistan conducted nuclear tests. In doing so, they broke no treaty, for neither had signed the NPT. But they violated the global antinuclear norm and were roundly criticized for doing so. Hence, too, the call in Resolution 1887 eleven years later for all non-NPT countries to sign the treaty.

Even if negotiated outside UN forums, treaties are often submitted to the UN machinery for formal endorsement that has no bearing on the legal standing of the treaty but does substantially enhance its moral weight. This has been true, for example, of the various regional nuclear-weapons-free zones. One of the clearest examples of the United Nations as a font of authority for global arms-control treaties came with the CTBT, which was approved by a vote of 158–3 by the General Assembly on September 10, 1996. Sometimes it is possible to be mesmerized by the illusion of a numerical majority in the United Nations for the weight of national security calculations in the real world of power politics. The resulting hardening of India's nuclear stance was predictable: "Faced with U.S.-led UN coercion, an isolated, sullen and resentful India is more likely to respond with an open nuclear program, including a . . . series of nuclear tests" (Thakur 1996). In Indian eyes the issue was no longer the clauses and substance of the CTBT but norms, sovereignty, and security. The General Assembly's adoption of the CTBT was taken as proof that the international security environment had deteriorated alarmingly against vital Indian interests.

The specific example of the politically counterproductive ploy with the CTBT in 1996 does not negate the general argument about the role of the United Nations as the legitimizing forum for demanding and enforcing compliance with global norms and regimes. Several international bodies are set within the UN framework as part of the implementation mechanism for disarmament, including but not limited to the IAEA. There are also ad hoc bodies like the UN inspection groups that, we now know conclusively, successfully disarmed Saddam Hussein (Findlay 2006, 140–159; Lewis 2006, 160–178). Even so, the Iran, Iraq, and North Korea experiences show the enormous difficulty of ensuring compliance with international norms and commitments.

The Responsibility to Protect

Going to war was an acknowledged attribute of state sovereignty, and war itself was an accepted institution of the Westphalian system with distinctive rules, etiquette, norms, and stable patterns of practices to govern armed conflicts (Holsti 1996). In that quasi-Hobbesian world, the main protection against aggression was countervailing power, which increased both the cost of victory and the risk of failure. Since 1945, the United Nations has spawned a corpus of law to stigmatize aggression and create a robust norm against it. The world organization exists to check the predatory instincts of the powerful—one of the most enduring but least endearing patterns in history—whether in domestic jurisdictions inside state borders or in international relations. Now there are significant restrictions on state use of force both domestically and internationally.

A second challenge to the Westphalian order came with the adoption of new standards of conduct for states in the protection and advancement of international human rights. There is an inherent tension between the intervention-proscribing principle of state sovereignty and the intervention-prescribing principle of human rights. Individuals became subjects of international law as bearers of duties and holders of rights under a rapidly proliferating array of human rights and international humanitarian law treaties, conventions, and instruments. Consequently, the "maintenance of international peace and security" (Article 24[1] of the UN Charter), for which primary responsibility is vested in the Security Council, needs to translate in practice into the protection of civilians in the midst of armed conflict. In a number of cases in the 1990s, the Security Council's imprimatur covered the use of force with the primary goal of humanitarian protection and assistance: in the protection of Kurds after the Gulf War, the proclamation of UN safe areas in Bosnia, the delivery of humanitarian relief in Somalia, the restoration of the democratically elected government of Haiti, and the deployment of the multinational Kosovo Force to Kosovo after the 1999 war (Lepard 2002, 7–23).

The interest in protecting civilians explains the adoption of the responsibility to protect norm. The actors who were critical in promoting and shepherding R2P through the maze of UN politics can be broken down into norm entrepreneurs, champions, and brokers. As a *norm entrepreneur*, the secretary-general is a unique international actor with distinctive characteristics and bases of authority and influence, if within limitations (Thakur 2006, 320–342; Chesterman 2007). In a speech in New York in March 2004 to commemorate the tenth anniversary of the Rwanda genocide, I recall Kofi Annan expressing regret at not having done more to try to stop it. He was driven similarly by his experience of being in charge of peacekeeping at the time of the Srebrenica massacre in 1995. Annan told an audience at Ditchley Park in 1998 that state frontiers "should no longer be seen as a watertight protection for war criminals or mass murderers" (1999, 7). He argued that human rights concerns transcended claims of sovereignty, a theme that he put forward more delicately at the Millennium Summit (Annan 2000). The reaction was loud, bitter, and predictable, especially from China, Russia, and many developing countries (Ayoob 2001, 225–230; Jackson 2000). Yet, Annan, the only UN insider to have held its top job, had an unmatched grasp of bureaucratic politics and was able to navigate his way through the complex maze and political hazards of the UN system and emerge triumphant. He subsequently described R2P as one of his most precious achievements (Annan 2006, 8) and claimed to have applied the R2P template in his successful mediation in Kenya in 2008 (Cohen 2008, 5–53). The other two significant norm entrepreneurs in the R2P story are the activist former foreign ministers of Canada and Australia, Lloyd Axworthy (2003) and Gareth Evans (2008).

R2P's state *champion* from start to finish was Canada, a country strongly committed to UN-centered multilateralism, with a history of close engagement with the world organization, political credibility in both the North and South, and a proud tradition of successful global initiatives. There were also several other like-minded countries like Norway and Switzerland, as well as major foundations like MacArthur and other actors like the International Committee of the Red Cross.

The *norm broker* was the International Commission on Intervention and State Sovereignty (ICISS). Its report consolidated a number of disparate trends and borrowed language first developed by Francis Deng and Roberta Cohen to help address the problem of internally displaced persons (Deng 1995; Cohen 1991). Its mandate was to find common ground for military intervention to support humanitarian objectives by reconciling the tension between intervention and state sovereignty. The ICISS final report was published with exceptionally bad timing in December 2001, when the world was preoccupied with the terrorist attacks of September 11. The subsequent invasion of Iraq and the ousting of Saddam Hussein by the U.S.-led coalition acting without UN authorization had a doubly damaging effect. First, as tensions mounted in 2002 and 2003, few had the time to focus on R2P. Second, as the weapons-of-mass-destruction justification for the war fell apart and claims of close links between Hussein's regime and Al Qaeda also proved spurious, the coalition of the willing began retroactively to use the language of humanitarian intervention and R2P as the main plank of justification for their actions in Iraq.

Contrary to the position taken by Australia, Britain, and the United States—the three main belligerent states—some of the ICISS commissioners argued strenuously in the public debate that Iraq would not have met the R2P test for intervention (Evans 2003; Thakur 2003, 2004). The Canadian government organized an extensive series of consultations with governments, regional organizations, and civil society forums, typically using the two cochairs, as well as Tom Weiss and me (and other ICISS members within their regions), to help promote the report. As the message resonated, many civil society organizations began advocacy and dissemination work on their own as well. Secretary-General Annan himself remained fully engaged with the issue.

The Secretary-General's High-Level Panel on Threats, Challenges and Change, which included ICISS cochair Gareth Evans, reaffirmed the importance of the change in terminology from the deeply divisive "humanitarian intervention" to "the responsibility to protect." It endorsed the ICISS argument that "the issue is not the 'right to intervene' of any State, but the 'responsibility to protect' of *every* State" (United Nations 2004). In his own report before the 2005 World Summit, Annan (2005) made an explicit reference to ICISS and R2P as well as to the high-level panel in urging endorsement of the responsibility to protect.

R2P was unanimously endorsed by heads of governments and states in September 2005 in paragraphs 138 and 139 of the *World Summit Outcome* (United Nations 2005). It contains a clear, unambiguous acceptance by all UN members of individual state responsibility to protect populations from genocide, war crimes, ethnic cleansing, and crimes against humanity. The assembled leaders further declared that they "are prepared to take collective action, in timely and decisive manner, through the Security Council . . . and in cooperation with relevant regional organizations as appropriate, should peaceful means be inadequate and national authorities are manifestly failing to protect their populations." Annan's successor, Ban Ki-moon, drawing on Special Adviser Edward Luck's wide-ranging consultations and reflections, published his own report on implementing R2P in January 2009.

Conclusion

In a book on the intellectual history of global governance, Tom Weiss and I have looked at the United Nations' contribution through the analytical lens of a series of gaps that the organization helps to fill (Weiss and Thakur 2010). With respect to knowledge gaps, for example, we argue that while in some cases the United Nations has generated new knowledge, more often it has provided an arena in which existing information can be collected and collated, a host of interpretations vetted, and differing interpretations of competing data debated. Thus, once again it has been both actor and site, albeit highly unequally.

With respect to normative gaps, the United Nations is an essential arena in which states actually codify norms in the form of resolutions and declarations (soft law) as well as conventions and treaties (hard law). It offers the most efficient forum for processing norms (i.e., standards of behavior) into laws (i.e., rules of behavior). Martha Finnemore and Kathryn Sikkink (1998) postulate a three-stage life cycle of norms: the emergence of a new norm and its advocacy by a norm entrepreneur; norm cascade when agreement among a critical mass of actors on an emergent norm creates a tipping point; and norm internalization so that it becomes taken for granted, and norm-conforming behavior becomes routine. The United Nations provides an organizational platform for advocacy in the first stage, then the forum of choice for cascade in the second, and affirmation and compliance in the final stages. In the Ottawa Treaty banning landmines, for example, norm generation by Western middle powers was underpinned by norm advocacy from NGOs and reinforced by norm promotion and standard setting by Secretary-General Annan (Thakur and Maley 1999; Price 1998).

This also applies to areas such as terrorism, environmental protection, and pandemics. A compendium of UN policies in these areas would include

- dissuasion of people from resorting to or supporting terrorism
- denial of access to funds and materials to terrorists
- deterrence of states from sponsoring terrorism
- capacity development so that states can defeat terrorism
- defense of human rights even when hunting down terrorists
- promotion of economic growth to satisfy the aspirations of the present generation without compromising the needs of future generations or irreversibly damaging the environment and the ecosystem
- promotion of economic growth in the poorest countries through technical and financial assistance and concessionary terms of trade in various iterations of partnerships of development
- protection of the ozone layer through the Montreal Protocol
- deceleration, halt, and reversal of global warming through the Kyoto Protocol, the UN Framework Convention on Climate Change, and successor regimes
- eradication of smallpox and polio
- control of the HIV/AIDS pandemic through the three-track strategy of prevention, treatment, and education

For all these issue areas, the UN system has made solid use of its unique legitimacy and helped initiate steps toward the formulation of coherent global policies.

UN-sponsored world conferences, heads-of-government summits, and blue-ribbon commissions and panels have been used for framing issues, outlining choices, and making decisions; anticipating and setting agendas; framing the rules; pledging and mobilizing resources; implementing collective decisions; and monitoring progress and recommending mid-term corrections and adjustments.

As a universal organization, the United Nations is an ideal forum in which to seek consensus about normative approaches that will govern global problems and work best with worldwide application. The host of problems, ranging from reducing greenhouse-gas emissions to impeding money laundering and halting pandemics, clearly provides instances for which universal norms and approaches are required and emerging. At the same time, the United Nations is a maddening forum because dissent by powerful states or even coalitions of less powerful ones means either no action or agreement only on a lowest common denominator.

This is especially true with respect to filling compliance gaps. Indeed, this particular type of gap often appears as a void because there exist no ways to enforce decisions. The charter notwithstanding, there are no standing UN military forces and no functioning Military Staff Committee. The United Nations has to beg for and borrow troops, which are always on loan and subject to operational control by national governments. Just as tellingly, the United Nations has no rapid reaction capability. As for the crucial issue of nuclear proliferation, as in recent years Iran and North Korea have repeatedly thumbed their noses at the IAEA and the Security Council, the compliance gap has been stark. In 2009 Sudan's president Omar al-Bashir did the same in defiance of international arrest warrants issued by the ICC on charges of war crimes and crimes against humanity. The case had been referred to the ICC by the UN Security Council.

The terrain on which the conceptual and policy contest over "humanitarian intervention" has been fought is essentially normative (Thakur 2006). Norm displacement has taken place from the entrenched norm of nonintervention to the new norm of the responsibility to protect. The United Nations lies at the center of this contest, both metaphorically and literally. The UN Charter encapsulates and articulates the agreed-on consensus regarding the prevailing norms that give structure and meaning to the foundations of world order. The international community of states comes together physically principally within the United Nations' hallowed halls. It is not surprising, therefore, that the organization should be the epicenter of the interplay between changing norms and shifting state practice.

The responsibility to protect is about the changing conceptions of the appropriate relations between citizens and states in an interdependent and globalizing world—the norms, laws, and practices that constitute those relations and the variety of civil society, governmental, and intergovernmental actors engaged in efforts to redefine and reconstitute the norms, laws, and practices. Most of these efforts posit the United Nations as the central reference point. ICISS was careful to embed R2P within the context of evolving Security Council practices and customary international law. The Canadian government formed and supported ICISS in direct response to Kofi Annan's challenge of humanitarian intervention and his call for the need to forge a new consensus. (I was an ICISS commissioner as a serving UN official.) The ICISS report was presented to the secretary-general and addressed primarily and self-consciously to the UN community. It was taken up by the high-level panel constituted by Annan, which included cochair Gareth Evans among its members. R2P was strongly endorsed by Annan himself ahead of its adoption by the world summit of government leaders in 2005. Taking all of the examples mentioned in this chapter into consideration, to insist on a rigid separation between the United Nations as site and actor in global governance would appear to be artificial to the point of silliness.

Notes

1. They are similar to policy declarations in another respect as well. At the national level, unless they are in the form of a "sense of the legislature" or equivalent, acts of parliament would be binding law. UN General Assembly resolutions, however, are not legally binding, any more than policy declarations by the political executive are at the national level.

2. This conceptual terminology comes from Margaret Joan Anstee, a former under-secretary-general of the United Nations, who proposed the categorization in the context of the UN Intellectual History Project (UNIHP). She and I are colleagues on the International Advisory Board of UNIHP.

References

Annan, K. A. 2006. A progress report on UN renewal, speech to the UN Association–UK, London, 31 January, *New World* (April–June): 6–11.

———. 2005. *In larger freedom: Towards development, security and human rights for all.* Report of the secretary-general. UN Document A/59/2005. United Nations. March 21. www.un.org/largerfreedom.

———. 2000. *The question of intervention and "we the peoples": The United Nations in the 21st century.* New York: United Nations.

———. 1999. *The question of intervention: Statements by the secretary-general.* New York: United Nations.

Aron, R. 1967. *Peace and war: A theory of international relations*, trans. Richard Howard and Annette Baker Fox. New York: Frederick A. Praeger.

Axworthy, L. 2003. *Navigating a new world: Canada's global future*. Toronto: Alfred A. Knopf Canada.

Ayoob, M. 2001. Humanitarian intervention and international society. *Global Governance 7*, no. 3: 225–230.

Ban, K. 2009. *Implementing the responsibility to protect*. Report of the secretary-general. UN Document A/63/677. United Nations. January 12. http://globalr2p.org/pdf/SGR2PEng.pdf.

Barnett, M., and M. Finnemore. 2004. *Rules for the world: International organizations in global politics*. Ithaca, NY: Cornell University Press.

Birkland, T. 2005. *An introduction to the policy process: Theories, concepts, and models of public policy making*. New York: M. E. Sharp.

Boulden, J., R. Thakur, and T. G. Weiss, eds. 2009. *The United Nations and nuclear orders*. Tokyo: United Nations University Press.

Chesterman, S., ed. 2007. *Secretary or general? The UN secretary-general in world politics*. Cambridge: Cambridge University Press.

Cohen, R. 2008. How Kofi Annan rescued Kenya. *New York Review of Books*. August 14, 51–53.

———. 1991. *Human rights protection for internally displaced persons*. Washington, DC: Refugee Policy Group.

Deng, F. M. 1995. Reconciling sovereignty with responsibility: A basis for international humanitarian action. In *Africa in world politics: Post–Cold War challenges*, ed. J. W. Harbeson and D. Rothschild, 295–310. Boulder, CO: Westview Press.

Evans, G. 2008. *The responsibility to protect: Ending mass atrocity crimes once and for all*. Washington, DC: Brookings.

———. 2003. Humanity did not justify this war. *Financial Times*, May 15, 15.

Evans, G., and J. Newnham. 1998. *The Penguin dictionary of international relations*. London: Penguin Books.

Findlay, T. 2006. Lessons of UNSCOM and UNMOVIC for WMD non-proliferation, arms control and disarmament. In *Arms control after Iraq: Normative and operational challenges*, ed. W. P. Singh Sidhu and R. Thakur, 140–159. Tokyo: United Nations University Press.

Finnemore, M., and K. Sikkink. 1998. International norm dynamics and political change. *International Organization* 52, no. 4: 887–917.

Hawkins, D., D. Lake, D. Nielson, and M. Tierney, eds. 2006. *Delegation and agency in international organizations*. New York: Cambridge University Press.

Hill, C. 2001. Foreign policy. In *The Oxford companion to the politics of the world*, ed. J. Krieger, 290–292. 2nd ed. Oxford: Oxford University Press.

Holsti, K. J. 1996. *War, the state, and the state of war*. Cambridge: Cambridge University Press.

Jackson, R. 2000. *The global covenant: Human conduct in a world of states*. Oxford: Oxford University Press.

Lepard, B. D. 2002. *Rethinking humanitarian intervention.* University Park: Pennsylvania State University Press.

Lewis, P. 2006. Why we got it wrong: Attempting to unravel the truth of bioweapons in Iraq. In *Arms control after Iraq: Normative and operational challenges,* ed. W. P. Singh Sidhu and R. Thakur, 160–178. Tokyo: United Nations University Press.

Morris, L. 2001. Public policy. In *The Oxford companion to the politics of the world,* ed. J. Krieger, 702–703. 2nd ed. Oxford: Oxford University Press.

Pande, S. 1996. *India and the nuclear test ban.* New Delhi: Institute for Defense Studies and Analyses.

Price, R. 1998. Reversing the gun sights: Transnational civil society targets land mines. *International Organization* 52, no. 3: 613–644.

Ramcharan, B. G. 2008. *Preventive diplomacy at the UN.* Bloomington: Indiana University Press.

Reinalda, B., and B. Verbeek, eds. 2004. *Decision making within international organizations.* London: Routledge.

Stein, J. G. 2008. Humanitarian organizations: Accountable—why, to whom, for what, and how? In *Humanitarianism in question: Politics, power, ethics,* ed. M. Barnett and T. G. Weiss, 124–142. Ithaca, NY: Cornell University Press.

Thakur, R. 2007. *War in our time: Reflections on Iraq, terrorism and weapons of mass destruction.* Tokyo: United Nations University Press.

———. 2006. *The United Nations, peace and security: From collective security to the responsibility to protect.* Cambridge: Cambridge University Press.

———. 2004. Iraq and the responsibility to protect. *Behind the Headlines* 62, no. 1: 1–16.

———. 2003. Chrétien was right: It's time to redefine a "just war." *Globe and Mail,* July 22, A13.

———, ed. 1998. *Nuclear weapons–free zones.* London/New York: Macmillan and St. Martin's Press.

———. 1996. Nuclear India needs coaxing, not coercion. *Australian* (Sydney), September 6, O11.

———. 1987. The treaty of Rarotonga: The South Pacific nuclear-free zone. In *Nuclear-free zones,* ed. D. Pitt and G. Thompson, 23–45. London: Croom Helm.

Thakur, R., A. F. Cooper, and J. English, eds. 2005. *International commissions and the power of ideas.* Tokyo: United Nations University Press.

Thakur, R., and E. Haru, eds. 2006. *The chemical weapons convention: Implementation, challenges and opportunities.* Tokyo: United Nations University Press.

Thakur, R., and W. Maley. 1999. The Ottawa convention on landmines: A landmark humanitarian treaty in arms control? *Global Governance* 5, no. 3: 273–298.

Thakur, R., and T. G. Weiss. 2009. United Nations "policy": An argument with three illustrations. *International Studies Perspectives* 10, no. 1 (January–April): 18–35.

United Nations. 2004. *A more secure world: Our shared responsibility.* Report of the secretary-general's High-Level Panel on Threats, Challenges and Change. UN Document A/59/565. United Nations. December 2. www.un.org/secureworld.

———. 2005. *World summit outcome*. UN Document A/RES/60/1. United Nations. October 24. http://daccess-dds-ny.un.org/doc/UNDOC/GEN/N05/487/60/ PDF/N0548760.pdf.

Weiss, T. G., T. Carayannis, and R. Jolly. 2009. The "third" United Nations. *Global Governance* 15, no. 1: 123–142.

Weiss, T. G., and R. Thakur. 2010. *Global governance and the UN: An unfinished journey*. Bloomington: Indiana University Press.

16

The Diplomacy of Specialized Agencies: High Food Prices and the World Food Program

Henk-Jan Brinkman and Masood Hyder

The rise in global food prices was sudden and unanticipated, with severe repercussions. The impact of the crisis was not uniform, hitting net importers particularly hard. At the household level, surging and volatile food prices affected those who could afford them the least. Globally, the numbers of the hungry began to rise toward the 1 billion mark. By 2007, it was clear that the crisis was not due to a temporary price spike and that structural forces would keep the cost of food high for years to come. Agencies working in the food and nutrition areas became very concerned about the impact of high food prices. Individual countries felt the pinch—Mexico was one of the first, leading to food riots in January 2007. Yet, at the global level, politicians were slow to react.

Several global summits put the food crisis on their agenda, and in April 2008, the Chief Executives Board (CEB) for Coordination of the United Nations established the High-Level Task Force (HLTF) on the Global Food Security Crisis under the leadership of the secretary-general, bringing together all concerned entities within the UN system. The primary aim of the HLTF was to promote a comprehensive and unified response.

Side by side with its participation in the task force, the World Food Program (WFP) continued its own advocacy for the hungry, aimed at three urgent tasks: raising additional funds to meet higher costs affecting its approved portfolio of projects for 2008, expanding its operations in order to cover the needs of the newly hungry, and coping with large new emergencies resulting from natural disasters. The WFP met all three objectives. Given that it fully relies on voluntary donations, it was an extraordinary achievement, not only in fund-raising but also in terms of operational efficiency and effective communication. In general, diplomatic efforts to mitigate the impact of high food prices and address the root causes have been successful only to a limited extent. What was achieved required a considerable effort on the part of many, and even that has been challenged by the global economic and financial crisis, which has drawn attention away from the food crisis.

This chapter sets the context of high food prices and then discusses the characteristics of the diplomacy of functional agencies of the United Nations, including their limitations and differences from traditional bilateral diplomacy. Following this, the chapter focuses on the WFP's diplomacy and concludes with an exploration of the WFP's role in specific issues related to the food-price crisis.

The Context of High Food Prices

Food prices had been increasing slowly but steadily since 2001, but hardly anyone was paying attention until the end of 2006 when maize (corn) prices began to increase more rapidly, followed by wheat in 2007 and rice in 2008. Figure 16.1 depicts the prices of three major cereal crops, but the price increases affected nearly all food commodities. The rice price hike in particular caused widespread panic. Rice prices had slowly doubled between 2001 and 2007, but then tripled to more than $1,000 per ton in the first few months of 2008. Traders were speculating that prices might reach $1,500 to $1,600 (Slayton 2009). Given that about 2 billion people in the world depend on rice, it is no surprise that such a price change caused extensive concern.

Figure 16.1   Cereal prices began to soar in 2006

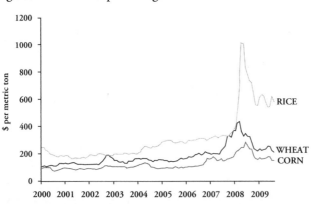

SOURCE: IMF data.

There is no consensus among economists about what caused the rise in food prices. Most agree that a combination of demand and supply factors played a role, but there is disagreement about the relative weight attributed to different factors, particularly for specific commodities and periods. Among the demand factors are higher incomes in rapidly growing economies, particularly Asia, population growth, biofuels, and, most controversially, large amounts of capital from institutional investors (see, for example, FAO 2008 and WFP 2009).

On the supply side, weather-related shocks caused small declines in global cereal production in 2005 and 2006. This happened at a time when cereal stocks were low and could not fully absorb the supply shocks. Stocks were low because supply had not kept pace with demand, partly because investments in agriculture had been low and the growth rate of yields had fallen. The supply situation was exacerbated by export restrictions imposed by dozens of countries, including major exporters. Higher energy prices also were a factor behind high food prices because some fertilizers and pesticides are based on hydrocarbons, and the production and transportation of food is energy intensive in many countries.

Many economists agreed that some of these factors, including high energy prices, income and population growth, and extreme weather events associated with climate change, are structural. As a result, they have forecasted high and volatile food prices for years to come. Yet, to many it was also clear that the extreme peaks in 2008 did not reflect fundamental economic factors but were a bubble fuelled by panic and speculation, even though the econometric evidence for this is mixed (WFP 2009).

The impact of high food prices has been severe. At the macro level, import bills increased, inflation rates went up, and budget deficits came under pressure. For households, the impact has been no less serious. The most vulnerable population groups have been those who buy more food than they sell (net buyers), spend a large share of their income on food, and have few coping strategies at their disposal. They switch to cheaper foods and reduce their expenditures on nonstaple foods, as well as the number and size of meals. Nonstaple foods are often the main sources of essential nutrients for a healthy and productive life. A lack of nutrients contributes to "hidden hunger." Even a few months of inadequate nutrition can do irreversible damage, especially for children under twenty-four months and pregnant women, in terms of health, learning, and productivity. The economic cost of hunger can be as high as 11 percent of gross domestic product (CEPAL 2007 and WFP 2007). Households also reduce expenditures on other basic needs, such as education and health, or sell productive assets, with negative effects on their current and future livelihoods. The consequences of high food prices, even if temporary, are long-term—even lifelong.

These effects were well known among economists and nutritionists. Yet, it was difficult to get the international community's attention until riots erupted and the political impacts became evident. The food riots in Haiti in April 2008, which brought down the government and also affected UN peacekeepers, were the trigger for political leaders around the world, including at the United Nations, to wake up. For a few months, at least, the food crisis was high on the diplomatic agenda. Disturbances, many of them labeled "food riots," occurred in dozens of countries. Food prices might have played a role, but often other broader or longer-lasting factors, such as political, economic, regional, and social elements, are required to cause riots to erupt. Nevertheless, "food riots" were instrumental in drawing the attention of political leaders to the food crisis, focusing on mitigating the impact and addressing the root causes.

The Diplomacy of Functional UN Agencies

The functional agencies of the UN system are often thought of as nonpolitical and are primarily concerned with humanitarian and developmental work (Claude 1965, 344). For that reason, they are involved in the management of relationships in the international political arena. The activities of their representatives do not appear to be very different from those of the professional diplomat. When it is taking an active part in negotiations in a diplomatic setting, an international organization and its officials are engaged in diplomacy. The diplomacy of international organizations takes place at different levels: multilaterally, bilaterally, and among international organizations themselves. Each arena has its own characteristics: The interpretation of the issue, the style of conducting business, and the objectives pursued vary accordingly from one forum to the other.

Multilateral Diplomacy

At the multilateral level, diplomacy is a collective activity, involving groups of countries (and international organizations). The food-price crisis figured as a major item on the agenda of several international conferences, including the Food and Agricultural Organization's (FAO) High-Level Conference on World Food Security of June 2008; the Group of Eight (G-8) Summit in Toyako, Japan, of July 2008; the Madrid High-Level Conference on Food Security for All in January 2009; the Group of Twenty (G-20) Summit in London of April 2009; and the G-8 Summit in L'Aquila, Italy, of April 2009. Such international gatherings can accomplish three objectives. First, they can create a climate of support: Summits are "moments of maximum communication" (Wight 1977, 32). The very act of placing it on the international agenda of a series of major conferences signals recognition of the food crisis as an issue of continuing international concern. Second, exposure in an international forum may subject the issue to a process of refinement or precision in which topics of particular significance or interest to the participants are identified. Thus, the 2008 G-8 Summit in Japan focused on feeding the hungry and promoting global partnerships; the Madrid conference pursued the idea of support for smallholder farming; and the G-20 proposed setting up a global alert system. Third, they can lead to the development of appropriate responses (such as the creation of coordination mechanisms), promises of funding, or recommendations to implement specific policies. The G-8 Summit of 2009, for example, committed $20 billion over three years in support of food security (later increased to $22 billion). In short, multilateral diplomacy is a means of enhancing communication whereby topics of common concern are identified, explored, and even promoted, but not necessarily resolved. The recommendations remain somewhat tentative, allowing member states a relatively free hand in taking them up or not.

Bilateral Diplomacy

If multilateral diplomacy is about clarifying policy, then bilateral diplomacy is about implementation. For donors, this means setting terms for committing resources; for recipient countries it means preparing for humanitarian interventions and other actions in their sovereign territories. For both, it means deciding the level of commitment to the policy in question, in light of their particular national interests.

Bilateral diplomacy between international agencies is conducted at headquarters and in capitals, operating through permanent representations and missions. In this way, the WFP deals on a regular basis with donor and recipient countries. Bilateral diplomacy is quieter, more focused, and more businesslike. The main concern in engaging donors is to ensure funding and support for WFP activities at the country level. The main concern with recipient countries is with gaining access to vulnerable groups and nurturing humanitarian space, an activity sometimes referred to as "humanitarian diplomacy" (Minear and Smith 2007). The

WFP also increasingly advocates for certain interventions, for example, regarding nutrition, through policies, projects, or programs and by developing partnerships in order to implement them. The WFP's main interlocutor in recipient countries is the government concerned (at various levels), its relevant ministries, and local communities (or the group or groups actually in power). The interceding parties include the UN resident coordinator or humanitarian coordinator, donor community representatives present in the country, humanitarian partners on the ground (e.g., nongovernmental agencies and agency partners), and agency headquarters, including the offices of the UN secretary-general, the Department of Political Affairs, and the Department of Safety and Security.

In the field, WFP officials share to a limited extent in the collegiality of the diplomatic profession (Mowat 1935). Their concerns are different in two respects. First, WFP officials have humanitarian rather than political concerns, being primarily interested in the people rather than what is happening to the government. Second, while both the WFP and the diplomats are interested in information, the purpose and methods are very different. The WFP has better—often unmatched—access to the hungry and the vulnerable throughout the country, whereas diplomats (who have an interest in intelligence gathering) operate mainly in the capitals, with quite limited access to the more affected areas of the country. This implies the need for the WFP to engage in "diplomacy" and negotiations at the local level with local governments, communities, and actors, sometimes leading to tensions with the central government.

Diplomacy Among International Organizations

While it is understandable to speak in terms of diplomacy and negotiation at the multilateral and bilateral levels, it could be argued that the relationship among international organizations is more cooperative, where common interests prevail and the process of diplomacy gives way to international technical management as a means of finding the most efficient way to achieve a given end. However, even among international agencies there has to be a process of bargaining and negotiation before common positions can be identified.

UN entities may share common interests and values, but they also have separate and distinct mandates. They are not part of a binding system of governance. The specialized agencies, including the Bretton Woods institutions (BWIs), are not directly supervised or controlled by the secretary-general or the UN General Assembly. The secretary-general chairs the UN CEB, which includes heads of all agencies within the United Nations, including the BWIs. The CEB focuses on coordination and information sharing. Interagency relations within the UN system display many characteristics of full-blown international diplomacy, including a willingness to work toward common goals and a reluctance to give up particular interests.

The process recalls Hedley Bull's observation that "the presentation of international problems as problems of international technical management often merely obscures the true position, which is that states have different interests, and that common interests have first to be identified by a process of bargaining before any question of maximization of them can arise" (1977, 170). The observation, though intended as a comment about interstate dealings, describes quite accurately the process by which the common interests of the UN entities were first identified and negotiated in the HLTF.

The United Nations and its funds, programs, and specialized agencies are intergovernmental bodies and, as such, not equal in status to sovereign states, the only full members of the international community. Strategic frameworks, budgets, policies, and often much more are all determined by the member states. Sometimes there are disagreements between the governing bodies and the secretariats about their respective roles concerning the extent to which the staff of secretariats should facilitate or participate in negotiations among member states. Some argue that diplomacy among international organizations is an oxymoron. This tension came to the surface regarding the HLTF: Some member states wanted to have control over it and pushed for a reporting function to the General Assembly. This attempt failed.

The High-Level Task Force on the Global Food Security Crisis

On April 29, 2008, the CEB decided to establish the High-Level Task Force on the Global Food Security Crisis under the leadership of the secretary-general, bringing together the heads of the UN funds, programs, and specialized agencies, including the BWIs, and senior officials from relevant parts of the UN Secretariat. The immediate aim of the HLTF was to create a plan of action for addressing the crisis. The plan, titled *Comprehensive Framework for Action* (CFA), was produced by July 2008. It set out the joint position of the HLTF members on the rise in food prices, offered recommendations for building resilience against future shocks, and made suggestions for improving country, regional, and global food security.

At first glance, the production of the CFA appears to be a good example of diplomacy, having given way to a collaborative, technical process. In May 2008, a drafting group of the HLTF prepared a common set of guidelines for dealing with the food crisis. Two months later, the CFA was finalized and presented to the General Assembly. The drafting of the CFA was a participatory process, and care was taken to ensure that the main operational agencies had a hand in its preparation. The CFA achieved something remarkable, representing in a fair and unbiased way the different and complementary functions that the main UN agencies might carry out in responding to the food crisis: providing food assistance, boosting agriculture, improving the global trade regime, enhancing the resilience of the system to price shocks, and so on. The proper roles of the agencies in undertaking these different tasks were recognized, not threatened. Care was taken to limit the authority of the task force secretariat. This was not merely technical management but also a demonstration of considerable political and diplomatic sensitivity by the task force coordinator and his team, who were responsible for managing the drafting process. Technical management did not drive out the diplomatic approach but incorporated it. The key was the sensitive promotion of common interests.

The CFA was widely praised as a balanced and sensible document produced in a timely fashion. It reflected well on the intention of the UN system to deal effectively with the food crisis. This success story should not hide the fact that it was nevertheless essentially a political process, characterized by decision making that is protracted and policy execution that is sometimes weak. It is in this light that we must consider the performance of the other UN institutions and arrangements concerned with the food crisis.

The CEB and HLTF are assemblies of semiautonomous UN agencies, funds, and programs. They may be described as consensus-driven bodies that struggle to reach decisions. The secretary-general is not the chief executive officer but primus inter pares. The CFA is not an action document but an advisory note. The HLTF Secretariat does not develop policy but is kept relatively weak to prevent it from assuming the policy-making and executive functions of the agencies. All these institutions have done remarkably well, given the constraints under which they operate.

In general, UN actors are at a certain disadvantage in a political arena dominated by member states interested in political outcomes rather than people-oriented humanitarian and developmental solutions. The United Nations' functional agencies are founded on the premise that economic and social welfare activities, such as the promotion of health and nutrition and the alleviation of hunger and poverty, will reinforce peace and security. The point is enshrined in the constitutional documents of some agencies and in the UN Charter (Article

55). For example, the constitution of the World Health Organization states, "The health of all peoples is fundamental to the attainment of peace and security."

However, the United Nations' experience shows that it is not possible to entirely separate political and nonpolitical matters in this way. Appeals to economic and social welfare are more effective in terms of national interest because loyalty to the state is usually stronger than any other international bond, including international agreements on human, economic, and social rights (Wight 1979, 25). Yet, it is not a question of choosing either the functional approach or the political approach. States appear to give priority to their own political interests while encouraging functionalism to the extent that domestic opinion and other considerations allow. The functional agencies appear to respond in kind, adhering to humanitarian, economic, and social principles but not hesitating, when negotiating in the political arena, to use the language of power politics and national interest to advance their cause.

Perhaps the clearest example of this flexible approach is the WFP's ability to present the food crisis using three types of argument: the humanitarian, the economic, and the political. In humanitarian terms, the case for fighting hunger is quite straightforward: It is a means of saving lives and reducing suffering. If we have the ability to help, we are morally bound to do so. The economic argument links hunger and poverty with undesirable economic, social, and political outcomes. Ending poverty and hunger will contribute to a higher standard of living and reinforce peace and security. The political argument is based on the perception of an imminent threat: Hunger, it is claimed, can lead to political instability. Of the three types of argument, the moral argument is sound because it is based on the humanitarian imperative. The economic argument is persuasive because it appeals to the common interest of all in the welfare of mankind. The political argument is perhaps less convincing, and yet perhaps most effective because it speaks directly to the survival of governments. The WFP has used all three types of argument to good effect.[1]

The Basis of the WFP's Diplomacy

The WFP's diplomacy is founded on its operational excellence and its actual achievements. Its reputation is the foundation of its diplomacy. Its diplomatic objectives in the food crisis have been pragmatic and limited. The WFP's diplomatic functions must be distinguished and derived from its operational activities, which constitute its chief concern. The WFP is engaged in a struggle to fight hunger, to save lives, and to sustain livelihoods. This is far removed from the rarified environments in which diplomats usually practice their craft. Yet, the WFP has been able to convey that authenticity of experience in its dealings in the diplomatic arena. The WFP's diplomacy is based on its strengths: its deep field presence; its knowledge of, and responsiveness to, humanitarian disasters and vulnerabilities; the scale of its operations; the intensity of its partnerships; and its ability to convey a positive image of its work. This makes the WFP a successful example of the exercise of "soft diplomacy" that elicits approval, enhances its attractiveness, and ensures support (Nye 2004). The WFP, we might say, undertakes hard operations at the country level and promotes soft diplomacy at the global level.

The WFP has been pragmatic in its diplomatic objectives. Its diplomatic goals are focused on important humanitarian concerns, whereas the food crisis is interpreted as an economic problem. The WFP's objectives are more humanitarian than economic: to feed the hungry, based on its concern with the impact of the price crisis on hunger and malnutrition. The question is, Is the fight against hunger generally perceived as the main objective of the food-price crisis? Are there other objectives as well, such as the political objective of maintaining political stability, or economic objectives, such as maintaining food-price stability or improving resilience to price shocks? How are these different objectives related?

The WFP deals with (humanitarian) symptoms, not (economic) causes. This narrow focus, it seems, is not a weakness but a strength. The diplomat has considerable admiration for the practitioner. The WFP does not do everything, but it does undertake important work, and what it undertakes it accomplishes very well. It has focused its advocacy on a select list of issues of direct relevance to its operations, such as funding for its emergency operations, humanitarian exemptions to export restrictions, or piracy off the Somali coast, and has taken a backseat on issues in which other agency partners have a more direct stake. The World Bank, for example, has focused more on trade policy and taxation and the subsidization of food, while the FAO concentrates on agricultural production and the need for fertilizers and seeds.

The WFP's actions are usually commensurate with the expected outcome. At the global level, the WFP has been interested in ensuring that the food crisis stays on the international agenda, the voices of the vulnerable are heard, and key issues of interest to the WFP figure on conference agendas. Conferences and summits are interested in the global architecture of food and are quite prolific in their suggestions for the creation of new coordination mechanisms. On such issues, the WFP has taken care to appear attentive without assuming a lead role in the comeback, encouraging instead a measured, negotiated, and joint response by the UN system (or more precisely, by the HLTF). Conferences also produce vague funding commitments, but the actual negotiations on this subject are usually undertaken bilaterally. The WFP has encouraged or lobbied for a commitment that pays due attention to the needs of the hungry.

Food-Price Diplomacy

During the food crisis, the WFP focused on one objective, feeding the hungry, which required resources. This had several components. First, feeding the hungry became more expensive because of the increase in food and fuel prices. Consequently, in March 2008 the WFP launched an extraordinary appeal for $755 million to cover the higher costs of its programs. Second, the WFP needed to do more because the number of hungry people was increasing. The expectation in 2008 was that the numbers would increase by 115 million in 2007 and 2008 as a result of high food prices, reaching 963 million. In 2009 these numbers were revised again to a total of 1.02 billion. This increase came on top of emergencies induced by natural disasters or violence, for example, in the Democratic Republic of Congo, Haiti, and Myanmar. Third, the depth of hunger and malnutrition deepened as vulnerable households reduced the quality and quantity of food consumption.

The WFP made ample use of public diplomacy—using public media and public opinion to indirectly influence the decisions of governments—to reach its objectives. This is not fundamentally new, but the Internet, mobile phones, blogs, and social-networking websites had expanded rapidly in recent years and increased the opportunity for public diplomacy. Using public diplomacy was an effective instrument to reach many actors at the same time with clear and important messages about the needs of the hungry and of the WFP to address those needs. Josette Sheeran, the executive director of the WFP, did a remarkable job of calling attention to the plight of the hungry. She appeared on the *Late Show with David Letterman*. Videos appeared on YouTube. She posted contributions to blogs. She testified before legislatures, gave interviews, and met with leaders of civil society. Public service announcements, featuring, for example, Sean Penn, aired on televisions across the world.

Public diplomacy was employed in addition to multilateral and bilateral diplomacy. The WFP staff met with donors, spoke at conferences, attended meetings at the United Nations, and worked behind the scenes on specific language in reports of the secretary-general and outcome documents of summits and conferences, including the G-8 Summit. The hard work of the executive director and WFP staff was supported by Robert Zoellick, president of the World Bank, and Ban Ki-moon, secretary-general of the United Nations, who repeatedly argued for the plight of the hungry and vulnerable and for increased funding for the WFP.

These efforts paid off. The WFP received $5 billion in 2008, up from $2.7 billion in 2007. Public diplomacy almost certainly contributed to this, and the single-largest contribution of $500 million from Saudi Arabia was most probably not the result of multilateral or bilateral diplomacy.

Access to and Availability of Food

The fight for the hungry could not be won without making a number of critical arguments. One of the key issues to emerge during the food crisis was the often-singular focus on food availability. The WFP argued hard that food security cannot be achieved, and hunger and malnutrition cannot be eliminated, by focusing on agricultural production alone. Food security involves availability, access, utilization, and stability. Yet, when a new global partnership among governments, civil society, and the private sector was proposed at the Madrid conference, it was focused on—or even restricted to—improving agricultural production. The WFP argued that it should focus on food security so that food access would also be addressed.

Ever since the seminal work of Amartya Sen (1981), it has been clear that famines, hunger, and malnutrition are related less to declines in food availability than to people's access to food, determined by such factors as wages, employment, and food and livestock prices (WFP 2009). The importance of access is illustrated by the fact that despite the enormous increase in food production in South Asia as a result of the Green Revolution, very high malnutrition levels still prevail, with stunting rates close to 50 percent in countries such as Bangladesh and India. "The persistence of malnutrition as a global health concern despite the successes in increasing agricultural production belies any notion that malnutrition and under-nutrition can be solved entirely from the supply side [by increasing agricultural production]" (World Bank 2007, xi).

The food-price crisis also supported the point. At no time during the crisis was there a shortage of food. People just did not have enough money to buy the food that was available. The WFP's executive director talked about the "new face of hunger," particularly referring to the urban poor, for example, at the European

Parliament Development Committee in March 2008. The WFP was able to rely on analysis it conducted itself through assessments and a timely flagship publication on hunger and markets (WFP 2009). Increasing production takes time. The gap could be as little as until the next harvest or as great as fifteen years, the time required to develop new high-yielding seeds. In the meantime, people need to eat. The CEB meeting in April 2008, therefore, concluded, "First, we must FEED THE HUNGRY. . . . Second, we must ensure FOOD FOR TOMORROW." The food and agriculture agencies of the United Nations (the FAO, WFP, and International Fund for Agricultural Development) have always accepted this twin-track approach, addressing availability and access issues, which formed the basis of the CFA as well. With additional resources, the WFP expanded and adjusted existing programs and rolled out new ones. It might have been the largest scale up in humanitarian history. For example, seventeen WFP school-feeding programs were upscaled in 2008, reaching 5 million more children and their families. An additional 31 million people in twenty-six countries were reached, increasing the total number of beneficiaries in 2008 to 102 million.

In 2009, however, the situation looked different. The global economic and financial crisis, which erupted in September 2008 in the United States and spread quickly across the world, took over the headlines. International food prices declined in the second half of 2008 (see Figure 16.1) but remained relatively high, especially at the local level. The WFP and other UN entities have struggled to keep the food crisis at the top of the international agenda. The WFP argued that the global economic and financial crisis made the situation worse for the hungry across the world as they not only faced higher food prices but now also lower incomes. Yet, contributions to the WFP as of mid-October 2009 amounted to only $2.9 billion against a program of work of $6.7 billion. This is probably partly a result of extensive budget pressures in donor countries, as they needed to support financial institutions, provide fiscal stimuli, and scale up social-protection programs while tax revenues have been declining. The argument that fighting hunger only amounts to a small percentage of the more than $20 trillion for financial institutions and fiscal stimuli has not yielded a very effective response.

Conclusion: The Limits of the Diplomacy of International Organizations

State actors dominate the international arena and focus on national interest. While international organizations may claim to support the international interest, processes driven by national governments impose constraints on outcomes. Management and diplomatic skills are generally of secondary importance. Yet, they can make a difference (Jolly, Emmerij, and Weiss 2009).

An international response to hunger is likely to be generated not so much by the diplomatic skills of the international organizations as by the perception of the risk that the situation poses to the interests of governments. Just as access to oil has influenced foreign policies, food security seems to have infiltrated the national security domain. In the United States, for example, the formulation of the new food-security strategy was led by the State Department. Because of the crisis, many countries across the world have focused on food sovereignty. However, it is not the moral, economic, or social imperative of fighting hunger that drives this, but the perceived threat to peace and security (see, for example, Natsios and Doley 2009). Economic constraints play an important part in determining the scale of international response to international crises. In the case of the current food crisis, there are sound economic arguments for helping the poor (e.g., the economic cost of undernutrition and the argument that helping the poor pays off if we can turn them into our business partners). Yet, the link is too hidden and long-term, and donors do not see a compelling argument that will win support from their domestic constituencies.

In practical terms, the WFP's achievements in 2008 owed little directly to the efforts of the high-level task force. Most of the funds were raised before the publication of the CFA. The UN secretary-general and the World Bank president went out of their way to appeal on behalf of the WFP, but this was largely done outside the HLTF context. The WFP's successful fund-raising did not stem from the coordination mechanisms that were created. Similarly, other UN agencies, such as the World Bank ($2 billion) and the European Commission (€1 billion and not a member of the HLTF), greatly expanded their commitments to address the food-security crisis.

If individual agency achievements and failures could be isolated in this way, what is directly attributable to the systemwide effort of the United Nations? Certainly the great achievement of 2008 was the preparation of the CFA. It is difficult to say if the CFA's recommendations helped the HLTF members in any practical way, although the symbolism was powerful: The UN system, including the BWIs, working together, had quickly produced an excellent document. But the CFA itself and the goodwill generated did very little in 2008 to help directly, for example, smallholder farmers (a major recommendation of the CFA). The planting season came and went without much notice being taken of their plight.

This was the great failure of 2008, which went largely unnoticed by the media. Direct results are very difficult to measure if the objectives are coordination and enhancing coherence. Whether the total is greater than the sum of its parts is difficult to assess.

It is too early to say what the coordinated interagency approach and the diplomacy of the HLTF agencies will produce in 2010. It will certainly be something of an achievement if, despite the preoccupations of the financial crisis, the food crisis is not overlooked. The secretary-general continued to be fully committed to keeping the food crisis on the global agenda. As of 2009, the HLTF continued to meet regularly, and the secretary-general never missed an HLTF meeting, indicating a determination to see the crisis through. Progress is discernible in operational terms as well. A secretariat has been established, the work goals of the HLTF have been defined, and country-level collaboration has been intensified in twenty-seven pilot countries. The members of the HLTF are acquiring the habit of consulting each other in preparing for conferences and summits. Yet, the question of whether the achievements of the HLTF are commensurate with its efforts remains an open one.

The food crisis was a hot topic on the agenda of diplomats for some time. International agencies, such as the WFP, certainly played a role in putting it there, although they might be less successful in keeping it there as other urgent topics compete for attention. The next critical test will be the delivery of results. Billions of dollars are being committed to food security, including by UN entities, the European Commission, the G-20, and others. Time alone will tell whether the current food crisis will be the last one that the world shall witness.

Note

1. See, for example, James Morris's briefing of the Security Council in December 2002 and April 2003 on the hunger crisis in Africa; see also Josette Sheeran's appeal to the G-8 (WFP news release of June 12, 2009). For a critique of the political argument, see M. Hyder (2007).

References

Bull, H. 1977. *The anarchical society*. New York: Colombia University Press.

Comision Economica para America Latina (CEPAL) and World Food Program (WFP). 2007. *El costo del hambre: Análisis del impacto social y económico de la desnutrición infantil en América Latina*. Santiago: CEPAL.

Claude, I. L. 1965. *Swords into plowshares: The problems and progress of international organization*. New York: Random House.

Food and Agricultural Organization (FAO). 2008. *Soaring food prices: Facts, perspectives, impacts and actions required. High-Level Conference on World Food Security: The Challenges of Climate Change and Bioenergy.* HLC/08/INF/1. Rome: FAO.

Hyder, M. 2007. Humanitarianism and the Muslim world. *Journal of Humanitarian Assistance* (August 22), http://jha.ac/2007/08/22/humanitarianism-and-the-muslim-world.

Jolly, R., L. Emmerij, and T. G. Weiss. 2009. *UN ideas that changed the world*. Bloomington: Indiana University Press.

Minear, L., and H. Smith. 2007. *Humanitarian diplomacy: Practitioners and their craft*. New York: United Nations University Press.

Mowat, R. B. 1935. *Diplomacy and peace*. London: William and Norgate.

Natsios, A., and K. W. Doley. 2009. The coming food coups. *The Washington Quarterly* 32, no. 1 (January): 7–25.

Nye, J. 2004. *Soft diplomacy: The means to success in world politics*. New York: Public Affairs.

Sen, A. 1981. *Poverty and famines: An essay on entitlement and deprivation*. Oxford: Oxford University Press.

Slayton, T. 2009. Rice crisis forensics: How Asian governments carelessly set the world rice market on fire. Working Paper No. 163, Center for Global Development, Washington, DC.

United Nations. 2008. *Comprehensive framework for action. United Nations High-Level Task Force on the Global Food Security Crisis.* New York: United Nations.

Wight, M. 1979. *Power politics*, ed. H. Bull and C. Holdbraad. Leicester, UK: Pelican Books and Leicester University Press.

———. 1977. *Systems of states*, ed. H. Bull. Leicester, UK: Leicester University Press.

World Bank. 2007. *From agriculture to nutrition: Pathways, synergies, and outcomes*. Washington, DC: World Bank.

World Food Program (WFP). 2009. *World hunger series—hunger and markets*. London: Earthscan.

PART FIVE
Reflections on
the New Dynamics
of Multilateralism

17

A Realist's Argument for Multilateral Diplomacy

Earl Sullivan

Political realism was developed as a school of thought in international relations theory in the mid-twentieth century. Its chief proponent and architect was Hans J. Morgenthau, a professor of political science and modern history at the University of Chicago. His seminal book, *Politics Among Nations: The Struggle for Power and Peace* (1973), was first published in 1948 and continued to be published in subsequent editions for several decades. This work influenced generations of scholars and also had an impact on policy makers, although perhaps not as much influence as its founder and other proponents would have wished. Political realism represents an important paradigm in international relations and is a useful framework for analyzing events and describing, at least in general terms, how diplomats and statesmen conduct themselves in the real world of international politics. It also has prescriptive value, as it contains a number of general guidelines for policy makers and practitioners. This chapter briefly reviews traditional realist thought of the last century, focusing on how realists have regarded multilateral diplomacy as a tool of statecraft. Following this, it shows how a contemporary realist in the early part of the twenty-first century would place a much higher value on the utility of multilateral diplomacy than did the traditional realists of the mid-twentieth century.

Traditional Realism

The essence of traditional political realism is that sovereign states dominate the international system. In this system, each state pursues what it perceives to be its national interest, and this interest is defined in terms of power; states pursue power in order to enhance and protect their interests. The world of sovereign states is highly decentralized, and there is no central authority to govern all states; the principal check against the power of one state is the countervailing power of another state or coalition of states. International law or a shared moral consensus might limit what states do in some cases, but in the realist paradigm, it is ultimately power, not morality or law, that constrains states (Morgenthau 1973, passim, especially 3–15).

Arguing in the mid-twentieth century, Morgenthau was especially concerned about the appeal of what he called "nationalistic universalism" to the leaders of his time (1973, 327–337). Nationalistic universalism is the belief that the values and interests of one state are presumed to be superior to the values and interests of all other states: "The nationalistic universalism of our age claims for one nation and one state the right to impose its own valuations and standards of action upon all the other nations" (Morgenthau 1973, 329). In a bipolar or multipolar world in which there is more than one such ideology, conflict is virtually impossible to avoid. Conflicting national interests between states need not lead to war, however, as diplomacy can be employed to reduce, if not entirely eliminate, war as an instrument of statecraft.

In Morgenthau's time the world of states was essentially bipolar, with the two superpowers vying against each other in virtually every arena possible, including in the contest for the minds of men. The major threat to peace in the latter half of the twentieth century was war between the superpowers, and the leading bulwark against this potentially catastrophic conflict was the rational and intelligent practice of traditional diplomacy. Morgenthau (1973, 455–475) argued convincingly that the United Nations was not able to deal with this threat and that contests between the superpowers should be kept *out* of the United Nations, rather than brought to it. Traditional diplomacy, the formation of military alliances, and a balance of power were the best, indeed only, tools available to avert war between the superpowers. When Morgenthau listed the "organized instruments of diplomacy" (1973, 520), he did not even mention diplomatic missions to international organizations and strongly implied that serious diplomacy was, by definition, bilateral. Henry Kissinger, both a theorist and a practitioner of international politics, also placed a high value on the practice of diplomacy but assigned very little importance to diplomacy in most multilateral arenas. In his view, diplomacy involved both threats and rewards: "In the practice of *Realpolitic*, statesmen shoulder the task of relating particular interests to general ones through a balance of incentives and penalties" (Kissinger 1994, 248). In traditional foreign policy, states form alliances to defend against common threats, usually involving the potential threat of war. For the most part, threats to national security are therefore thought of in military terms, with war or the threat of war as the ultimate instrument of diplomacy. The implication is clear: Unless multilateral agencies can be used to mobilize allies against putative enemies, they should be avoided if possible.

Although international organizations are not the only arenas for multilateral diplomacy, they are the principal ones, and they tend to make decisions by means of voting. In the case of the UN General Assembly, this means one vote for each state, no matter how rich or poor, powerful or weak it may be. This fits with the doctrine of sovereign equality, but it does not comport well with political reality, and realists have tended to view what they call parliamentary diplomacy with disdain. (For a useful definition of parliamentary diplomacy, see Freeman 1997, 77.) As Morgenthau pointed out, one of the evils of UN diplomacy is that it forces diplomats to couch the argument for the resolution on the agenda in highly moralistic and ideological "supranational terms" rather than in the cold but more truthful and realistic terms of realpolitik. Furthermore, it sets in motion a process of bargaining that "necessitates a search for a common denominator, which is bound to be below the maximum desired by the originator" of the resolution (Morgenthau 1973, 472). This problem can occur even in cases in which a weighted majority is employed, for example, one in which greater voting power is given to states with more financial and economic weight than others, as is the case in the World Bank and the International Monitory Fund. Inis L. Claude Jr., a noted specialist on international organizations stated, "Excessive emphasis on the power to mobilize a voting majority obscures the fundamental truth that, in the world as it really is, voting [in international organizations] does not solve problems or resolve conflicts" (1971, 140).

One of the most basic principles of political realism is that all states have a hierarchy of interests, some of which are vital to the survival of the state and hence not subject to compromise. As Morgenthau put it, "Nations must be willing to compromise on all issues that are not vital to them" (1973, 542). This automatically raises the question of how vital interests are to be distinguished from secondary and tertiary interests, and while classical geopolitics provides some guidance here—all states can be expected to regard secure borders and noninvolvement in their internal affairs as vital interests—this principle is admittedly somewhat vague, and it is an issue to which we return in the next section of this chapter. However, one way to understand the issue of hierarchy of interests is to consider the distinction between the *high politics* of national security and the *low politics* of all other issues. National security issues traditionally involve such issues as the protection of borders and other geopolitical interests as strategic waterways and other vital trade routes as well as the principle of noninvolvement in the internal affairs of the state (Kaplan 2009). The significance of this distinction for our topic is that realists traditionally argue that national security issues can seldom, if ever, be compromised on and are therefore not appropriate for most multilateral venues, except for the diplomacy that takes place in military alliances. Bilateral diplomacy and alliance diplomacy are the most, if not the only, appropriate forms of diplomacy for national security issues. Social, environmental, and even economic topics, by implication, are more amenable to solution by negotiation, persuasion, or compromise, and in some cases for submission to relevant multilateral venues and organizations.

What Is a Contemporary Realist to Do?

From this brief review it is easy to conclude that traditional political realism places a relatively low value on most forms of multilateral diplomacy. Virtually the only multilateral venue that realists have tended to value highly is the traditional military alliance. These theories were developed several decades ago, and it is reasonable to ask if the conclusions that political realism reached about the value of multilateral diplomacy are still valid. One principle of realism is pragmatism: Policies must change as circumstances and interests change (Morgenthau 1973, 8–9). Therefore, within the realist paradigm the best way to address this question is to consider how the world of international politics has changed since the theory was first formulated.

In what ways is the agenda of global politics fundamentally different in the early years of the twenty-first century from the basic patterns of politics in the latter half of the twentieth century? How do the changes that have occurred affect the way a contemporary realist would view the relative utility of multilateral diplomacy versus traditional bilateral diplomacy and the diplomacy needed to sustain traditional military alliances? Five major factors are relevant to this issue: (1) the end of the Cold War, (2) the relative decline of the economic power of the United States, (3) the growing salience of social, environmental, and economic issues, (4) globalization, (5) and the end of the presidency of George W. Bush.

The end of the Cold War brought with it the end of the bipolar system that dominated international politics for decades and ushered in a new system in which there is a single superpower and a number of other states of increasing economic and political significance. It has become commonplace to read about meetings of the Group of Eight (G-8; Britain, Canada, France, Germany, Italy, Russia, and the United States), the Group of Twenty (G-20; all members of the G-8 plus Brazil, China, India, and nine other states). It is now normal for such meetings to include a variety of social, economic, and environmental topics high on the agenda, along with the traditional discussion of military and security issues. In short, many of the issues that were considered low politics have become topics of high politics.

The scope and pace of globalization has also had a profound effect on international politics; international trade and commerce now affect virtually every state in ways that are central rather than marginal to their well-being. Communications are now global and instantaneous, and no country can totally close its borders to information from outside; nor can it prevent its citizens from communicating to the world. All countries are now penetrated from the outside, and no country can isolate itself from the assets and liabilities of being part of a global network. States remain as key actors in the global system, but multinational corporations, international organizations, and international nongovernmental organizations are also major actors rather than bit players in the emerging global order.

As demonstrated in the chapters of this book dealing with international secretariats, one fact that contemporary realists must recognize is that the leaders of international organizations are *legitimate* actors in their own right in the debates and discussions that take place in the international arena. As such, they condition and help shape policies and the behavior of states, even on issues of high strategic importance. The first objective of a realist is to recognize reality for what it is, warts and all, and this is part of the new reality.

It may seem odd, and to some it will seem inappropriate, to mention the Bush presidency in this context, but it is relevant in a number of ways. In the early years of his administration, the second President Bush and his leading neoconservative advisors attempted to change the terms of the relationship between the sole superpower and all other states. This new set of rules could be summed up by a simple phrase: You are either with us, or you are against us. This tendency was dictated by ideology, not by pragmatism. This extreme Manichaean perspective produced a profound backlash, even, or indeed especially, among most of the closest allies of the United States, and it ultimately failed. The United States was not able to have everything its own way, and the failure was so clear that it seems highly probable that future U.S. administrations will be much less likely or able to revert to an attempt to dictate the terms of reference to other states. Conversely, they will be more likely to operate within the norms of traditional diplomacy. One of the hallmarks of the Bush presidency was open disdain for working within multilateral venues unless it could be done totally on Washington's terms. As this approach to international politics also clearly failed, succeeding administrations will be more likely to take a more pragmatic and constructive approach to participation in international organizations and to remain more open to engaging in diplomacy in multilateral venues.

As Henry Kissinger, one of the most ardent realists of recent times, has pointed out, "What *is* new about the emerging world order is that, for the first time, the United States can neither withdraw from the world nor dominate it" (1994, 19). As the United States can neither dictate norms and behavior to others nor withdraw behind its now porous borders, what roles would contemporary realists assign to it?

The Role of the United States in the Emerging World Order

One of the most interesting contemporary realists is Fareed Zakaria, an Indian-born American citizen who serves as the editor of *Newsweek International* and hosts *Fareed Zakaria GPS* on CNN. He is also an author, and his widely read book *The Post-American World* contains some trenchant observations and policy recommendations regarding the emerging world system. One of his most important proposals is that the United States should not attempt to serve as the balancer in the post–Cold War world. This runs contrary to the predisposition of realists in the earlier era. In classical realism, the United States, as the leading superpower of the time, was called upon to balance against the rising, and hence threatening, power of the Soviet Union. In the early years of the twenty-first century, the United States is still the leading power of the contemporary order and is highly likely to remain so for many decades. In this new system, with a single superpower and a number of rising powers, the United States should not automatically "balance" against rising powers—Brazil, China, India, Russia, and so forth. Rather it should work to integrate them into the system. In this new emerging system, the United States should emulate Otto von Bismarck, who "chose to engage all the great powers. His goal was to have better relations with all of them than any of them had with each other—to be the pivot of . . . [the new] international system"; balancing against rising powers, in this case, "would be a dangerous, destabilizing and potentially self-fulfilling policy" (Zakaria 2009, 241). Rising powers should be accommodated as they grow in significance and strongly encouraged to abide by the norms of the global order, as they are increasingly able to benefit from full membership in the system. Balancing is always an option but should not be the first or the automatic option.

One key characteristic of the emerging system is the growing salience of social, environmental, and economic issues on the agenda of international politics. The old hierarchy of interests, in which security concerns that are at least potentially open to military action are intrinsically more important than all other issues, has been replaced by a much more fluid set of interests, many of which are vital to a large number of states but nevertheless do not lend themselves to military responses. These global issues are by definition multilateral ones, and this implies that the relative salience of multilateral diplomacy has increased along with the relative salience of environmental, social, and economic issues on the global agenda. Global issues need to be addressed on a global basis and are not susceptible to solution by unilateral action, even by global or regional superpowers.

Times change, and interests change, and states in the twenty-first century must address an increasingly large number of global issues that do not involve the threat of nuclear conflict between superpowers. Although war between the leading nuclear powers has certainly not been eliminated as a threat, the threat has significantly abated, and other threats to the security and well-being of all states compete for the attention of diplomatists with traditional geopolitical and military problems. Among these threats are issues such as global warming, global environmental degradation, global pandemics, and the functioning, or mal-functioning, of the global financial system. For a realist in the twenty-first century, global issues must be dealt with pragmatically, on a global basis, and multilateral diplomacy must be an essential tool of realist statecraft. As Henry Kissinger has stated,

> The international system of the twenty-first century will . . . contain at least six major powers—the United States, Europe, China, Japan, Russia, and probably India—as well as a multiplicity of medium-sized and smaller countries. At the same time, international relations have become truly global for the first time. Communications are instantaneous; the world economy operates on all continents simultaneously. A whole set of issues has surfaced that can only be dealt with on a worldwide basis, such as nuclear proliferation, the environment, the population explosion, and economic interdependence." (1994, 23–24)

Contemporary and traditional realists urge policy makers and diplomatists to be pragmatic. This admonition carries with it certain risks, as Kissinger pointed out many years ago: "American pragmatism produces a penchant for examining issues separately: to solve problems on their merits, without a sense of time or context or the seamless web of reality. . . . Yet in foreign policy there is no escaping the need for an integrating conceptual framework. . . . The most difficult challenge for a policymaker in foreign affairs is to establish priorities. A conceptual framework—which 'links' events—is an essential tool" (1979, 130). That "tool" is "a firm conception of the national interest." Does this mean that a state may do anything in the name of national interest? Not according to the father of political realism, who urged statesmen to be guided by the political virtue of prudence and to consider the long-term consequences of all actions. As Morgenthau said, "There can be no political morality without prudence, that is, without consideration of the political consequences of seemingly moral action. Realism, then, considers prudence—the weighing of the consequences of alternative political actions—to be the supreme virtue in politics" (1973, 10).

In traditional ways of thinking about foreign policy, all states pursue what they conceive to be their national interest, and in so doing they often form alliances to defend against common threats, usually involving the potential threat of war. For the most part, threats to national security are therefore thought of in military terms, with war or the threat of war as the ultimate instrument of diplomacy. In our time, however, there are numerous vital national interests at stake and many challenges for which the threat of war is essentially irrelevant. States cannot go to war to solve a global financial crisis or prevent the threat of a global pandemic or deal with the congeries of issues related to global warming. They can, however, form very broad-based alliances to address common threats such as these. The United Nations and other international organizations can provide a useful platform for such alliances, but they are not the only multilateral options that contemporary realists would consider.

Working with the United Nations and Other Venues of Multilateral Diplomacy

The leading power of our time, the United States, has, for several of the early years of the twenty-first century, belittled, ignored, or otherwise downplayed the importance of the United Nations and many other international organizations. Unilateralism was pursued as a policy of first choice for ideological reasons. This was not in the American national interest and, as stated above, produced a serious backlash against American leadership. Rather than acting against the United Nations and other international organizations, the United States should actively support reform of the United Nations and thus bolster the use of international institutions and compliance with international norms. It is important to note, however, that for those who advocate what is called "smart power," multilateralism is a pragmatic choice, not an ideological one (Nossel 2004, 140–142). Multilateralism should not be pursued "as a sacred ideal, but as a choice dictated by the logic of smart power. Washington should seek the blessing of the UN not because it confers otherwise unattainable legitimacy, but because of its pragmatic benefits" (Nossel 2004, 140).

Realists believe that voting arrangements in international organizations should reflect real power whenever possible. Although in some cases the one state, one vote rule may be unavoidable, major states will take international organizations more seriously if they have votes appropriate to their real ability to make things happen, or to prevent them from happening, in the real world. They are also more likely to take international organizations seriously if they have votes that are weighted to reflect their real role in the international system. This applies especially to international financial institutions, such as the World Bank and the International Monetary Fund, but it may also be applied to other international organizations in the future.

Inis Claude pointed out many years ago that "the management of power in international relations looms as the central issue of our time" (1962, 5). What Claude said then remains true in the early years of the twenty-first century, and multilateral diplomacy is usually the most efficient way to manage power when the issues at stake are essentially multilateral ones. Andrew Bacevich, a contemporary realist, proposes a modern version of what he calls "enlightened realism" in which states are able to achieve the national interest "more easily when those interests are compatible with the interests of others" (2009, 174). Most global issues are such that the wisest course of action is to identify the common ground and seek agreement on "those interests [that] are compatible with the interests of others" (Bacevich 2009, 175). In so doing, a realist would never argue that multilateral diplomacy is the only venue to address global issues; nor would a realist argue that multilateral venues are never appropriate. As another analyst put it, "Americans should regard this new [pragmatic] multilateralism not as a surrender but as an opportunity. By acknowledging how it contributes to the existence of the global problems, by recognizing how much it stands to gain from their solution, and by assuming a leadership role in international efforts to deal with them, the United States can advance its own interests while also creating the solidarity it needs with other nations" (Chua 2009, 341). Realists should use whichever venue is most appropriate for the problem at hand. "No one institution or organization is always right, no one framework ideal. The UN might work for one problem, NATO for another, the [Organization of American States] for a third. . . . Being accommodating, flexible, and adaptable is likely to produce better results on the ground than insisting on a pure approach" (Zakaria 2009, 243).

While realists would argue that the United States and other leading powers should work to reform the United Nations, they should also be prepared to seek creative ways to work together in other multilateral venues. Amy Chua goes on to say that "the United States must look for ways to foster multilateral, coordinated campaigns with other nations. This does not necessarily mean working within the confines of the existing international legal and political framework, which is centered on the United Nations. The UN may be useful, but the United States might also pursue bilateral or multilateral agreements with like-minded countries outside the UN framework, or even create brand new international institutions" (2009, 341). A more pointed argument has been advanced by Moises Naim, managing editor of the influential journal *Foreign Policy*: "The pattern is clear: Since the early 1990s, the need for effective multicountry collaboration has soared, but at the same time multilateral talks have inevitably failed. . . . These failures represent not only the perpetual lack of international consensus, but also a flawed obsession with multilateralism as the panacea for all the world's ills" (2009). His solution to this problem is to seek what he calls "minilateralism"— "bring to the table the smallest number of countries needed to have the largest possible impact on solving a particular problem" (2009). Thus, contemporary realists are likely to favor groupings of states like the G-20 and other ad hoc gatherings of states over traditional bodies like the United Nations, where the need for a very broad consensus may actually block effective action and the one state, one vote rule does not reflect real power.

Although the world has changed a great deal in recent decades, political realists acknowledge that international politics is still about power and competition for resources, that the principal means by which the system is regulated is still diplomacy, and that military threats to peace will still be susceptible to being countered by military actions. However, a variety of multilateral venues for diplomatic action will become increasingly important as the century unfolds and as the salience of nontraditional threats to the security and welfare of states and their citizens increases. Diplomacy, whether multilateral or bilateral, calls for accommodation and compromise and eschews a winner-take-all approach to the various interests and issues at hand. Realists should continue to resist what Morgenthau called "nationalistic universalism" and the "crusading zeal" of states and statesmen who try to impose on others their sense of right and wrong and of what is to be done. Those who say, "It's my way or the highway" and "If you are not with us you are against us," are threats to the stability of the international system, and their policy perspectives should be rejected.

References

Bacevich, A. J. 2009. *The limits of power: The end of American exceptionalism.* New York: Holt.

Chua, A. 2009. *Days of empire: How hyperpowers rise to global dominance—and why they fail.* New York: Anchor Books.

Claude, I. L. 1971. *Swords into plowshares: The problems and progress of international organization.* 4th ed. New York: Random House.

———. 1962. *Power and international relations.* New York: Random House.

Freeman, C. W. 1997. *The diplomat's dictionary.* Washington, DC: The U.S. Institute of Peace.

Kaplan, R. D. 2009. The revenge of geography. *Foreign Policy* 172 (May–June): 96–106.

Kissinger, H. 1994. *Diplomacy.* New York: Simon and Schuster.

———. 1979. *The White House Years.* New York: Little Brown.

Morgenthau, H. J. 1973. *Politics among nations: The struggle for power and peace.* 5th ed. New York: Alfred A. Knopf.

Naim, M. 2009. Minilateralism: The magic number to get to real international action. *Foreign Policy* (June 22), www.foreignpolicy.com/articles/2009/06/18/mini lateralism?print=yes&hidecomments=yes&page=full.

Nossel, S. 2004. Smart power. *Foreign Affairs* 83, no. 2 (March–April): 131–142.

Zakaria, F. 2009. *The post-American world.* New York: W. W. Norton & Company.

18

The Role of Nonstate Actors

JoAnn Fagot Aviel

Globalization has increased the influence of nonstate actors in multilateral diplomacy. In contrast to 1947, when member states were virtually the sole actors in the international process, former UN Secretary-General Kofi Annan (1997) noted, "Non-governmental organizations [NGOs] are now seen as essential partners of the United Nations, not only in mobilizing public opinion, but also in the process of deliberation and policy formulation and—even more important—in the execution of policies, in work on the ground." NGOs and other nonstate actors, especially businesses and foundations, are involved not only with the United Nations but with other multilateral organizations as well and have even formed their own multilateral associations.

The need for global action on transnational problems and the increasing ease of instant communication have helped to expand the number of NGOs at the global level and increased their role in multilateral diplomacy and global governance. Even though estimated numbers of NGOs vary widely, as do definitions of what constitutes an NGO, all agree that—no matter how defined—their numbers and influence have increased tremendously in recent years. In 1949, the UN Economic and Social Council (ECOSOC) under Article 71 of the UN Charter—the only specific mention of NGOs in the charter—had granted only 90 NGOs consultative status, whereas by 2009, there were over 3,290 organizations with consultative status with ECOSOC, including some business associations, such as the International Chamber of Commerce, and certain private foundations, such as the United Nations Foundation.[1]

All of the UN entities and specialized agencies have established variously denominated units responsible for relations with NGOs and other civil society actors and the private sector. The size of these units ranges from a single staff member to the World Bank's staff of 120. However, there is no single standard approach to granting NGOs accreditation or formal relations with nonstate actors. In 1996, ECOSOC opened accreditation to regional and national NGOs as well as international NGOs, including organizations sponsored by governments to defend their position (government-operated NGOs, or GONGOs) (McKeon 2009, 123–124). The UN Global Compact, launched in July 2000, involves six UN agencies and now has over 5,200 businesses in 130 countries and many business associations as members who pledge to follow a list of principles involving human rights, labor, the environment, and anticorruption and make annual financial contributions to the United Nations. It also involves many NGO, academic, and public-sector participants (UN Global Compact 2009). All multilateral organizations have had to make arrangements for dealing with the increasing number of nonstate actors that seek to participate in policy making. For example, the European Commission has established a voluntary register of organizations wanting to consult with it. It lists 2,127 organizations, including businesses, labor unions, professional associations, and NGOs (European Commission 2009). The Association of Southeast Asian Nations (2009) lists fifty-eight civil society organizations affiliated with it, each of which comprises a network of NGOs in member countries.

A Variety of Roles

Nonstate actors play a variety of roles in multilateral diplomacy. For example, the roles played by the U.S. Chamber of Commerce include that of convener, facilitator, advocate, information provider, negotiator, and watchdog (see Chapter 12). These are roles played by many other NGOs as well. Nonstate actors play important roles in negotiations and decision making before, during, and after international conferences and in policy making on issues with other international actors—states and international secretariats—even without international conferences. They also play a key role in implementing policy and agreements on important international issues.

NGOs have learned over the past few years that for multilateral negotiations to succeed, ideas must be tested and a public consensus formed on the existence of a problem and possible solutions well before a conference begins. They have found that the best time to influence a world conference is during the preparatory process—at least 60 percent of the final outcome of a UN world conference is determined during the preparatory process—often through expert-group meetings, which are most open to NGO participation (UNIFEM 1995, 13). The women's movement, for example, achieved notable success by mounting global campaigns, building coalitions and consensus, and drafting its own policy documents to influence the composition of official delegations before conferences even began (Alter Chen 1996, 151). Some NGOs work on the outside of multilateral conferences, staging protests and demonstrations to influence the conference proceedings, some work on the inside as members of national delegations or as official observers, and still others do both. At the Earth Summit at least fourteen countries had environmental NGO representatives in their national delegations (Conca 1996, 111). At the Cairo Population Conference in 1994, NGO representatives constituted a large part of many official delegations—half in the case of the U.S. delegation (Alter Chen 1996, 149; Higer 1996, 34). Representatives of private firms are also involved before, during, and after such conferences as well as during regular UN sessions (McKeon 2009). Like NGOs, private companies can be incorporated into the national delegations of member governments themselves, especially when the issues at hand are of concern to them. Of the twenty-three members of the U.S. delegation to the July 2008 meeting of the joint Food and Agricultural Organization–World Health Organization Codex Alimentarius Commission, which sets the standards applied by the World Trade Organization for international trade in food production, ten represented food corporations or private firms that consult for them (McKeon 2009, 172).

NGOs have insured their being from the beginning by joining with governments and international organizations to sponsor conferences as well as calling conferences on their own. For example, the heads of the United Nations Development Program, the United Nations Educational, Scientific, and Cultural Organization, the United Nations Children's Fund (UNICEF), and the World Bank invited governments, intergovernmental organizations (IGOs), and NGOs to participate in the preparatory process and in the World Conference on Education for All in 1990 on the basis of complete equality of status and decision making among all participants (Ritchie 1996, 184). NGOs also play an important role after conferences—building public support for the agreements, monitoring commitments made, and coordinating activities through networking. Nora McKeon (2009, 135) states that one respondent to a survey of UN civil society liaison offices reported that civil society organizations are explicitly authorized to signal breaches in implementation of guidelines and to act as watchdogs. Stanley Burgiel's case study in this volume (see Chapter 11) illustrates the role of one NGO before, during, and after negotiations on the issue of invasive species and analyzes the comparative advantage of NGOs in negotiations. He considers most important their "ability to gather and process technical information into a strategic set of policy priorities." Their networks, which extend across a range of countries as well as issue-specific programs, provide broader levels of expertise than most individual governments can provide.

The NGO role in policy making is perhaps most prominent in regards to humanitarian-relief issues but can be found in all international policy issues. Since 1994 the New York representative of the International Committee of the Red Cross has met monthly with the serving president of the Security Council in an informal and confidential atmosphere that allows both sides to exchange information and concerns (Ritchie 1996, 186). Since 1997 the NGO Working Group on the Security Council, which includes about thirty NGOs, has met regularly with the presidents of the Security Council and delegations to the Security Council as well as with UN Secretariat officials in informal, off-the-record consultations (Global Policy Forum 2009). In Chapter 9 of this volume, Peter D. Bell and Sherine S. Jayawickrama describe how CARE used the Arria Formula meeting format, which enables a member of the Security Council to invite other members to an informal meeting held outside the council chamber to enable civil society groups in conflict-torn countries to make presentations to the Security Council. The heads of prominent NGOs have frequent meetings with the secretary-general.

The UN Secretariat and agencies have chosen to take NGOs on as partners. The Inter-Agency Standing Committee (IASC) was established in 1992 to coordinate the work of UN agencies and NGOs involved in complex humanitarian emergencies. Its emergency-relief coordinator chairs the twice yearly meetings of the committee as well as ad hoc meetings with the heads of major UN agencies and NGOs involved in humanitarian relief, such as the International Committee of the Red Cross, InterAction, Oxfam, and the International Council of Voluntary Agencies (IASC 2009). The UN Office for the Coordination of Humanitarian Affairs (OCHA) has stated that it "is firmly committed to improving its global humanitarian partnerships with both UN and non-UN actors acting on an equal basis"; in 2007, OCHA convened the Global Humanitarian Platform "that brought together some 40 NGOs, Red Crescent/Red Cross societies and UN agencies as equal partners seeking to improve cooperation and communication based on mutually agreed upon principles" (United Nations 2009b). The Joint United Nations Program on HIV/AIDS (UNAIDS 2009), established in 1996, was the first UN agency to include NGOs as part of its governing structure, which now includes twenty-two governments, ten UN agencies, and five NGOs. New coalitions on global issues have emerged based on equality among the partners involved. For example, the Global Alliance for Vaccines and Immunization involves, in addition to NGOs, multinational and bilateral agencies, international development banks, foundations, the pharmaceutical industry, and national government health programs (see Chapter 13). In 2003 about half of World Bank–financed projects involved NGOs (United Nations 2003). According to the 2007–2009 World Bank–Civil Society Engagement Review, civil society organizations were involved in different ways in the design and preparation of 792 of the 1,059 projects funded (or 75 percent) over the last three years. Civil society participation has also increased to 87 percent in the formulation of the country assistance strategies and to 100 percent in consultations on poverty-reduction strategy papers. The increase in the number of civil society organizations attending annual and spring meetings of the World Bank has been facilitated by its Civil Society Sponsorship Program, which extends invitations to executive officers of civil society organizations to attend. The World Bank (2009) has also sponsored a series of policy round tables with civil society organizations on the food and financial crises.

Key Issues for Nonstate Actors' Influence

Nonstate actors are involved in all areas of multilateral diplomacy, with individual NGOs usually specializing in key issue areas, such as the focus of Human Rights Watch on human rights issues and of the U.S. Chamber of Commerce on core business issues. NGOs have been particularly influential in the framing of issues. Their influence is greater on issues in which the political stakes of the negotiations are relatively low, as in negotiations over nonbinding principles or framework agreements with few demands for behavioral change (Betsill and Corell 2008, 16). A comparative study of six global conferences during the 1990s found that "the more states link conference topics to sovereignty issues, the less ready states are to permit the open contestation and mutual accountability at the UN conferences" (Friedman, Hochstetler, and Clark 2005, 130). It found that at conferences on population and development (1994), social development (1996), and human settlements (1996), NGO participation did not threaten state sovereignty, and NGOs were permitted a greater role than at conferences on the environment and development (1992), human rights (1993), and women (1995). McKeon notes, "There is a relatively high degree of consensus in literature on civil society and global summits that civil society has been more successful in gaining international attention and setting agendas than in getting results, and that the impact of civil society is stronger on . . . highly salient low policy issues than on hardcore economic questions" (2009, 132).

NGOs' influence is enhanced when they form alliances with key states, regional and other technical agencies, and key international secretariats. On most issues coalitions are formed, either in support of or in opposition to proposals, and comprise various nonstate actors as well as states and often international secretariats. For example on the issue of banning landmines, all the permanent members of the UN Security Council were opposed, as were many rebel or terrorist groups, but a middle power, Canada, led an effort to promote the ban through a coalition of NGOs (the International Campaign to Ban Landmines) and of like-minded states, which resulted in 123 states signing the Ottawa Treaty in December 1997. As of May 2009, 156 states had signed, but not China, Russia, or the United States (Gilboa 2009). In a similar way, a coalition, cochaired by Steve Goose of Human Rights Watch, Grethe Ostern of Norwegian People's Aid, and Simon Conway of Landmine Action, formed to achieve a ban on cluster munitions in a treaty signed in December 2008. Bell and Jayawickrama in this volume describe how CARE helped to form an effective coalition to unify advocacy efforts for one country, which included other international NGOs, such as Save the Children UK, Oxfam International, International Rescue Committee, Tearfund, and Christian Aid (see Chapter 9).

Burgiel (2008) has analyzed the influence of environmental NGOs (ENGOs) and industry associations on the negotiation of the Cartagena Protocol on Biosafety in which each worked with different key states to influence the outcome. He concluded that ENGOs were most influential at the early stages of the negotiations in educating developing country delegates and keeping issues such as liability and socioeconomic considerations on the agenda, while industry groups exerted most influence in the middle and late stages by working with the Miami Group countries (six agricultural exporting countries: Argentina, Australia, Canada, Chile, the United States, and Uruguay) to limit the protocol's scope and keep detailed documentation and identification requirements off the agenda (Burgiel 2008, 99). The influence of ENGOs and industry associations is greatest when they are able to unite their members behind an issue. On the issue of climate change, it has been reported that some members of the U.S. Chamber of Commerce who are members of the U.S. Climate Action Partnership, a coalition of businesses and environmental groups, have left over the positions the U.S. Chamber of Commerce has taken on climate change (*New York Times* 2009).

Nonstate actors have been very prominent on the issue of human rights. According to Esther Brimmer, U.S. assistant secretary of state for international organization affairs, human rights is the issue on which NGOs have had the most influence (Brimmer 2009). Carroll Bogert in this volume describes the rising influence of Human Rights Watch (HRW), indicated by its executive director's meetings with heads of state and with Ban Ki-moon in 2006, when he was campaigning to be secretary-general, reaching a level at which, as Justice Richard Goldstone recently remarked, "Human Rights Watch is roughly as influential on the world stage as a middle-sized country" (see Chapter 10). Human rights NGOs have been criticized for focusing on abuses in democratic countries and countries in transition to democracy, in which they have the most access to information and can be most effective in bringing about changes, but not in authoritarian countries where abuses may be greater. For example, the founding chairman emeritus of HRW criticized its recent record of writing "far more condemnations of Israel for violations of international law than of any other country . . . in a region populated by authoritarian regimes with appalling human rights records" (Bernstein 2009). In assessing the effectiveness of foundations on the issue of human rights, Joan Spero writes in Chapter 13 of this volume that "foundations played a meaningful supporting role in protecting human rights in Eastern Europe, Latin America, and South Africa and facilitating the transition to democracy and free markets in Eastern Europe." Nonstate actors have also been especially influential regarding global health issues. The World Health Organization's regular two-year operating budget for 2006 and 2007 was $1 billion, with voluntary contributions of $2.2 billion. This compares with $3 billion in grants that the Bill and Melinda Gates Foundation will be making each year in global health. Of even greater influence are the pharmaceutical companies, with product sales for the fifty largest totaling about half a trillion dollars a year (Waldman 2007, 102–104).

NGOs have perhaps been most effective concerning issues regarding the delivery of humanitarian assistance since governments depend on NGOs, which are the main actors in its delivery. In Chapter 12 Stephen Jordan and Taryn Bird argue that from the private sector's perspective, the field of humanitarian assistance and development is "the most promising area for multisector multilateralism," which involves both public- and private-sector actors in broad coalitions to respond to humanitarian emergencies. Moreover, in an Organization for Economic Cooperation and Development (OECD) comparison of the international solidarity action of big NGOs with state action, "the most important NGOs compete in equal terms with the European states" (Calame 2008, 6). Bell and Jayawickrama point out that in 2008, CARE USA had a budget of over $700 million and that, collectively, the twelve major U.S.-based international relief and development organizations represented in the NGO Leaders Forum have a combined annual budget equal to, or exceeding, the agencies of the United Nations engaged in international relief and development. They warn, however, that because (with the notable exception of Oxfam) these NGOs depend heavily on government funding, their influence in opposition to governments can be limited since governments can turn to their own military organizations or to commercial contractors to deliver humanitarian relief, as the George W. Bush administration did in Iraq and Afghanistan (see Chapter 9).

Changes in Multilateral Diplomacy

Multilateral diplomacy has changed greatly due to the increase in influence of the unprecedented number and variety of civil society– and business-related organizations and their globalization. Bogert states that the critical change in HRW's advocacy was internationalization, which was made possible by a global fundraising strategy and necessary because of new international organizations (see Chapter 10). Jordan and Bird note that there has been an "extraordinary explosion in national, sectoral, and organizational diversity" over the last forty years and a shift in general attitudes about the role of government. They quote a UN official at a conference in 2005 who remarked, "Ten years ago, we thought of the private sector as part of the problem. Now we look at it as part of the solution" (see Chapter 12). As one analyst put it, "At the political level, the UN has shifted from an organization in which only governments spoke to only governments, to one that now brings together the political power of governments, the economic power of the corporate sector, and the 'public opinion' power of civil society (and the global communication and information media) as participants in the global policy dialogue" (Hill 2004).

While nonstate actors were involved in the past, the increase in their numbers and the growing importance of their involvement represent a major change in multilateral diplomacy. Both state and international secretariat actors have had to adjust to their importance. As discussed previously, government departments and foreign ministries now consult with relevant nonstate actors on major issues throughout the negotiation process and often include NGO and private-sector members as part of official state delegations. International secretariats not only have offices devoted to relations with civil society but also consult with civil society representatives frequently as well as make use of NGOs to administer aid and monitor agreements.

One of the most significant changes in how diplomacy is conducted is the decreasing use of formal votes and traditional institutional arrangements and the increasing use of informal agreements and coalitions in which nonstate actors can play an important role. Even within the United Nations, formal votes are often not taken; instead, resolutions are often approved by consensus, leaving it up to a coalition of the willing to implement what it wishes. Informal groups can be ad hoc or relatively permanent. They can be small but influential, such as the Group of 8, or large networks, partnerships, or coalitions of the willing containing a wide range of actors and including UN agencies and nonstate actors in both the formulation and implementation of policy. These arrangements have been both praised and criticized. They can be seen as an efficient means to bypass the United Nations and its voting, budgetary, and reform constraints. When the United Nations or its specialized agencies are involved, they can also be considered as a means to expand the United Nations' reach and capacity without needing to go through a formal reform process. These arrangements can be seen in all areas of international concern. In the area of security, the Bill Clinton administration formed a coalition of the willing to intervene in Kosovo based on the North Atlantic Treaty Organization (NATO) without Security Council authorization. After the end of the conflict, the Security Council authorized a peace-enforcement force of thirty-five NATO and non-NATO nations and created a UN mission there to coordinate reconstruction efforts involving the European Union and a range of governments, private companies, and NGOs. The Bush administration formed a coalition of the willing to support its decision to invade Iraq without Security Council authorization, but the UN later became involved in efforts to reconstruct Iraq together with willing governments, private companies, and NGOs. Private security forces such as Blackwell, the Dyn Corp, and MPRI have formed a part of the coalition in both Kosovo and Iraq as well as elsewhere, and private corporations such as Halliburton and Bechtel have been heavily involved in reconstruction together with NGOs such as CARE and Mercy Corps. Instead of the United Nations alone being involved in mediation of disputes, it often works with support coalitions in various areas that include NGOs. For example, the Center for Humanitarian Dialogue, an NGO that receives 98 percent of its funding from nine governments, "was charged with negotiating and implementing the peace accord between Indonesia and Aceh, with several nations committing peacekeepers for that effort" (Forman and Segaar 2006, 207), and it has been involved in different coalitions dealing with conflicts in the Central African Republic, the Philippines, Sudan, and Timor Leste.

The United Nations has promoted partnerships in a number of areas. In the area of development, the UN Fund for International Partnerships works with many UN agencies, businesses, foundations, and NGOs to help promote the Millennium Development Goals (MDGs) (United Nations 2009a). The Millennium Campaign is led by a core coalition—the Global Call to Action Against Poverty—promoted by international NGOs and networks (McKeon 2009, 159). More and more development projects are partnerships of donor and recipient government agencies, domestic and international NGOs, and increasingly private companies. UN agencies and donor government agencies such as the U.S. Agency for International Development's call for bids on projects by both international NGOs as well as for-profit international-development consultancy companies such as Creative Associates International based in the United States, GOPA-Consultants based in Germany, and Cowater based in Canada. The lines between public and private are often blurred. One study of 1,832 European development NGOs found that 42 percent of their income came from government and multilateral agencies with voluntary donations from private sources comprising another 42 percent and self-financing through trading and consultancy services 16 percent (Stubbs 2003, 143). After the heads of state adopted development goals at the UN Millennium Summit in September 2000, the head of the UN Development Program called for coalitions to be formed similar to the successful Coalition against Landmines to implement the goals. The OECD's Development Assistance Committee (DAC) had developed a strategy for development cooperation that was based on partnerships on development plans owned and led by developing countries and civil society to accomplish the MDGs by 2015. The OECD reported that in 2008, total net official development assistance from OECD DAC countries rose by 10.2 percent in real terms to US$119.8 billion and was the highest annual aid figure ever recorded, representing 0.3 percent of members' combined gross national income. It also warned, however, that the economic crisis still threatened the achievement of the MDGs (OECD 2009). Moreover, at a time when government budgets are reduced and the work of nonstate actors is even more important, the economic crisis threatens to decrease their role. It is reported that nonprofit organizations and NGOs are laying off staff and cutting back aid programs. "In 2009, we're estimating that giving from foundations will decline in the range of the high single digits to the low double digits," said Steven Lawrence, senior director of research at the Foundation Center, a leading U.S.

authority on philanthropy, noting that foundation assets declined double that amount, almost 22 percent, in 2008 (IRIN 2009).

In the area of public health, broad coalitions and alliances have been formed to solve particular global health problems. Spero in this volume points out that one of the earliest such partnerships was the International AIDS Vaccine Initiative, which was created by the Rockefeller Foundation in 1996 with support from several private and corporate foundations, an NGO, and the World Bank (see Chapter 13). Another is the Global Alliance for Vaccines Initiative, whose board includes renewable members from the World Health Organization, UNICEF, the World Bank, and the Bill and Melinda Gates Foundation, as well as rotating members from three OECD countries, two developing countries, two businesses, one foundation, one NGO, one research institute, and one technical health institute; the initiative has a secretariat housed in the Geneva offices of UNICEF. The boards of directors for the Global Fund to Fight AIDS, Tuberculosis, and Malaria (GFATM) and the Global Alliance for Improved Nutrition also include diverse members but have differing structures (Ollila 2003, 48–55). In January 2008 GFATM announced the launch of the Corporate Champions Program. Chevron Corporation, a major international energy company, is the program's inaugural Corporate Champion, making a commitment to invest $30 million over three years in Global Fund–supported programs in parts of Asia and Africa. "Global companies with large, long-term investments in developing countries understand that fighting disease is a necessary part of their strategic investments," said Rajat Gupta, chairman of the fund's board of directors. Since its creation in 2002, the fund has become the dominant source of multilateral financing of programs to fight AIDS, tuberculosis, and malaria, providing well over 20 percent of all international finance against AIDS and two-thirds of global financing for tuberculosis and malaria (United Nations News Service 2008). While these coalitions can be praised for bringing together diverse actors to focus on serious health problems in innovative ways, they have also received criticism. In each, industry is involved in policy making and agenda setting, but there are no mechanisms to deal with conflicts of interests. According to one study, corporations have tended to give earmarked funding only and to have more of an interest in solutions that can be sold and that are more expensive. Lines of public accountability are unclear, and there is a lack of transparency (Ollila 2003, 63).

The increasing focus on accountability and transparency has made multinational corporations (MNCs) prefer standardized rules to avoid problems that may arise from inconsistencies and has increased their role in multilateral diplomacy.

The same focus on accountability also has transferred to relationships between NGOs and IGOs. This has also produced changes in private sector–NGO relations. As one analyst states, "Rather than waiting for states to address among themselves a problem, NGOs and MNCs are in fact engaging with each other, where they used to be sworn enemies, wouldn't be seen in the same room together, let alone the same conference or convention" (Katz 2006). In this new diplomacy, NGOs and MNCs work toward a solution together and then attempt to impose it on IGOs and states. "Sort of turning the whole system upside-down, so rather than a top-down system, much more bottom-up," Owen Pell said. "It's definitely something that you would argue is in its infancy, but I think it's hard to say there isn't a trend" (Katz 2006). Many of the issues these new MNC-NGO alliances have been focusing on are those avoided by states in the past due to states' own self-interest. Because NGOs and MNCs have different agendas from states, they are able to tackle these problems. To be successful generally requires NGOs to unify several MNCs in order to represent a large market share. For example, in the case of the Cocoa Harvesting Accord, NGOs united companies representing 99 percent of cocoa buyers to form a cartel to negotiate child-labor practices. The MNCs agreed to buy cocoa only from areas with minimal use of child labor, as determined by a survey of local labor markets funded by the MNCs. Ultimately, around twenty African states agreed to participate. Similarly, the Kimberly Accord on Mercenary Diamonds aimed to eliminate the use of child labor to mine diamonds that fund African civil wars. The Equator Principles originated under the auspices of the World Bank and ultimately resulted in an agreement between approximately fifty banks worldwide—representing 80 to 90 percent of the project finance market—not to lend money to projects exceeding $50 million that violate certain UN conventions. Lenders also made an unprecedented pledge to monitor the compliance of these projects (Katz 2006).

In a speech before the U.S. Chamber of Commerce in June 1999, UN Secretary-General Annan stated, "A fundamental shift has occurred in recent years in the attitude of the United Nations towards the private sector. Confrontation has taken a back seat to cooperation. Polemics have given way to partnerships" (Knight 2000). For example, at the World Summit on Sustainable Development in September 2002, the presence of business and industry was unprecedented, and more than two hundred partnerships were launched (Bull and McNeill 2007, 9–10). The Business Humanitarian Forum (BHF) was established in 1999 to encourage dialogue between relief organizations and corporations and to gain business support for humanitarian projects. It has an impressive international board of advisors consisting of former high-ranking officials of international agencies, business executives of global corporations and industries, and leaders of major humanitarian-relief NGOs, and it has organized several public-private partnerships in postconflict areas such as Afghanistan, Bosnia, and southern Africa. Some NGOs have criticized BHF for including oil companies that have been cited for human rights abuses (Knight 2000).

The Global Compact was formed to promote voluntary adoption of the international standards included in ten core principles by international businesses (Bull and McNeil 2007, 17). McKeon and other analysts have criticized the lack of a serious monitoring process incorporated into the Global Compact as well as the public-private partnerships launched around the World Conference on Sustainable Development (McKeon 2009, 173). In opposition to the Global Compact aimed at businesses, an international coalition of NGOs proposed a Citizens Compact. Signatories include the Third World Network, Washington's Institute for Policy Studies, Zimbabwe's International South Group Network, India's International Group for Grassroots Initiatives, and John Sellers of the Ruckus Society. The alternative compact outlines nine principles aiming to "safeguard the image, mission and credibility of the United Nations as it deals with the private sector" (CorpsWatch 1998). While the United Nations should help companies improve their human rights and environmental records, the Citizens Compact states, this should not be seen as a "partnership." As Kenny Bruno of the California-based Transnational Resource and Action Center maintains, "The United Nations is our best hope to monitor and hold accountable the giant companies that control so much of our economies and our lives" (Knight 2000). At the same time, Benedicte Bull and Desmond McNeil's examination of public-private partnerships (PPPs) concludes that "the influence that the private sector gains in the multilateral organizations through PPPs varies greatly, and so does the degree to which the PPPs affect the multilateral system's legitimacy, in its different forms. . . . Including the private sector in the multilateral system has the potential to add to, rather than detract from, the long-term goal of creating multilateral institutions that are better at solving the pressing development problems of today" (2007, 175–177). These informal arrangements have the advantage of responding to problems quickly, flexibly, without institutional restraints, and with those actors who are most committed, including nonstate actors. However, these informal arrangements often have few or no mechanisms of public accountability or oversight. No public records exist of their meetings and discussions. They often focus on narrow issues or a limited number of countries deemed important and lack the permanent authority and ongoing financial and normative commitments needed to address global problems and legitimize solutions to them. By permitting those willing to take action to do so outside the United Nations or with minimal UN participation, less attention is paid to strengthening the United Nations.

Looking to the Future

Some have called for substantial reform of the United Nations and other multilateral organizations to better take into account these changes in multilateral diplomacy involving nonstate actors. Proposals include creating a new global environmental organization as well as a People's Assembly with NGO representatives. So far, however, there has not been any major reform of existing arrangements in multilateral organizations. Shepard Forman and Derk Segaar point out that there is a lack of "a generally agreed pragmatic and normative framework for global governance that recognizes the broad range of actors along the public-private spectrum, their respective capabilities and responsibilities, and their complementary roles in shaping the global public policy agenda" (2006, 222). In recognition of this need, the secretary-general authorized the Panel of Eminent Persons on United Nations–Civil Society Relations, which issued a report (the so-called Cardoso Report) in June 2004 recommending various reforms, including incorporating the Global Compact into a proposed UN Office of Constituency Engagement and Partnerships. NGOs expressed substantial reservations about incorporating multinational companies into the office but have called for the appointment of a high-level officer in the secretary-general's office to handle relations with NGOs (Garcia-Delgado 2004; Global Policy Forum 2006). Following the release of the Cardoso Report, the secretary-general issued a report that contained a set of proposals incorporating some of its recommendations to bring greater coherence and consistency to UN-NGO relations. Those included simplifying the accreditation process, increasing financial support for the participation of southern NGOs, improving country-level engagement of UN representatives with NGOs, and opening further the General Assembly to NGOs. In response the General Assembly has started to hold informal hearings with NGOs and a trust fund has been established to support UN country teams' work with civil society (UN-NGLS 2009).

NGOs have called for a permanent formal role for NGOs in the General Assembly, particularly with its standing committees, and for more assistance of NGOs from the South to enable their participation. They have criticized the current use of "multistakeholder dialogues" as ineffective and poorly attended by member states and have called for a return to the model of the global conferences of the 1990s for all substantive decision-making processes. They would like plans for reform of ECOSOC to take into account new ways for NGOs to consult with the council as well as reinforce existing arrangements (Global Policy Forum 2006). While many NGOs would like to see a People's Assembly become a permanent feature of the UN system, they recognize that some states are calling for curtailing the influence of NGOs, and many more are opposed to expanding their influence. When asked about UN reforms that would expand the role of nonstate actors, the U.S. assistant secretary of state for international organization stated that some states are opposed, but the United States itself always consults with relevant nonstate actors before any conference (Brimmer 2009). Thus, only minor reforms in NGO relations with the United Nations are likely to be implemented.

Relatively minor reforms have also been recommended in regards to the United Nations' relations with the private sector. The secretary-general's report titled "Enhanced Cooperation Between the United Nations and All Relevant Partners, in Particular the Private Sector" cautioned that "efforts are needed to develop a more strategic and coherent approach to partner selection and engagement, integrate small companies and those from low-income countries, align global partnerships with country development agendas, build an enabling framework for partnerships, build capacity of staff, enhance mechanisms to share best practices and improve evaluation and impact assessment" (UN Secretary-General 2009). A group of NGOs has formed the Alliance for a Corporate-Free United Nations, which is opposed to such partnerships and calls instead for strengthening the United Nations' ability to control corporations (CorpsWatch 2001). A panel of experts convened by the UN General Assembly, chaired by Joseph Stiglitz, called for the drastic overhaul of international finance structures in the face of the global economic crisis. Included in the panel's recommendations is the creation of a financial regulatory board and competition authority "which could prevent the expansion of multi-national firms that threaten competition or become problematic when they become too big to fail" (UN News Center 2009). Raymond Saner and Lichia Yiu call for "special efforts to be made to support the creation of an international economic governance structure that could help provide a policy framework for the interaction between state and non-state actors" (2008, 102). However, such a formal expansion of global governance is unlikely to take place. Instead, global economic governance will continue to be conducted in the frequent meetings of the finance ministers and heads of state of the Group of Eight and Group of Twenty more than in formal multilateral organizations. Nonstate actors can attempt to influence these proceedings through contact with the participating government ministries and departments ahead of the meetings and demonstrations during, but the important decisions will continue to be made during closed meetings of government ministers.

Reforms are likely to be relatively minor as well in regards to the relations between NGOs, foundations, and businesses and other multilateral organizations. The current use of ad hoc arrangements and partnerships of those interested in a particular issue, including nonstate actors as well as states and international secretariats, is likely to continue and multiply in spite of the coordination and accountability problems that are often involved. As one study of such arrangements dealing with microfinance states, "It is often easier to agree on broad goals and visions than on the specific actions needed to implement them"; yet, networks often include NGOs and donors with differing goals and objectives (Ohanyan 2008, 5–8). In spite of some of these difficulties, the cumulative effect of these partnerships, as well as the increased participation of nonstate actors in multilateral organizations, has already changed multilateral diplomacy and global governance. More substantial reform, however, will depend on greater political will than currently exists.

Notes

1. The number of NGOs with official consultative status is much smaller than the number with some relationship to the United Nations. While not giving a specific definition of an NGO, the ECOSOC has endeavored to regulate the type of organization to be given consultative status. ECOSOC Resolution 1996/31 states that the organization shall have an established headquarters, a democratically adopted constitution, and a representative structure with appropriate mechanisms of accountability to its members, as well as other requirements. For a list of NGOs in consultative status with the ECOSOC and more information on the relationship between the United Nations and NGOs, see the United Nations website (www.un.org/en/civilsociety/19-ch19index.shtml).

References

Alger, C. 2002. The emerging roles of NGOs in the UN system: From Article 71 to a People's Millennium Assembly. *Global Governance* 8, no. 1 (January–March): 93–117.

Alter Chen, M. 1996. Engendering world conferences: The international women's movement and the UN. In *NGOs, the UN, and global governance*, ed. T. G. Weiss and L. Gordenker, 139–155. Boulder, CO: Lynne Rienner.

Annan, K. 1997. "Opening address to the Fiftieth Annual Department of Public Information/Nongovernmental Organization (DPI/NGO) Conference." United Nations Press Release, SG/SM/6320,PI/1027. September 10. http://mirror .undp.org/magnet/e-list/archive/25.txt.

Association of Southeast Asian Nations (ASEAN). 2009. Register of ASEAN affiliated CSOs. ASEAN. March 24. www.aseansec.org/6070.pdf.

Bernstein, R. L. 2009. Rights watchdog, lost in the Mideast. *New York Times*, October 20, A31.

Betsill, M. M., and E. Corell. 2008. Introduction to NGO diplomacy. In *NGO diplomacy: The influence of nongovernmental organizations on international environmental negotiations*, ed. M. M. Betsill and E. Corell, 1–18. Cambridge, MA: MIT Press.

Brimmer, E. 2009. Interview with author, October 29.

Bull, B., and D. McNeill. 2007. *Development issues in global governance, public-private partnerships and market multilateralism.* London: Routledge.

Burgiel, S. W. 2008. Non-state actors and the Cartagena Protocol on Biosafety. In *NGO diplomacy: The influence of nongovernmental organizations on international environmental negotiations*, ed. M. M. Betsill and E. Correl, 67–100. Cambridge, MA: MIT Press.

Calame, P. 2008. Non-state actors and world governance. Forum for a New World Governance, June 2. www.world-governance.org/spip.php?article297.

Clark, A. M. 1995. Non-governmental organizations and their influence on international society. *Journal of International Affairs* 48, no. 2: 507–525.

Conca, K. 1996. Greening the UN: Environmental organizations and the UN system. In *NGOs, the UN, and global governance*, ed. T. G. Weiss and L. Gordenker, 102–119. Boulder, CO: Lynne Rienner.

CorpsWatch. 2001. Alliance for a corporate free United Nations campaign profile. CorpsWatch. March 22. www.corpwatch.org/article.php?id=927.

———. 1998. Citizens compact on the United Nations and corporations. Corps Watch. January 28. www.corpswatch.org/article.php?id=992.

European Commission. 2009. Statistics for register. EUROPA. https://webgate.ec .europa.eu/transparency/regrin/consultation/statistics.do.

Forman, S., and D. Segaar. 2006. New coalitions for global governance: The changing dynamics of multilateralism. *Global Governance* 12, no. 2 (April–June): 205–225.

Friedman, E. J., K. Hochstetler, and A. M. Clark. 2005. *Sovereignty, democracy and global civil society: State-society relations at UN world conferences.* Albany: State University of New York Press.

García-Delgado, V. 2004. Too close for comfort: Should civil society and the Global Compact live under the same UN roof? Global Policy Forum. September–October. www.globalpolicy.org/component/content/article/226/32334.html.

Gilboa, E. 2009. The public diplomacy of middle powers. *PD Magazine* 2 (summer). http://publicdiplomacymagazine.com/category/past-issues/issue-summer-2009.

Global Policy Forum. 2009. NGO working group on the security council. Global Policy Forum. www.globalpolicy.org/security-council/ngos-and-the-council/ngo -working-group-on-the-security-council.html.

————. 2006. Paper on NGO participation at the United Nations. Global Policy Forum. March 28. www.globalpolicy.org/component/content/article/177/31756.html.

Higer, A. J. 1996. International women's activism and change: Understanding feminist influence at UN population conferences. Paper presented at the American Political Science Association meeting, August, San Francisco, California.

Hill, T. 2004. Three generations of UN–civil society relations: A quick sketch. Global Policy Forum. April. www.globalpolicy.org/component/content/article/177-un/31824-three-generations-of-un-civil-society-relations.html.

Integrated Regional Information Networks (IRIN). 2009. Humanitarian news and analysis. IRIN. July 11. www.irinnews.org.

Inter-Agency Standing Committee (IASC). 2009. About the Inter-Agency Standing Committee. IASC. www.humanitarianinfo.org/iasc.

Katz, E. 2006. Business-NGO alliance marks new diplomacy, Pell says. Virginia Law. February 10. www.law.virginia.edu/html/news/2006_spr/pell.htm.

Knight, D. 2000. United MacNations? The UN's growing alliance with multinational corporations. *Dollars and Sense* 230 (July–August): 34–37.

McKeon, N. 2009. *The United Nations and civil society: Legitimating global governance—whose voice?* London: Zed Books.

Nelson, P. 2000. Whose civil society? Whose governance? Decision making and practice in the new agenda at the Inter-American Development Bank and the World Bank. *Global Governance* 6, no. 4 (October–November): 405–431.

New York Times. 2009. Way behind the curve. *New York Times*, September 30, A30.

Ohanyan, A. 2008. *NGOs, IGOs, and the network mechanisms of post-conflict global governance in microfinance.* New York: Palgrave Macmillan.

Ollila, E. 2003. Health-related public-private partnerships and the United Nations. In *Global social governance: Themes and prospects*, ed. P. Deacon, E. Ollila, M. Koivusalo, and P. Stubbs, 36–68. Helsinki: Ministry of Foreign Affairs Finland.

Organization for Economic Cooperation and Development (OECD). 2009. Development aid: The funding challenge. *OECD Observer* 272 (April), www.oecdobserver.org/news/fullstory.php/aid/2866/Development_aid:_The_funding_challenge.html.

Ritchie, C. 1996. Coordinate? Cooperate? Harmonize? NGO policy and operational coalitions. In *NGOs, the UN, and global governance*, ed. T. G. Weiss and L. Gordenker, 177–188. Boulder, CO: Lynne Rienner.

Saner, R., and L. Yiu. 2008. Business-government-NGO relations: Their impact on global economic governance. In *Global governance and diplomacy: Worlds apart?* ed. A. F. Cooper, B. Hocking, and W. Maley, 85–103. New York: Palgrave Macmillan.

Stubbs, P. 2003. International non-state actors and social development policy. In *Global social governance: Themes and prospects*, ed. P. Deacon, E. Ollila, M. Koivusalo, and P. Stubbs, 130–153. Helsinki: Ministry of Foreign Affairs Finland.

United Nations. 2009a. Partnerships. United Nations. www.un.org/partnerships/YAboutUs.htm.

———. 2009b. Reform at the United Nations: Strengthening humanitarian action. United Nations. www.un.org/reform/humanitarian.shtml.

———. 2003. UN system and civil society—an inventory and analysis of practices. United Nations. May. www.un.org/reform/civilsociety/practices.shtml.

United Nations AIDS Agency (UNAIDS). 2009. Governance. www.unaids.org/en/AboutUNAIDS/Governance/default.asp.

United Nations Development Fund for Women (UNIFEM). 1995. *Putting gender on the agenda: A guide to participating in UN world conferences.* New York: UNIFEM.

United Nations Global Compact. 2009. Participants and stakeholders. UN Global Compact. June 30. www.unglobalcompact.org/ParticipantsAndStakeholders/index.html.

United Nations News Center. 2009. Global financial structures must be revamped, says UN expert panel. United Nations News Center. March 26. www.un.org/apps/news/story.asp?NewsID=30309&Cr=financial+crisis&Cr1=.

United Nations News Service. 2008. Major corporations to invest in UN-backed fight against AIDS, TB, Malaria. *United Nations Daily News,* January 21, 10–11.

United Nations Nongovernmental Liaison Service (UN-NGLS). 2009. Brief history. UN-NGLS. www.un-ngls.org/spip.php?page=article_s&id_article=796).

United Nations Secretary-General. 2009. Enhanced cooperation between the United Nations and all relevant partners, in particular the private sector. UN Document A/64/337. November 5. www.unglobalcompact.org/NewsAndEvents/news_archives/2009_11_05.html.

Waldman, R. 2007. Global health governance. In *Global governance reform: Breaking the stalemate,* ed. C. I. Bradford Jr. and J. F. Linn. Washington, DC: Brookings Institution Press.

World Bank. 2009. World Bank–civil society engagement: A review of years 2007–2009. http://go.worldbank.org/Y74DYAIEV0.

19

Power, the State, Multilateral Diplomacy, and Global Governance

Richard Reitano

As many of our contributors have observed in this book, the issues surrounding state sovereignty and the use of national power to advance state interests are nothing new in world history. The Westphalian system of states created after 1648, if anything, has only exacerbated the inherent conflict between sovereignty and multilateral diplomacy and between sovereignty and the concept and reality of global governance.

The increase in the number of independent nation-states after World War II, the creation of the United Nations, and the establishment of hundreds of inter-governmental organizations[1] have all dramatically expanded the opportunities for multilateral diplomacy and created opportunities for global governance.[2] Nevertheless, the assertion of state sovereignty is still a major factor in whether or not states will participate in multilateral diplomatic efforts and work through international organizations and institutions to deal with and resolve the complex and difficult problems confronting the international community in the twenty-first century.

Ambassador Joseph Melrose and Andrew Melrose remind us in this volume that the United Nations, after all, was only designed to be a collection of sovereign states that occasionally delegate collective authority to that body. They also point out that "Nothing in the [UN] charter explicitly authorized action in matters essentially within the domestic jurisdiction of the state" (see Chapter 4). Also in this volume, however, Stephen Rock observes that state sovereignty need not always preclude swift action by the international community. The detonation of a nuclear device in 2006 by North Korea, widely regarded as a "rogue state," resulted in an almost immediate response by the UN Security Council, which adopted a resolution critical of North Korea's action and also sanctioned the regime in Pyongyang (see Chapter 5).

John Rourke and Mark Boyer (2008, 141) offer several reasons for when and why multilateral diplomacy is employed and the global consequences when it either fails or is not utilized. They believe that the advent of technology has made us more aware of problems within and among nations. Absent modern communication, how many people would be interested in human rights violations in China and Zimbabwe, the use of torture by the United States in Iraq or Guantánamo, or the AIDS crisis in South Africa? Rourke and Boyer also cite problems, such as global climate change, that by their very nature must lend themselves to multilateral action and possible solutions. The empowerment of smaller states by collective action is another impetus, they suggest, for multilateral diplomacy, although the influence of these states may be more rhetorical than real. Finally, they note that global diplomacy and actions were conspicuously absent and global governance failed when the George W. Bush administration invaded Iraq in March 2003. Without concerted action by the global community, as in the first Gulf war (1990–1991), the "coalition of the willing" (used to describe UN peacekeeping operations since the early 1990s) in Iraq became the "coalition of the piddling," with only the British contributing significant military forces and offering major diplomatic backing.

In this chapter, I briefly explore several case studies regarding state sovereignty and national power, multilateral diplomacy, and global governance. The cases involve a major success for concerted diplomatic and military action through the United Nations, the 1990–1991 Gulf War; one of the more conspicuous failures with devastating consequences, the genocide in Rwanda in 1994; and the ongoing efforts by the international community to restrain Iran in its efforts either to build nuclear weapons or to allow the use of nuclear energy for peaceful purposes (Iran's stated position). I will also offer some insights about the future of multilateral diplomacy and global governance in the twenty-first century.

The 1990–1991 War in the Persian Gulf

On August 2, 1990, Iraq invaded Kuwait. The UN Security Council, determining that a breach of international peace and security existed as a result of the invasion and acting under Articles 39 and 40 of the UN Charter, adopted twelve major resolutions from August 1990 through November 1990. These resolutions condemned Iraq and demanded its immediate withdrawal from Kuwait (Security Council Resolution 660, the first resolution) and imposed mandatory sanctions against Iraq; finally, Resolution 678 (the last resolution) authorized "member states cooperating with the government of Kuwait . . . to use all necessary means to uphold and implement Security Council Resolution 660 and all subsequent resolutions and to restore international peace and security in the area."

Why was multilateral diplomacy so successful in the Gulf War, and why did the usual suspects, state sovereignty and national interests, not prevail?

With the end of the Cold War and a greatly weakened Soviet Union (the country did not collapse until December 1991), there was no ideological barrier or great power struggle to prevent collective security from being employed as envisioned by the UN Charter. The United States had neutralized a possible Chinese veto in the Security Council by President George H. W. Bush's opposition to (and vetoes of) sanctions imposed by the U.S. Congress over the massacre at Tiananmen Square in 1989. China either voted with the United States or abstained in the Security Council. Saddam Hussein's actions frightened the more conservative Arab states (and the wealthiest) so that there was no support for Iraq except from Jordan and Libya. Hussein obviously received no support from his enemies in Syria and Iran. In addition, none of the twelve Security Council resolutions called for the overthrow of the Iraqi leader. This allowed the anti-Hussein coalition to remain united (i.e., they all agreed he had to get out of Kuwait or be thrown out); only some UN members, such as the United States, had other longer-term goals. Unlike the Korean War, the various forces that participated in Operations Desert Shield and Storm did not come under the command of the United Nations. They were all ultimately placed under American command because the United States was the dominant military force in the military coalition against Iraq. The problems of national sovereignty and command and control, then, were never at issue.[3]

As part of the cease-fire agreement, Iraq agreed to disclose the "locations, amounts, and types" of biological and chemical weapons it possessed and to furnish similar information about ballistic missiles with a range of more than 150 kilometers. Iraq agreed to destroy these weapons and to accept ongoing international supervision through a UN special commission (UNSCOM). Security Council Resolution 687 also called for International Atomic Energy Agency (IAEA) inspection of Iraq's nuclear facilities. Sanctions would be lifted when Iraq destroyed these weapons under appropriate UN and IAEA supervision. Iraq did not comply and eventually kicked out the IAEA and the UNSCOM inspectors.

Critics contended that Hussein undermined the United Nations by successfully flouting its authority. U.S. and British warplanes, however, continued to enforce no-fly zones in the northern and southern parts of the country. In short, multilateral diplomatic efforts failed, neoconservatives in the United States argued, and the United States had no choice but to act in March 2003. Moreover, the United Nations was in danger, President George W. Bush charged in February 2003 prior to the war, of becoming "an irrelevant, debating society" if it did not enforce its own resolutions on disarming Iraq. The sanctions were lifted only after "regime change" in Iraq resulted in the removal of Hussein and his cohorts from power.

Thus, the Gulf War, although a successful effort in the use of multilateral diplomacy and military power, proved not to be a model for future UN collective-security actions (or, as President George H. W. Bush proclaimed at the time, "a New World Order"), because the George W. Bush administration adopted what became known as the "Bush Doctrine" based on the United States' essentially taking unilateral actions internationally and acting preemptively after 9/11. As the only remaining superpower, the United States would not feel constrained to act when its vital interests and national security were threatened, the Bush administration argued, even if many of America's allies and a majority of UN members opposed the action (the Iraq War). The economic collapse in 2008 and the reluctance of the American public to support America's "forgotten wars" may reflect what historian Paul Kennedy (1987) described as "imperial overstretch." He argued that history is replete with examples of dominant world powers engaging in self-destructive behavior because of their external wars and commitments. This behavior eventually resulted in the decline of "great powers" because their adventures abroad ultimately diminished their economic and military strength and their political influence.

The 1994 Genocide in Rwanda

In 1994, the United Nations failed to act in Rwanda when the Hutu majority began a systematic slaughter, or genocide, of the minority Tutsi. In one hundred days' time, between April and July, an estimated 800,000 people were killed. The murder rate was five times faster than anything the Nazis did before or during World War II. The United Nations failed to act because it was "another African bloody war" and because the United States and the Western powers were reluctant to intervene after the debacle in Somalia in 1994 (even though a relatively small UN force, many believe, would have prevented the slaughter). It was, as Edmund Burke once wrote, a situation in which "evil triumphs when good men do nothing."

The 1999 Report of the Independent Inquiry into the Actions of the United Nations During the 1994 Genocide in Rwanda concluded in part, "The failure by the United Nations to prevent, and subsequently, to stop the genocide in Rwanda was a failure by the United Nations system as a whole. The fundamental failure was the lack of resources and political commitment devoted to developments in Rwanda and to the United Nations presence there. There was a persistent lack of political will by Member States to act, or to act with enough assertiveness" (United Nations 1999, 3).

There are still arguments in some quarters that a rescue mission by the international community through the United Nations would have required over 100,000 troops, an altogether unrealistic goal. Gen. Romeo Dallaire, the UN commander in Rwanda, disputes this contention. He continues to claim that a small UN peacekeeping force would have saved thousands of lives. This much is not in dispute. The 1999 independent inquiry report was correct (i.e., for whatever reasons, the United Nations did not act before or during the genocide). Alan Kuperman also suggests, "If the West is unwilling to deploy . . . robust forces [in advance of a humanitarian disaster], it [also] must refrain from coercive diplomacy" because of an often "tragic backlash" (2000, 117).

Why did the United Nations not act? Was it another example of states being unwilling to intervene in another state's internal affairs because of precedents that could be used against so many nations that have deplorable human rights records? Was it about unintended consequences, "crossing the Mogadishu line," as was the case with UN intervention in Somalia in 1992? Or was it a reflections of Senator Robert Dole's statement that "I don't think we have any national interest here [in Rwanda]. I hope we don't get involved there"? And, by extension, did the powers that be in other states come to the same conclusion? A more cynical, but perhaps more realistic, view of humanitarian interventions has been offered by political scientist Ronald Steel: "Intervention (by the UN) will occur where it can be done relatively cheaply, against a weak nation, in an area both accessible and strategic, where the public's emotions are aroused, and where it does not get in the way of other political, economic or military needs" (1999).

In Chapter 6 of this volume, Donna Schlagheck also observes that "state sovereignty continues to thwart development of an effective and rapid response to genocide." However, by contrast, when a state's existence is threatened by the acquisition of nuclear weapons by a rogue state or by terrorism, states, she argues, are more likely to "collaborate" in dealing with these perceived life-and-death issues.

I would suggest that all of these factors came into play when the international community essentially ignored the ensuing disaster, even though many governments and their intelligence agencies were fully aware of what was happening in Rwanda. Many states continued to assert the Westphalian principle of nonintervention based on state sovereignty. An interesting twist is provided by Singapore's Kishore Mahbubani (2008), who has made a case that the West's insistence on promoting and protecting human rights is an ill-disguised effort to impose Western values on non-Western societies. President Bill Clinton, who inherited a U.S. military commitment as part of a UN peacekeeping force from his predecessor, President George H. W. Bush, acquiesced when Congress legislated that all U.S. troops had to be withdrawn from Somalia in order to avoid a repetition of the incidents involving the murder in Mogadishu of American troops who were part of the UN peacekeeping mission. They got into harm's way when the United States concluded that nation building was an essential element in preventing a repetition of what had previously occurred in Somalia and what had initially prompted UN intervention. Senator Dole spoke for many Americans who could not have found Somalia on a map if their lives depended on it. Why risk American lives with an intervention without a clear cut U.S. political, strategic, or economic interest? Lastly, Professor Steel may be correct in that the situation in Rwanda was complex and involved, and it would have been difficult at best to stop the warring factions in a civil conflict from continuing to kill each other. In the final analysis, no one really cared until it was too late, and Rwanda's coffee crop hardly qualified as an irreplaceable resource.[4]

The Iranian Nuclear-Program Crisis

Iran's national objectives and strategies are shaped by its regional political aspirations, threat perceptions, and the need to preserve its Islamic government. Mohsen Milani points out that "in fact, Tehran's foreign policy [is] . . . based on Iran's ambitions and Tehran's perception of what threatens them. Tehran's top priority is the survival of the Islamic Republic" (2009, 46).

In the past, and within the framework of its national goals, Iran gave high priority to expanding its nuclear, biological, and chemical weapons and missile programs. Thus, in 1991 Ayatollah Mohajerani, one of then president Akbar Hashemi Rafsanjani's deputies, said in a statement widely quoted online that "since the enemy has atomic capabilities, Islamic countries must be armed with the same capacity."

The Iran-Iraq War (1980–1988), the worst war in modern Middle Eastern history, exposed Iranian military and strategic weakness and vulnerability, for which a nuclear weapons capability could compensate. Iran's emphasis on pursuing independent production capabilities for special weapons and missiles was driven by its experience in the war, during which it was unable to respond adequately to Iraqi chemical and missile attacks and suffered the effects of an international arms embargo. The war was probably the greatest influence on Iran's decision to pursue special weapons capabilities.

In his 2003 State of the Union address, President Bush labeled Iran as part of an "axis of evil" along with Iraq and North Korea. From its perspective Iran concluded that nuclear weapons could prove useful, therefore, in deterring the United States, and a nuclear weapons capability could constitute a balance to Israel. Iran's president, Mahmoud Ahmadinejad, who first took office in 2005 and was re-elected in a much disputed election in 2009, has repeatedly emphasized that Iran has the right to peacefully use nuclear energy and that Iran will act to protect its security against the Great Satan, meaning the United States. In December 2009, *The Economist* noted, "Iran is much further on with its enrichment plans. . . . [It] has done warhead development, besides other experiments whose purpose can only be to build a nuclear weapon, or enable one to be assembled at speed."[5]

The foundation of the nuclear nonproliferation regime has been the Nuclear Nonproliferation Treaty (NPT) in effect since 1970 and renewed indefinitely in 1995. NPT signatories are legally bound to fulfill specific obligations to prevent proliferation. In the view of many Western governments, although Iran remains a signatory to the treaty, it has sought nuclear weapons in violation of its nonproliferation and safeguards obligations under the NPT. In fact, inspectors from the IAEA, the NPT's enforcement arm, have warned that Iran's nuclear-enrichment efforts are in an "advanced state of construction" (quoted in *The Economist* 2009). Fareed Zakaria reminds us that Iran "has a right to civilian nuclear energy, as do all nations. But Tehran has signed the Nuclear Non-Proliferation Treaty, submitting itself to the jurisdiction of the International Atomic Energy Agency. The IAEA says Iran has exhibited a pattern of deception and non-cooperation involving its nuclear program for 20 years—including lying about its activities and concealing sites" (2009).

Charles D. Ferguson notes,

> To make nuclear fuel, an enrichment facility is not enough. A country needs adequate supplies of natural uranium to begin the process. Also, it needs a fuel fabrication facility to turn the enriched uranium into fuel that can be placed inside the core of a nuclear reactor. Iran has

neither. . . . Therefore, Iran cannot run a peaceful nuclear program alone. In order to build commercial nuclear reactors, Iran must rely on the major reactor producers, including France, Russia, and the U.S.— some of the same countries working to prevent Iran from making nuclear bombs. It must also rely on international suppliers of natural uranium and international fuel fabrication facilities. (2008, 9)

UN Security Council Resolution 1540 (2004) requires all states to enact and enforce legal and regulatory measures against the proliferation of weapons of mass destruction by state and nonstate actors. The United States and the United Kingdom have called for implementation of Resolution 1540, which declares that all member states "resolve to take appropriate and effective actions against any threat to international peace and security caused by the proliferation of nuclear, chemical and biological weapons and their means of delivery, in conformity with its primary responsibilities, as provided for in the United Nations Charter . . . [and to support] multilateral treaties whose aim is to eliminate or prevent the proliferation of nuclear, chemical or biological weapons."

Leslie H. Gelb (2009) has argued that even great powers such as the United States must work with other nations in order to build coalitions to confront and respond to global problems. The Lone Ranger approach so famously adopted and employed by the George W. Bush administration never really worked, as evidenced by the disastrous 2003 war in Iraq. With the end of this very brief "unipolar moment,"[6] working with other countries may be the only effective way to deal with a potential disaster resulting from a nuclear-armed Iran.

How should the international community respond to Iran? Using the framework for governance recommended above (common interests, leadership by major powers, and effective enforcement mechanisms), there are possible alternatives to a preemptive strike by the United States, Israel, or both, and the consequences that would necessarily result.

First, there has to be a consensus among the great and interested powers. They include Britain, China, France, Germany, Russia, and the United States. In December 2009, a senior Russian diplomat observed, "We will not stand aside" if others agree on sanctions. At least initially, this requires that the major powers disavow regime change in Tehran and offer trade and contact incentives to the Iranian government.

Second, the major powers must be clear and resolute in their determination to prevent Iran from becoming armed with nuclear weapons. In 2009, the IAEA's board voted 25–3, with the support of both China and Russia, to censure Iran for its latest safeguards breaches and to refer the matter, yet again, to the UN Security Council. This means that the major powers must present a united front on Iran, and they must be willing to support additional and harsher sanctions if warranted by Tehran's intransigence and its continued defiance of the Security Council and a united global community. In addition, the United States must lean hard on Israel to discourage a preemptive strike against Iran. Ariel Ilan Roth suggests that the "Israelis know better than anyone else that the trick to developing a nuclear weapon as a small power is to drag out the process of diplomacy and inspections long enough to produce sufficient quantities of fissionable material" (2009).

Nevertheless, he discounts this potential development because "Tehran's expanding influence in Iraq and the fear that it inspires in the Persian Gulf states are already advancing the first goal. Iran needs only to possess nuclear weapons, not to use them, in order to further enhance its international prestige and force adversaries to take it seriously" (2009).

The United States must also consider reevaluating its policy toward Iran essentially since the hostage crisis of 1979. It is unlikely, given the current state of American domestic politics, that full U.S. engagement with Iran is a viable option. Some scholars, however, have suggested that opening the door to cultural and educational exchanges, developing economic relationships on a small-scale basis, and encouraging political dialogues and contacts, especially with opposition Iranian domestic political actors, may be a good start by the United States in an effort to normalize relations between the two countries. In short, the United States must begin to think about détente with Iran and reject the "axis of evil" approach favored by George W. Bush and Dick Cheney.

An important note here involves the role of nongovernmental organizations (NGOs), particularly those involved in human rights issues, regarding Iran. Amnesty International, Human Rights Watch, and the Fédération International des Ligues des Droits de l'Homme have been outspoken in their condemnation of the Iranian government's efforts to suppress continuing opposition to the results of the June 2009 presidential election. This NGO focus on Iran is important, should continue, and must be encouraged and supported. NGOs have an enormously productive role to play in global governance.

Third, the recommendations of the IAEA must be supported by the UN Security Council. A nuclear-armed Iran is in no nation's interest, including Iran's. And, as former president Richard Nixon used to say, this must be made "perfectly clear" to all of the parties involved. Any additional sanctions imposed by the

Security Council against Iran must be targeted so that the Iranian government and those associated with it are directly effected and not the Iranian people.

The Future: State Power and Global Governance

So, what is the future of state power and global governance through intergovernmental organizations in this new century? Will we ever experience even a reasonable balance between state sovereignty and national power (often unilaterally asserted, for example, by the Americans in countries such as Iraq or the Russians in nations such as Georgia) and global governance as a means through which the international community acts to address global problems and crises? We are certainly aware of the "responsibility to protect," the notion that state sovereignty comes with certain obligations, and the much older notion of "cooperative security," the idea that states need to work together to advance their security goals. We also know that whatever the problems we confront now or in the future, including continuing environmental degradation, terrorism conducted by groups or sponsored by so-called rogue states, or global economic collapse, they all lend themselves to cooperative behavior between and among nation-states and have enhanced the need to build institutions and a framework for global governance. Unilateralism is not dead, but we are aware that America's unilateral war in Iraq made the United States few friends internationally, set back America's national and diplomatic interests, and clearly demonstrated the necessity for multilateral military and diplomatic action (NATO) in other trouble regions of the world, including the war in Afghanistan and the spill over conflict in the border region with Pakistan.

A Framework for Global Governance

The idea of global governance is nothing new in international politics. In his 1795 essay "Perpetual Peace," Immanuel Kant observed, "Reason without exception absolutely condemns war as a mean of right, and makes a state of peace an absolute duty; and since this peace cannot be effected or be guaranteed without a compact among nations, they must form an alliance of a peculiar kind [a federation]" (Kant 1795, 24–25). Many theorists and political leaders have long supported Kant's contention that global peace and stability rest on "democratic governance" within states, which is the key, in turn, to a "sustainable peace" internationally because democracies are unlikely to make war against other democratic states.

It should also be noted that a community of interest does not always lend itself to combined diplomatic action, even when national interests converge. The so-called BRIC countries (Brazil, Russia, India, and China) have many common economic concerns, but Russia and China, in particular, often agree only on when to oppose multilateral action regarding countries such as Iran. They rarely engage in united diplomatic action in response to major global issues. In fact, John Lewis Gaddis even suggests that "an expansion of 'poles' within the international system . . . [or] shifts toward bipolarity or multipolarity, are dangerous" (1992, 23). Gaddis also subscribes to Stephen Rock's conclusion that a "state of peace is most likely to emerge among states that are heterogeneous in the exercise of national power . . . in their economic activities, [and] in their societal attributes" (Rock 1989, 12, 15).

It should be noted, as David Kennett concludes in his contribution to this volume, that there is often no "agreement on the exact nature of the disease and on the appropriate medicine" when it comes to global economic problems (see Chapter 7). The same conclusion is valid when it comes to the myriad of political, social, and economic problems confronting humankind in the twenty-first century.

Wilsonian Democracy and the United Nations

The Wilsonian notion that only democracies could provide a framework for a stable and peaceful world was unintentionally confirmed by the failure of the League of Nations to prevent another global conflict after World War I. The history and the failures of the league, which helped consolidate the coming to power of the European dictators Adolf Hitler and Benito Mussolini, are well documented. The UN Charter drafted in San Francisco in 1945 reflected a more realistic view of the world as it actually was and not how it ideally should be. The UN Security Council, in particular, was a functional manifestation of what Hans Morgenthau later called "political realism." Nevertheless, this post–World War II concept that the great powers could manage the peace by acting collectively was deeply flawed.

Stanley Hoffman (1994) points out that identifying an aggressor, subordination of national interests to a greater good, and imposing and enforcing sanctions on nations have often prevented the United Nations from functioning as it was intended by at least some of the fifty-one nations assembled in San Francisco after the war. He also points out that regional organizations "cannot be effective" unless they are supported politically and militarily by a great power. The NATO intervention in Afghanistan is a good example of where the effort to isolate and destroy the Taliban and Al Qaeda would not work at all if the United States did not provide the bulk of the military forces involved in the fighting. In addition, collective security as an aspect of global or regional governance is an expensive proposition not only in terms of lives but also in the cost to national taxpayers. The estimated cost to the American taxpayer for 30,000 U.S. troops being deployed to Afghanistan in the coming years, for example, is about $1 million per soldier, or approximately $30 billion annually.

Mark Malloch Brown also suggests, however, that "if members of a society are . . . unable to sit down across various boundaries—ethnic, religious, social, or cultural—and develop common plans" (2003, 142), it is unlikely that their nation will support global efforts to resolve crises and disputes among nations. And, of course, we are always confronted by what Hans Morgenthau characterized as the "anarchic" state of the international political system and the subsequent and continuing struggle for power (and domination) in global politics.

The Case for Global Governance

So, is global governance even a remote possibility in the twenty-first century, or is it a notion debated and discussed by those advocates who, in general, do not understand the real nature of the world in which we live?

In discussing and evaluating a structure for global governance in the twenty-first century, Robert Keohane makes some very useful starting points. He believes that international cooperation, the basis of global governance, does not "necessarily depend on altruism, idealism, personal honor, common purposes, internalized norms, or a shared belief in a set of values embodied in a culture" (1988, 380). Here, we are really referring to a common set of interests as a starting point and as a basis for global governance. In late December 2009, nearly two hundred nations met in Copenhagen, Denmark, to agree on common action in dealing with climate change. The nations assembled included big producing and big polluting nations such as China and the United States, poor nations that claim they bear little or no responsibility for global environmental damage, and nations that are skeptical of the science of climate change, including Saudi Arabia. Whether or not political agreements or effective action eventually emerge depends on bringing together nations that recognize the common long-term dangers and are willing to join with other nations in order to create the global institutional framework necessary to deal with climate change.

Any real prospect of dealing with reducing greenhouse-gas emissions will ultimately rely on the degree of support for these efforts by China and the United States. This example illustrates a second major factor in global governance. If the United States assumes a leadership role, and if China adopts energy-efficient methods together with slowing the growth of emissions, there is a chance that developing nations can be persuaded to go along as well. In short, the leadership and support of the major powers is a prerequisite for global action. In the final analysis, global governance, as a general principle, depends on support from the world's major economic, military, and political powers that share common interests.

The third major aspect of global governance must involve enforcement. As we know, the devil is always in the details. Political agreements regarding climate change are a beginning, but they must be followed by defined goals and, more importantly, by the creation of enforcement mechanisms. Timothy Longman and Natalie Zähringer point out in Chapter 8 that there is hope regarding enforcement, even when violations of human rights are involved. They believe that not only have minimum standards of "decent treatment" for all human beings "become an increasingly important influence on international affairs," but enforcement, individual accountability, and humanitarian intervention have occurred more frequently and have seriously challenged the principle of state sovereignty. The tragic situation in Haiti in 2010 is an important reminder that the international community, led by the United States in this case, can react positively to a natural disaster with terrible consequences for the people affected.

In summary, three essential aspects of global governance have been identified. In order for global governance to work, common purposes must be identified, the great powers must support measures that are responsive and effective, and the international community must engage in enforcement efforts by supporting and strengthening existing institutions and creating new institutions if necessary, by participating in peacemaking and peacekeeping activities, by upholding sanctions, and by providing the financial resources required to do the job.

Regarding strengthening international institutions, for example, Kishore Mahbubani has observed,

> Democracy, the foundation of government in the West, is based on the premise that each human being in a society is an equal stakeholder in the domestic order. Thus, governments are selected on the basis of "one person, one vote." . . . In order to produce long-term stability and order worldwide, democracy should be the cornerstone of global society, and

the planet's 6.6 billion inhabitants should become equal stakeholders. . . .
The problem today is that . . . many Western actors . . . are reluctant to
strengthen the UN's core institution, the UN General Assembly . . . the
most representative body on the planet, and yet many Western countries
are deeply skeptical of it. (2008, 123)

Finally, it is important also to remember what can be accomplished when states
act in concert through alliances, international organizations and institutions, and
multilateral cooperative behavior. *New York Times* writer David Brooks in one of
his columns recalled a broadcast on National Public Radio originally recorded
the day after Japan surrendered in 1945. An actor was featured who read what
Ernie Pyle, the American World War II correspondent, had written about who
won the war. Pyle wrote, "We won this war because our men are brave and because of many things . . . because of Russia, England and China. . . . We did not
win it because destiny created us better than other peoples" (Brooks 2009). Na-
tionalism and state sovereignty may always be factors in global politics. The real
question is whether they can be controlled and channeled to benefit all of humankind or history will continue to repeat itself.

Notes

1. Scholars often use different criteria in identifying IGOs, so the exact number of
IGOs is debatable.

2. While definitions of global governance may vary, it is useful to note the following
excerpt from the Commission on Global Governance: "Governance is the sum of
the many ways individuals and institutions, public and private, manage their common affairs. It is a continuing process through which conflicting or diverse interests
may be accommodated and co-operative action may be taken. It includes formal institutions and regimes empowered to enforce compliance, as well as informal arrangements that people and institutions either have agreed to or perceive to be in their
interest. . . . At the global level, governance has been viewed primarily as intergovernmental relationships, but it must now be understood as also involving non-governmental
organizations (NGOs), citizens' movements, multinational corporations, and the
global capital market. Interacting with these are global mass media of dramatically
enlarged influence. There is no single model or form of global governance, nor is there
a single structure or set of structures. It is a broad, dynamic, complex process of interactive decision-making that is constantly evolving and responding to changing circumstances" (1995, 2–3).

3. The United Nations itself considers the action it authorized in the Gulf War to
be an example of what it calls "peace enforcement," where the Security Council authorizes member states to "take all necessary measures to achieve a stated objective."

There is no UN command, and the consent of the warring parties is not necessarily required. Many scholars, however, consider the Gulf War to be an example of the collective-security provisions of the UN Charter.

4. Critics argued that the nation-building effort in Somalia was an either good or bad (and inevitable) example of "mission creep" (i.e., going far beyond the original UN mandate). Others argued that the United Nations had few options in Somalia and only reluctantly became involved in a civil conflict.

5. Quoted in *The Economist* 2009.

6. Charles Krauthammer first wrote about a "unipolar moment" in a *Foreign Affairs* article in 1990. He argued that after the Cold War, the United States being the only remaining superpower, it should act accordingly, and that internationalism had replaced isolationism among the majority of the American public.

References

Brooks, D. 2009. High-five nation. *New York Times*, September 15, A33.

Brown, M. M. 2003. Democratic governance: Toward a framework for sustainable peace. *Global Governance* 9, no. 2 (April–June): 141–146.

Commission on Global Governance. 1995. *Our global neighbourhood*. New York: Oxford University Press.

Economist, The. 2009. An Iranian nuclear bomb, or the bombing of Iran? *The Economist*, December 5, 27–30.

Ferguson, C. D. 2008. A new approach to Iran's nukes. *Christian Science Monitor*, September 8, 9.

Gaddis, J. L. 1992. International relations theory and the end of the Cold War. *International Security* 17, no. 3 (winter): 5–58.

Gelb, L. H. 2009. *Power rules: How common sense can rescue American foreign policy*. New York: Harper/HarperCollins.

Hoffman, S. 1994. Delusions of world order. In *At issue: Politics in the world arena*, ed. S. Spiegel and D. Pervin, 13–26. New York: St. Martin's Press.

Kant, Immanuel. 1795. Project for a perpetual peace. A philosophical essay. Google Books. http://books.google.ca/books?id=LykHAAAAQAAJ&dq=kant+perpetual +peace+text.

Kennedy, P. 1987. *The rise and fall of the great powers*. New York: Random House.

Keohane, R. 1988. International institutions: Two approaches. *International Studies Quarterly* 32, no. 4 (December): 379–396.

Kuperman, A. 2000. Rwanda in retrospect. *Foreign Affairs* 79, no. 1 (January–February): 94–118.

Mahbubani, K. 2008. The case against the West. *Foreign Affairs* 87, no. 3 (May–June): 111–125.

Milani, M. 2009. Tehran's take. *Foreign Affairs* 88, no. 4 (July–August): 46–63.

Rock, S. 1989. *Why peace breaks out*. Chapel Hill: University of North Carolina.

Roth, A. I. 2009. The root of all fears. *Foreign Affairs*, November 24, www.foreign affairs.com/articles/65692/ariel-ilan-roth/the-root-of-all-fears.

Rourke, J., and M. Boyer. 2008. *International politics on the world stage.* New York: McGraw-Hill.

Steel, R. 1999. East Timor isn't Kosovo. *New York Times*, September 12.

United Nations. 1999. *Report of the independent inquiry into the actions of the United Nations during the 1994 genocide in Rwanda.* S/1999/1257. United Nations. December 16. www.un.org/News/dh/latest/rwanda.htm.

Zakaria, F. 2009. Containing a nuclear Iran. *Newsweek.* October 3. www.newsweek .com/id/216702.

20

Multilateralism's New Mix: Implications for Diplomacy, International Organizations, and Global Governance

James P. Muldoon, Jr.

Multilateralism has reached the proverbial crossroad. The world in which it was created and developed has radically and fundamentally changed. From a historical perspective, multilateralism has come to reflect much of what Woodrow Wilson envisioned for a new world order. The array of multilateral structures built since the end of World War II has "brought a measure of law and reciprocity to international politics" and "bred some measure of trust among sovereign states that had eyed each other warily at least since Westphalia" (Kennedy 2010, 93–94). Multilateralism has become an "internalized" norm of interstate relations and a defining characteristic of the international community of independent states. Today, however, the international system is no longer simply about interstate relations and the community of independent sovereign states. Globalization and the global communications revolution have made the world a smaller place, taking interdependence to a significantly new level and changing the patterns of interaction between states, market actors, and civil society on the international level. Hence, the world order that Wilson and others had sought to bring about over the course of the twentieth century does not necessarily reflect the new political, economic, and social landscape of a globalizing international system that has started to unfold in the twenty-first century. This in turn raises the question, Whither multilateralism in this brave new world?

For the past two decades, scholars and practitioners of international relations have been engrossed by the dramatic global changes that have happened and the impact these changes are having on the structural and functional characteristics of the international system and order. A growing number of scholars and analysts point out that breakthroughs in telecommunications and transportation have undermined state authority by ending the state's monopoly on information; that there is an increasing reliance on nonstate entities, such as nongovernmental organizations (NGOs), for focus and direction, drafting, and implementation of declarations, platforms, and treaties on crucial international issues, including landmines, human rights, and the environment; and that there is a renewed emphasis on working through the UN system to deal with the growing number of intrastate conflicts and new definitions of human security. Many contend that a new world order is both needed and emerging. But, as Henry Kissinger once argued, "[The new world order] is still in a period of gestation, and its final form will not be visible until well into the [twenty-first] century. Part extension of the past, part unprecedented, the new world order, like those which it succeeds, will emerge as an answer to three questions: What are the basic units of the international order? What are their means of interacting? What are the goals on behalf of which they interact?" (1994, 806). Whereas Kissinger remained fixed on states, particularly "continental-type states" (e.g., China, the European Union, India, the Russian Federation, and the United States) as "the basic units of the new world order" (1994, 807), others have realized that globalization and the technological revolution have enabled nonstate actors to become important elements of world order too (cf. Keck and Sikkink 1998; Cutler, Haufler, and Porter 1999; Florini 2000; Mendelson and Glenn 2002; Muldoon 2003; Barnett and Finnemore 2004; DeMars 2005).

As has been pointed out throughout this volume, the role played by nonstate actors in contemporary international relations is an important dimension largely missing in traditional notions of multilateralism, which minimize or ignore nonstate actors' interactions with states and multilateral organizations and their influence on intergovernmental decision making. Due to the dramatic growth and increasing activities of nonstate actors, it is no longer practical to exclude this dimension of global politics. But the answer to the initial question above is not simply to add nonstate actors to the mix; it is more complicated than that since the interactive dynamics between international actors are so fluid and their affects on the institutional and organizational structure of the global system are still unfolding. In addition, at least four important developments in the international system must be taken into account:

(1) The existing state system is being transformed into a multi-level pattern of political actors, including macro and microeconomic entities; (2) dominant neo-liberal economic 'globalization' is polarizing rich and poor, included and excluded, both among countries—especially those in Africa—and within societies; (3) threats to people's lives include forces, like the biosphere, which are not contained by territorially based political entities; and (4) current concepts of world order, including Pax Americana and the United States' vaguely articulated preferred new world order, are open to challenge. (Schechter 1999, 2)

Changing Roles, Many Multilateralisms

The last two decades have been a terribly turbulent period for the world, economically, politically, and socially. This has resulted in considerable changes in the way societal actors interact with and relate to each other. States, businesses, and civil society at all levels, from the local to the global, are having to adapt their respective roles to the increasingly complex reality of today's globalizing environment. This, in turn, is shaping the institutional and organizational structure of the international system and global governance. Moreover, as the traditional divides between the private and public and the national and international increasingly blur, the roles played by states, nonstate actors, and international organizations in the governance of the international system are being reconfigured.

In the case of states and their governments, the last twenty years have been particularly rough. Their ability to "control" the forces unleashed by the revolution in information and communications technologies and the effects of globalization has diminished; their resources, financial and otherwise, have declined; and, their authority and legitimacy have been seriously challenged. According to P. Cerny,

> The governments of nation-states are no longer able to make foreign policies autonomously, based primarily on "national interests," whether benevolent or domineering. Nor is foreign policy today about the projection of power, whether "hard" or "soft" (*pace* Joseph Nye and David Milibrand). In a globalizing world it is increasingly about co-operating and co-ordinating both foreign and domestic policies for the purpose of making what international relations theorists call "absolute" or "positive sum" gains. . . . Multilateralism and "civilian superpowers" increasingly trump nationalistic foreign policies in terms of global effectiveness. (2007, 12)

The role of states has clearly changed since the end of the Cold War, but it is not so much a lesser role as a different one. Although no longer necessarily the sole determinants of the international system, states and the power(s) they continue to wield remain both significant and crucial to the international system's stability and governance. In other words, states are still the dominant actors on the world stage, and the state system continues to be the foundation upon which the emerging global order is being built.

It has also been a tough time for nonstate actors, particularly international business and civil society, primarily due to the changing fortunes of the private sector in the global economy and the rise of "uncivil" society (e.g., Al Qaeda and transnational networks of organized crime). NGOs and civil society groups—an amorphous, fluid, and fractious collectivity of actors—have struggled with the increasing diversity of their ranks and goals, power asymmetries, and funding, resulting in intense competition and fragmentation. Even though NGOs and civil society enjoy high levels of "trust" vis-à-vis government and business in most countries, their legitimacy and accountability have been challenged; this is especially true for humanitarian and development NGOs involved in postconflict areas and in disaster-relief operations (cf. Terry 2002; Juma and Suhrke 2002; Cooley and Ron 2002; DeMars 2005). This has limited their effectiveness and ability to contend in global politics. Likewise, the credibility and influence of international business has been undermined by high-profile corporate scandals (e.g., Enron and Worldcom) and reckless risk taking by global banks and private financial institutions (e.g., American International Group, Goldman Sachs, and Merrill Lynch), which precipitated the current global financial crisis. At the same time, civil society groups, NGOs, and their private-sector counterparts (i.e., multinational corporations and business associations) have graduated from their marginal position within the international system to become key partners and consequential participants in global processes. They no longer simply "lobby" or "inform" governments on global issues and problems but have the resources and capacity to act independently and to protect or promote their own interests and policies. "Civil society organizations as well as corporations have successfully reorganized themselves on a transnational scale, using various forms and varying degrees of influence to make their interests count in international politics. In some cases, transnational non-state interests have managed to almost fully transcend control of nation-states" (Witte, Reinicke, and Benner 2002, 4; Cooper 2002; Langhorne 1998). The role of nonstate actors has definitely grown in the international system, filling in some of the political and economic space that states have abandoned or were failing to maintain control over, and despite their limitations or perceived (or actual) deficiencies of accountability, legitimacy, or capability, nonstate actors are indeed "units" of the new world order and proactively involved in defining and setting the goals, rules, and terms of engagement of the international system.

Finally, the effects of global change and pluralized international politics on international organizations have been just as profound. Since the end of the Cold War, international organizations have been struggling to stay abreast of global events and developments, as well as to meet the growing demands made of them for services (e.g., peacekeeping, development, and humanitarian assistance) (Kennedy and Russett 1995). As Paul Diehl has pointed out,

> The prospects for expanding the roles, functions, and powers of international organizations in global governance seemed bright at the beginning of the 1990s. Yet a series of events underscored the problems and limitations of international organizations as they approached the twenty-first century. . . . [International organizations] now struggle with the new environment and the redefinition of their roles as their original purposes have been significantly altered or rendered obsolete. [They] play a greater role than they ever have in history. Yet we are still reminded that state sovereignty and lack of political will by members inhibit the long-term prospects of those organizations for creating effective structures of global governance. (1997, 3; see also Elliott 2000)

Most importantly, international organizations have had difficulty in balancing their two major roles: forum and service provider. As Robert Cox and Harold Jacobson note,

> Some organizations are established to provide a forum or framework for negotiations and decisions, others to provide specific services. . . . In reality, of course, many international organizations fall into both categories. ILO, for example, has an extensive technical assistance program, but also provides a framework for the negotiation of International Labor Conventions. Similarly, ITU, UNESCO, WHO, IAEA, and IMF execute services in their own right and at the same time provide frameworks for discussion and negotiations among their member states. (1997, 75–76)

While the two roles are interrelated, each is distinct, demanding different organizational capabilities—political and diplomatic for the former and managerial for the latter—that are sometimes contradictory and always difficult to link effectively (Dijkzeul and Beigbeder 2003). Although international organizations have been slow to adjust to the shifting patterns of interaction between state and nonstate actors and the new global environment, they have grown stronger, more focused, and more capable as they gradually move away from the fragmented, "silo-ed," decentralized bureaucratic structure toward a more coherent, networked, and coordinated one. Interorganizational dynamics among international organizations are certainly an important dimension of today's multilateral system and reinforce the intermediary role international organizations have and do play in the international system and its governance.

As these three sets of actors engage one another, their roles are inevitably shaped and altered. Brian Hocking and Dominic Kelly argue that there is "strong impetus" for this engagement, which "affects both governmental and nongovernmental actors in ways which, whilst related, are differentiated by their distinctive organizational characteristics (their 'actorness')":

> In the case of business, this is reflected in the growing concern with corporate citizenship which, by its nature, focuses on redefining a firm's relations with an expanded range of "stakeholders." In the case of governments, it is reflected in the reform of diplomatic services to enhance their interaction with civil society and reinforce and redefine the "public diplomacy" function. In the case of NGOs, it is reflected in debates about purpose, strategies, and engagement with both business and government, and for multilateral organizations, in reaching out beyond the realm of states in a search for funds, expertise, and legitimacy. (2002, 207)

The interests that each set of actors brings to bear on its relationships with the others, as well as the complex set of interactions between them, contribute to the growing complexity of the international operating environment. These varied interests also reflect the different changes within each set of actors—for example, the power shifts within the interstate system with the rise of new major political and economic powers (e.g., China and India); the rise of transnational movements of civil society and NGO networks, the rise (and fall) of global business power over the global economy, and the trend toward "partnerships" between business and civil society; and the emergence of innovative interorganizational arrangements and coordinating mechanisms among international organizations—that inform and drive their respective behaviors and goals in the international system and the emerging global order. It is this interactive dynamic that creates myriad constellations of actors in free-flowing networks and ad hoc arrangements that pervade the international policy milieu and animates international institutions and existing and emergent forms of multilateralism.

Multilateralism in its traditional guise as an institutional form of coordination of relations among three or more states is still pertinent to the system of states and international governmental organizations (e.g., the UN system, Bretton Woods institutions, the North Atlantic Treaty Organization, the European Union, and other regional bodies like the Organization of American States, the African Union, and the Association of Southeast Asian Nations). The Westphalian order of states is still intact and increasingly relies on institutions of multilateralism to manage the inherent "anarchy" of the interstate system and soften "the rough edges of power" of states (Thakur 2002, 283), especially the great powers, like the Russian Federation or the United States. Even though U.S. policies of the last several years have shaken "the foundations of mutual trust that a half century of multilateral life cemented" and eroded confidence in multilateral institutions, multilateralism provides "the world the very tools it needs most to manage the ever more interdependent global order of the 21st century. It would be folly to abandon those tools, or let them rust through inattention, particularly as new great powers arise to rival the last century's hegemon. To do so would leave all nations, including the United States, markedly less secure" (Kennedy 2010, 94). However, limiting multilateralism to intergovernmental relations creates an incomplete picture of the international system. As James Orbinski argues, "Today, competing and overlapping state alliances and blocks (Chimerica vs. G8/G5 + Egypt vs. G20 vs. UN Fora vs. BRIC), multinational corporations, intergovernmental organizations like the WTO and WHO, transnational public-private partnerships, foundations like Gates, one-man states like Bono, the UN, big and small NGOs, and transnational civil society networks are all powerful forces that shape and reshape contemporary international relations" (2009, 32). Now that crowds of private actors are in the international public arena and so deeply involved in how international public policy is made and implemented, it no longer makes sense to think of multilateralism only in terms of states and interstate relations or of intergovernmental organizations and regimes.

Other multilateralisms are emerging that both challenge and complement the statecentric multilateral system. Shepard Forman and Derk Segaar point out,

Just as a multitude of alternative intergovernmental arrangements [e.g., the Group of Twenty or ad hoc coalitions of the willing, multinational forces, and "friends of" arrangements] have emerged to address issues that are presumed to be underattended or mishandled by the formal multilateral institutions, so too have NGOs and multinational corporations sought to expand their influence and inputs into the making of international public policy and the delivery of essential goods and services that national governments and intergovernmental institutions seem unable or unwilling to provide. (2006, 214)

Through multistakeholder arrangements like NGO coalitions and networks, public-private partnerships, and a variety of nonstate forums such as the World Economic Forum, World Social Forum, and the parallel gatherings of NGOs at world conferences and summits, nonstate actors have become an essential part of the international system. Similarly, Thomas Weiss, Tatiana Carayannis, and Richard Jolly argue that the extensive relationships and interaction between nonstate actors and the two United Nations—one composed of member states and the other of the secretariats—have created what they call a third United Nations:

This "additional" UN consists of certain nongovernmental organizations (NGOs), external experts, scholars, consultants, and committed citizens who work closely with the UN's intergovernmental machinery [the first UN] and secretariats [the second UN]. The third UN's roles include advocacy, research, policy analysis, and idea mongering. Its elements often combine forces to put forward new information and ideas, push for new policies, and mobilize public opinion around UN deliberations and operations. . . . These circles—a third UN—are independent of and provide essential inputs into the other two UNs. Such "outside-insiders" are an integral part of today's United Nations. What once seemed marginal for international relations now is central to multilateralism. (2009, 123)

Multistakeholder arrangements and multisector networks offer an alternative approach for transnational problem-solving. According to Jan Witte, Wolfgang Reinicke, and Thorsten Benner, "Multisector networks create bridges on a transnational scale among the public sector (national, regional or state, and local governments as well as inter-governmental groups), the private sector and civil society. They (a) reflect the changing roles and relative importance among them; (b) pull diverse groups and resources together; and (c) address issues that no group can solve by itself" (2002, 10). Nonstate actors and international secretariats have turned to these new forms and structures of multilateralism primarily out of frustration with the inflexibility of states to reform the intergovernmental machinery and decision making of the traditional multilateral system, but these alternative forums and modalities have not emerged to replace intergovernmental multilateralism. Rather, they complement and supplement existing multilateral institutions, enlarging their capacity and increasing their capability to respond to a range of global and transnational problems. Moreover, intergovernmental organizations like the United Nations have regained relevance in global governance by assuming "the role of nodal points in complex networks of governance emerging from the multitude of private-public partnerships now being developed . . . [and] by placing them[selves] at center stage in a new structure of world governance based on public-private partnerships organized along lines of overlapping networks of governance" (Bull, Bøås, McNeill 2004, 495).

Conclusion

Although the mix of actors is unsettled and the roles of states, nonstate actors, and international organizations are still being negotiated, there is little doubt that the institutions and structures of world order are in transition, moving from the international order established after World War II to a global order for the twenty-first century. A number of factors are driving the transition—structural changes in the international system; periodic crises and disasters (e.g., inter- and intrastate conflicts, economic collapse or depression, and catastrophic environmental events) that shock the system; shifts in the international system's characteristics or nature due to competitive pressures for resources and mandates, new and expanded norms, and domestic politics; and organizational leadership and learning—and creating distinctively new conditions and pressures for institutional change (Kapur 2002). One of the more important consequences of this transition has been the pluralization of international relations, which is causing the shift away from the state-centered institutional forms and mechanisms of governance and shaping the contours of twenty-first-century world politics. But, despite these pressures, most mechanisms for international decision making are exclusive to states, and governments continue to resist formalizing or institutionalizing the role and influence of nonstate actors in intergovernmental bodies or expanding the roles and powers of international organizations in contemporary international relations. While this arrangement is increasingly untenable in the complex global realities of today's world, the interstate system is not likely to relinquish its privileged position, though it may well be forced by circumstances to accept a role for nonstate actors and international organizations in the system of global governance.

The new dynamics of world politics arising out of this period of transition are forcing existing multilateral institutions to expand their institutional boundaries to manage relations among a wider set of global actors and creating the new mix of participants and roles in the structure and governance of the international system and order. Clearly, the cast of characters on the multilateral stage is large and growing, and the roles they play in contemporary world politics are both diverse and complex. Multilateralism encompasses this complexity; anchors the practices and means of interaction of states, nonstate actors, and international organizations; and enables states and nonstate actors to tackle transnational and global problems collectively and to realize common goals. In the end, perhaps most significant about multilateralism today is its salience in the evolution of the emerging global order and governance in the twenty-first century.

References

Barnett, M., and M. Finnemore. 2004. *Rules for the world: International organizations in global politics.* Ithaca, NY: Cornell University Press.

Bull, B., M. Bøås, and D. McNeill. 2004. Private sector influence in the multilateral system: A changing structure of world governance? *Global Governance* 10, no. 4 (October–December): 481–498.

Cerny, P. 2007. Letter to *Financial Times. Financial Times*, November 21, 12.

Cooley, A., and J. Ron. 2002. The NGO scramble: Organizational insecurity and the political economy of transnational action. *International Security* 27, no. 1 (summer): 5–39.

Cooper, R. 2002. Foreign policy, values and globalization. *Financial Times*, January 31, 21.

Cox, R., and H. K. Jacobson. 1997. The framework for inquiry. In *The politics of global governance: International organizations in an interdependent world*, ed. P. Diehl, 75–90. Boulder, CO: Lynne Rienner Publishers.

Cutler, A. C., V. Haufler, and T. Porter, eds. 1999. *Private authority and international affairs.* Albany: State University of New York Press.

DeMars, W. E. 2005. *NGOs and transnational networks: Wild cards in world politics.* London: Pluto Press.

Diehl, P. 1997. Introduction to *The politics of global governance: International organizations in an interdependent world*, ed. P. Diehl, 1–6. Boulder, CO: Lynne Rienner Publishers.

Dijkzeul, D., and Y. Beigbeder, eds. 2003. *Rethinking international organizations: Pathology and promise.* New York: Berghahn Books.

Elliott, L. 2000. Multilateral thinking. *Guardian*, November 29, www.guardian
.co.uk/comment/story/0,3604,404230,00.html.

Florini, A. M., ed. 2000. *The third force: The rise of transnational civil society.* Washington, DC: Carnegie Endowment for International Peace.

Forman, S., and D. Segaar. 2006. New coalitions for global governance: The changing dynamics of multilateralism. *Global Governance* 12, no. 2 (April–June): 205–225.

Hocking, B., and D. Kelly. 2002. Doing the business? The International Chamber of Commerce, the United Nations, and the Global Compact. In *Enhancing global governance: Towards a new diplomacy?* ed. A. F. Cooper, J. English, and R. Thakur, 203–228. Tokyo: United Nations University Press.

Juma, M. K., and A. Suhrke, eds. 2002. *Eroding local capacity: International humanitarian action in Africa.* Uppsala, Sweden: Nordiska Afrika Institutet.

Kapur, D. 2002. Processes of change in international organizations. In *Governing globalization: Issues and institutions,* ed. D. Nayyar, 334–355. New York: Oxford University Press.

Keck, M. E., and K. Sikkink. 1998. *Activists beyond borders: Advocacy networks in international politics.* Ithaca, NY: Cornell University Press.

Kennedy, D. M. 2010. What would Wilson do? *The Atlantic* 305, no. 1 (January–February): 90–94.

Kennedy, P., and B. Russett. 1995. Reforming the United Nations. *Foreign Affairs* 74, no. 5 (September–October): 56–71.

Kissinger, H. 1994. *Diplomacy.* New York: Simon & Schuster.

Langhorne, R. 1998. Diplomacy beyond the primacy of the state. DSP Discussion Papers No. 43. Leicester, UK: Center for the Study of Diplomacy.

Mendelson, S., and J. Glenn, eds. 2002. *The power and limits of NGOs.* New York: Columbia University Press.

Muldoon, J. P. 2003. *The architecture of global governance: An introduction to the study of international organizations.* Boulder, CO: Westview Press.

Orbinski, J. 2009. Who's to lead? *Global Brief* 2 (fall): 30–35.

Rieff, D. 2002. *A bed for the night: Humanitarianism in crisis.* New York: Simon and Schuster.

Schechter, M. G. 1999. Introduction to *Future multilateralism: The political and social framework,* ed. M. G. Schechter, 1–11. New York: United Nations University Press.

Terry, F. 2002. *Condemned to repeat? The paradox of humanitarian action.* Ithaca, NY: Cornell University Press.

Thakur, R. 2002. Security in the new millennium. In *Enhancing global governance: Towards a new diplomacy?* ed. A. F. Cooper, J. English, and R. Thakur, 268–286. Tokyo: United Nations University Press.

Weiss, T. G., T. Carayannis, and R. Jolly. 2009. The "third" United Nations. *Global Governance* 15, no. 1 (January–March): 123–142.

Witte, J. M., W. Reinicke, and T. Benner. 2002. Networked governance: Developing a research agenda. Paper presented at the annual meeting of the International Studies Association, March 24–27, New Orleans, Louisiana.

About the Editors

James P. Muldoon, Jr. is a senior fellow with the Center for Global Change and Governance, Rutgers University, Newark, conducting research on multilateral diplomacy, international organizations, and global governance. Prior to joining the center, he was a senior research fellow at the Carnegie Council on Ethics and International Affairs (1999–2000), visiting scholar at the Shanghai Academy of Social Sciences in China (1996–1999), and director of education programs with the United Nations Association of the United States of America (1986–1996). His publications include *Multilateral Diplomacy and the United Nations Today* (2005) and *The Architecture of Global Governance: An Introduction to the Study of International Organizations* (2004). He has also contributed to major newspapers and academic journals on contemporary international relations and global issues.

JoAnn Fagot Aviel is a professor of international relations at San Francisco State University, where she also serves as the faculty advisor of the Model United Nations program. She is vice president of the United Nations Association of San Francisco. She served as a Fulbright professor in 2008 at the University of Piura, Peru; in 1999 at the University of Costa Rica; and in 1984 at the Diplomatic Academy of Peru. She is a coeditor of and contributor to *Multilateral Diplomacy and the United Nations Today* (2005) and has published numerous articles in comparative foreign policy and international relations.

Richard Reitano is an emeritus professor of government at Dutchess Community College and an adjunct professor of political science at Vassar College. He is the recipient of the 2007 State University of New York's Chancellor's Award for Excellence in Teaching. His publications include articles in the *Magazine of History* (by the Organization of American Historians) and *PS: Political Science & Politics* (by the American Political Science Association). He is a coeditor of and contributor to *Multilateral Diplomacy and the United Nations Today* (2005). In 2002, the Carnegie Foundation for the Advancement of Teaching selected his course on the Model United Nations, offered jointly at Dutchess Community College and Vassar College, as part of a three-year study on students and political involvement in the United States. He is president of the board of directors of the

National Collegiate Conference Association, which sponsors annual National Model UN (NMUN) simulations in New York City and Washington, D.C. Other NMUN venues include NMUN China (2008), NMUN Latin America in Quito, Ecuador (2010), and NMUN Europe (2010). Since 2008, Reitano has been the director of the Dutchess County Summer Scholars Program for area high school students.

Earl Sullivan has been a professor of political science at the American University in Cairo (AUC) since 1973. He received his BA in political science from Seattle University and his PhD in international relations and government from Claremont Graduate University. He initiated the Cairo International Model United Nations and the Cairo International Model Arab League at AUC and was the faculty advisor of both programs for many years. He served as provost of AUC from 1998 to 2008 and is now professor and provost emeritus. For most of 2010 he served as the interim president of the American University of Kuwait. His major publications include *Women in Egyptian Public Life* (1986) and *The Contemporary Study of the Arab World: Critical Perspectives on Arab Studies* (1991); he is a coeditor of and contributor to *Multilateral Diplomacy and the United Nations Today* (2005).

About the Contributors

Peter D. Bell is a senior research fellow at the Hauser Center for Nonprofit Organizations at Harvard University and chairs the facilitation group for the NGO Leaders Forum, a semiannual retreat for chief executives of the major U.S.-based international relief and development NGOs. He was president and chief executive officer of CARE USA, the international relief and development NGO, from 1995 to 2006 and served as chair of its board during the five preceding years.

Taryn Bird runs the Global Corporate Citizenship Program of the Business Civic Leadership Center (BCLC). She joined BCLC in January 2008 and is responsible for developing its global corporate citizenship reports and events and executing related projects. Prior to joining BCLC, she was on staff with the Association of American Chambers of Commerce in Latin America, an affiliate of the U.S. Chamber of Commerce.

Carroll Bogert is the associate director of Human Rights Watch, where she has worked since 1998. Previously, she spent a dozen years as a foreign correspondent for *Newsweek* magazine in China, Southeast Asia, and the former Soviet Union. She holds a BA and an MA in East Asian studies from Harvard University.

Henk-Jan Brinkman is a senior adviser for economic policy in the World Food Program (WFP), based in New York. Previously, he was chief of economic analysis and chief of food-security policy and markets at the WFP in Rome, Italy. From 2001 to 2006 he was an adviser on economic, social, and environmental issues to Secretary-General Kofi Annan and Deputy Secretary-General Louise Fréchette. Between 1989 and 2001, he was in the Department of Economic and Social Affairs of the United Nations Secretariat, where, inter alia, he contributed to the *World Economic and Social Survey*. He holds a BA and an MA in economics from the University of Groningen in the Netherlands and a PhD in economics from the New School for Social Research in New York City. He has written on such topics as economic adjustment in Africa. He is the lead author of the WFP's *World Hunger Series—Hunger and Markets* (2009) and the author of *Explaining Prices in the Global Economy: A Post-Keynesian Model* (1999).

Stanley (Stas) W. Burgiel currently serves as policy director for the Global Invasive Species Program. He has more than fifteen years experience with international environmental policy issues and has worked with a range of nongovernmental, intergovernmental, and governmental organizations. His work has addressed a wide range of issues, including invasive species, biodiversity conservation and sustainable use, trade, and the interface between science and policy making. He received his doctorate from the School of International Service at the American University in Washington, D.C., where he focused on the intersection of international environmental and trade policies.

Masood Hyder, an Indian national, joined the World Food Program (WFP) in 1984 and has since held various senior positions in that and other UN agencies. During 2008 and 2009, he represented the WFP on the Senior Steering Group of the High-Level Task Force on the Global Food Crisis.

Sherine S. Jayawickrama manages the humanitarian and development domain of practice at the Hauser Center of Harvard University and serves as executive director of the NGO Leaders Forum. From 1999 to 2008, she held a variety of positions at CARE USA, including deputy regional director for Asia and senior policy analyst.

Stephen Jordan is senior vice president and executive director of the U.S. Chamber of Commerce Business Civic Leadership Center (BCLC) and has served in this capacity since the organization's founding as the Center for Corporate Citizenship in May 2000. He leads BCLC's engagement with a broad spectrum of companies and chambers of commerce in the United States and overseas. He has produced numerous conferences, policy papers, and other projects and programs related to the fields of corporate citizenship, business and society relations, global development, education, disaster assistance, military quality of life, critical infrastructure protection, homeland security, and public-private partnerships.

David A. Kennett is a professor of economics at Vassar College. He has been a consultant to the Organization of Economic Cooperation and Development, the U.S. Department of Energy, the World Bank, and the Aspen Institute. At Vassar College, he has served as the director of the Program in International Studies. His publications include *A New View of Comparative Economics* (2003) and *The Road to Capitalism: Economic Transformation in Eastern Europe and the USSR* (1992, coeditor).

Andreas Kruck is a teaching and research associate at the Institute of Political Science, University of Munich, Germany. His research focuses on global governance, the transformation of the advanced Organization of Economic Cooperation and Development states, and the reallocation of political authority to private actors. He is a coauthor of *Grundzüge der Weltpolitik* (*Fundamentals of World Politics*) (2010, with Volker Rittberger and Anne Romund).

Timothy Longman is a visiting associate professor and director of the African Studies Center at Boston University. Before accepting that position, he was a professor of political science at Vassar College. Longman is a past Rwanda research director for the Human Rights Center at the University of California, Berkeley, and a past head of the field office for Human Rights Watch and the Fédération International des Ligues des Droits de l'Homme in Butare, Rwanda; he has served as a consultant to Human Rights Watch, the International Center for Transitional Justice, the U.S. Agency for International Development, and the State Department working on human rights issues related to Burundi, Congo, and Rwanda. He has been a contributor to many publications, including *Transitional Justice in the Twenty-First Century* (2006), *My Neighbor, My Enemy: Justice and Community in the Aftermath of Mass Atrocity* (2004), and *Women in African Parliaments* (2006).

John Mathiason is a professor of international relations at the Maxwell School of Citizenship and Public Affairs of Syracuse University. A former official of the United Nations Secretariat, he is author of *Invisible Governance: International Secretariats in Global Politics* (2007), *Internet Governance: The New Frontier of Global Institutions* (2009), and many articles on global governance.

J. Andrew Melrose, a lawyer (George Washington Law School, 2002) and vice president of Melrose Associates LLC, focuses on economic issues in developing nations. He has traveled extensively throughout the developing world, where he has had frequent dealings with international organizations.

Joseph H. Melrose Jr. is the former U.S. ambassador to Sierra Leone. He is currently a senior advisor to the U.S. Mission to the United Nations. Melrose is the program chair in international relations, a professor of international relations, and ambassador in residence at Ursinus College in Pennsylvania. He is a former board president of the National Collegiate Conference Association. After leaving Sierra

Leone in 2001, he was coordinator for the Post–September 11 Task Force with the Department of State and was a senior consultant on counterterrorism for the Office of the Secretary of State's Coordinator for Counterterrorism.

Volker Rittberger is an emeritus professor of political science and international relations at the Institute of Political Science, University of Tübingen, Germany. He has published widely on international institutions, peace and conflict research, foreign policy analysis, and global governance. His recent publications include *International Organization—Polity, Politics and Policies* (2006, with Bernhard Zangl), *Authority in the Global Political Economy* (2008, coeditor with Martin Nettesheim and coauthor), and *Grundzüge der Weltpolitik* (*Fundamentals of World Politics*) (2010, with Andreas Kruck and Anne Romund).

Stephen R. Rock is a professor of political science at Vassar College. He has been a visiting professor of political science at Yale University and a research fellow on the Avoiding Nuclear War Project at the Belfer Center for Science and International Affairs at Harvard University. Rock is the author of *Appeasement in International Politics* (2000). He is currently writing a book on the influence of religion on foreign policy, with an emphasis on the differences in foreign policy preferences among Roman Catholics, Evangelical Protestants, and mainline Protestants in the United States.

Michael G. Schechter is a professor at James Madison College of Michigan State University. An award-winning teacher of international relations, he has taught about international law and organization for over thirty years. He is the author, editor, or coeditor of more than a dozen books, most recently, the second edition of the *Historical Dictionary of International Organizations* (2010) and *International Governance of Fisheries Ecosystems: Learning from the Past, Finding Solutions for the Future* (2008).

Donna M. Schlagheck is a professor in and chair of the Department of Political Science at Wright State University and adjunct professor at the Defense Institute of Security Assistance. She serves as president of the Dayton, Ohio, Council on World Affairs and as a board member of the National Collegiate Conference Association. She is the author of *International Terrorism: An Introduction to the Concepts and Actors* (1988) and coauthor of *Issues in American Political Life: Money, Violence and Biology* (2005).

Joan E. Spero is a visiting scholar at the Foundation Center. From 1997 to 2008, she was president of the Doris Duke Charitable Foundation, which makes grants in the performing arts, environmental preservation, medical research, and prevention of child abuse. Previously, Spero served as undersecretary of state for economic, business, and agricultural affairs in the U.S. Department of State (1993–1997) and U.S. ambassador to the United Nations for economic and social affairs (1980–1981), as a corporate executive at American Express Company (1981–1993), and as an assistant professor at Columbia University (1973–1979). She graduated from the University of Wisconsin and holds an MA and PhD from Columbia University. Her publications include *The Politics of International Economic Relations* (7th ed., 2010) and *The Failure of the Franklin National Bank: Challenge to the International Banking System* (1980, reissued 1999).

Ramesh Thakur is director, Balsillie School of International Affairs; distinguished fellow, Center for International Governance Innovation; and professor of political science at the University of Waterloo in Canada. He was vice rector and senior vice rector of the United Nations University (and assistant secretary-general of the United Nations) from 1998 to 2007. He was a commissioner and one of the principal authors of *The Responsibility to Protect* and senior adviser on reforms and principal writer of the UN secretary-general's second reform report. His books include *The United Nations, Peace and Security: From Collective Security to the Responsibility to Protect* (2006), winner of the ACUNS 2008 award for the best recent book on the UN system, and *Global Governance and the United Nations: An Unfinished Journey* (2010, cowritten with Thomas G. Weiss).

Geoffrey Wiseman is a professor of the practice of international relations at the University of Southern California (USC) in Los Angeles. He was previously director of the USC Center on Public Diplomacy, principal officer in the Strategic Planning Unit of the Executive Office of the UN Secretary-General, peace and security program officer at the Ford Foundation, and a diplomat—with postings to Brussels, Hanoi, and Stockholm—in the Australian Foreign Service. He has published on international security, Asia-Pacific regional security, and diplomacy.

Natalie Zähringer is a lecturer in international relations at the University of Witwatersrand, Johannesburg, South Africa, teaching both undergraduate and postgraduate courses on a variety of topics, including international political economy, the European Union, and public international law. She is currently the South African–based academic director of the International Human Rights Exchange, a program coordinated by Bard College in New York and the University of Witwatersrand.

Index

European Union (EU), 11, 14, 24,
26, 38, 60n6, 96, 110, 117, 137,
141, 156, 174, 179, 199, 202,
305, 334, 339
Evans, Gareth, 231, 258, 259, 262
Extractive Industries Transparency
Initiative (EITI), 55

Failed states, 138, 203, 234, 243
Fair Labor Association, 205
Farmer, Paul, 212
Ferguson, Charles D., 323
Ferguson, Niall, 119
Fiji, 254
Financial crisis, 235, 268, 279, 281,
292, 336
Financial Stability Board (FSB), 122
Finnemore, Martha, 260
Food, 78, 269, 278
crisis, 232, 233, 234, 267–268,
270–271, 274–278, 281, 301
rising prices of, 267–270, 277, 279
production, 214, 278
riots, 267, 270
security, 164, 215, 267, 271, 273,
278, 280, 281
Food and Agricultural Organization
(FAO), 214, 232, 270, 276, 279,
299
Ford Foundation, 156, 173, 210, 214
Foundation Center, 221n2, 222n12,
306
Foundations, 151, 207–212, 218–221,
297, 301, 303, 306, 312, 339
corporate, 199, 211, 307
European, 208, 210, 211, 216
private, 54, 151, 153, 207, 212,
215, 221, 297, 307
U.S., 207–208, 216, 217
Forman, Shepard, 35, 310, 339
France, 11, 101, 109, 140, 289, 324
Franklin, Benjamin, 73
Frederick the Great, 73
Free riding, 37, 71, 123, 126–127

Functional agencies, 232, 268, 270,
274–275. *See also* Specialized
agencies
Functionalism, 232, 275

Gaddis, John Lewis, 327
Gates, Bill, 74
Gates Foundation, 60n8, 212, 214,
221n2, 303, 307, 339
Gelb, Leslie H., 72, 324
General Agreement on Tariffs and
Trade (GATT), 49, 84–85, 239,
242
Geneva Conventions, 133, 143
Genocide, 69, 70–71, 103, 104, 110–
114, 133, 134, 143, 203, 259,
321
against Kurdish population in Iraq,
140
in Darfur, Sudan, 103, 104, 140
in Rwanda, 134, 135, 142, 257,
318, 320–321
Georgia, 178–179, 182n4, 326
Germany, 11, 103, 108–109, 112,
116, 133, 172, 289, 324
Gesellschaft für Technische
Zusammenarbeit, 200
Gill, Bates, 26
Global Alliance for Improved
Nutrition (GAIN), 307
Global Alliance for Vaccines and
Immunization (GAVI), 54, 212,
301, 307
Global Business Council on
HIV/AIDS, 199
Global Call to Action Against Poverty,
306
Global Compact, the UN, 30, 54,
199, 205, 298, 309, 310
Global Development Alliance, 200,
202
Global Fund to Fight AIDS,
Tuberculosis and Malaria
(GFATM), 53–54, 307